ADVANCED LEVEL
APPLIED MATHEMATICS

Additional and Advanced Level Mathematics Series

ADDITIONAL APPLIED MATHEMATICS
F. G. J. Norton and L. H. Clarke

ADVANCED LEVEL APPLIED MATHEMATICS
F. G. J. Norton

ADDITIONAL PURE MATHEMATICS (third edition)
L. H. Clarke and F. G. J. Norton

PURE MATHEMATICS AT ADVANCED LEVEL (third edition)
L. H. Clarke and F. G. J. Norton

Also by L. H. Clarke and F. G. J. Norton

OBJECTIVE TESTS IN 'O' LEVEL MATHEMATICS

OBJECTIVE TESTS IN C.S.E. MATHEMATICS

Advanced Level Applied Mathematics

F. G. J. NORTON

Head of the Mathematics Department, Rugby School

HEINEMANN EDUCATIONAL BOOKS
LONDON

Heinemann Educational Books Ltd
22 Bedford Square, London WC1B 3HH
LONDON EDINBURGH MELBOURNE AUCKLAND
HONG KONG SINGAPORE KUALA LUMPUR NEW DELHI
IBADAN NAIROBI JOHANNESBURG
EXETER (NH) KINGSTON PORT OF SPAIN

ISBN 0 435 51660 4

First published 1974
Reprinted with corrections 1977
Reprinted 1979, 1981

Printed and bound in Great Britain by
Richard Clay (The Chaucer Press) Ltd,
Bungay, Suffolk

Preface

This book is a sequel to *Additional Applied Mathematics*, and completes the course in Applied Mathematics that is likely to be covered, whether studied to Advanced or Scholarship level or for University Scholarships. The earlier book has proved suitable for introducing applied mathematics in the fifth or lower sixth forms, and this volume is intended for students towards the end of the first post certificate year and in subsequent years.

Recently there have been considerable changes in Applied Mathematics and these are reflected in the examination syllabuses. The traditional preoccupation with mechanics has been reduced and applications of mathematics are now taken from biology, chemistry, and economics, as well as physics. Examples of these are considered in Chapter 3 on differential equations.

Chapter 10 on statics aims to give a thorough understanding of the moment of a force about an axis before considering the rotation of moving bodies, and also of the manner in which friction affects the motion or equilibrium of bodies. There are not, however, any problems requiring artificially complicated trigonometry. Some of the topics included later in the chapter, such as Bow's notation, shearing force and bending moment, still form part of some 'A' level syllabuses, but many think that they are more properly studied in university engineering courses, and these sections can readily be omitted.

Vector analysis is used throughout the book, and Chapter 1 ensures that the reader has knowledge adequate for later work. The chapters can be read in the order in which they occur, parts marked * in the list of contents being postponed for a second reading.

I should like to express my indebtedness to the Second Report of the Mathematical Association on the teaching of Mechanics in schools; and my most sincere thanks to Professor A. Geary, formerly of The City University, London, for reading the manuscript and for many suggestions; to Mr J. W. Norton, of The King's

School, Bruton, for help in many ways; finally to Mr Hamish MacGibbon and all at Heinemann Educational Books for their encouragement in the writing of this book.

Questions are reprinted from papers set by many examining boards and I should like to thank these boards for permission to reprint the questions. Such questions are indicated in the text by the following abbreviations:

Associated Examining Board	A.E.B.
Joint Matriculation Board	J.M.B.
Oxford and Cambridge Examining Board	O. & C.
Oxford and Cambridge Examining Board M.E.I. project	M.E.I.
Oxford and Cambridge Examining Board S.M.P. project	S.M.P.
Oxford Delegacy for Local Examinations	O.
Cambridge University Local Examinations Syndicate	C.
Southern Universities Joint Board	S.U.
Welsh Joint Education Committee	W.J.E.C.
Cambridge University Scholarships	C.S.
Oxford University Scholarships	O.S.

These questions are designed for a variety of syllabuses, and should not be expected to be of equal difficulty.

1974 F.G.J.N.

Abbreviations used

s	seconds
mm	millimetres
cm	centimetres
m	metres
km	kilometres
cm s^{-1}	centimetres per second
m s^{-1}	metres per second
km h^{-1}	kilometres per hour
m s^{-2}	metres per second per second

The SI unit of force is 1 newton (1 N)
of work or energy is 1 joule (1 J)
of power is 1 watt (1 W)

1 newton = 1 kg m s^{-2}
1 joule = 1 newton metre, 1 N m
1 watt = 1 joule per second, 1 J s^{-1}

Notation used

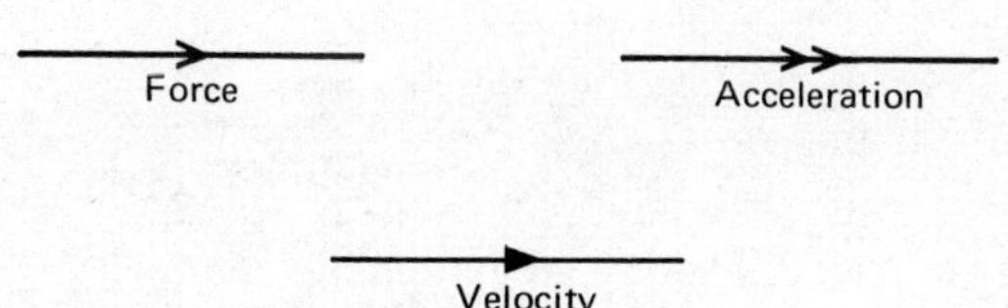

Contents

* Indicates topics likely to be more suitable for a second reading.

* Indicates topics likely to be more suitable for a second reading.

* Indicates topics likely to be more suitable for a second reading.

* Indicates topics likely to be more suitable for a second reading.

* Indicates topics likely to be more suitable for a second reading.

Dimensions

Almost all the quantities we consider in mechanics have to be expressed in terms of units, e.g. velocity in metres per second, force in newtons, momentum in newton-seconds. There are a few exceptions, e.g. the measure of an angle in radians, which is the ratio of two lengths, the length of the arc subtended by that angle at the centre of a circle to the radius of the circle, and the coefficient of restitution (page 43), which is the ratio of two speeds. The fundamental units in which other quantities are usually measured are mass, length, and time. Each is independent of the other two and our unit of mass does not in any way affect our choice of unit of length or of time. It is interesting to note that they are to a certain extent arbitrary, and astronomers use speed instead of length. They take the unit of time as a year, and the unit of speed as the speed of light so that distances are measured in light-years.

From our basic units mass, length, and time all other units can be derived. A unit of speed is such that a unit of distance is covered in a unit of time; a unit of acceleration is such that speed increases by one unit in one unit of time. If we denote mass, length, and time by the symbols M, L, T, this suggests that velocity will have the symbol

$$\frac{\mathrm{L}}{\mathrm{T}}$$

and acceleration the symbol

$$\left(\frac{\mathrm{L}}{\mathrm{T}}\right) \div \mathrm{T}$$

written $\mathrm{L\,T^{-1}}$ and $\mathrm{L\,T^{-2}}$ respectively. These are called the *dimensions* of the physical quantities. To take a less familiar example, density is the mass per unit volume and so has the symbol $\mathrm{M\,L^{-3}}$. Note that the SI units in which all quantities are measured correspond closely to the dimensions, e.g. velocity in $\mathrm{m\,s^{-1}}$, acceleration in m s^{-2}, density in kg m^{-3}. Sometimes of course the derived units obscure the dimensions, e.g. the unit of force, dimensions M L T^{-2}, is the newton, the unit of work, dimensions M L^2 T^{-2}, is the joule.

Since mass, length, and time are independent quantities, it is not possible to equate numerical multiples of them. It is meaningless to say that 2 cm is greater than 3 seconds, or to talk about 'adding' 2 kg to 3 cm. All the terms in mechanical equations must have the same dimensions. Thus in

$$v^2 = u^2 + 2as$$

u and v have dimensions L T^{-1}, so u^2 and v^2 have dimensions L^2 T^{-2},
a has dimensions L T^{-2},
and s has dimensions L,
so the dimensions of all the terms are the same, L^2 T^{-2}. The dimensions of some of the commoner quantities are listed in the table below and in Exercise 1

Velocity	L T^{-1}
Acceleration	L T^{-2}
Force	M L T^{-2}
Momentum	M L T^{-1}
Energy	M L^2 T^{-2}

Exercise 1

Verify the dimensions given of the following physical quantities:

Angular acceleration	T^{-2}
Power	M L^2 T^{-3}
Frequency	T^{-1}
Pressure	M L^{-1} T^{-2}

Dimensions as a check on accuracy

Since the dimensions of all terms in an equation must be the same, if we can identify the dimensions of terms in algebraic solutions to problems, we have an easy check that an equation *may* be correct.

If we think the period of oscillation of a simple pendulum is

$$\frac{2\pi}{g}\sqrt{l}$$

where l is the length of the pendulum and g the acceleration due to gravity, this has dimensions

$$\frac{\mathrm{L}^{1/2}}{\mathrm{L\,T}^{-2}}, \quad \text{i.e.,} \quad \mathrm{L}^{-1/2}\,\mathrm{T}^{2}$$

so cannot be an interval of time. Likewise if the constant acceleration formula is recalled incorrectly as $s = ut + \frac{1}{2}at$, the term at has dimensions $(\mathrm{L\,T}^{-2})\,\mathrm{T}$, i.e. $\mathrm{L\,T}^{-1}$, so is not a length. Many such checks are indicated in the text (e.g. pages 102, 216); the reader is urged to apply them frequently to his own work.

Exercise 2

Show that, with the usual notation, only one of the following 'equations' is dimensionally correct.

(a) $s = \dfrac{v-u}{2a}$

(b) $a = \dfrac{M+g}{m}$

(c) $a = \left(\dfrac{M+m}{Mm}\right) g$

(d) $t = \pi\sqrt{\dfrac{l^3}{4g}}$

(e) $s = ut + at^2$.

Dimensions as an aid to solving problems

Knowing that the terms of an equation must have the same dimensions can often help in solving physical problems. For example it was said that if two bodies, masses m_1, m_2 were a distance d apart, the gravitational attraction exerted by each on the other was proportional to m_1m_2/d^2. What are the dimensions of the constant of proportion, usually denoted by G?

Since the gravitational attraction is a force, $G(m_1m_2/d^2)$ must have dimensions M L T^{-2}. But m_1m_2/d^2 has dimensions M^2 L^{-2}, so the dimensions of G are M^{-1} L^3 T^{-2}.

Again, it was thought by some early experimenters on the flow of fluids that the volume of fluid that did flow through a capillary tube in a unit of time was proportional to the pressure-gradient and some power of the radius r of the tube, and inversely proportional to the viscosity ν of the fluid. This gives a formula

$$V \propto \frac{1}{\nu}\left(\frac{\mathrm{d}p}{\mathrm{d}x}\right) r^n$$

where V is the volume per unit time, $\mathrm{d}p/\mathrm{d}x$ the pressure gradient.

The dimensions of V are L^3 T^{-1} (volume per unit time), those of $\mathrm{d}p/\mathrm{d}x$ are M L^{-2} T^{-2} (since pressure is M L^{-1} T^{-2}), and the dimensions of viscosity were known to be M L^{-1} T^{-1}. Thus

$$\frac{1}{\nu}\left(\frac{\mathrm{d}p}{\mathrm{d}x}\right) r^n$$

has dimensions (M^{-1} L T)(M L^{-2} T^{-2})(L)^n, i.e. L^{n-1} T^{-1}. This must equal L^3 T^{-1}, so $n = 4$.

Notice that if they had thought that the flow was proportional to the viscosity, instead of being inversely proportional, they would have had a term M^2 in the dimensions of the right hand side of the equation. This does not appear in the left hand side, therefore the equation cannot possibly be correct and the original hypothesis must be false.

Exercise 3

(a) It is thought that the force necessary to cause a body mass m to describe a circle radius r with velocity v is proportional to $m^\alpha r^\beta v^\gamma$. Show that $\alpha = 1, \beta = -1$ and $\gamma = 2$.

(b) The frequency n of the note given by an organ pipe length l depends on the air pressure p and the air density ρ. If n is proportional to $l^\alpha p^\beta \rho^\gamma$, show that $\alpha = -1, \beta = \frac{1}{2}, \gamma = -\frac{1}{2}$.

(c) A fluid is flowing steadily along a wide horizontal channel and the velocity at height y above the bottom of the channel is u. The traction force F per unit area between the fluid above and below the layer at height y is given by $F = k(du/dy)$, where k is a constant. Show the dimensions of k are $M L T^{-1}$. (S.M.P.)

(d) A new system of dimensions is proposed in which the fundamental quantities are momentum P, energy Q, and frequency R. Show that the dimensions of density in this system are $P^5Q^{-4}R^{-5}$. (S.M.P.)

(e) The height h at which a hovercraft hovers above the ground might be thought to depend only on the volume F of air which is pumped per second through the fans, and on the speed v at which the air escapes from under the skirt. Show that h, F, and v could be related by the equation $h = k\sqrt{(F/v)}$. (S.M.P.)

1. Vectors

Scalars and vectors

Physical quantities which are determined completely by one variable are called *scalars*: examples of such are mass, time, area, and temperature. Physical quantities which require more than one variable to determine them, and which are such that any two are added by the parallelogram law of addition, are called *vectors*. Examples of vectors are displacement, velocity, acceleration, force, and momentum. Since any one type of vector can serve to illustrate the laws governing all of them, we can often think most conveniently of vectors as lines of given length with specific directions. The vector represented by the line from the point A to a point B we shall write $\overrightarrow{AB}$, or sometimes denote by a single letter **a**. (Some writers use **AB** or $\overline{AB}$; the advantage of our notation is that it emphasizes the difference between $\overrightarrow{AB}$ and $\overrightarrow{BA}$, that they are in opposite directions.) Thus a line in two dimensions will be determined completely if we know its magnitude and direction, e.g. 10 km north-east. In three dimensions it is more difficult to describe the direction. We could say 10 km north-east, 40° above the horizontal.

The reader may later wish to generalize his work on vectors, and may wish to redefine them in a more abstract way. The above definition is most suitable for the present work.

Parallelogram law of addition

As stated in *Additional Applied Mathematics*, page 67, if $\overrightarrow{AB}$ and $\overrightarrow{AC}$ are two vectors in space, their sum is found by completing the parallelogram ABDC, the sum being represented in magnitude, direction, and position by the diagonal $\overrightarrow{AD}$, as shown in Fig. 1.1.

Many properties follow directly from this definition. Although they were nearly all in *Additional Applied Mathematics*, they are listed again here, partly for completeness but more so as the reader

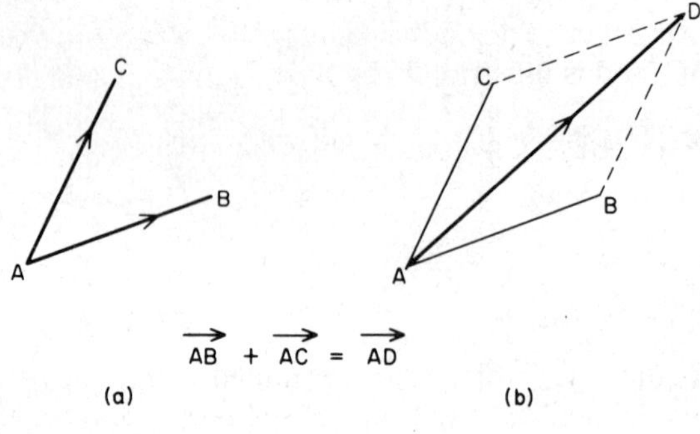

Fig. 1.1

is now better able to appreciate the significance of some of them. For example, vector addition is commutative,

i.e. $$\overrightarrow{AB} + \overrightarrow{AC} = \overrightarrow{AC} + \overrightarrow{AB}$$

and associative,

i.e. $$\overrightarrow{AB} + (\overrightarrow{AC} + \overrightarrow{AD}) = (\overrightarrow{AB} + \overrightarrow{AC}) + \overrightarrow{AD}$$

even if the vectors are not coplanar.

Subtraction of vectors

The subtraction of vectors is defined by

$$\overrightarrow{AB} - \overrightarrow{AC} = \overrightarrow{AB} + (-\overrightarrow{AC}),$$

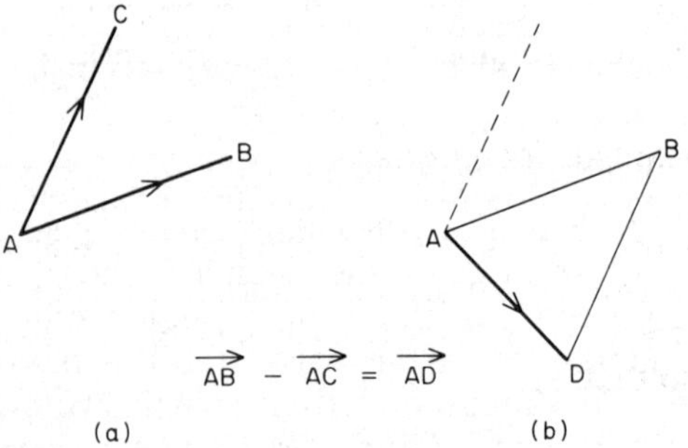

$\overrightarrow{AB} - \overrightarrow{AC} = \overrightarrow{AD}$

(a) (b)

Fig. 1.2

where $-\overrightarrow{AC}$ is the vector equal in magnitude but opposite in direction to $\overrightarrow{AC}$, and is illustrated in Fig. 1.2,

$$\text{where} \qquad \overrightarrow{BD} = \overrightarrow{CA} \text{ in magnitude and direction}$$
$$= -\overrightarrow{AC}.$$

Multiplication by a scalar

The multiplication of a vector by an integer k is the abbreviation used for repeated addition, e.g.

$$\overrightarrow{AB} + \overrightarrow{AB} = 2\overrightarrow{AB}$$

and

$$\overrightarrow{AB} + \overrightarrow{AB} + \overrightarrow{AB} + \cdots \text{ to } k \text{ terms} = k\overrightarrow{AB}$$

Similarly

$$\frac{1}{k}\,\overrightarrow{AB} + \frac{1}{k}\,\overrightarrow{AB} + \frac{1}{k}\,\overrightarrow{AB} + \cdots \text{ to } k \text{ terms} = \overrightarrow{AB}$$

defines division by an integer. Combining these two generalizes, so that k can be any rational number, not just an integer.

Magnitude of a vector

The magnitude (or modulus) of a vector is the positive number which is the measure of the length of the line which represents the vector. Thus the magnitude of the displacement from the origin O to the point P, coordinates (3, 4), is five units; in three dimensions the magnitude of the displacement from O to the point Q(3, 4, 12) is thirteen units. A vector of zero magnitude is called a zero (or null) vector, and a vector whose magnitude is 1 is called a unit vector. Often it is convenient to denote unit vectors along three mutually perpendicular lines, which are taken as axes Ox, Oy, and Oz, by $\mathbf{i}$, $\mathbf{j}$, $\mathbf{k}$ respectively. A unit vector in the direction of a more general vector $\mathbf{a}$ is usually written $\hat{\mathbf{a}}$, and the magnitude of $\mathbf{a}$ is written a, so that

$$\mathbf{a} = a\hat{\mathbf{a}},$$

a giving the magnitude and $\hat{\mathbf{a}}$ the direction of the vector $\mathbf{a}$.

Free vectors, localized vectors, position vectors

Vectors as defined so far are usually called free vectors, for their values are dependent only on their magnitudes and directions, and not on their positions in space. By contrast, the position vector of a point P relative to an origin O represents in magnitude and direction the line from O to P and is an example of a localized vector. The words 'relative to the origin' are often omitted unless this omission will cause ambiguity.

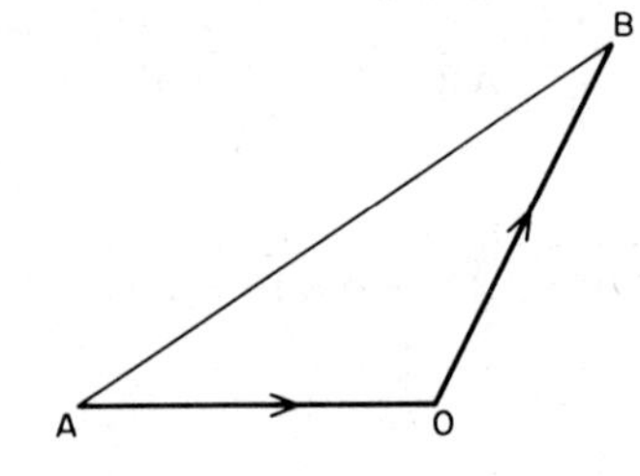

Fig. 1.3

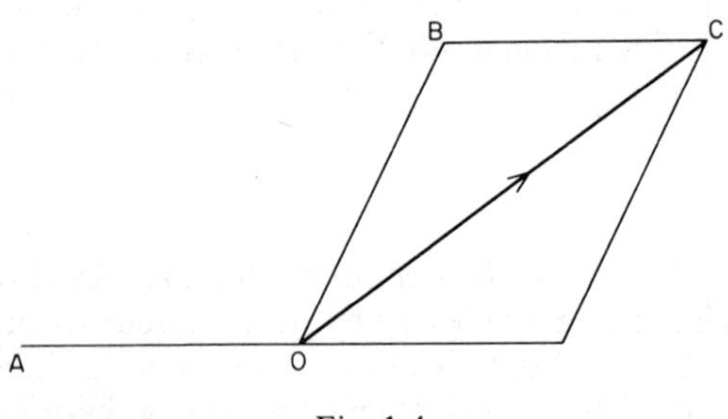

Fig. 1.4

This distinction between free and localized vectors is important. Thus vectors $\overrightarrow{AO}$ and $\overrightarrow{OB}$ represented in Fig. 1.3 are such that

$$\overrightarrow{AO} + \overrightarrow{OB} = \overrightarrow{AB}$$

in magnitude and direction, but as the sum, or resultant of $\overrightarrow{AO}$ and $\overrightarrow{OB}$ must act through O, $\overrightarrow{AB}$ does not give the position of the resultant. The resultant is given in magnitude, direction and position by $\overrightarrow{OC}$ (Fig. 1.4), where OC and AB are equal and parallel.

Components, resolved parts

If a vector $\overrightarrow{OC}$ is the sum of two vectors $\overrightarrow{OA}$ and $\overrightarrow{AC}$, $\overrightarrow{OA}$ and $\overrightarrow{AC}$ may be called the components of $\overrightarrow{OC}$ in the directions $\overrightarrow{OA}$ and $\overrightarrow{OB}$. (The directions $\overrightarrow{AC}$ and $\overrightarrow{OB}$ are the same.) The resolved parts of $\overrightarrow{OC}$ in these directions are $\overrightarrow{OA}$ and $\overrightarrow{OB}$ (Fig. 1.5). It can be shown that this resolution is unique if the directions are prescribed; if the directions are not prescribed, of course, there is an infinite number of possible resolutes, a few of which are illustrated in Fig. 1.6.

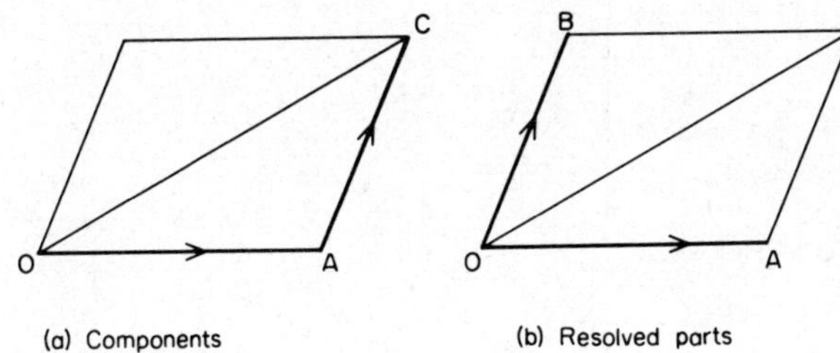

Fig. 1.5

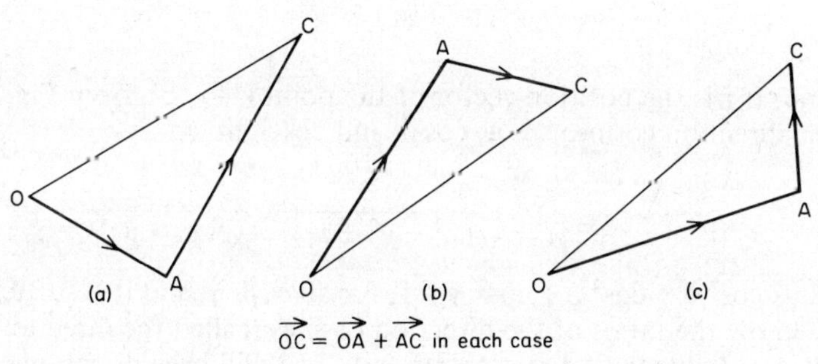

Fig. 1.6

It is usually desirable to resolve a vector into two or three resolutes along perpendicular coordinate axes. Thus the position vector of Q(3, 4, 12), has as resolved parts, vectors three units along Ox, four along Oy and twelve along Oz,

i.e. $$\overrightarrow{OQ} = 3\mathbf{i} + 4\mathbf{j} + 12\mathbf{k}$$

Direction cosines

We have seen that it is not easy to describe the direction of a vector **r** in three dimensions. Even if we know the angle between **r** and a fixed vector **a**, this merely tells us that **r** is parallel to a generator of a certain cone. The commonest method is to give the direction cosines of the angles made by **r** with three suitable coordinate axes.

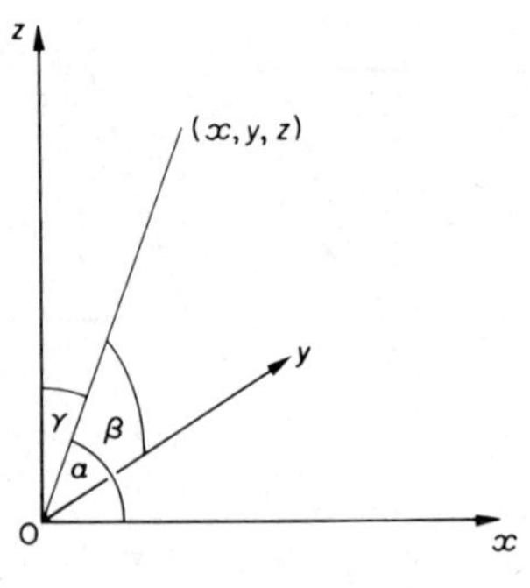

Fig. 1.7

Thus if **r** is the position vector of the point (x, y, z), from Fig. 1.7, the direction cosines $\cos\alpha$, $\cos\beta$, and $\cos\gamma$ are

$$\frac{x}{\sqrt{(x^2+y^2+z^2)}}, \quad \frac{y}{\sqrt{(x^2+y^2+z^2)}}, \quad \frac{z}{\sqrt{(x^2+y^2+z^2)}}$$

Thus $\cos^2\alpha + \cos^2\beta + \cos^2\gamma = 1$, for all α, β, γ, and it is sufficient to know the ratios of the direction cosines (called the direction ratios). A line with direction ratios $1:2:3$ will have direction cosines

$$\frac{1}{\sqrt{14}}, \quad \frac{2}{\sqrt{14}}, \quad \frac{3}{\sqrt{14}}$$

Section theorem

If P is the point of AB (Fig. 1.8) such that $\text{AP}:\text{PB} = l:m$,

$$\overrightarrow{\text{AP}} = \frac{l}{l+m}\,\overrightarrow{\text{AB}}$$

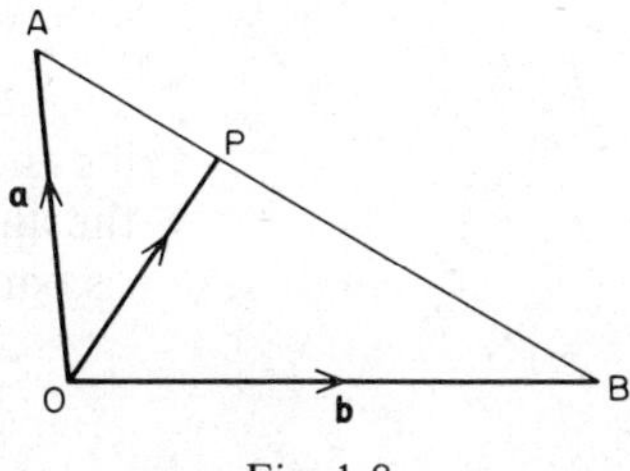

Fig. 1.8

But $\overrightarrow{OP} = \overrightarrow{OA} + \overrightarrow{AP}$, so denoting $\overrightarrow{OA}$ and $\overrightarrow{OB}$ by **a** and **b** respectively

$$\overrightarrow{OP} = \mathbf{a} + \frac{l}{l+m}(\mathbf{b} - \mathbf{a})$$

$$= \frac{m\mathbf{a} + l\mathbf{b}}{l+m}$$

Thus the position vector of the point dividing AB in the ratio $l : m$ is

$$\frac{m\mathbf{a} + l\mathbf{b}}{l+m}$$

Deductions

1. The midpoint of AB has position vector $\frac{1}{2}(\mathbf{a} + \mathbf{b})$
2. Any point of AB can be represented by a position vector $k\mathbf{a} + (1 - k)\mathbf{b}$ for suitable k.
3. Points with position vectors **a**, **b**, and $p\mathbf{a} + q\mathbf{b}$ are collinear if and only if $p + q = 1$.

Example 1.1. *P, Q, R, and S are four points in space. Prove that the midpoints of PQ, QR, RS, and SP are the vertices of a parallelogram.*

If the position vectors (Fig. 1.9) of the points P, Q, R, and S are **p**, **q**, **r**, and **s** respectively, then

the position vector of the midpoint A of PQ is $\frac{1}{2}(\mathbf{p} + \mathbf{q})$
the position vector of the midpoint B of QR is $\frac{1}{2}(\mathbf{q} + \mathbf{r})$
the position vector of the midpoint C of RS is $\frac{1}{2}(\mathbf{r} + \mathbf{s})$
the position vector of the midpoint D of SP is $\frac{1}{2}(\mathbf{s} + \mathbf{p})$

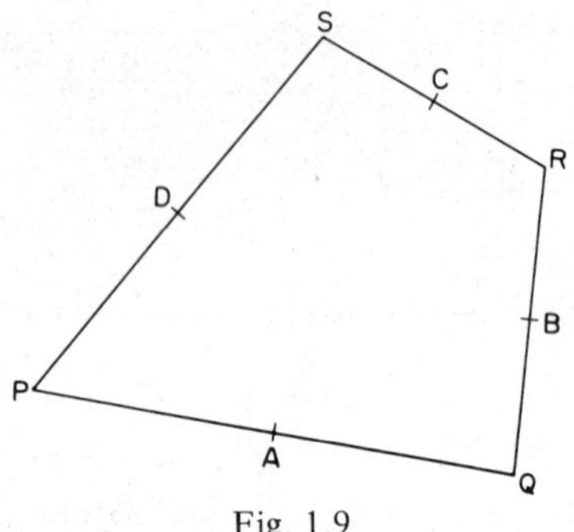

Fig. 1.9

$$\therefore \qquad \overrightarrow{AB} = \tfrac{1}{2}(\mathbf{q} + \mathbf{r}) - \tfrac{1}{2}(\mathbf{p} + \mathbf{q})$$
$$= \tfrac{1}{2}(\mathbf{r} - \mathbf{p})$$

and
$$\overrightarrow{DC} = \tfrac{1}{2}(\mathbf{r} + \mathbf{s}) - \tfrac{1}{2}(\mathbf{s} + \mathbf{p})$$
$$= \tfrac{1}{2}(\mathbf{r} - \mathbf{p})$$

So $\overrightarrow{AB}$ is equal and parallel to $\overrightarrow{DC}$,

i.e. ABCD is a parallelogram.

This result was proved in *Additional Applied Mathematics* when P, Q, R, and S were coplanar. The proof above shows how easily vectors can be applied to problems in three-dimensional geometry.

Example 1.2. *A, B, C, and D are four points in space. Prove that the lines from any one of these points to the centroid of the triangle formed by the other three are concurrent.*

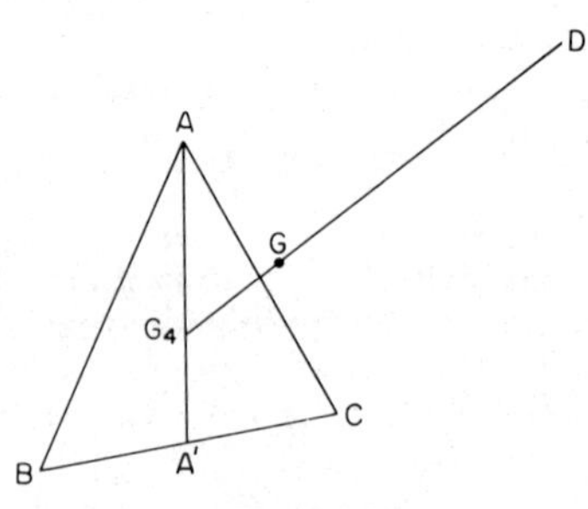

Fig. 1.10

If A′ is the midpoint of BC (Fig. 1.10), the position vector of A′ is $\tfrac{1}{2}(\mathbf{b} + \mathbf{c})$. If G_4 is the centroid of the triangle which does not contain D as a vertex, i.e.

triangle ABC, G_4 divides AA′ in the ratio 2:1, so the position vector of G_4 is $\frac{1}{3}(\mathbf{a}+\mathbf{b}+\mathbf{c})$. If G is the point dividing DG_4 in the ratio 3:1, the position vector of G is

$$\frac{3\times\frac{1}{3}(\mathbf{a}+\mathbf{b}+\mathbf{c})+\mathbf{d}}{3+1}$$

i.e.

$$\tfrac{1}{4}(\mathbf{a}+\mathbf{b}+\mathbf{c}+\mathbf{d})$$

The symmetry of the result proves that G also lies on the lines AG_1, BG_2, and CG_3, G_1, G_2, and G_3 being defined in a similar manner to G_4.

Centroid, centre of mass, centre of gravity

We can define the centroid of n points, position vectors $\mathbf{r}_1, \mathbf{r}_2, \mathbf{r}_3, \ldots$ as the point whose position vector $\bar{\mathbf{r}}$ is given by

$$\bar{\mathbf{r}} = \frac{1}{n}(\mathbf{r}_1+\mathbf{r}_2+\mathbf{r}_3+\cdots)$$

i.e.

$$\bar{\mathbf{r}} = \frac{1}{n}\sum \mathbf{r}_i$$

This definition is not dependent on any idea of mass or weight. So defined, the centroid is the centre of mass of equal bodies placed at points position vectors $\mathbf{r}_1, \mathbf{r}_2, \mathbf{r}_3, \ldots$. In Example 1.2, G is the centre of mass of equal bodies placed at A, B, C, and D, and G is also the centre of mass of the uniform solid tetrahedron ABCD. Similarly, the centroid of points position vectors $\mathbf{r}_1, \mathbf{r}_2, \mathbf{r}_3$ is the centre of mass of the triangular lamina whose vertices have position vectors $\mathbf{r}_1, \mathbf{r}_2, \mathbf{r}_3$ and also of equal masses placed at these points.

If we ignore variations in the gravitational field, which we can invariably do at this stage, the weight of a body acts at its centre of mass, and so this point is often called the centre of gravity. But if the body is so large (or the system of particles so widely dispersed) that the gravitational field is not uniform, the resultant gravitational force does not act through the centre of mass. Since the existence of a centre of mass is not dependent even on there being a gravitational field, we shall generally use the term ‘centre of mass’ when referring to bodies having mass; in examples which do not even require the existence of masses, as here, the term ‘centroid’ is more appropriate.

Determining the centre of mass

In *Additional Applied Mathematics* (page 127), we found that the coordinates $(\bar{x}, \bar{y})$ in two dimensions of the centre of mass of masses $m_1, m_2, m_3, \ldots$ at points $(x_1, y_1), (x_2, y_2), \ldots$ were

$$\bar{x} = \frac{m_1x_1 + m_2x_2 + m_3x_3 + \cdots}{m_1 + m_2 + m_3 \cdots} \qquad \text{i.e. } \bar{x} = \frac{\Sigma\, m_\text{i}x_\text{i}}{\Sigma\, m_\text{i}}$$

and $$\bar{y} = \frac{m_1y_1 + m_2y_2 + m_3y_3 + \cdots}{m_1 + m_2 + m_3 \ldots} \qquad \text{i.e. } \bar{y} = \frac{\Sigma\, m_\text{i}y_\text{i}}{\Sigma\, m_\text{i}}$$

and that this could be written

$$\bar{x}\mathbf{i} + \bar{y}\mathbf{j} = \frac{\Sigma\, m_\text{i}x_\text{i}\mathbf{i} + \Sigma\, m_\text{i}y_\text{i}\mathbf{j}}{\Sigma\, m_\text{i}}$$

i.e. $$(\Sigma\, m_\text{i})\bar{\mathbf{r}} = \Sigma\, m_\text{i}\mathbf{r}_\text{i}, \quad \text{summed for } i = 1, \ldots, n$$

This can be generalized to determine the position in three dimensions of the centre of mass of bodies or systems of masses.

Example 1.3. *Small bodies, mass m, 2m, 3m have position vectors* (−**i** −**k**), (2**i** + 3**j** − **k**), *and* (3**i** + 2**j** + 3**k**) *respectively. Find the position vector of the centre of mass of the system.*

The position vector $\bar{\mathbf{r}}$ of the centre of mass is given by

$$(m + 2m + 3m)\bar{\mathbf{r}} = m(-\mathbf{i} - \mathbf{k}) + 2m(2\mathbf{i} + 3\mathbf{j} - \mathbf{k}) + 3m(3\mathbf{i} + 2\mathbf{j} + 3\mathbf{k})$$
$$= 12m\mathbf{i} + 12m\mathbf{j} + 6m\mathbf{k}$$

i.e. $$\bar{\mathbf{r}} = 2\mathbf{i} + 2\mathbf{j} + \mathbf{k}$$

Equivalent systems of forces

If the lines of action of forces $\mathbf{F}_1$, $\mathbf{F}_2$, meet in a point P (Fig. 1.11), the resultant of these two forces is $(\mathbf{F}_1 + \mathbf{F}_2)$ through P. But if $\mathbf{F}_1$ and $\mathbf{F}_2$ are parallel and in the same direction (Fig. 1.12), their resultant $(\mathbf{F}_1 + \mathbf{F}_2)$ acts along the line dividing the distance between the lines of action of $\mathbf{F}_1$ and $\mathbf{F}_2$ in the ratio $\mathbf{F}_2 : \mathbf{F}_1$, since the components of the two systems in any direction are equal and the moments about an axis perpendicular to the plane of $\mathbf{F}_1$ and $\mathbf{F}_2$ are equal. But if $\mathbf{F}_2 = -\mathbf{F}_1$, the forces are equivalent to a couple

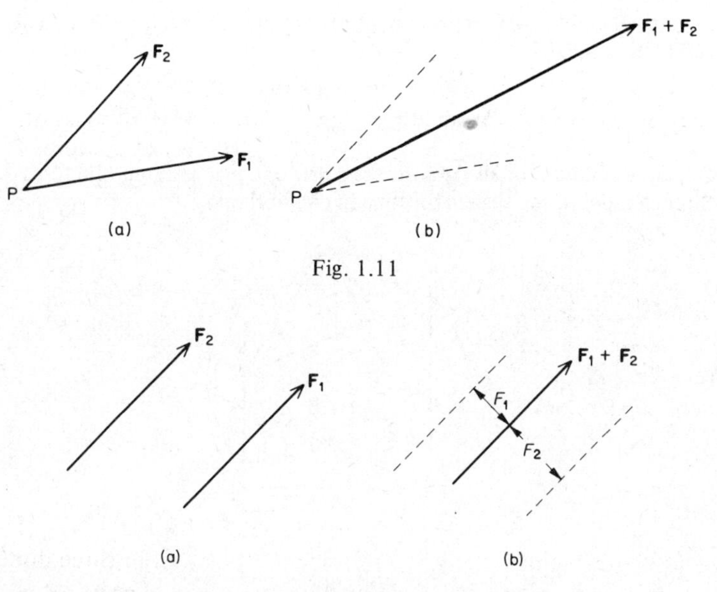

Fig. 1.11

Fig. 1.12

(unless the lines of action are coincident), since the vector sum $\mathbf{F}_1 + \mathbf{F}_2 = 0$, yet the moment of the system about any axis (e.g. an axis perpendicular to the plane of $\mathbf{F}_1$ and $\mathbf{F}_2$ through a point on the line of action of $\mathbf{F}_1$ or $\mathbf{F}_2$) is not zero. The next example illustrates this.

Example 1.4. *A circle centre O passes through the four vertices of a square ABCD. P is any other point on the circle. Show that the forces represented by the vectors* $\overrightarrow{PA}$, $\overrightarrow{BP}$, $\overrightarrow{PC}$, *and* $\overrightarrow{DP}$ *are in equilibrium. What is the resultant of the system of forces represented by* $\overrightarrow{PA}$, $\overrightarrow{PB}$, $\overrightarrow{PC}$, *and* $\overrightarrow{PD}$?

By vector addition (Fig. 1.13),

$$\overrightarrow{BP} + \overrightarrow{PA} = \overrightarrow{BA}$$

Since $\overrightarrow{PA}$ and $\overrightarrow{BP}$ pass through the point P, their resultant must pass through P, so the resultant of $\overrightarrow{PA}$ and $\overrightarrow{BP}$ is a force given in magnitude and direction by $\overrightarrow{BA}$, but passing through P.

Similarly the resultant of $\overrightarrow{PC}$ and $\overrightarrow{DP}$ is a force given in magnitude and direction by $\overrightarrow{DC}$, passing through P.

But $\overrightarrow{AB}$ and $\overrightarrow{DC}$ are opposite sides of a square and so are equal in magnitude and direction, i.e.

$$\overrightarrow{AB} = \overrightarrow{DC}$$
$$\overrightarrow{BA} + \overrightarrow{DC} = O$$

Since the resultant of all the forces is a pair of equal and opposite forces through a point, the system must be in equilibrium.

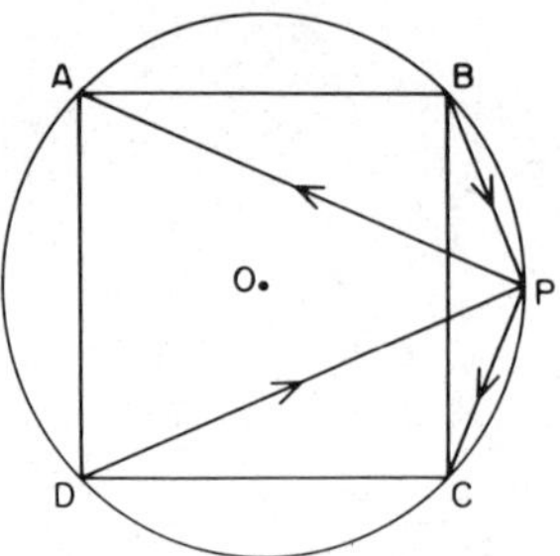

Fig. 1.13

Notice that we had to establish the lines of action of the forces. Forces represented by $\overrightarrow{BA}$ and $\overrightarrow{DC}$ acting along BA and DC respectively would be equivalent to a couple.

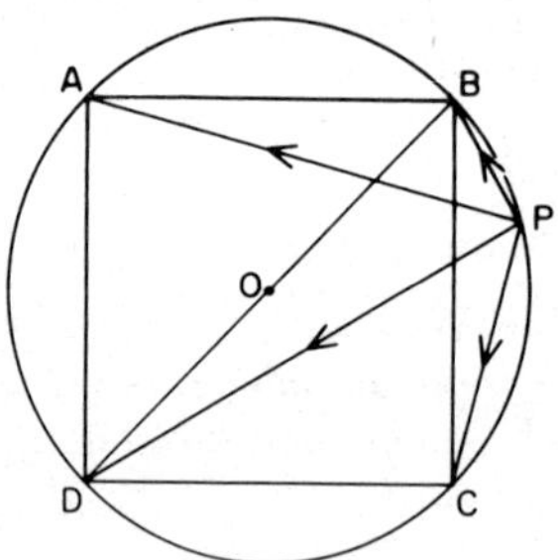

Fig. 1.14

When two of the forces are reversed in direction, the system is shown in Fig. 1.14. Now,

$$\overrightarrow{PA} + \overrightarrow{PB} + \overrightarrow{PC} + \overrightarrow{PD} = \overrightarrow{PA} + \overrightarrow{BP} + \overrightarrow{PC} + \overrightarrow{DP} + 2(\overrightarrow{PB} + \overrightarrow{PD})$$

and we have just seen

$$\overrightarrow{PA} + \overrightarrow{BP} + \overrightarrow{PC} + \overrightarrow{DP} = O$$

so that

$$\overrightarrow{PA} + \overrightarrow{PB} + \overrightarrow{PC} + \overrightarrow{PD} = 2(\overrightarrow{PB} + \overrightarrow{PD})$$

But O is the midpoint of BD, so that

$$\overrightarrow{PB} + \overrightarrow{PD} = 2\overrightarrow{PO}$$

i.e.

$$2(\overrightarrow{PB} + \overrightarrow{PD}) = 4\overrightarrow{PO}$$

Since all the original forces pass through P, their resultant must pass through P, i.e. $\overrightarrow{PA} + \overrightarrow{PB} + \overrightarrow{PC} + \overrightarrow{PD}$ are equivalent to a single force $4\overrightarrow{PO}$ through P.

EXERCISE 1(a)

The reader who feels in need of some easy examples for revision is reminded that there are many such in Exercises 10 and 11 of *Additional Applied Mathematics.*

1. Show that the points whose position vectors are $\mathbf{i} + \mathbf{j}$, $\mathbf{i} + 2\mathbf{j}$, $2\mathbf{i} + 4\mathbf{j}$, and $-\mathbf{i} - 3\mathbf{j}$ are the vertices of a trapezium whose parallel sides are in the ratio 1 : 2.

2. If the position vectors of A, B, and C are $3\mathbf{i}$, $2\mathbf{i} + \mathbf{j}$, and $3\mathbf{i} - 4\mathbf{j}$, respectively, D is the midpoint of BC and H has position vector $8\mathbf{i} - 3\mathbf{j}$, show that $\overrightarrow{AH} = 2\overrightarrow{OD}$, where O is the origin.

3. Find the value of λ if the points with position vectors $3\mathbf{i} + 4\mathbf{j}$, $\lambda\mathbf{i}$, and $\mathbf{i} - 2\mathbf{j}$ are collinear.

4. Find the value of μ if the points with position vectors $\mathbf{i} + \mathbf{j}$, $\mu\mathbf{j}$, and $-2\mathbf{i} + 7\mathbf{j}$ are collinear.

5. Find the value of λ if the points whose position vectors are $\mathbf{a} + \mathbf{b}$, $\frac{3}{2}\mathbf{a} + \lambda\mathbf{b}$, and $2\mathbf{a} + 4\mathbf{b}$ are collinear.

6. Find the position vector of the point K which divides AB in the ratio 1:2, if the position vectors of A and B are $\mathbf{i} - \mathbf{j}$ and $4\mathbf{i} + 5\mathbf{j}$ respectively.

7. OABC is a square with sides 1 unit in length. X and Y are the midpoints of OA and AB respectively. Find the position vector of P, the point of intersection of BX and OY, in terms of unit vectors $\mathbf{i}$ and $\mathbf{j}$ along OA and OC respectively.

8. With the data of Question 7, if L divides AB in the ratio 1:2, and M divides BC in the ratio 1:3, find the position vector of the point of intersection of OL and AM.

9. OABC is a square of side $2a$; **i** and **j** are unit vectors along OA, OC. The midpoint of AB is L; the midpoint of BC is M; OL, AM meet at P; BP meets OA at N. Show that the segment OP can be measured by the vector $\lambda(2a\mathbf{i} + a\mathbf{j})$ and also by the vector $2a\mathbf{i} + \mu(2a\mathbf{j} - a\mathbf{i})$. Hence determine λ and μ, and prove that ON = $\frac{2}{3}$OA. (O. & C.)

10. Two unit vectors $\hat{\mathbf{a}}$ and $\hat{\mathbf{b}}$ are such that the line of action of $\hat{\mathbf{b}}$ makes an angle of $+60°$ with the line of action of $\hat{\mathbf{a}}$. If $\mathbf{v}_1 = 2\hat{\mathbf{a}} - \hat{\mathbf{b}}$, $\mathbf{v}_2 = -\hat{\mathbf{a}} + 3\hat{\mathbf{b}}$, and $\mathbf{v}_3 = 3\hat{\mathbf{a}} + \hat{\mathbf{b}}$,
    (a) find $\mathbf{v}_3$ in terms of $\mathbf{v}_1$ and $\mathbf{v}_2$,
    (b) prove that $2\mathbf{v}_1 + 2\mathbf{v}_2 + \mathbf{v}_3$ is of magnitude $5\sqrt{3}$. (O. & C.)

11. Find the magnitude and the direction cosines of the vector $2\mathbf{i} + 10\mathbf{j} + 11\mathbf{k}$.

12. Find the magnitude and the direction cosines of the vector $\mathbf{i} - 4\mathbf{j} - 8\mathbf{k}$.

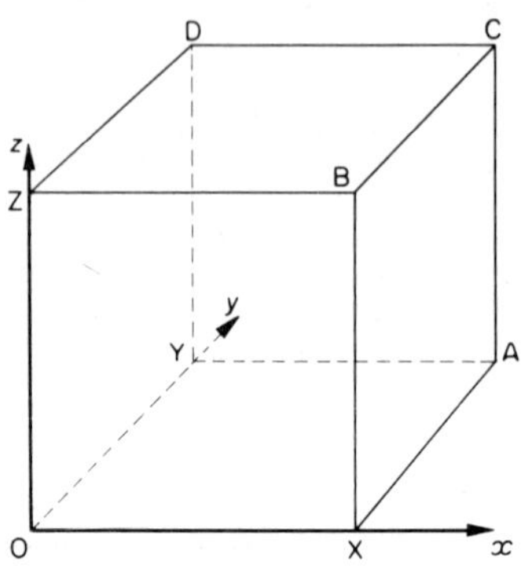

Fig. 1.15

Questions 13, 14, and 15 refer to the cube, edge 12 units, illustrated in Fig. 1.15. Take **i**, **j**, **k** *as unit vectors along Ox, Oy, Oz.*

13. If L is the midpoint of BC and M the midpoint of XL, find the cosine of the angle between OM and Ox.

14. If R divides BC in the ratio 1:2, find the cosine of the angle between OR and Oy.

15. If S divides DA in the ratio 1:3, find the cosine of the angle between ZS and Oz.

In Questions 16–20 A, B, C, and D are the vertices of a square.

16. Forces are represented completely by the vectors $\overrightarrow{AB}$, $\overrightarrow{AD}$. To what single force are they equivalent?

17. To what single force are the forces represented by $\overrightarrow{AB}$ and $\overrightarrow{DA}$ equivalent?

18. E is the midpoint of BC. To what single force is the system $2\overrightarrow{AE} + \overrightarrow{AD}$ equivalent?

19. To what single force is the system given completely by $2\overrightarrow{AE} + \overrightarrow{DA}$ equivalent?

20. Show that the system given completely by $\overrightarrow{AB} + 2\overrightarrow{BC} + \overrightarrow{CD} + 2\overrightarrow{DA}$ is not in equilibrium.

21. A, B, C, and D are any four points in space. X and Y are the midpoints of BC and DA respectively. If two forces given in magnitude and direction by $\overrightarrow{AB}$ and $\overrightarrow{DC}$ act at any point, show that they are equivalent to a force $2\overrightarrow{YX}$ at that point.

22. D, E, and F are the midpoints of the sides AB, BC, CA of a triangle. O is any point, not necessarily in the plane of the triangle. Prove that $\overrightarrow{OA} + \overrightarrow{OB} + \overrightarrow{OC} = \overrightarrow{OD} + \overrightarrow{OE} + \overrightarrow{OF}$.

23. OABCDE is a regular hexagon. If OA = **a** and AB = **b**, find the position vectors of B, C, D, and E in terms of **a** and **b**.

24. Find the position vector of the centroid of the points O, A, B, C, D, and E in Question 23.

25. Masses m, $2m$, m are placed at points whose position vectors are $\mathbf{i} + \mathbf{j} + \mathbf{k}$, $2\mathbf{i} - 2\mathbf{j} + 2\mathbf{k}$, and $-\mathbf{i} - \mathbf{j} + 3\mathbf{k}$ respectively. Find the centre of mass of the system.

26. Masses m, $2m$, $3m$ are placed at points whose position vectors are $3\mathbf{i} + 3\mathbf{j} + 4\mathbf{k}$, $-3\mathbf{i} - 5\mathbf{k}$, and $\mathbf{i} - \mathbf{j} + \mathbf{k}$ respectively. Find the centre of mass of the system.

27. Unit masses are placed at points A, B, C, D, and E whose position vectors are $\mathbf{a}$, $\mathbf{b}$, $3\mathbf{a} + 2\mathbf{b}$, $3\mathbf{a} - 2\mathbf{b}$, $\lambda\mathbf{a} + \mu\mathbf{b}$ respectively. G_1 is the centre of mass of the particles at A, B, C, and E; G_2 is the centre of mass of the particles at A, B, D, and E; G_3 is the centre of mass of the particles at C, D, and E. Find the values of λ and μ if G_1, G_2, and G_3 are collinear and $G_1G_2 = G_2G_3$. (S.U.)

28. Particles of mass $m_1, m_2, m_3, \ldots m_n$ are placed at the n points A_1, A_2, $A_3, \ldots, A_n$, respectively, whose position vectors relative to an origin O are $\mathbf{a}_1, \mathbf{a}_2, \ldots, \mathbf{a}_n$ respectively. The centre of mass of the particles is the point G with position vector $\mathbf{g}$ defined by

$$\frac{\Sigma m_i \mathbf{a}_i}{\Sigma m_i}$$

Prove that the position of G relative to the points A_i is independent of the choice of O.
Prove also that if forces $km_i\overrightarrow{OA_i}$, $i = 1, 2, 3, \ldots, n$ act at O, then the resultant force is $k\mathbf{g}\,\Sigma m_i$. (S.U.)

29. A triangle ABC is given; M is the point of trisection of AB nearer to A, and N is the point of trisection of AC nearer to C. If the force acting along MN and represented by the vector $\overrightarrow{MN}$ is equivalent to three forces acting along the sides of the triangle and represented by the vectors $\alpha\overrightarrow{BC}$, $\beta\overrightarrow{CA}$, and $\gamma\overrightarrow{AB}$, find α, β, and γ. (O. & C.)

30. Two vectors **a** and **b**, such that **b** is not a multiple of **a**, are given in a plane. Two other vectors **c** and **d** are defined by the equations $\mathbf{c} = \gamma_1\mathbf{a} + \gamma_2\mathbf{b}$, $\mathbf{d} = \delta_1\mathbf{a} + \delta_2\mathbf{b}$. Prove that any vector $\alpha\mathbf{a} + \beta\mathbf{b}$ can be expressed in terms of **c** and **d** provided $\gamma_1\delta_2 - \gamma_2\delta_1 \neq 0$. Find the coefficients of **c** and **d**. Explain the geometrical significance of the condition $\gamma_1\delta_2 - \gamma_2\delta_1 \neq 0$. (O. & C.)

31. The midpoints of the sides BC, CA, and AB of a triangle ABC are L, M, and N respectively. The centroid of this triangle is G, and O is any point in the plane of the triangle. Show that
(a) the resultant of the forces $\overrightarrow{OA}$, $\overrightarrow{OB}$, and $\overrightarrow{OC}$ is $3\,\overrightarrow{OG}$,
(b) the resultant of the forces $\overrightarrow{AB}$, $\overrightarrow{BC}$, and $\overrightarrow{CA}$ is a couple whose magnitude can be represented by twice the area of the triangle ABC.

Find the resultant of each of the following systems of forces:
(c) $\overrightarrow{OL}$, $\overrightarrow{OM}$, and $\overrightarrow{ON}$,
(d) $\overrightarrow{AL}$, $\overrightarrow{BM}$, and $\overrightarrow{CN}$. (A.E.B.)

32. Two triangles ABC and A′B′C′ are coplanar, and a point O is in the same plane; G and G′ are the centroids of the triangles ABC and A′B′C′ respectively. Show that
(a) $\overrightarrow{AO} + \overrightarrow{BO} + \overrightarrow{CO} = 3\overrightarrow{GO}$,
(b) $\overrightarrow{OA'} + \overrightarrow{OB'} + \overrightarrow{OC'} = 3\overrightarrow{OG'}$,
(c) $\overrightarrow{AA'} + \overrightarrow{BB'} + \overrightarrow{CC'} = 3\overrightarrow{GG'}$. (A.E.B.)

33. If A, B, and C are three non-collinear points, find the resultant force or the resultant couple for each of the following systems of forces:
(a) $\overrightarrow{AB}$, $\overrightarrow{BC}$, $\overrightarrow{CA}$,
(b) $\overrightarrow{AB}$, $\overrightarrow{AC}$, $\overrightarrow{CB}$. (L.)

34. O is the circumcentre of an acute angled triangle ABC. Forces of magnitudes proportional to the lengths of BC, CA, AB act along the perpendicular bisectors of the sides BC, CA, AB respectively, all directed towards O. Prove that this system of forces is in equilibrium. ABCDE is a plane convex polygon. Prove that the system of forces $\overrightarrow{AB}$, $\overrightarrow{BC}$, $\overrightarrow{CD}$, $\overrightarrow{DE}$, $\overrightarrow{EA}$ is equivalent to a couple.
Prove that, if the line of action of each force is turned through one right angle in the same sense about the midpoint of the side along which it was acting, the magnitude remaining unaltered, the new force system is in equilibrium. (L.)

35. The points A, B, and C are fixed, and P is any point on a fixed straight line. Three forces are represented by $\lambda\overrightarrow{PA}$, $\mu\overrightarrow{PB}$, $\nu\overrightarrow{PC}$ where λ, μ, and ν are constants, and $\overrightarrow{PQ}$ represents their resultant. Show that apart from one exceptional case, the locus of the point Q is a straight line. (L.)

Vector equation of a straight line

Every straight line has the property that it passes through some one point and is in a fixed direction. This enables us to write down the vector equation of the straight line.

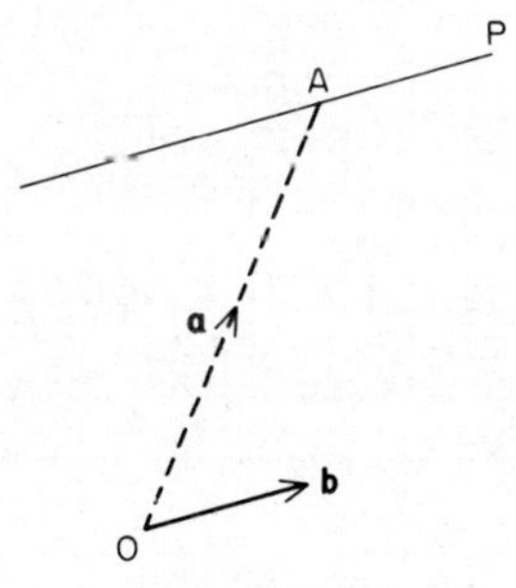

Fig. 1.16

Let the line (Fig. 1.16) pass through a point A, position vector **a**, and be parallel to a fixed vector **b**. Any point P on the line can be reached by going to A, and then a convenient distance in the direction of **b**. If **r** is the position vector of P,

$$\overrightarrow{OP} = \overrightarrow{OA} + \overrightarrow{AP}$$

i.e. $\mathbf{r} = \mathbf{a} + t\mathbf{b}$, where t is a parameter

This is the vector equation of the straight line. If the line passes through O instead of A, the equation is merely

$$\mathbf{r} = t\mathbf{b}$$

Equation of the straight line through two points

If P is any point on the straight line through A, B (Fig. 1.17),

$$\overrightarrow{OP} = \overrightarrow{OA} + \overrightarrow{AP}$$

$$= \overrightarrow{OA} + t\overrightarrow{AB}, \quad \text{where } t \text{ is again a parameter}$$

i.e. $\mathbf{r} = \mathbf{a} + t(\mathbf{b} - \mathbf{a})$, with the usual notation

i.e. $\mathbf{r} = t\mathbf{b} + (1 - t)\mathbf{a}$

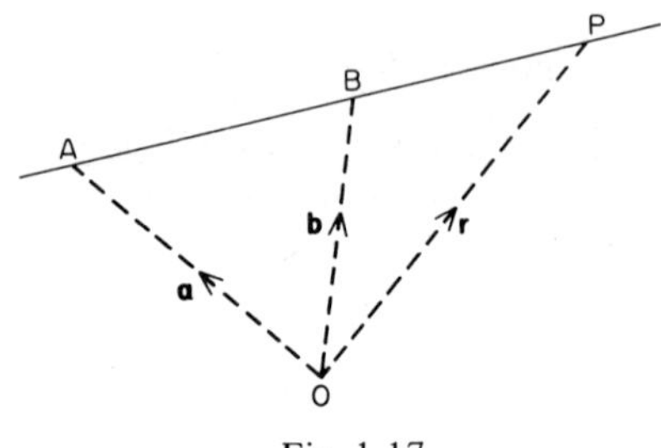

Fig. 1.17

Example 1.5. *Find the equation of the straight line through the point whose position vector is* **i** + **j**, *parallel to the x axis.*

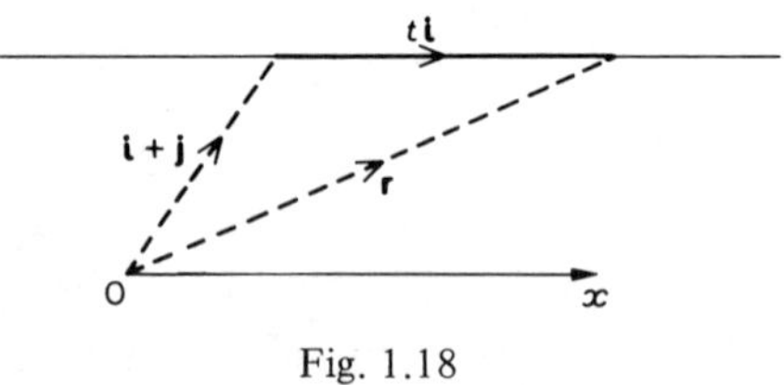

Fig. 1.18

Any vector parallel to the x axis can be expressed as $t\mathbf{i}$ (Fig. 1.18). Thus the position vector of any point on the line is

$$\mathbf{r} = \mathbf{i} + \mathbf{j} + t\mathbf{i}$$

or

$$\mathbf{r} = (1 + t)\mathbf{i} + \mathbf{j}$$

Example 1.6. *Find the equation of the straight line through the point (1, −2, 3) parallel to the line joining the origin to (1, 1, 1).*

The position vector of (1, −2, 3) is $\mathbf{i} - 2\mathbf{j} + 3\mathbf{k}$, and the line joining the origin to (1, 1, 1) may be represented by $\mathbf{i} + \mathbf{j} + \mathbf{k}$. Thus the position vector $\mathbf{r}$ of any point on the line is

$$\mathbf{r} = \mathbf{i} - 2\mathbf{j} + 3\mathbf{k} + t(\mathbf{i} + \mathbf{j} + \mathbf{k})$$

Example 1.7. *L_1 is the straight line through (1, −2, 3) parallel to the line joining the origin to (1, 1, 1): L_2 is the straight line through (2, −1, 3) parallel to the line joining the origin to (1, 1, 2). Prove that L_1 and L_2 meet.*

If $\mathbf{r}_1$ is the position vector of any point on L_1,

$$\mathbf{r}_1 = \mathbf{i} - 2\mathbf{j} + 3\mathbf{k} + t(\mathbf{i} + \mathbf{j} + \mathbf{k})$$

Similarly

$$\mathbf{r}_2 = 2\mathbf{i} - \mathbf{j} + 3\mathbf{k} + s(\mathbf{i} + \mathbf{j} + 2\mathbf{k})$$

gives the position vector of any point on L_2.
If L_1 and L_2 intersect, it must be possible to find values of t and s for which $\mathbf{r}_1$ and $\mathbf{r}_2$ give the same point.
Since the unit vectors **i**, **j**, and **k** are independent of each other, equating the values of each given by $\mathbf{r}_1$ and $\mathbf{r}_2$,

$$\begin{aligned} 1 + t &= 2 + s, && \text{from } \mathbf{i} \\ -2 + t &= -1 + s, && \text{from } \mathbf{j} \\ 3 + t &= 3 + 2s, && \text{from } \mathbf{k} \end{aligned}$$

Solving these, we see they are all satisfied by $t = 2$, $s = 1$, so the position vector of the point of intersection of L_1 and L_2 is $3\mathbf{i} + 5\mathbf{k}$.
(See Questions 7–10 in Exercise 1 (b) for similar examples, including skew lines.)

Applications to mechanics; concurrent forces, colliding particles; relative velocity

Two forces, whose lines of action meet, are either in equilibrium or are equivalent to a single force: two particles collide if they are at the same point at the same time. Having found the vector equation of a straight line we are now able to consider these and similar mechanics problems. All physical quantities in these examples are measured in kilogrammes, metres, seconds, and derived units.

Example 1.8. *A particle, initially at rest at the point whose position vector is (***i** *–* 2**j** *+* **k***) has constant velocity given by the vector* **i** *+* **j**. *Find the position of the particle after 5 s.*

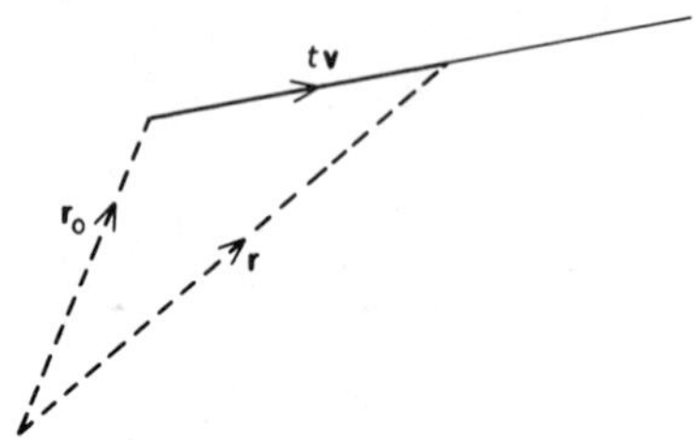

Fig. 1.19

Fig. 1.19 illustrates the change in position of a particle which has constant velocity **v** for time t. In this example the initial position vector was **i** – 2**j** + **k**, and the change in position due to a velocity **i** + **j** for 5 s is 5(**i** + **j**). The new position vector **r** of the particle is

$$\begin{aligned}\mathbf{r} &= \mathbf{i} - 2\mathbf{j} + \mathbf{k} + 5(\mathbf{i} + \mathbf{j}) \\ &= 6\mathbf{i} + 3\mathbf{j} + \mathbf{k}\end{aligned}$$

More generally, its position vector after time t is

$$\mathbf{r} = \mathbf{i} - 2\mathbf{j} + \mathbf{k} + t(\mathbf{i} + \mathbf{j})$$

Example 1.9. *A particle A has position vector* **i** – 2**j** + **k** + t(**i** + **j**), *where t is the time measured from some fixed instant. A second particle B has position vector* –**i** – 2**j** – **k** + t(**i** + 2**k**). *Find their shortest distance apart.*

The displacement vector from A to B is –2**i** – 2**k** + t(–**j** + 2**k**),

i.e. $$-2\mathbf{i} - t\mathbf{j} + (2t - 2)\mathbf{k}$$

The magnitude m of this vector is

$$\sqrt{[4 + t^2 + (2t - 2)^2]}$$

To find the minimum value of m we can more easily consider m^2, where

$$\begin{aligned}m^2 &= 4 + t^2 + 4t^2 - 8t + 4 \\ &= 5t^2 - 8t + 8 \\ &= 5\left(t - \frac{4}{5}\right)^2 + \frac{24}{5}\end{aligned}$$

The least value of m^2 is 24/5, so the shortest distance apart of the particles is $\sqrt{(24/5)}$. This occurs when $t = 4/5$. Of course, calculus could have been used, but it is often easier to find the minimum value of a quadratic function as we have done here.

Example 1.10. *Two forces* $\mathbf{F}_1 = \mathbf{i} - \mathbf{j} + \mathbf{k}$ *and* $\mathbf{F}_2 = 2\mathbf{i} - \mathbf{j} + 2\mathbf{k}$ *act at points whose position vectors are* $\mathbf{i} + 2\mathbf{k}$ *and* $4\mathbf{i} - \mathbf{j} + 5\mathbf{k}$ *respectively. Prove that they are equivalent to a single force and find the magnitude of this force and the vector equation of its line of action.*

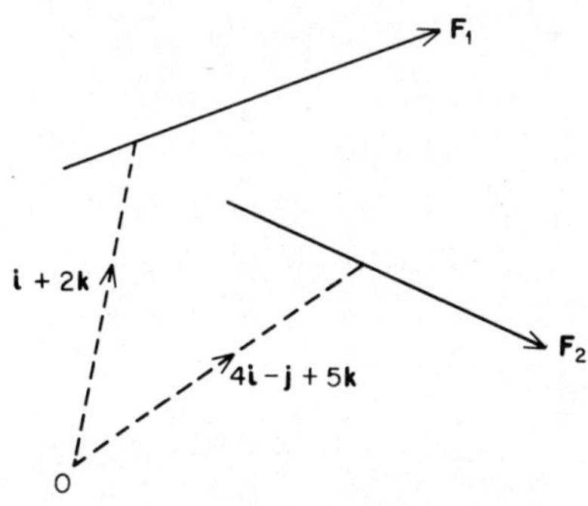

Fig. 1.20

Any point (Fig. 1.20) on the line of action of $\mathbf{F}_1$ has position vector

$$\mathbf{i} + 2\mathbf{k} + s(\mathbf{i} - \mathbf{j} + \mathbf{k})$$

Any point on the line of action of $\mathbf{F}_2$ has position vector

$$4\mathbf{i} - \mathbf{j} + 5\mathbf{k} + t(2\mathbf{i} - \mathbf{j} + 2\mathbf{k})$$

If these lines have a common point, values of s and t exist satisfying

$$1 + s = 4 + 2t \quad \text{from } \mathbf{i}$$

$$-s = -1 - t \quad \text{from } \mathbf{j}$$

$$2 + s = 5 + 2t \quad \text{from } \mathbf{k}$$

Solving these, $t = -2$, $s = -1$ satisfy all three equations, i.e. the lines of action meet at the point whose position vector is $\mathbf{j} + \mathbf{k}$.

Since their lines of action intersect, $\mathbf{F}_1$ and $\mathbf{F}_2$ are equivalent to a single force $\mathbf{F}_1 + \mathbf{F}_2$ through $\mathbf{j} + \mathbf{k}$, i.e. a force $3\mathbf{i} - 2\mathbf{j} + 3\mathbf{k}$. The magnitude of this force is

$$\sqrt{[3^2 + (-2)^2 + 3^2]}$$

i.e. $$\sqrt{22}$$

and the vector equation of its line of action is

$$\mathbf{r} = \mathbf{j} + \mathbf{k} + t(3\mathbf{i} - 2\mathbf{j} + 3\mathbf{k})$$

Example 1.11. *Find the position vector of the points of intersection of the curves given by*

$$\mathbf{r} = 3a \cos \theta \mathbf{i} + a\sqrt{2} \sin \theta \mathbf{j}$$

and $$\mathbf{r} = at^2\mathbf{i} + at\mathbf{j}$$

At the points where these meet,

$$3a \cos \theta = at^2 \quad \text{from } \mathbf{i}$$

and $$a\sqrt{2} \sin \theta = at \quad \text{from } \mathbf{j}$$

i.e. $$3 \cos \theta = 2 \sin^2 \theta$$

$$= 2 - 2 \cos^2 \theta$$

$$\Rightarrow 2 \cos^2 \theta + 3 \cos \theta - 2 = 0$$

$$\Rightarrow (2 \cos \theta - 1)(\cos \theta + 2) = 0$$

The only real values of t come from $\cos \theta = \frac{1}{2}$,

$$\Rightarrow \sin \theta = \pm \tfrac{1}{2}\sqrt{3}$$

so the points of intersection have position vectors

$$\mathbf{r}_1 = \tfrac{3}{2}a\mathbf{i} + a\sqrt{\tfrac{3}{2}}\,\mathbf{j}$$

and $$\mathbf{r}_2 = \tfrac{3}{2}a\mathbf{i} - a\sqrt{\tfrac{3}{2}}\,\mathbf{j}$$

The first curve is the ellipse

$$\frac{x^2}{9} + \frac{y^2}{2} = 1$$

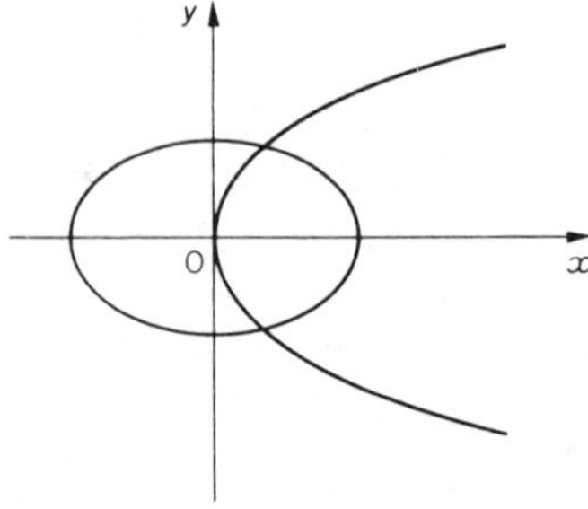

Fig. 1.21

and the second the parabola

$$y^2 = ax$$

Their points of intersection are shown in Fig. 1.21.

Example 1.12. *The position vector* **r** *of a particle is given by*

$$\mathbf{r} = a \cos t\mathbf{i} + a \sin t\mathbf{j} + bt\mathbf{k}.$$

Describe the path executed by the particle.

Expressing the position vector **r** in terms of its components,

$$\mathbf{r} = x\mathbf{i} + y\mathbf{j} + z\mathbf{k}$$

Equating the corresponding components,

$$x = a \cos t$$

$$y = a \sin t$$

$$z = bt$$

For any value of t the point is always a constant distance from the z axis, and the z coordinate increases uniformly with time. Thus the particle describes a helix (Fig. 1.22).

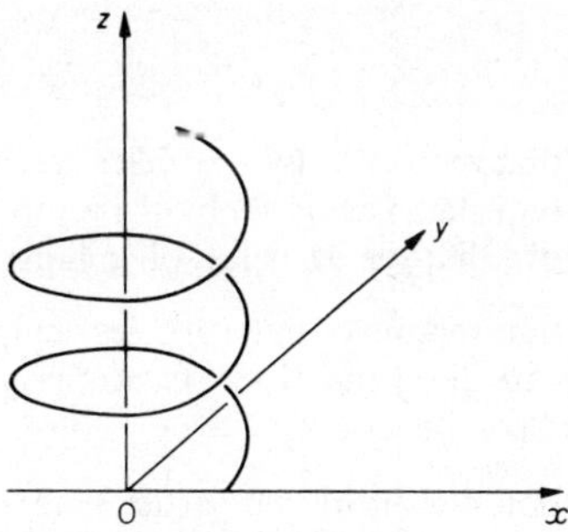

Fig. 1.22

Example 1.13. *At noon two ships A and B, each moving with constant velocity have position vectors* $3\mathbf{i} + 4\mathbf{j}$ *and* $9\mathbf{i} - 4\mathbf{j}$ *and velocity vectors* $17\mathbf{i} - 4\mathbf{j}$ *and* $5\mathbf{i} + 12\mathbf{j}$ *respectively, the units of distance being kilometres and units of velocity being kilometres per hour. Show that the ships will collide if they do not alter course or speed.*

At time t hours after noon, the position vector of A is

$$3\mathbf{i} + 4\mathbf{j} + t(17\mathbf{i} - 4\mathbf{j})$$

and that of B is

$$9\mathbf{i} - 4\mathbf{j} + t(5\mathbf{i} + 12\mathbf{j})$$

The ships collide if a value of t can be found for which the position vectors are equal,

i.e. $\quad 3 + 17t = 9 + 5t, \quad$ from **i**

and $\quad 4 - 4t = -4 + 12t, \quad$ from **j**

The solution of the first equation is $t = \frac{1}{2}$, which satisfies the second equation, so the ships would collide at 12.30 hours.

Alternative method of solution

The position vector of B relative to A is

$$9\mathbf{i} - 4\mathbf{j} - (3\mathbf{i} + 4\mathbf{j}), \quad \text{i.e. } 6\mathbf{i} - 8\mathbf{j}$$

The velocity of B relative to A is

$$5\mathbf{i} + 12\mathbf{j} - (17\mathbf{i} - 4\mathbf{j}), \quad \text{i.e. } -12\mathbf{i} + 16\mathbf{j}$$

Thus the velocity of B relative to A is along the line $\overrightarrow{BA}$, so the ships will collide if they maintain the same courses and velocities.

EXERCISE 1(b)

1. The initial position vectors of two particles are $3\mathbf{i} + 2\mathbf{j}$ and $\mathbf{i} - 4\mathbf{j}$, and their velocities (constant) are given by the vectors $-\frac{1}{2}\mathbf{i} - \mathbf{j}$ and $\frac{1}{2}\mathbf{i} + 2\mathbf{j}$ respectively. Prove that the particles will collide.

2. The initial position vectors of two particles are $\mathbf{i} + 2\mathbf{j}$ and $-2\mathbf{i} - \mathbf{j}$. Their velocity vectors are $2\mathbf{i} + \mathbf{j}$ and $3\mathbf{i} + 2\mathbf{j}$ respectively. Investigate whether the particles will collide.

3. The initial position vectors of two particles are $-\mathbf{i} + 2\mathbf{j}$ and $-2\mathbf{i} - \mathbf{j}$, and their velocity vectors are $\mathbf{i} + \mathbf{j}$ and $3\mathbf{i} + 2\mathbf{j}$ respectively. Find when they are closest together and their minimum distance apart.

4. A boat A at a point with position vector $2\mathbf{i} + \mathbf{j}$ is sailing with velocity $4\mathbf{i} + 3\mathbf{j}$, and at the same time a boat B at a point with position vector $8\mathbf{i} + 9\mathbf{j}$ sails with velocity $-3\mathbf{i} + 2\mathbf{j}$. If the boats continue on their courses with the given velocities, find their shortest distance apart and after how long this occurs. (Distances are in kilometres and velocities in kilometres per hour.) (W.J.E.C.)

5. The initial position vector of a particle is $8\mathbf{i}$ and the velocity vector at time t is $(1 + 2t)\mathbf{j}$. After how long is the particle 10 units from O?

6. The initial position vector of a particle is $7\mathbf{j}$ and its velocity vector is $6t\mathbf{i}$. After how long is the particle 25 units from O?

7. The initial position vectors of two particles are $\mathbf{i} + \mathbf{j}$ and $-\mathbf{i} + \mathbf{j} + 2\mathbf{k}$ and their constant velocity vectors are $\mathbf{i} + \mathbf{j} + 2\mathbf{k}$ and $2\mathbf{i} + \mathbf{j} + \mathbf{k}$ respectively. After how long do they collide?

8. The position vectors initially of two particles are $\mathbf{i} + \mathbf{j} + \mathbf{k}$ and $\mathbf{i} + 2\mathbf{j} + \mathbf{k}$. Their constant velocity vectors are $2\mathbf{i} + \mathbf{j} + \mathbf{k}$ and $4\mathbf{i} - \mathbf{j} + \mathbf{k}$ respectively. Show that the particles do not collide.

9. The position vectors initially of two particles are $\mathbf{i} - \mathbf{j} - \mathbf{k}$ and $2\mathbf{i} + \mathbf{j} + \mathbf{k}$ and their constant velocity vectors are $2\mathbf{i} + \mathbf{j} + \mathbf{k}$ and $\mathbf{i} + \mathbf{j} + \mathbf{k}$ respectively. Find their minimum distance apart.

10. The position vectors initially of two particles are $\mathbf{i} - \mathbf{j} + 3\mathbf{k}$ and $2\mathbf{i} + \mathbf{j} + \mathbf{k}$. Their constant velocity vectors are $2\mathbf{i} + \mathbf{j} + \mathbf{k}$ and $\mathbf{i} + 2\mathbf{j} + 3\mathbf{k}$ respectively. Find their minimum distance apart.

11. At time $t = 0$ the position vectors of two particles P and Q are $\mathbf{i} + \mathbf{j} + 3\mathbf{k}$ and $4\mathbf{i} + 5\mathbf{j} + \mathbf{k}$ respectively. The particles have constant velocity vectors $2\mathbf{i} + \mathbf{j} + 2\mathbf{k}$ and $-4\mathbf{j} + 3\mathbf{k}$ respectively. Find the position vector of Q relative to P when $t = T$. Show that the distance between the two particles is a minimum when $t = 14/15$ and find the minimum distance. Also find the position vector of Q relative to P at this instant. (L.)

12. The position vectors of the vertices A and B of a triangle ABC are $\mathbf{i} - 2\mathbf{j}$ and $5\mathbf{i}$ respectively. A particle starts to move from A to B with constant speed $\sqrt{5}$ units and a second particle starts simultaneously to move from B to C with constant velocity vector $\mathbf{i} - \mathbf{j}$. Find the velocity vector of the second particle relative to the first and find the shortest distance between the particles in the subsequent motion. (A.E.B.)

13. Two forces $\mathbf{i} + \mathbf{j}$ and $2\mathbf{i} + 3\mathbf{j}$ act at points whose position vectors are $\mathbf{i} + 2\mathbf{j}$ and $\mathbf{i} + \mathbf{j}$ respectively. Show that they are equivalent to a single force, and find the vector equation of its line of action.

14. Two forces $\mathbf{i} + \mathbf{j}$ and $2\mathbf{i} + 2\mathbf{j}$ act at points whose position vectors are $\mathbf{i} + 2\mathbf{j}$ and $\mathbf{i} + 5\mathbf{j}$ respectively. Show that they are equivalent to a single force, and find the vector equation of its line of action.

15. Two forces $\mathbf{i} + \mathbf{j}$ and $-\mathbf{i} - \mathbf{j}$ act at points whose position vectors are $\mathbf{i} + 2\mathbf{j}$ and $\mathbf{i} + \mathbf{j}$ respectively. Show that they are *not* equivalent to a single force but are not in equilibrium.

16. Two forces $\mathbf{i} + \mathbf{j}$ and $-\mathbf{i} - \mathbf{j}$ act at points whose position vectors are $\mathbf{i} + 2\mathbf{j}$ and $4\mathbf{i} + 5\mathbf{j}$ respectively. Show that they are in equilibrium.

17. Two forces $\mathbf{i} + \mathbf{j} + \mathbf{k}$ and $2\mathbf{i} + 3\mathbf{j} + 4\mathbf{k}$ act at points whose position vectors are $\mathbf{i} + 2\mathbf{j} + 3\mathbf{k}$ and $\mathbf{i} + \mathbf{j} + \mathbf{k}$ respectively. Show that they are equivalent to a single force, and find the vector equation of its line of action.

18. Two forces $\mathbf{i} + \mathbf{j} - \mathbf{k}$ and $2\mathbf{i} + 2\mathbf{j} - 2\mathbf{k}$ act at points whose position vectors are $\mathbf{i} + 2\mathbf{j} + \mathbf{k}$ and $\mathbf{i} + 5\mathbf{j} + \mathbf{k}$ respectively. Show that they are equivalent to a single force, and find the equation of its line of action.

19. Two forces $\mathbf{i} + \mathbf{j} + \mathbf{k}$ and $2\mathbf{i} + 2\mathbf{j} - \mathbf{k}$ act at points whose position vectors are $-\mathbf{i} + \mathbf{j} - \mathbf{k}$ and $3\mathbf{i} - \mathbf{j} + \mathbf{k}$ respectively. Are they equivalent to a single force?

20. A particle is acted on by a force $3\mathbf{i} + 4\mathbf{j} - 5\mathbf{k}$. If the particle was initially at rest at the point whose position vector is $\mathbf{i} + \mathbf{j} + \mathbf{k}$, what is its least distance in the subsequent motion from the point whose position vector is $3\mathbf{i} + 2\mathbf{j} + \mathbf{k}$?

21. OA, OB, and OC are the three edges of a cube that meet at a vertex O. Forces 1N, 2N, 3N act along OA, OB, OC respectively. Find the magnitude of the single force to which they are equivalent.

22. Two forces $\mathbf{F}_1$ and $\mathbf{F}_2$ are such that $\mathbf{F}_1$ is perpendicular to $\mathbf{F}_1 + \mathbf{F}_2$ and $\mathbf{F}_1$ is equal in magnitude to $\mathbf{F}_1 + \mathbf{F}_2$. Find F_2 in terms of F_1.

23. A particle of mass m which is free to move in the $\mathbf{i}, \mathbf{j}$ plane has position vector $\mathbf{r} = 0$ and velocity $\mathbf{v} = v\mathbf{i}$ when time $t = 0$. If it is acted upon by a force $mu\mathrm{e}^{-t}\mathbf{j}$ throughout the motion, show that when $t = \log_e 2$,

$$\mathbf{v} = v\mathbf{i} + \frac{u}{2}\mathbf{j}$$

Show also that the path of the particle is asymptotic to

$$\mathbf{r} = vt\mathbf{i} + u(t - 1)\mathbf{j}$$ (L.)

24. Show that the equation

$$\mathbf{r} = 4(\mathbf{i} \cos t + \mathbf{j} \sin t)$$

where t is a parameter, represents a circle. Find the position vectors of the points on this circle which are nearest to and farthest from the point whose position vector is $3\mathbf{i} + 4\mathbf{j} + 5\mathbf{k}$.

Products of vectors

So far we have defined only addition and subtraction of vectors. In considering work done and kinetic energy, however, we need the product of two vectors, and again in finding the moment of a force we need the product of two vectors. Although one of these quantities, energy, is a scalar, we notice that the other is a vector, so that there are two different types of products required.

Scalar product

The scalar product of two vectors **a**, **b** is defined as $ab \cos \theta$, where θ is the angle between **a** and **b**, and a, b are the moduli of the two vectors (Fig. 1.23). It is usually written **a . b**, so that by definition,

$$\mathbf{a} \cdot \mathbf{b} = ab \cos \theta$$

From the definition we see that the scalar product is commutative, i.e. $\mathbf{a} \cdot \mathbf{b} = \mathbf{b} \cdot \mathbf{a}$.

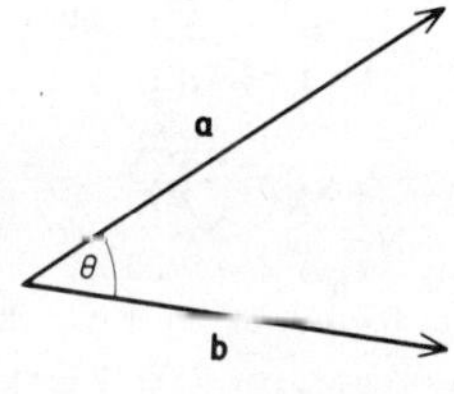

Fig. 1.23

If two vectors are perpendicular, their scalar product is zero; in particular,

$$\mathbf{i} \cdot \mathbf{j} = \mathbf{j} \cdot \mathbf{k} = \mathbf{k} \cdot \mathbf{i} = 0$$

If two vectors are parallel, their scalar product is the product of their moduli; in particular,

$$\mathbf{a}^2 = a^2 \quad \text{for all } \mathbf{a} \quad \text{and} \quad \mathbf{i}^2 = \mathbf{j}^2 = \mathbf{k}^2 = 1$$

It can easily be proved that the scalar product is distributive over addition,

i.e. $$\mathbf{a} \cdot (\mathbf{b} + \mathbf{c}) = \mathbf{a} \cdot \mathbf{b} + \mathbf{a} \cdot \mathbf{c}$$

From this it follows that the scalar product of two vectors is equal to the sum of the products of their rectangular components,

i.e. if $$\mathbf{a} = x_1\mathbf{i} + y_1\mathbf{j} + z_1\mathbf{k}$$

and $$\mathbf{b} = x_2\mathbf{i} + y_2\mathbf{j} + z_2\mathbf{k}$$

$$\mathbf{a} \cdot \mathbf{b} = x_1x_2 + y_1y_2 + z_1z_2$$

Since $\mathbf{a} \cdot \mathbf{b} = ab \cos \theta$, we can find the angle between two vectors **a**, **b**. Here,

$$a = \sqrt{(x_1^2 + y_1^2 + z_1^2)} \quad \text{and} \quad b = \sqrt{(x_2^2 + y_2^2 + z_2^2)}$$

so that $$\cos \theta = \frac{x_1x_2 + y_1y_2 + z_1z_2}{\sqrt{(x_1^2 + y_1^2 + z_1^2)}\sqrt{(x_2^2 + y_2^2 + z_2^2)}}$$

Example 1.14. *Find the cosine of the angle between the two vectors* $\mathbf{i} + \mathbf{j} + \mathbf{k}$ *and* $2\mathbf{i} + 3\mathbf{j} + 4\mathbf{k}$.

The modulus of $\mathbf{i} + \mathbf{j} + \mathbf{k}$ is $\sqrt{3}$ and of $2\mathbf{i} + 3\mathbf{j} + 4\mathbf{k}$ is $\sqrt{29}$. But

$$(\mathbf{i} + \mathbf{j} + \mathbf{k}) \cdot (2\mathbf{i} + 3\mathbf{j} + 4\mathbf{k}) = 9,$$

so if θ is the angle between the two vectors

$$\sqrt{3}\sqrt{29} \cos \theta = (\mathbf{i} + \mathbf{j} + \mathbf{k}) \cdot (2\mathbf{i} + 3\mathbf{j} + 4\mathbf{k}) = 9$$

$$\Rightarrow \cos \theta = \frac{3\sqrt{3}}{\sqrt{29}}$$

Cosine formula

Scalar products give a neat proof of the cosine formula (Fig. 1.24), for if **a**, **b**, and **c** represent the sides of the triangle ABC,

$$\mathbf{c} = \mathbf{a} + \mathbf{b}$$

$$\Rightarrow \mathbf{c} \cdot \mathbf{c} = (\mathbf{a} + \mathbf{b}) \cdot (\mathbf{a} + \mathbf{b})$$

$$\Rightarrow \quad c^2 = a^2 + b^2 + 2\mathbf{a} \cdot \mathbf{b}$$

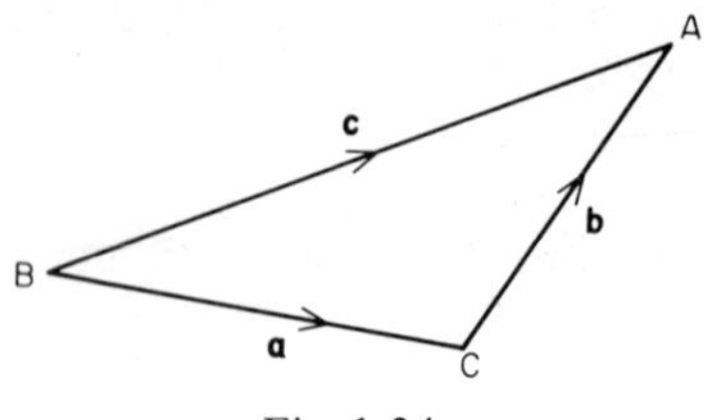

Fig. 1.24

But $\mathbf{a} \cdot \mathbf{b} = ab \cos(180° - C)$, if C is the angle BCA,

$$\Rightarrow c^2 = a^2 + b^2 - 2ab \cos C$$

Equation of a plane

If **n** is the vector from the origin perpendicular to a given plane (Fig. 1.25), and **r** is the position vector of any point in the plane, (**r** – **n**) is contained in the plane,

i.e. $$(\mathbf{r} - \mathbf{n}) \cdot \mathbf{n} = 0$$

$$\Rightarrow \mathbf{r} \cdot \mathbf{n} = n^2$$

This gives us a form for the vector equation of a plane.

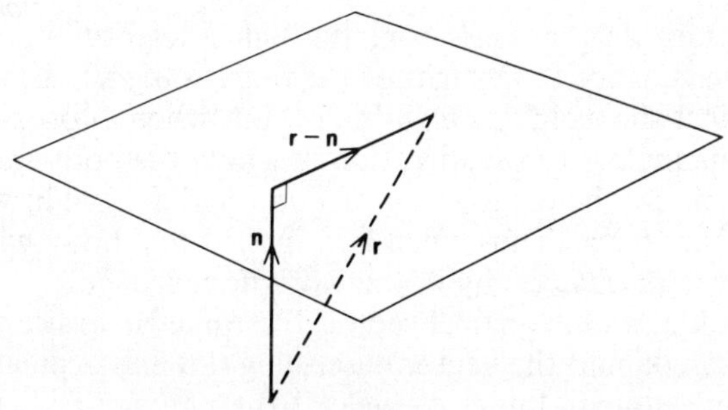

Fig. 1.25

Angle between two planes

The angle θ between two planes $\mathbf{r} \cdot \mathbf{m} = m^2$ and $\mathbf{r} \cdot \mathbf{n} = n^2$ is equal to the angle θ_1 between the vectors **m** and **n** (since each vector is perpendicular to one of the planes) (Fig. 1.26).

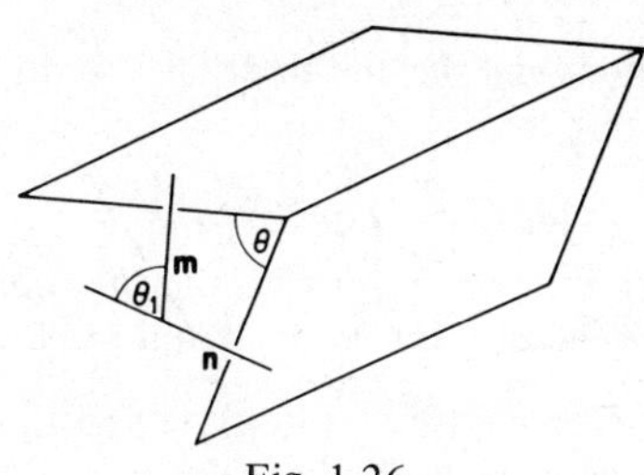

Fig. 1.26

Since $$\mathbf{m} \cdot \mathbf{n} = mn \cos \theta$$

$$\cos \theta = \frac{\mathbf{m} \cdot \mathbf{n}}{mn}$$

Components of a force

When the line of action of a force **F** makes an angle θ with the direction of a unit vector $\hat{\mathbf{a}}$, the component of **F** in the direction of $\hat{\mathbf{a}}$ is $F \cos \theta$. This can now be written $\mathbf{F} \cdot \hat{\mathbf{a}}$, since we have defined $\mathbf{F} \cdot \hat{\mathbf{a}}$ as $F \cos \theta$, $\hat{\mathbf{a}}$ being a unit vector.

Work done by a force

When we raise a body mass m kg through a height h metres at a steady speed, since the weight of the body is mg newtons, the work done against the weight is mgh joules. But when a force **F** acts on a body at an angle θ to the direction in which the body moves, work is only done by the component of **F** in the direction in which motion takes place. Thus when **F** is applied to a body while its position vector changes by **d**, the work done is $\mathbf{F} \cdot \mathbf{d}$.

Taking **k** as a unit vertical vector, the force that raises the body mass m is $mg\mathbf{k}$, and the vector describing the displacement is $h\mathbf{k}$, so the work done in joules is $(mg\mathbf{k}) \cdot (h\mathbf{k})$, i.e. mgh.

Example 1.14. *Find the work done by a force* $3\mathbf{i} + 4\mathbf{j} + 5\mathbf{k}$ *acting on a body which moves from the origin to the point position vector* $\mathbf{i} + \mathbf{j} + 2\mathbf{k}$.

The displacement vector is $\mathbf{i} + \mathbf{j} + 2\mathbf{k}$, so

$$\begin{aligned} \mathbf{F} \cdot \mathbf{d} &= (3\mathbf{i} + 4\mathbf{j} + 5\mathbf{k}) \cdot (\mathbf{i} + \mathbf{j} + 2\mathbf{k}) \\ &= 17 \end{aligned}$$

If the force is in newtons and the unit of distance is the metre, the work done is 17 J.

Example 1.15. *A force of* $(2\mathbf{i} + 3\mathbf{j} + 4\mathbf{k})$ *newtons acts on a body mass 2 kg while the body moves from rest at the origin to the point P, position vector* $(\mathbf{i} + \mathbf{j} + \mathbf{k})$ *m. Find the speed of the body when it reaches P.*

The work done by the force is $(2\mathbf{i} + 3\mathbf{j} + 4\mathbf{k}) \cdot (\mathbf{i} + \mathbf{j} + \mathbf{k})$ joules i.e. 9 J. This increases the kinetic energy of the body, which was initially zero, so that if the speed is v m s^{-1} at P,

$$\tfrac{1}{2}(2)v^2 = 9$$

the speed at P is 3 m s^{-1}.

Conservative field of force

If the work done by a field of force displacing a particle from a point A to a point B is independent of the path taken from A to B, such a field of force is called conservative. All fields of force studied at this level are conservative.

Work done by a variable force

Any variable force **F** can be expressed in terms of its components (which will themselves vary in magnitude) in fixed directions, say **i**, **j**, **k**, i.e.

$$\mathbf{F} = X\mathbf{i} + Y\mathbf{j} + Z\mathbf{k}$$

The work done δW by such a force in a small displacement $\delta\mathbf{s}$ is $\mathbf{F} \cdot \delta\mathbf{s}$. But $\delta\mathbf{s}$ can also be expressed in terms of its components in fixed directions,

i.e. $$\delta\mathbf{s} = \delta x\mathbf{i} + \delta y\mathbf{j} + \delta z\mathbf{k}$$

so that $$\delta W = (X\mathbf{i} + Y\mathbf{j} + Z\mathbf{k}) \cdot (\delta x\mathbf{i} + \delta y\mathbf{j} + \delta z\mathbf{k})$$

$$= X\,\delta x + Y\,\delta y + Z\,\delta z$$

i.e. $$W = \int X\,\mathrm{d}x + \int Y\,\mathrm{d}y + \int Z\,\mathrm{d}z$$

Example 1.16. *A force $\lambda x\mathbf{i}$ acts on a body while it is displaced from the origin to the point whose position vector is $k\mathbf{i}$. Find the work done by the force.*

The work done W is

$$\int_0^k (\lambda x\mathbf{i}) \cdot (\mathrm{d}x\mathbf{i})$$

the limits being determined by the displacement from the origin to the point position vector $k\mathbf{i}$.

$\therefore$ $$W = \left[\tfrac{1}{2}\lambda x^2\right]_0^k$$

$$= \tfrac{1}{2}\lambda k^2$$

The remainder of this chapter is more suitable for a second reading. Exercise 1(c), Questions 1–28 may now be attempted.

Vector product

We now define the vector product of two vectors **a**, **b** as a vector of magnitude $ab \sin \theta$, where θ is the angle between **a** and **b**, perpendicular to the plane containing the vectors **a**, **b**. As this is a vector it is necessary to specify the direction which is positive, and it is customary to adopt the 'right hand' convention; if θ is measured from **a** to **b**, the positive direction is the one in which a right-handed screw would advance when turned from **a** to **b**, as illustrated in Fig. 1.27.

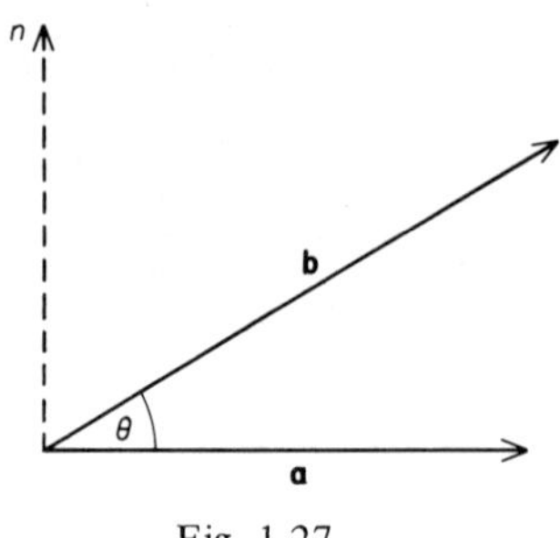

Fig. 1.27

The vector product of **a** and **b** is usually written **a x b** (occasionally **a** ∧ **b**), thus by definition

$$\mathbf{a} \times \mathbf{b} = ab \sin \theta \mathbf{n}$$

where **n** is a unit vector perpendicular to **a** and **b**. Considering a rotation from **b** to **a** in the opposite sense through the angle θ, **b x a** is in the opposite direction to **a x b**, so that

$$\mathbf{b} \times \mathbf{a} = -ab \sin \theta \mathbf{n} = -\mathbf{a} \times \mathbf{b}$$

The same result would be obtained by rotating from **b** to **a** in the anticlockwise sense through $(360° - \theta)$, when

$$\mathbf{b} \times \mathbf{a} = ab \sin (360° - \theta)\mathbf{n} = -ab \sin \theta \mathbf{n} = -\mathbf{a} \times \mathbf{b}$$

Thus the vector product is not commutative. It can be shown, however, that it is distributive over addition,

i.e. $$\mathbf{a} \times (\mathbf{b} + \mathbf{c}) = \mathbf{a} \times \mathbf{b} + \mathbf{a} \times \mathbf{c}$$

From our definition it follows that

$$\mathbf{i} \times \mathbf{i} = \mathbf{j} \times \mathbf{j} = \mathbf{k} \times \mathbf{k} = 0$$

and $$\mathbf{i} \times \mathbf{j} = -\mathbf{j} \times \mathbf{i} = \mathbf{k}, \text{ etc.}$$

also that $\mathbf{a} \times \mathbf{b} = 0 \Rightarrow \mathbf{a}$ or $\mathbf{b}$ or both equal 0 or that $\mathbf{a}$ is parallel to $\mathbf{b}$.

Sine formula

As we proved the cosine formula using scalar products, it is interesting to note that the sine formula can be proved using vector products. With the notation of Fig. 1.28,

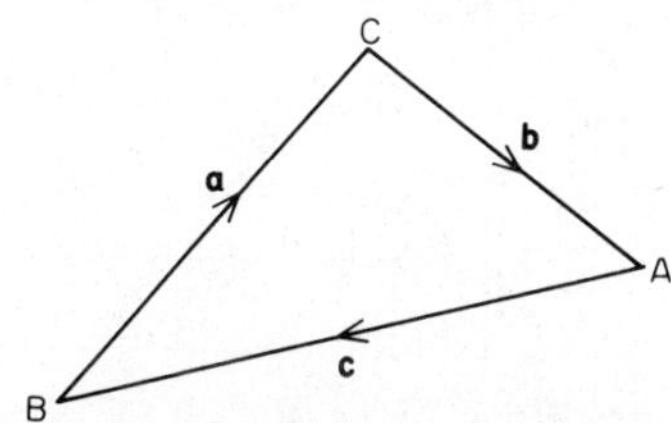

$$\mathbf{a} + \mathbf{b} + \mathbf{c} = \mathbf{0}$$

$\therefore$ $$\mathbf{a} \times (\mathbf{a} + \mathbf{b} + \mathbf{c}) = \mathbf{0}$$

i.e. $$\mathbf{a} \times \mathbf{b} + \mathbf{a} \times \mathbf{c} = \mathbf{0}, \quad \text{since } \mathbf{a} \times \mathbf{a} = \mathbf{0}$$

i.e. $$\mathbf{a} \times \mathbf{b} = \mathbf{c} \times \mathbf{a}$$

Similarly $$\mathbf{c} \times \mathbf{a} = \mathbf{b} \times \mathbf{c}$$

$$\mathbf{a} \times \mathbf{b} = \mathbf{b} \times \mathbf{c} = \mathbf{c} \times \mathbf{a}$$

But $\mathbf{a} \times \mathbf{b} = ab \sin \mathrm{C}\mathbf{n}$, where $\mathbf{n}$ is a unit vector perpendicular to the plane of the triangle ABC; similarly $\mathbf{b} \times \mathbf{c} = bc \sin \mathrm{A}\mathbf{n}$, $\mathbf{c} \times \mathbf{a} = ca \sin \mathrm{B}\mathbf{n}$.

$\therefore$ $$ab \sin \mathrm{C} = bc \sin \mathrm{A} = ca \sin \mathrm{B}$$

i.e. $$\frac{a}{\sin \mathrm{A}} = \frac{b}{\sin \mathrm{B}} = \frac{c}{\sin \mathrm{C}}.$$

Moment of a force about a point

We define the moment about the origin of the force **F** through the point P, position vector **r**, as **r x F** in a direction perpendicular to the plane containing **r** and **F**. Using the right hand convention, **r x F** acts as shown in Fig. 1.29.

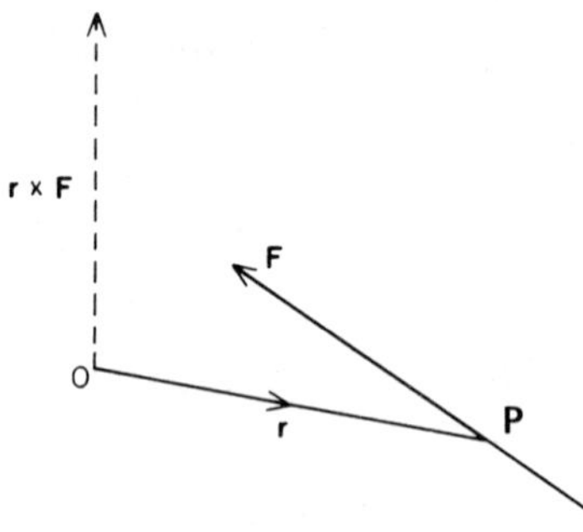

Fig. 1.29

This moment is independent of the point we choose on the line of action of **F**. For if $\mathbf{r}_1$ and $\mathbf{r}_2$ are the position vectors of two points on the line of action of **F**,

$$(\mathbf{r}_1 - \mathbf{r}_2) \text{ is along } \mathbf{F}$$
$$\Rightarrow (\mathbf{r}_1 - \mathbf{r}_2) \times \mathbf{F} = \mathbf{0}$$
$$\mathbf{r}_1 \times \mathbf{F} - \mathbf{r}_2 \times \mathbf{F} = \mathbf{0}$$
$$\mathbf{r}_1 \times \mathbf{F} = \mathbf{r}_2 \times \mathbf{F}$$

The moment of a force (and later, of other vectors) about a point is needed to investigate the motion of bodies free to move in three dimensions.

Moment of a force about an axis

By contrast, in *Additional Applied Mathematics*, we emphasized that the moment of a force then was about an axis, because at that stage we were only concerned with bodies free to move in two dimensions, and we took the axis perpendicular to the plane in which motion was possible. The moment of a force about an axis l we now define as the resolved part in the direction of l of the moment about a point on l, i.e., if $\hat{\mathbf{l}}$ is a unit vector along l, and **r** is the position vector of a point on l, the moment of a force **F** about the axis l is $(\mathbf{r} \times \mathbf{F}) \cdot \hat{\mathbf{l}}$.

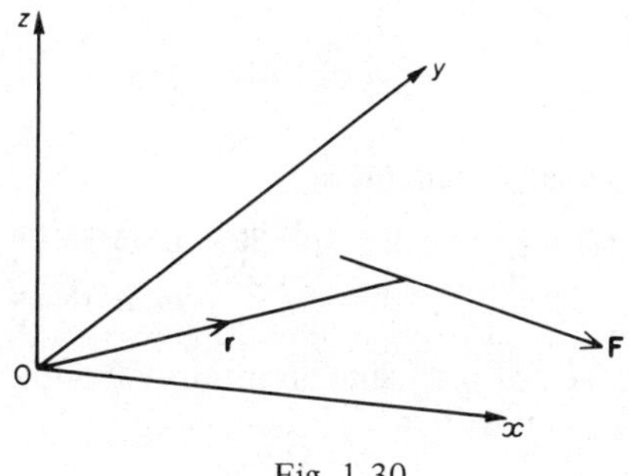

Fig. 1.30

This is a scalar quantity, as we expected, since it is a resolved part. If **F** lies in the plane Oxy and l is the z axis, let

$$\mathbf{F} = F_x\mathbf{i} + F_y\mathbf{j} \quad \text{and} \quad \mathbf{r} = x\mathbf{i} + y\mathbf{j}$$

Then the moment of **F** about the z axis is

$$[(x\mathbf{i} + y\mathbf{j}) \times (F_x\mathbf{i} + F_y\mathbf{j})] \cdot \mathbf{k} = (xF_y\mathbf{k} - yF_x\mathbf{k}) \cdot \mathbf{k}$$
$$= xF_y - yF_x$$

a result with which we are familiar. Thus our new definition of the moment of a force about an axis is consistent with our former use of the word 'moment'.

Example 1.17. *Find the moment about the point B, position vector* $2\mathbf{i} - \mathbf{j} - \mathbf{k}$ *of the force* $\mathbf{F} = 3\mathbf{i} + -\mathbf{j} + \mathbf{k}$ *acting at the point A, position vector* $\mathbf{i} + \mathbf{j} + \mathbf{k}$.

The position vector of A relative to B (Fig. 1.31) is $\mathbf{a} - \mathbf{b}$, with the usual notation,

i.e. $$-\mathbf{i} + 2\mathbf{j} + 2\mathbf{k}$$

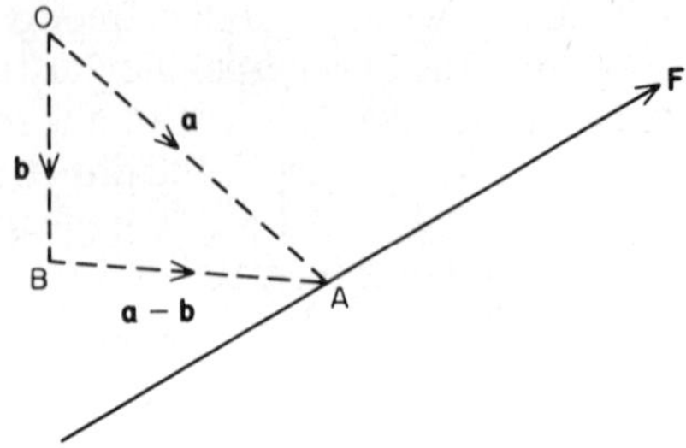

Fig. 1.31

The moment of **F** about B therefore is

$$(-\mathbf{i} + 2\mathbf{j} + 2\mathbf{k}) \times (3\mathbf{i} - \mathbf{j} + \mathbf{k}) = 4\mathbf{i} + 7\mathbf{j} - 5\mathbf{k}, \quad \text{using } \mathbf{i} \times \mathbf{j} = \mathbf{k}, \text{ etc., and } \mathbf{i} \times \mathbf{i} = \mathbf{j} \times \mathbf{j} = \mathbf{k} \times \mathbf{k} = \mathbf{0}$$

The reader who is familiar with determinants may find the arithmetic of the vector product simpler if written

$$(-\mathbf{i} + 2\mathbf{j} + 2\mathbf{k}) \times (3\mathbf{i} - \mathbf{j} + \mathbf{k}) = \begin{vmatrix} \mathbf{i} & \mathbf{j} & \mathbf{k} \\ -1 & 2 & 2 \\ 3 & -1 & 1 \end{vmatrix}$$

$$= \begin{vmatrix} 2 & 2 \\ -1 & 1 \end{vmatrix} \mathbf{i} - \begin{vmatrix} -1 & 2 \\ 3 & 1 \end{vmatrix} \mathbf{j} + \begin{vmatrix} -1 & 2 \\ 3 & -1 \end{vmatrix} \mathbf{k}$$

$$= 4\mathbf{i} + 7\mathbf{j} - 5\mathbf{k}$$

Example 1.18. *Find the moment of the force* **F** *in Example 1.17 about an axis through B parallel to the vector* **i** + **j** + 2**k**.

From the definition of the moment about an axis, this is

$$[(\mathbf{a} - \mathbf{b}) \times \mathbf{F}] \cdot \hat{\mathbf{l}}$$

where $\hat{\mathbf{l}}$ is a unit vector parallel to **i** + **j** + 2**k**.

But the magnitude of **i** + **j** + 2**k** is $\sqrt{6}$ so that the required unit vector is

$$\frac{1}{\sqrt{6}}(\mathbf{i} + \mathbf{j} + 2\mathbf{k})$$

Thus the moment of the force about the axis is

$$(4\mathbf{i} + 7\mathbf{j} - 5\mathbf{k}) \cdot \frac{1}{\sqrt{6}}(\mathbf{i} + \mathbf{j} + 2\mathbf{k}) = \frac{1}{\sqrt{6}}$$

Equivalent systems of forces

We have seen (*Additional Applied Mathematics*, page 101) that the necessary and sufficient condition for two systems of forces to be equivalent is that their vector sums should be equal, and that the sums of their moments about any axis should be equal. Since the moments about any axes have to be equal, the components of the moments about any point are equal, that is, the vector sums of the moments about any point are equal.

Example 1.19. *Forces* $\mathbf{i}+\mathbf{j}+\mathbf{k}$ *and* $2\mathbf{i}+3\mathbf{j}+4\mathbf{k}$ *act at points whose position vectors are* $\mathbf{i}+2\mathbf{j}+3\mathbf{k}$ *and* $\mathbf{i}+\mathbf{j}+\mathbf{k}$ *respectively. Given that they are equivalent to a single force, find the line of action of this force.*

The resultant force $\mathbf{F}$ must be equal to the vector sum of the original forces,

i.e. $$\mathbf{F} = 3\mathbf{i}+4\mathbf{j}+5\mathbf{k}$$

If $\mathbf{r}$ is any point on the line of action of $\mathbf{F}$,

$$\begin{aligned}\mathbf{r}\times\mathbf{F} &= (\mathbf{i}+2\mathbf{j}+3\mathbf{k})\times(\mathbf{i}+\mathbf{j}+\mathbf{k})+(\mathbf{i}+\mathbf{j}+\mathbf{k})\times(2\mathbf{i}+3\mathbf{j}+4\mathbf{k})\\ &= \mathbf{0}\end{aligned}$$

Thus $\mathbf{r}$ must be parallel to $\mathbf{F}$, so the vector equation of the line of action of $\mathbf{F}$ is

$$\mathbf{r} = \lambda(3\mathbf{i}+4\mathbf{j}+5\mathbf{k})$$

EXERCISE 1(c)

Problems requiring vector products are confined to Questions 28–40.

1. Find the following scalar products:
   (a) $(\mathbf{i}+\mathbf{j}+\mathbf{k}).(\mathbf{i}+2\mathbf{j}+3\mathbf{k})$
   (b) $(-\mathbf{i}+2\mathbf{j}+\mathbf{k}).(2\mathbf{i}-\mathbf{j}+4\mathbf{k})$
   (c) $(2\mathbf{i}+\mathbf{j}-2\mathbf{k}).(3\mathbf{i}-4\mathbf{j}+\mathbf{k})$
   (d) $(\mathbf{i}-\mathbf{j}-\mathbf{k}).(\mathbf{i}+\mathbf{j})$
   What can you deduce about the directions of the vectors in (b), (c) and (d)?
2. Find a unit vector perpendicular to $2\mathbf{i}+\mathbf{j}-\mathbf{k}$ and $-3\mathbf{i}-4\mathbf{j}-\mathbf{k}$.
3. Prove that the vector equation of the sphere on points, position vectors $\mathbf{a}$, $\mathbf{b}$ as diameter is $(\mathbf{r}-\mathbf{a}).(\mathbf{r}-\mathbf{b}) = 0$.

4. Find the Cartesian equation of the plane through the point whose position vector is **i** + **j** + 4**k** perpendicular to the vector –**i** + 2**j** – 3**k**.

5. Find the Cartesian equation of the plane through the point whose position vector is –**i** – **j** + 2**k** perpendicular to the vector **i** – **j** + 2**k**.

6. Find the cosine of the angle between the two forces **i** – 2**j** + 2**k** and 2**i** + 2**j** + **k**.

7. Find the cosine of the angle between the two forces 3**i** + 4**j** + 5**k** and **i** + **j** – 2**k**.

8. Find the cosine of the angle between the planes **r** . (**i** – **j** + **k**) = 3 and **r** . (**i** + **j** – **k**) = 4.

9. Find the cosine of the angle between the planes **r** . (**i** + 2**j** – 2**k**) = 1 and **r** . (**i** – **j** + **k**) = 2.

10. Find the cosine of the angle between the planes **r** . (**i** + 2**j** – 2**k**) = 1 and **r** . (4**i** – **j** + **k**) = 1.

11. Find the sine of the angle made by the force **i** + 2**j** + 2**k** with the plane **r** . (2**i** – **j** – **k**) = 1.

12. Find the sine of the angle made by the force **i** – **j** – 4**k** with the plane **r** . (**i** – **j** – 2**k**) = 1.

13. Two rods each of length 13 cm are placed, not side by side, inside a rectangular box 3 cm by 4 cm by 12 cm. Find by vector methods, the cosine of the largest possible angle between the rods.

In Questions 14, 15, and 16, OABCXYZW is a rectangular framework, edge 1 unit, in which X is vertically above O, Y above A, and Z above B.

14. Find the angle between the lines of action of a force along OZ and a force along OX.

15. Find the magnitude of the force equal to a force of $\sqrt{3}$ units along OZ and a force of $\sqrt{2}$ units along OY.

16. Find the resultant of forces 4 units along YW and 4 units along OY.

17. A particle of mass 3 units is acted on by the forces $\mathbf{F}_1$ = 2**i** + 3**j**, $\mathbf{F}_2$ = 3**j** + 4**k**, and $\mathbf{F}_3$ = **i** + 2**k**, and is initially at rest at the point **i** – **j** – **k**. Find the position and the momentum of the particle after 2 s. Find also the work done on the particle in that time. (L.)

18. If **u** = a**i** + b**j** + c**k**, where **i**, **j**, and **k** are mutually perpendicular unit vectors, show that a = **u** . **i**, b = **u** . **j**, and c = **u** . **k**.

If

$$\mathbf{u} = \frac{1}{\sqrt{3}}(\mathbf{i} + \mathbf{j} + \mathbf{k}), \quad \mathbf{v} = \sqrt{\frac{2}{3}}(\mathbf{i} - \tfrac{1}{2}\mathbf{j} - \tfrac{1}{2}\mathbf{k})$$

and

$$\mathbf{w} = \frac{1}{\sqrt{2}}(\mathbf{j} - \mathbf{k})$$

show that **u**, **v**, and **w** are mutually perpendicular unit vectors, and express **i** in the form

$$p\mathbf{u} + q\mathbf{v} + r\mathbf{w}$$

(J.M.B.)

19. If **a**, **b**, and **c** are the vectors OA, OB, and OC, and

$$\mathbf{c} = \frac{\alpha\mathbf{a} + \beta\mathbf{b}}{\alpha + \beta}$$

show that A, B, and C are collinear; for what values of α and β does C lie between A and B? Verify algebraically that given any three distinct points on a line one and only one of them can lie between the other two.
Express the angle AOC in terms of the scalar product of vectors, and show that if the angles AOC and BOC are equal, then

$$\frac{AC}{BC} = \frac{OA}{OB}$$

(O.S.)

20. Two forces, represented by $2\mathbf{i} + 3\mathbf{j}$ and $\mathbf{i} - 2\mathbf{j}$ respectively, move a particle of mass 3 units from rest at a point with position vector $\mathbf{i} + \mathbf{j}$. These are the only forces acting on the particle. Find the position vector of the point reached by the particle after 4 s, and the velocity of the particle at this time. Calculate the total work done by the forces. What force is required to bring the particle to rest in the next 3 s? Sketch the speed-time curve for the first 7 s of motion. (A.E.B.)

21. A particle is acted on by forces $4\mathbf{i} + \mathbf{j} - 3\mathbf{k}$ and $3\mathbf{i} + \mathbf{j} - \mathbf{k}$ as it is displaced from the point position vector $\mathbf{i} + 2\mathbf{j} + 3\mathbf{k}$ to the point $5\mathbf{i} + 4\mathbf{j} + \mathbf{k}$. Find the work done on the particle.

22. A constant force $2\mathbf{i} + 3\mathbf{j} + 6\mathbf{k}$ acts on a particle of unit mass as it is displaced from the point position vector $\mathbf{i} + \mathbf{j} + 2\mathbf{k}$ to the point $3\mathbf{i} - \mathbf{j} + 3\mathbf{k}$. If the particle was initially at rest find its velocity when it reaches the point position vector $3\mathbf{i} - \mathbf{j} + 3\mathbf{k}$.

23. A constant force **F** has magnitude 10 units and its direction is the same as that of the vector $2\mathbf{i} + 3\mathbf{j} + 6\mathbf{k}$. The force acts on a particle of unit mass which moves on a smooth rail connecting the points A and B

whose position vectors are $\mathbf{i} + \mathbf{j} + 2\mathbf{k}$ and $3\mathbf{i} - \mathbf{j} + 3\mathbf{k}$ respectively. If the particle is initially at rest at A find its speed when it reaches B.

(J.M.B.)

24. Two forces $\mathbf{F}_1 = 5\mathbf{i} + 2\mathbf{j} + 7\mathbf{k}$ and $\mathbf{F}_2 = 4\mathbf{i} + \mathbf{j} - \mathbf{k}$ act at points whose position vectors are $\mathbf{r}_1 = -3\mathbf{i} + 3\mathbf{j} - 2\mathbf{k}$ and $\mathbf{r}_2 = 10\mathbf{i} + 7\mathbf{j} + 3\mathbf{k}$ respectively. Show that the lines of action of these forces are coplanar. Find the magnitude of their resultant and the vector and Cartesian equations of the line of action of this resultant. Write down the unit vectors which lie in the lines of action of $\mathbf{F}_1$ and $\mathbf{F}_2$ and hence find the cosine of the angle between these lines of action. (A.E.B.)

25. Forces $\mathbf{P}_i$ act at coplanar points whose displacement vectors are $\mathbf{r}_i$ $(i = 1, 2, \ldots, n)$ and produce equilibrium. Investigate the possible values of the constant scalars λ, μ and constant vectors $\mathbf{Q}$ and $\mathbf{a}$ such that forces $(\lambda\mathbf{P}_i + \mathbf{Q})$ acting at $(\mu\mathbf{r}_i + \mathbf{a})$ produce equilibrium. Illustrate your result by starting with four forces which are in equilibrium and obtaining another set of forces by giving appropriate values to the constants. (M.E.I.)

26. If $\mathbf{n}$ and $\mathbf{r}$ are two vectors, prove that the resolved part of $\mathbf{r}$ in the direction of $\mathbf{n}$ is

$$\left(\frac{\mathbf{n}\,.\,\mathbf{r}}{|\mathbf{n}|^2}\right)\mathbf{n}$$

Hence show that the perpendicular distance of the point whose position vector is $\mathbf{a}$ from the straight line $\mathbf{r} = \mathbf{b} + t\mathbf{n}$ is the square root of

$$|\mathbf{b} - \mathbf{a}|^2 - \frac{[\mathbf{n}\,.\,(\mathbf{b} - \mathbf{a})]^2}{|\mathbf{n}|^2}$$

27. Show that the distance of the point a from the plane $\mathbf{r}\,.\,\mathbf{n} = p$, where n is a unit vector, is $|\mathbf{a}\,.\,\mathbf{n} - p|$. A circle S is defined by the intersection of the surfaces

$$\mathbf{r}\,.\,\mathbf{n} = p, \quad (\mathbf{r} - \mathbf{c})^2 = R^2$$

Show that, if $\mathbf{c}\,.\,\mathbf{n} = p$, the distance between the point $\mathbf{a}$ and the closest point of S is

$$\{(\mathbf{a} - \mathbf{c})^2 + R^2 - 2R[(\mathbf{a} - \mathbf{c})^2 - (\mathbf{a}\,.\,\mathbf{n} - p)^2]^{1/2}\}^{1/2} \qquad \text{(C.S.)}$$

28. These equations occur in the Theory of Relativity:

$$\mathbf{r}' = \mathbf{r} + \left(\frac{\gamma - 1}{\mathbf{v}^2}\mathbf{v}\,.\,\mathbf{r} - \gamma t\right)\mathbf{v}; \quad t' = \gamma\left(t - \frac{\mathbf{v}\,.\,\mathbf{r}}{c^2}\right)$$

where $\gamma = \dfrac{c}{\sqrt{(c^2 - \mathrm{v}^2)}}$.

Prove the reciprocal equations:

$$\mathbf{r} = \mathbf{r}' + \left(\frac{\gamma - 1}{\mathrm{v}^2}\mathbf{v} \cdot \mathbf{r}' + \gamma t'\right)\mathbf{v}; \quad t = \gamma\left(t' + \frac{\mathbf{v} \cdot \mathbf{r}'}{c^2}\right)$$

29. Find the following vector products:
(a) $(\mathbf{i} + \mathbf{j} - \mathbf{k}) \times (2\mathbf{i} + 3\mathbf{j} + \mathbf{k})$
(b) $(\mathbf{i} + \mathbf{k}) \times (\mathbf{i} - \mathbf{j})$
(c) $(\mathbf{i} + \mathbf{j} + \mathbf{k}) \times (\mathbf{i} - \mathbf{j} - \mathbf{k})$
(d) $(2\mathbf{i} - \mathbf{j} - \mathbf{k}) \times (-\mathbf{i} + \frac{1}{2}\mathbf{j} + \frac{1}{2}\mathbf{k})$

30. Find the moment about the origin of the force $3\mathbf{i} - \mathbf{j} - \mathbf{k}$ acting at the point $\mathbf{i} - \mathbf{j} - \mathbf{k}$.

31. Find the moment about the point $\mathbf{i} - \mathbf{j} - 2\mathbf{k}$ of the force $2\mathbf{i} - 4\mathbf{j} - \mathbf{k}$ at the point $\mathbf{i} + \mathbf{j} + \mathbf{k}$.

32. Find the moment of the force in Question 30 about a line through the origin parallel to $\mathbf{i} - \mathbf{j}$.

33. Find the moment of the force in Question 31 about a line through $\mathbf{i} - \mathbf{j} - 2\mathbf{k}$ parallel to $\mathbf{i} - \mathbf{j} - \mathbf{k}$.

34. The position vectors of the vertices of a tetrahedron are **a**, **b**, **c** and **d**. Find the volume of the tetrahedron.

35. Show that the perpendicular distance from a point C, position vector **c**, to the straight line through A and B, position vectors **a**, **b** is

$$\frac{|\mathbf{b} \times \mathbf{c} + \mathbf{c} \times \mathbf{a} + \mathbf{a} \times \mathbf{b}|}{|\mathbf{b} - \mathbf{a}|}$$

36. A force of magnitude 10 units acts along a diagonal of a face of a cube whose edges have length 2 units. Calculate the moment of the force about one of the diagonals of the cube which it does not intersect. (S.M.P.)

37. A light tetrahedron has its vertices at O, the origin, and at points A, B, and C whose position vectors are $3\mathbf{j} + 4\mathbf{k}$, $4\mathbf{i} + 4\mathbf{j} + 2\mathbf{k}$, and $2\mathbf{i} + 10\mathbf{j} + 11\mathbf{k}$. Three forces, each of magnitude P, act at O in the directions OA, OB, and OC. Find the magnitude of the resultant and the point where its line of action meets the face ABC of the tetrahedron. If the tetrahedron is smoothly hinged along the edge AC, find the magnitude of the couple required to maintain equilibrium. (A.E.B.)

38. The following forces act through the centre of a uniform sphere: $\mathbf{F}_1$, magnitude 9 N, in the direction of the vector $\mathbf{i} + 2\mathbf{j} - 2\mathbf{k}$; $\mathbf{F}_2$, magnitude 7 N, in the direction of the vector $6\mathbf{i} + 3\mathbf{j} - 2\mathbf{k}$; $\mathbf{F}_3$, and the sphere's own weight, 5 N, in the direction $-\mathbf{k}$. The centre of the sphere starts from rest at A (4, 3, 2) and is moved by this system of forces to B (8, 7, 6) in 1 second. Given that the unit of length is the metre, find the work done by each of the forces $\mathbf{F}_1$, $\mathbf{F}_2$, as the centre of the sphere moves from A to B. Find also the magnitude and direction of the force $\mathbf{F}_3$ and the resultant of the system. (L.)

39. A force of magnitude 10 N acts along the line AB from A (−11, 6, 2) to B (7, 7, −4). Determine the magnitude of the moment of this force about a line passing through the points (3, 3, 3) and (−3, 7, 13). All coordinates are in metres. (C.S.)

40. Three forces **P**, **Q** and **R** act at points whose position vectors are **p**, **q**, **r** respectively. Given that

$$\mathbf{P} = (4\mathbf{i} - 3\mathbf{j} + 2\mathbf{k}) \quad \text{acting at } \mathbf{p} = 9\mathbf{i}$$
$$\mathbf{Q} = (3\mathbf{i} + 2\mathbf{j} - 4\mathbf{k}) \quad \text{acting at } \mathbf{q} = (-\mathbf{i} - \mathbf{j} + 6\mathbf{k})$$
$$\mathbf{R} = (-7\mathbf{i} + \mathbf{j} + 2\mathbf{k}) \quad \text{acting at } \mathbf{r} = (-2\mathbf{i} + \mathbf{j} - 3\mathbf{k})$$

show that the forces reduce to a couple and calculate its magnitude. The force **R** is now removed from the system and replaced by the force **S** which is such that the forces **P**, **Q**, and **S** are in equilibrium. Find the magnitude of **S** and the equation of the line along which it acts. (A.E.B.)

2. Impacts of Elastic Bodies: Impulsive Tensions in Strings

Direct impact of elastic bodies

Newton found by experiment that when two small smooth spheres collide, the ratio

$$\frac{\text{velocity of separation}}{\text{velocity of approach}}$$

is independent of the velocities of the spheres before impact, providing these velocities are neither very small nor very large. Using the notation of Fig. 2.1

$$\frac{v_2 - v_1}{u_1 - u_2} = \text{constant}$$

This constant is called the coefficient of restitution, and is denoted by e. In practice, the equation is usually written

$$v_2 - v_1 = e(u_1 - u_2)$$

The value of e depends on the nature of both bodies. The coefficient of restitution between two billiard balls is different from the coefficient of restitution between one of the billiard balls and a tennis ball. Bodies for which $e = 1$ are said to be perfectly elastic; for which $e = 0$ perfectly inelastic. The value $e = 1$ is not attained by any physical bodies.

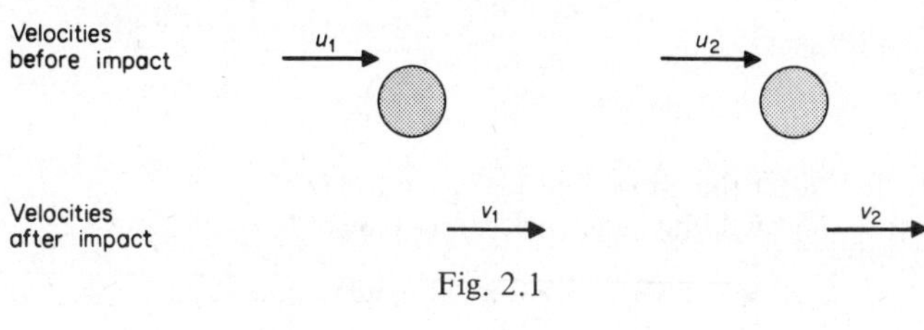

Fig. 2.1

Care must be taken that the quantities equated are positive, and it is most important to draw a diagram showing clearly the directions of the velocities in each problem.

In general, the velocities of the bodies before impact will be known, and we saw in *Additional Applied Mathematics* (page 149) that momentum is conserved during impacts. Thus we have two equations for the two unknown velocities after the impact.

We consider at this stage only impacts between smooth spheres which do not roll and which are sufficiently small so that we can ignore their size. By direct impact we mean that all motion takes place along the line of centres of the spheres.

Example 2.1. *Two small smooth spheres, mass 1 kg and 2 kg, are moving in the same direction along the same straight line with velocities 3 m s^{-1} and 1 m s^{-1} respectively (Fig. 2.2). If the coefficient of restitution e between the spheres is $\frac{1}{2}$, find the velocities of the spheres after impact.*

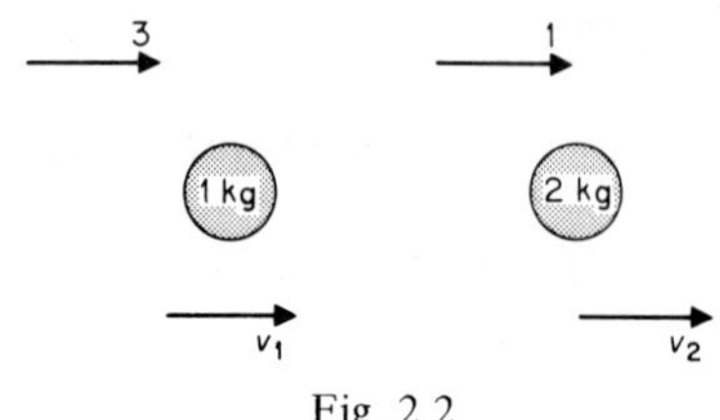

Fig. 2.2

From the conservation of linear momentum ($m\mathbf{v}$),

$$1 \times 3 + 2 \times 1 = 1 \times v_1 + 2 \times v_2$$

From Newton's experimental law,

$$\tfrac{1}{2}(3 - 1) = v_2 - v_1$$

$$\Rightarrow v_1 + 2v_2 = 5$$

and

$$-v_1 + v_2 = 1$$

$$\Rightarrow v_1 = 1, \quad v_2 = 2$$

the velocities after the impact are 1 m s^{-1} and 2 m s^{-1}.
Notice that the total kinetic energy before impact is

$$\tfrac{1}{2} \times 1 \times (3)^2 + \tfrac{1}{2} \times 2 \times (1)^2 \text{ joules, i.e. } 5\tfrac{1}{2} \text{ J}$$

After impact the total kinetic energy is

$$\tfrac{1}{2} \times 1 \times (1)^2 + \tfrac{1}{2} \times 2 \times (2)^2 \text{ joules}, \quad \text{i.e. } 4\tfrac{1}{2} \text{ J}$$

There is a loss of kinetic energy of 1 J. Kinetic energy is always lost in impacts (except for theoretical impacts when $e = 1$), in contrast to momentum which is conserved.

Example 2.2. *Two small smooth spheres A, B, mass 3 kg and 2 kg, have velocities* $2\mathbf{i}$ *m s*$^{-1}$ *and* $-\mathbf{i}$ *m s*$^{-1}$ *respectively, where* $\mathbf{i}$ *is a unit vector in the direction AB. If* $e = \frac{1}{4}$, *find their velocities after the impact.*

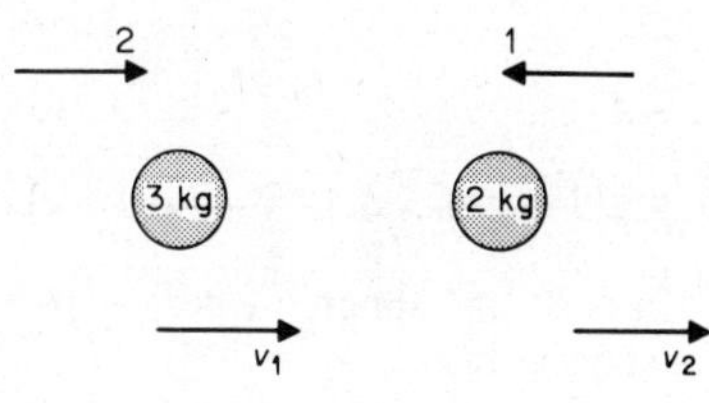

Fig. 2.3

From the conservation of linear momentum,

$$3 \times 2 + 2(-1) = 3v_1 + 2v_2$$

and from Newton's law,

$$\tfrac{1}{4}[2 - (-1)] = v_2 - v_1$$

$$\Rightarrow 3v_1 + 2v_2 = 4$$

and

$$-v_1 + v_2 = \tfrac{3}{4}$$

$$\Rightarrow v_1 = 0.5 \quad \text{and} \quad v_2 = 1.25$$

their velocities are $0.5\,\mathbf{i}$ m s^{-1} and $1.25\,\mathbf{i}$ m s^{-1}.

The direction of all the velocities is clearly shown in Fig. 2.3. If v_1 had been negative, that would merely have meant that A was moving to the left after the impact.

Example 2.3. *A small smooth sphere, velocity u, strikes an identical sphere initially at rest. Find the subsequent velocities of the two bodies.*

Denoting the mass of each body by m and the coefficient of restitution by e,

$$mu = mv_1 + mv_2, \quad \text{conservation of momentum,}$$

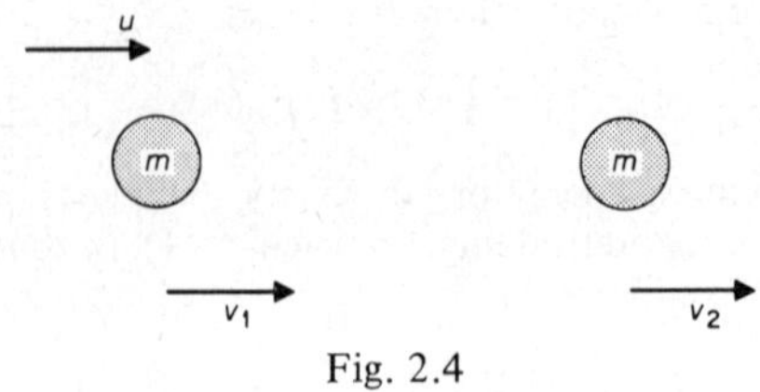

Fig. 2.4

and

$$eu = v_2 - v_1, \quad \text{Newton's law,}$$

$$\Rightarrow v_1 + v_2 = u$$

and $$-v_1 + v_2 = eu$$

$$\Rightarrow v_1 = \tfrac{1}{2}(1 - e)u \quad \text{and} \quad v_2 = \tfrac{1}{2}(1 + e)u$$

Notice that, when $e = 1$, the second sphere moves away with velocity u, whereas the first sphere stays at rest.

Loss of kinetic energy in impacts

In Example 2.1 we saw that there was a loss of 1 J of kinetic energy. To find the loss of kinetic energy in the general problem in which two spheres masses m_1 and m_2, velocities u_1 and u_2 collide, from the conservation of momentum

$$m_1u_1 + m_2u_2 = m_1v_1 + m_2v_2$$

and from Newton's law,

$$v_2 - v_1 = e(u_1 - u_2)$$

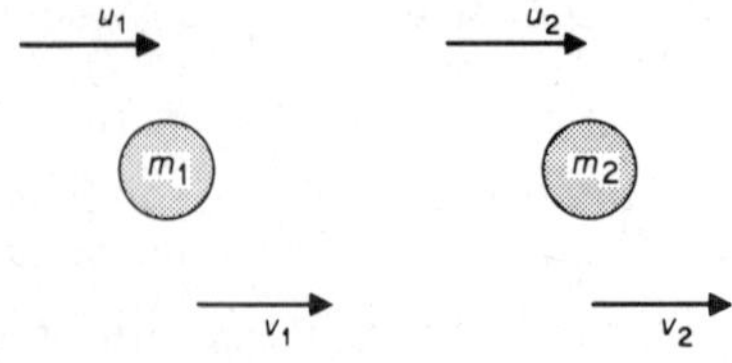

Fig. 2.5

We could solve these equations to find v_1 and v_2 in terms of the known quantities, but the algebra is much easier if we notice that the kinetic energy initially,

$$\tfrac{1}{2}m_1u_1^2 + \tfrac{1}{2}m_2u_2^2 = \frac{1}{2}\,\frac{(m_1^2u_1^2 + m_1m_2u_1^2) + (m_1m_2u_2^2 + m_2^2u_2^2)}{m_1 + m_2}$$

$$= \frac{1}{2}\,\frac{(m_1u_1 + m_2u_2)^2 + m_1m_2(u_1 - u_2)^2}{m_1 + m_2}$$

Similarly the final kinetic energy

$$\tfrac{1}{2}m_1v_1^2 + \tfrac{1}{2}m_2v_2^2 = \frac{1}{2}\,\frac{(m_1v_1 + m_2v_2)^2 + m_1m_2(v_1 - v_2)^2}{m_1 + m_2}$$

But

$$m_1u_1 + m_2u_2 = m_1v_1 + m_2v_2$$

so the loss of kinetic energy is

$$\frac{1}{2}\,\frac{m_1m_2(u_1 - u_2)^2 - m_1m_2(v_1 - v_2)^2}{m_1 + m_2}$$

$$= \frac{1}{2}\,\frac{m_1m_2}{m_1 + m_2}\,(u_1 - u_2)^2(1 - e^2)$$

since

$$v_2 - v_1 = e(u_1 - u_2)$$

Notice that the terms which are equal in each expression

$$\frac{1}{2}\,\frac{(m_1u_1 + m_2u_2)^2}{m_1 + m_2} \quad \text{and} \quad \frac{1}{2}\,\frac{(m_1v_1 + m_2v_2)^2}{m_1 + m_2}$$

are each equal to the kinetic energy of a body mass $(m_1 + m_2)$ moving with the velocity of the centre of gravity of the two smaller bodies.

Impacts on a fixed body

When one of the bodies is fixed (Fig. 2.6), its velocity before and after the impact is obviously zero. Newton's experimental law is still valid, so that $\mathbf{v} = -e\mathbf{u}$. The change in momentum of the body,

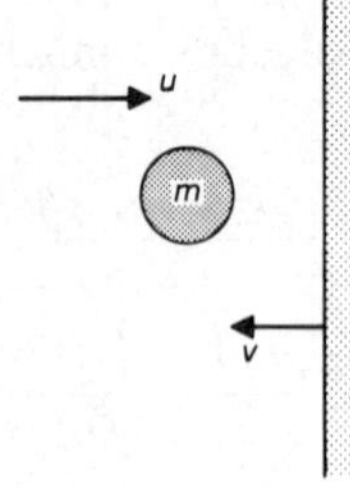

Fig. 2.6

mass m, is $mu + mv$, since the direction of the velocity has been changed,

i.e. $\qquad mu + meu, \quad$ i.e., $mu(1 + e)$

This is the impulse exerted by the wall on the body, as shown in Fig. 2.7, illustrating the changes of momentum of a body colliding with a fixed wall.

momentum before impact + impulse = momentum after impact

The impulse exerted by the wall on the body of course is equal and opposite to the impulse of the ball on the wall.

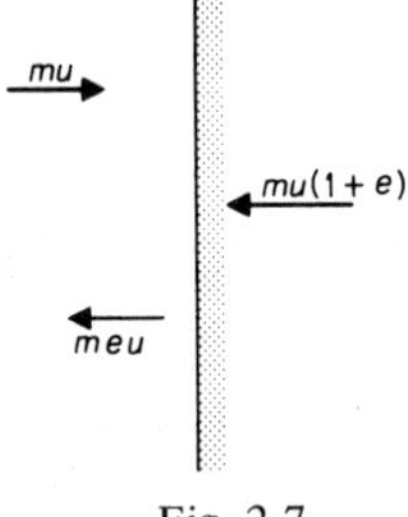

Fig. 2.7

Impact inclined to a fixed surface

When a body strikes a smooth wall or similar object there is not a change in the component of the velocity parallel to the wall, so that the motion in that direction is unaltered by the impact. Thus in Fig. 2.8, the component of velocity parallel to the wall is unaltered.

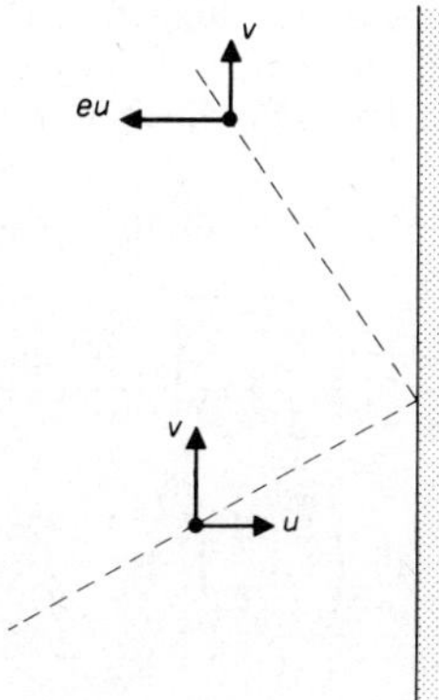

Fig. 2.8

Example 2.4. *A ball is projected with velocity U at an angle α above the horizontal from a point in the middle of a rackets court, width 2a, so that it strikes one side wall, then the other side wall, then returns to the point from which it was projected. Show that*

$$\sin 2\alpha = \frac{ag}{U^2}\left(1 + \frac{1}{e}\right)^2$$

where e is the coefficient of restitution.

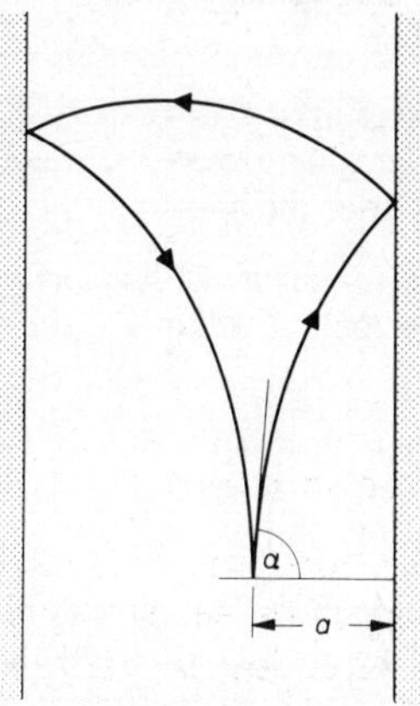

Fig. 2.9

Since the ball is projected from the middle of a court of width $2a$, the time to reach the first wall is $a/U\cos\alpha$; to go from the first wall to the second is $2a/eU\cos\alpha$; to go from the second wall back to the point of projection is $a/e^2U\cos\alpha$.

The vertical motion is not affected by the impacts, so the total time of flight is $2U\sin\alpha/g$.

$$\therefore \qquad \frac{a}{U\cos\alpha}\left(1+\frac{2}{e}+\frac{1}{e^2}\right)=\frac{2U\sin\alpha}{g}$$

$$\text{i.e.} \qquad \frac{a}{U\cos\alpha}\left(1+\frac{1}{e}\right)^2=\frac{2U\sin\alpha}{g}$$

$$\sin 2\alpha=\frac{ag}{U^2}\left(1+\frac{1}{e}\right)^2.$$

EXERCISE 2(a)

1. A small smooth sphere, mass 2 kg, moving with velocity 3 m s^{-1} strikes a similar sphere, mass 1 kg, initially at rest. If $e=\frac{1}{2}$, find the velocity of each sphere after the impact.

2. A small smooth sphere, mass 2 kg, moving with velocity 3$\mathbf{i}$ m s^{-1} strikes a similar sphere, mass 10 kg, moving with velocity $\mathbf{i}$ m s^{-1}. If $e=0.2$, find the velocity of each sphere after the impact.

3. A small smooth sphere mass 3 kg velocity 4$\mathbf{i}$ m s^{-1} collides with a similar sphere mass 2 kg velocity $-\mathbf{i}$ m s^{-1}. If $e=\frac{1}{2}$, find the subsequent velocity of each sphere.

4. A small smooth sphere mass 4 kg velocity 20$\mathbf{i}$ m s^{-1} overtakes and collides with a similar sphere mass 3 kg velocity 16$\mathbf{i}$ m s^{-1}. If $e=0.75$ find their velocities after the impact.

5. A small smooth sphere moving with velocity 24$\mathbf{i}$ m s^{-1} meets an equal body moving with velocity $-18\mathbf{i}$ m s^{-1}. If $e=\frac{1}{3}$, find the velocities after the impact.

6. A small smooth sphere mass 3 kg velocity $\mathbf{i}$ m s^{-1} collides with a similar body mass 2 kg velocity $-3\mathbf{i}$ m s^{-1}. If $e=\frac{1}{4}$ show that the second body is brought to rest by the impact.

7. A small smooth sphere mass 2 kg velocity $u\mathbf{i}$ m s^{-1} collides with a similar body mass 1 kg initially at rest. If the second body moves away with velocity $u\mathbf{i}$ m s^{-1}, find the coefficient of restitution between the two bodies.

8. Three small smooth spheres masses 0.1 kg, 0.3 kg and 0.6 kg, velocities $12\mathbf{i}$ m s^{-1}, $4\mathbf{i}$ m s^{-1} and $2\mathbf{i}$ m s^{-1} respectively are moving equally-spaced in a straight line in the above order. If $e = 1$, show that the first and second spheres are brought to rest by the subsequent collisions.

9. A body mass m strikes an equal body at rest. Find the ratio of their subsequent velocities after the impact.

10. A body mass $2m$ velocity $u\mathbf{i}$ strikes a body mass m, velocity $-u\mathbf{i}$. Find their subsequent velocities in terms of e and u.

11. Two equal masses moving in the same straight line collide. Show that if $e = 1$, they exchange velocities. Show also the converse result, that if they exchange velocities, $e = 1$.

12. A small smooth sphere, mass 2 kg, moving with velocity 3 m s^{-1} strikes a similar sphere mass 10 kg, moving in the same direction with velocity 1 m s^{-1}. If $e = 0.8$, find the velocity of each sphere after the impact.

13. A small smooth sphere, mass 4 kg, moving with velocity $3\mathbf{i}$ m s^{-1} strikes a similar sphere, mass 1 kg, moving with velocity $-2\mathbf{i}$ m s^{-1}. If $e = 0.4$, find the velocity of each sphere after the impact.

14. A golf ball is dropped from a height of 1 m onto a concrete pavement. If $e = 0.7$, find the height to which the golf ball rebounds.

15. A tennis ball is dropped from a window 10 metres above a garden path. If $e = 0.4$, find the time that elapses before the tennis ball comes to rest and the motion ceases.

16. A small smooth sphere mass m, velocity u, strikes an identical sphere moving in the same direction with velocity v ($u > v$). Find the impulse exerted by each sphere on the other, in terms of m, e, u and v.

17. Three identical smooth small balls A, B, and C are at rest in a straight line. A is projected towards B with velocity u. What is the velocity of B after the first impact? Show that A will always strike B after B has hit C, and find the range in which the value of e must lie if B strikes C a second time.

18. A ball is thrown with velocity V at an angle of inclination α above the horizontal so as to hit a vertical wall at a horizontal distance d from the point of projection and at right angles to the plane in which the ball is moving. The ball rebounds from the wall and returns to the point from which it was thrown. Prove that

$$V^2 \sin 2\alpha = gd(1 + e)/e$$

19. Two small balls A and B, of equal radii and masses m and $2m$ respectively, lie at rest on a smooth horizontal table in a line perpendicular to a vertical wall, B being nearer to the wall than A; A is given a velocity u so as to impinge directly on B, and after B rebounds from the wall it is brought to rest on its second impact with A. If the coefficient of restitution between A and B is $\frac{1}{4}$, find the coefficient of restitution between B and the wall. (O. & C.)

20. Two small marbles are at rest in a smooth horizontal circular tube, one at each end of a diameter. One is projected along the tube and strikes the other after time t. How long elapses before the second impact? (Use e to denote the coefficient of restitution.)

21. A certain game involves projecting a circular brass disc along a horizontal slate surface so as to strike a similar disc at rest. In any such impact, momentum is conserved, but a fraction k ($<\frac{1}{2}$) of the energy is lost. One disc A is moving directly towards the centre of another B with speed u just before impact, and the discs separate at a relative speed $2w$ after impact: prove (a) that A's motion after impact is in the same direction as before, and (b) that $w = \frac{1}{2}u\sqrt{(1 - 2k)}$.
If $k = 0.095$ and the motion of each disc over the slate after impact is resisted by a constant horizontal force, prove that the ratio of the distances moved after impact is about 1 to 360. (M.E.I.)

22. Two parallel walls are built on horizontal ground. A ball is projected from a point A on one wall at a height a metres above the ground so that it travels in a vertical plane perpendicular to the walls and hits the second wall at right angles at a point B at a height $2a$ metres from the ground. It bounces back and hits the ground at the foot of the first wall. Find the coefficient of restitution between the ball and the wall. If the point X of the ball's path from A to B is $(2a - x)$ metres above the ground, prove that when the ball is vertically below X on its return it is $(2a - 2x)$ metres above the ground. (O. & C.)

23. The masses of three perfectly elastic spheres A, B, and C are M, M, and m respectively ($M > m$). The spheres are initially at rest with their centres in a straight line, C lying between A and B. If C is given a velocity towards A along the line of centres, show that after colliding first with A and then with B it will not collide a second time with A if $M < (\sqrt{5} + 2)m$.
Find the ratios of the kinetic energies of the three spheres after the second collision and verify that no energy has been lost. (L.)

24. Two particles, each of mass m, are threaded on a fixed smooth horizontal circular wire of radius a. The particles are placed side by side

and one is projected away from the other with speed u. If the coefficient of restitution between the particles is e, find their speed when $2n$ collisions have taken place and the time for this to happen.
Show that the total loss in kinetic energy due to these collisions is

$$\tfrac{1}{4}mu^2(1 - e^{4n}) \qquad \text{(A.E.B.)}$$

Oblique impact

We have considered so far only impacts for which the size of the bodies could be ignored, or ones in which all the motion was along the line of centres. In discussing more general problems, oblique

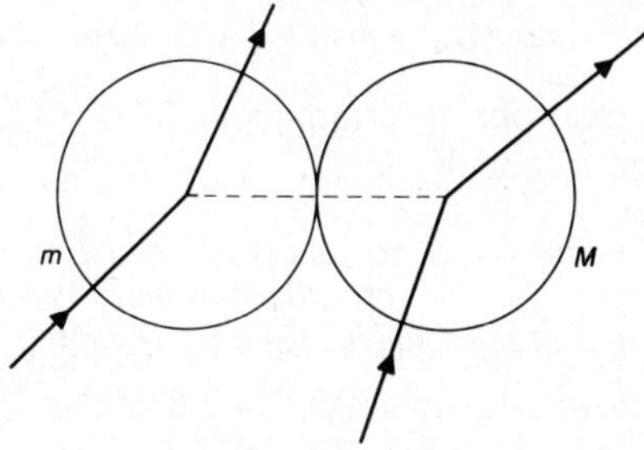

Fig. 2.10

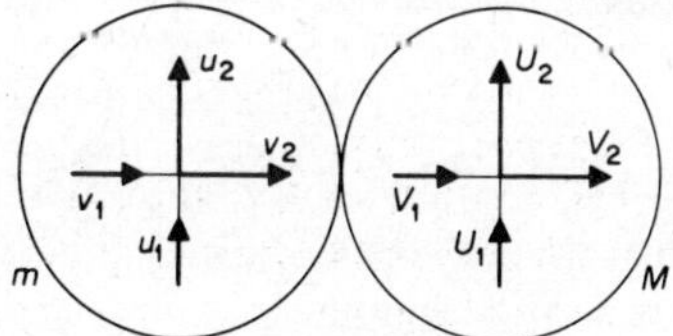

Fig. 2.11

impact, we can consider problems in which all the relative motion is not along the line of centres (Fig. 2.10) by considering separately the motion along and at right angles to the line of centres (Fig. 2.11).

Let u_1, v_1, U_1, V_1, denote the components of the velocities of m and M before impact; u_2, v_2, U_2, V_2 the components of velocity after the impact. Since the two spheres are smooth, there is no impact perpendicular to the line of centres, so the momentum of each sphere in that direction is unaltered,

i.e. $$mu_1 = mu_2 \quad \text{and} \quad MU_1 = MU_2$$
$$\Rightarrow u_2 = u_1 \quad \text{and} \quad U_2 = U_1$$

Considering the motion along the line of centres as before, since the momentum of the system is conserved,

$$mv_1 + MV_1 = mv_2 + MV_2$$

and from Newton's law,

$$e(v_1 - V_1) = V_2 - v_2$$

The first two equations determine u_2 and U_2, and from the second two we can find v_2 and V_2.

Example 2.5. *Two smooth spheres, mass 1 kg and 2 kg, have velocities* $(2\mathbf{i} + \mathbf{j})$ *m s*$^{-1}$ *and* $(\mathbf{i} + 2\mathbf{j})$ *m s*$^{-1}$ *respectively, where* **i** *is a unit vector parallel to the line of centres of the spheres at impact. If e = 0.2, find the subsequent velocity of each sphere.*

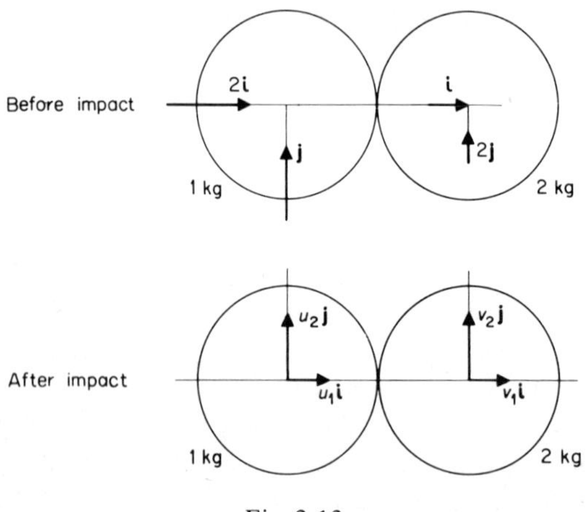

Fig. 2.12

Since the momentum is unchanged perpendicular to the line of centres,

$$u_2 = 1 \quad \text{and} \quad v_2 = 2$$

where $(u_1\mathbf{i} + u_2\mathbf{j})$ m s^{-1} and $(v_1\mathbf{i} + v_2\mathbf{j})$ m s^{-1} are the final velocities. From the conservation of momentum along the line of centres

$$1 \times 2 + 2 \times 1 = 1 \times u_1 + 2 \times v_1$$

and from Newton's law

$$0.2(2 - 1) = v_1 - u_1$$

$$\Rightarrow u_1 + 2v_1 = 4$$

and

$$-u_1 + v_1 = 0.2$$

$$\Rightarrow v_1 = 1.4 \quad \text{and} \quad u_1 = 1.2$$

the subsequent velocities are $(1.2\mathbf{i} + \mathbf{j})$ m s^{-1} and $(1.4\mathbf{i} + 2\mathbf{j})$ m s^{-1}.

Instead of knowing the components of the velocities we may know their magnitude and initial directions. In which case we resolve along and perpendicular to the line of centres.

Example 2.6. *A smooth sphere strikes an identical sphere initially at rest. If the velocity of the moving sphere before the impact is 2 m s^{-1} at 45° to the line of centres AB, and e = 0.6, find the velocities of the spheres after the impact.*

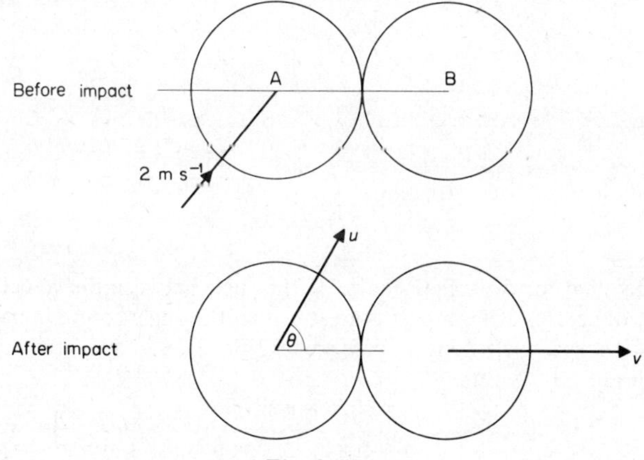

Fig. 2.13

Since the second sphere was initially at rest and the impulse it receives is along AB, its final velocity must be along AB.

Considering the momentum of the first sphere perpendicular to AB,

$$m \times 2 \sin 45° = mu \sin \theta, \quad \text{where } m \text{ is the mass of a sphere}$$

$$\Rightarrow u \sin \theta = \sqrt{2}$$

From the conservation of momentum along AB,

$$m \times 2 \cos 45^\circ = mu \cos \theta + mv$$

and from Newton's law,

$$0.6 \times 2 \cos 45^\circ = v - u \cos \theta$$

$$\Rightarrow v + u \cos \theta = 2 \cos 45^\circ$$

and $$v - u \cos \theta = 1.2 \cos 45^\circ$$

$$\Rightarrow v = 1.6 \cos 45^\circ \quad \text{and} \quad u \cos \theta = 0.4 \cos 45^\circ$$

i.e. $$v = 1.13 \quad \text{and} \quad u \cos \theta = 0.283 \text{ approximately}$$

Since $$u \sin \theta = \sqrt{2}, \quad \tan \theta = 5$$

$$\Rightarrow \theta \simeq 79^\circ \quad \text{and} \quad u = 1.44$$

Thus the velocity of the second sphere is 1.13 m s^{-1} along AB, and that of the first sphere is 1.44 m s^{-1} at 79° to AB.

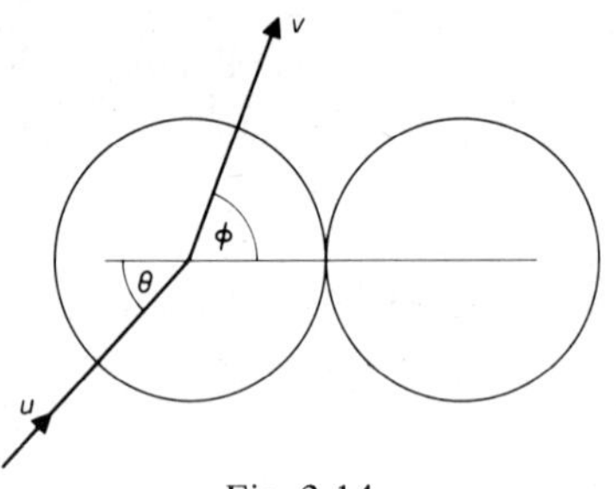

Fig. 2.14

Notice that for the sphere centre A, the angle between the velocity and the line of centres after impact is greater than the angle before impact. For, if θ and ϕ respectively denote these angles (Fig. 2.14), and u and v are the velocities,

$$u \sin \theta = v \sin \phi$$

and $$u \cos \theta > v \cos \phi$$

$$\Rightarrow \tan \theta < \tan \phi$$

$$\Rightarrow \theta < \phi$$

Deflection

In Example 2.6, the first sphere was deflected by the impact through 34°. In algebraic problems concerning the angle of deflec-

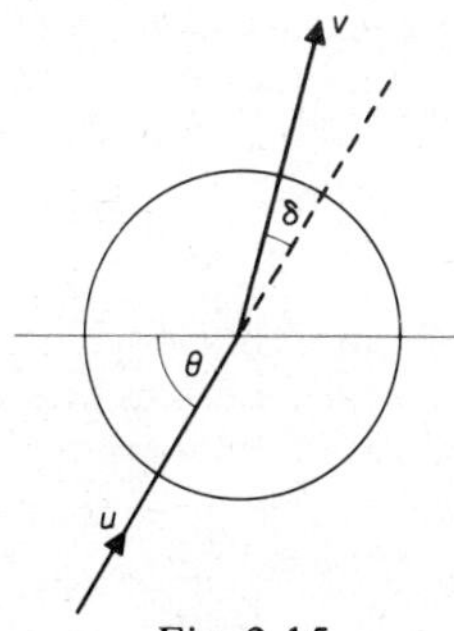

Fig. 2.15

tion, it is better to take the angles as θ and $(\theta + \delta)$, where δ is the deflection. This angle δ can be identified more easily than the $(\theta + \delta)$ which the notation of Fig. 2.14 would suggest.

EXERCISE 2(b)

In Questions 1–4 of this exercise, **i** *is a unit vector along the line of centres and* **j** *a unit vector at right angles to the line of centres. e denotes the coefficient of restitution.*

1. Two smooth spheres each of mass 1 kg collide with velocities $(\mathbf{i} + 3\mathbf{j})$ m s^{-1} and $(-2\mathbf{i} + \mathbf{j})$ m s^{-1}. If $e = \frac{1}{3}$, find the velocities of the spheres after the impact and the loss of kinetic energy caused by the impact.

2. Two smooth spheres, mass 2 kg and 3 kg collide with velocities $(2\mathbf{i} - 3\mathbf{j})$ m s^{-1} and $(\mathbf{i} + \mathbf{j})$ m s^{-1} respectively. If $e = \frac{1}{4}$, find the velocities after the impact.

3. Two smooth spheres mass 3 kg and 1 kg collide with velocities $(4\mathbf{i} - \mathbf{j})$ m s^{-1} and $(-2\mathbf{i} + \mathbf{j})$ m s^{-1}. If $e = \frac{1}{3}$, find the velocities after the impact. Use the scalar product to find the cosine of the angle through which each sphere is deflected by the impact.

4. Two smooth spheres of equal mass collide with velocities $(\mathbf{i} + \mathbf{j})$ m s^{-1} and $(-2\mathbf{i} + \mathbf{j})$ m s^{-1}. If their velocities after the impact are at right angles to each other, find the coefficient of restitution between the spheres.

5. A smooth sphere centre A, mass 2 kg strikes a similar sphere centre B, mass 3 kg initially at rest. If the velocity of A before the impact was 4 m s^{-1} at 60° to AB, find the velocities of the spheres after the impact, if $e = \frac{2}{3}$.

6. A smooth sphere centre A mass 3 kg, velocity 5 m s^{-1} strikes a similar sphere centre B mass 2 kg, velocity 13 m s^{-1}. If the directions of motion at impact are inclined at $\tan^{-1}\frac{3}{4}$ with $\overrightarrow{AB}$ and $\tan^{-1}(5/12)$ with $\overrightarrow{BA}$ respectively, and $e = 0.5$, find the subsequent velocities of the spheres after the impact.

7. A smooth sphere strikes an identical sphere at rest. If the angle which the direction of the first sphere makes with the line of centres is θ before the impact and ϕ after the impact, prove that ϕ is given by

$$\tan\phi = \frac{2}{1-e}\tan\theta$$

8. A ball bounces down a long flight of identical stairs, height h and breadth b. It hits each stair at the same distance from each edge, at the same angle and with the same velocity. Find the angle which the ball makes with the vertical when it strikes a stair.

9. A shallow rectangular box has a smooth base and sides, and the length and breadth of the box are a and b respectively. The box is fixed with its base horizontal and a particle is projected in the plane of the box at the midpoint M of one of the longer sides. It rebounds off a shorter side and then off the other sides in succession, hitting the original side again at M. Show that it must have left M in a direction making an angle θ with the longer side, where

$$\tan\theta = \frac{2eb}{a(1+e)}$$

e being the coefficient of restitution.
Show also that the particle will leave M for the second time round in the same direction and with a speed e^2 times the original speed.
(O. & C.)

10. Two identical smooth balls are moving on a smooth horizontal table with the same speeds in opposite directions, along parallel straight lines. After they collide, their directions of motion are perpendicular to the original directions of motion. Show that the distance between the parallel lines along which they were originally moving is

$$2a\sqrt{\left(\frac{e}{1+e}\right)}$$

where a is the radius of each sphere and e is the coefficient of restitution between the spheres.

11. Two smooth spheres of equal radii but of masses m and λm are sliding on a smooth horizontal table, with velocity vectors $3\mathbf{i} + \mathbf{j}$ and $\mathbf{i} + 2\mathbf{j}$ respectively. They collide when their line of centres is parallel to the vector $\mathbf{i}$. The coefficient of restitution between them is e ($\leqslant 1$). If after the collision the spheres move in parallel directions show that $\lambda \geqslant \frac{1}{3}$. (L.)

12. A smooth sphere A, of mass m, moving with speed ku ($k > 1$), collides obliquely with a smooth sphere B, of equal mass, moving with speed u, the coefficient of restitution being e. Before the impact, A is moving in a direction making an acute angle α with the line of centres, and B is

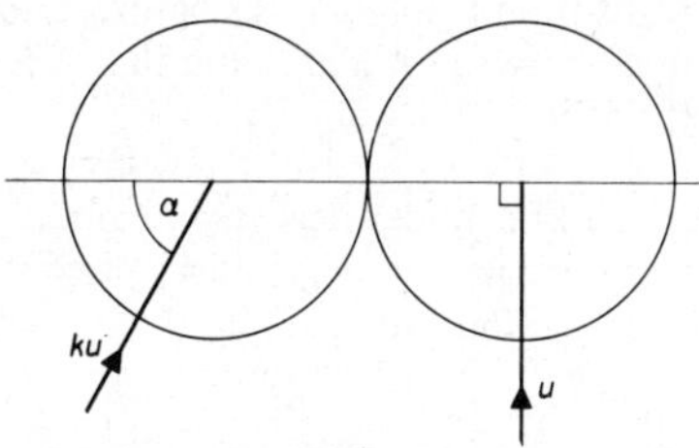

Fig. 2.16

moving in a direction at right angles to the line of centres, as shown in Fig. 2.16. After the impact, B moves in a direction making an angle α with the line of centres. Prove that $\operatorname{cosec} \alpha \leqslant k \leqslant 2 \operatorname{cosec} \alpha$.
Given that $k = (3/2) \operatorname{cosec} \alpha$, find the value of e and show that an amount $\frac{1}{2}mu^2 \cot^2 \alpha$ of kinetic energy has been lost in the impact. (J.M.B.)

13. A smooth sphere mass em strikes a similar smooth sphere mass m initially at rest. Prove that after the impact the spheres are moving at right angles to each other.

14. A particle of mass m is moving with velocity

$$\mathbf{V} = u\mathbf{i} + v\mathbf{j}$$

where $\mathbf{i}$ and $\mathbf{j}$ are unit vectors parallel to Ox and Oy respectively, when an impulse $I\mathbf{i} + J\mathbf{j}$ is applied. Find the subsequent velocity of the particle and prove that, if the blow causes the direction of motion of the particle to be turned through a right angle,

$$2T + uI + vJ = 0$$

where T is the kinetic energy of the particle before the impulse is applied. Prove further that in this case the gain in kinetic energy is

$$\frac{1}{2m}(I^2 + J^2) - 2T \qquad \text{(M.E.I.)}$$

15. A smooth ball A of mass m is at rest on a smooth table when it is hit directly by a similar ball B of mass M which is moving with velocity u; after impact the velocities are u and $\frac{1}{2}u$ for A and B respectively. Find the ratio of $m : M$ and show that a quarter of the energy is lost in the impact.
The ball A hits a vertical wall at right angles to its motion and the coefficient of restitution is the same as before. Show that there will be three impacts in all between A and B and that A is finally at rest. Find the final velocity of B. (M.E.I.)

16. A smooth sphere strikes an identical sphere initially at rest. The path of the moving sphere makes an angle of 45° with the line of centres. If $e = 0.5$, find the deflection produced by the impact in the path of the moving sphere.

17. A smooth sphere strikes an identical sphere initially at rest. The path of the moving sphere makes an angle α with the line of centres. If $e = 0.5$, find the value of α for which the deflection is greatest.

18. With the data in Question 17, find the value of α for which the deflection is greatest, for a general value e of the coefficient of restitution.

19. A smooth small ball A of negligible radius lies at rest on a smooth horizontal plane. A similar ball B, of the same mass as A, moves along the plane with velocity V and strikes A so that the latter proceeds to hit a smooth vertical wall. At the moment of first impact the line BA makes an angle of α with the wall, and the direction of motion of B makes an angle β with the wall ($\alpha > \beta$). The coefficient of restitution for both impacts is e. Find the velocities of the balls along and perpendicular to the line BA after the first impact.
Hence show that the conditions that the balls should collide again, after A has struck the wall, are

$$\tan(\alpha - \beta) = e \cot \alpha$$

and

$$(1 + e^2)\tan^2 \alpha > 2e \qquad \text{(O. \& C.)}$$

20. A ball is dropped from the roof of a lift ascending with an acceleration a m s^{-2}. If the height of the lift is h metres and the coefficient of restitution between the ball and the floor of the lift is e, show that the time which elapses before the ball stops bouncing is

$$\frac{1+e}{1-e}\sqrt{\left(\frac{2h}{a+g}\right)} \text{ seconds} \qquad \text{(W.J.E.C.)}$$

Impulsive tensions in strings

If a body X is connected by an inelastic string XY to another body at Y and is jerked into motion by the string becoming taut, the impulse given to the body must be along the line of the string, and so the body must begin to move along the line of the string, with

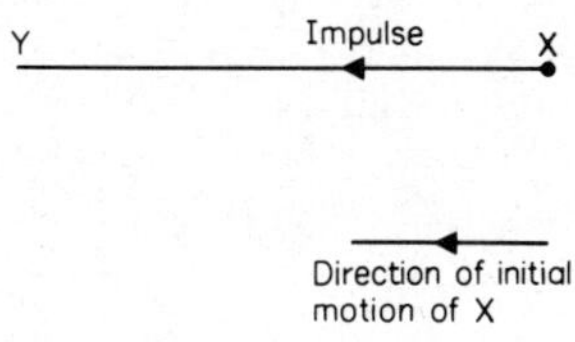

Fig. 2.17

the same velocity along the string as the component of the other end Y of the string. XY may rotate, so that the velocity of Y may have a component at right angles to XY, but the component along XY will always be equal to the velocity of X.

Example 2.7. *Two particles A, B, of equal mass are at rest on a smooth horizontal table, joined by a string which is just taut. A is projected with velocity u at 45° to AB, as in Fig. 2.18. Find the velocities of A and B immediately the string becomes taut.*

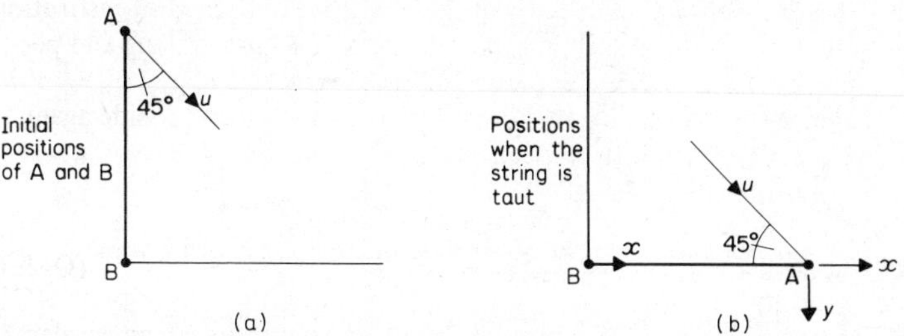

Fig. 2.18

Let the velocity of B when the string is again taut be x; then the component of the velocity of A along the string is also x. Let the component of the velocity of A at right angles to the string be y.

Then by the conservation of momentum for the system along the line of initial motion,

$$mu = m(y \sin 45^\circ + x \cos 45^\circ) + mx \cos 45^\circ$$

and at right angles to the line of initial motion,

$$0 = m(y \cos 45^\circ - x \sin 45^\circ) - mx \sin 45^\circ$$

$$\Rightarrow u = y\frac{1}{\sqrt{2}} + 2x\frac{1}{\sqrt{2}}$$

and $$0 = y\frac{1}{\sqrt{2}} - 2x\frac{1}{\sqrt{2}}$$

$$\Rightarrow y = \frac{u}{\sqrt{2}} \quad \text{and} \quad x = \frac{u}{2\sqrt{2}}$$

The velocity of B is $u/2\sqrt{2}$ along the string; the velocity of A is

$$\frac{u}{2}\sqrt{\frac{5}{2}}$$

making an angle of $\tan^{-1} 2$ with the line joining A to B, when the string becomes taut.

Example 2.8. *Three particles A, B, and C, each of mass m, are at rest on a smooth horizontal table (Fig. 2.19). A, B and B, C are joined by light inextensible strings, so that angle ABC = 60°. A is given a velocity v parallel to CB. Find the velocity with which C moves when AB is again taut.*

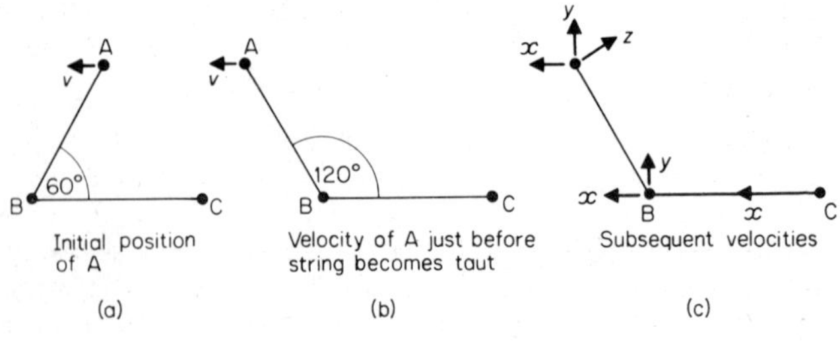

Fig. 2.19

Let the velocity of C be x. Then the velocity of B is x along CB and y at right angles to CB. The velocity of A is the velocity of B plus the velocity of A relative to B, which must be at right angles to AB, as AB is a constant length.

Considering the conservation of momentum of the whole system in the direction CB,

$$mv = mx + mx + m(x - z \sin 60^\circ)$$

and at right angles to CB,

$$0 = my + m(y + z \cos 60^\circ)$$

The impulse given to the pair of particles B and C is along AB, so their momentum at right angles to AB is conserved,

$$0 = mx \sin 60^\circ + m(x \sin 60^\circ - y \cos 60^\circ)$$

From these equations we have

$$v = 3x - \frac{\sqrt{3}}{2} z \qquad (2.1)$$

$$0 = 2y + \tfrac{1}{2} z \qquad (2.2)$$

and $$0 = x\sqrt{3} - \tfrac{1}{2} y \qquad (2.3)$$

from equations 2.1 and 2.2 $\quad v = 3x + 2\sqrt{3}y$

and from equation 2.3, $\quad 0 = 12x - 2\sqrt{3}y$

$$\Rightarrow x = \tfrac{1}{15} v$$

If the other velocities are required, we can obtain them easily by substitution.

EXERCISE 2(c)

Questions 6–10 are more suitable for a second reading.

1. Two small bodies A, B, masses 1 kg and 2 kg respectively are placed side by side on a smooth horizontal table, and are joined by a light inextensible string. A is projected horizontally with a velocity of 6 m s^{-1}. Find the velocity of B after the string has become taut, the impulsive tension in the string, and the loss of kinetic energy.

2. Two identical small smooth spheres A, B are connected by a light inextensible string. They are placed on a smooth horizontal table, a distance a apart, so that the string is just taut. A is projected towards B with velocity U. The coefficient of restitution between the spheres is 0.5. Find (a) the velocities of A and B after the impact, (b) the time after the projection of A before the string becomes taut, (c) the final velocities of A and B.

3. Two bodies A and B of equal mass, connected by a light inextensible string, are placed on a smooth horizontal table with the string just taut. A is projected with velocity U at 45° to $\overrightarrow{AB}$. Find the impulse in the string when the string becomes taut.

4. Two bodies A and B, masses 1 kg and 2 kg respectively, are connected by a light inextensible string and placed on a smooth horizontal table, with the string just taut. A is projected with velocity 4 m s^{-1} at 45° to $\overrightarrow{AB}$. Find the velocities of A and B after the string becomes taut again.

5. Two bodies A and B, masses m and M respectively, are placed on a smooth horizontal table and connected by a light inextensible string. Initially the string is just taut. A is projected with velocity U at 30° to $\overrightarrow{AB}$. Find the velocities of A and B after the string becomes taut again.

6. Two particles of equal mass are joined by an inextensible string and lie on a smooth horizontal table. The ratio of their distance apart to the length of the string is 3 : 5. One particle is projected along the table at right angles to the line joining them. Show that 32 per cent of the initial kinetic energy is lost when the string tightens. (M.E.I.)

7. Particles A, B, C, and D are placed at the four corners of a rhombus, A and B, B and C, C and D, and A and D being joined by light inextensible strings of equal length. Angle $D\hat{A}B = 60°$. A is given a velocity U in the direction $\overrightarrow{CA}$. Prove that C begins to move with velocity $\frac{1}{3}U$.

8. Two identical particles are at points A and B which are l metres apart on a smooth horizontal table. The particles are connected by a light inextensible string of length $2l$ metres. The particle at A is projected with a speed of u m s^{-1} in a direction perpendicular to the line AB. Find the speed with which the particle at B starts to move when the string becomes taut.
Find also the magnitude and direction of the velocity of each particle when the string is perpendicular to AB. (A.E.B.)

9. Three particles A, B, and C of equal mass m lie on a horizontal surface at the vertices of an equilateral triangle; they are joined by light inextensible strings. An impulse I is applied to C in the direction BC. Calculate the ratio of the initial speeds of B and A. (C.S.)

10. Four particles A, B, C, and D, each of mass m, are joined by light inextensible strings of length a to form a square ABCD which lies on a smooth horizontal plane. An impulse I is applied to particle A in the direction of the diagonal CA. Find the velocities with which the particle begins to move.

If at a time t subsequent to the start of the motion $\mathrm{B\hat{A}D} = 2\theta$, show that the kinetic energy of the system is

$$\frac{I^2}{8m} + ma^2\left(\frac{\mathrm{d}\theta}{\mathrm{d}t}\right)^2$$

provided that B and D have not collided.
Hence, or otherwise, determine the time at which B and D first collide.
Show that the centre of mass of the whole system will then have travelled a distance

$$\frac{\pi a}{4\sqrt{2}}$$

(C.S.)

3. Differential Equations

If at time t the distance x of a particle from a fixed point is given by

$$x = a \cos \omega t$$

differentiating twice we have

$$\frac{d^2x}{dt^2} = -a\omega^2 \cos \omega t$$

Eliminating $\cos \omega t$ between these equations,

$$\frac{d^2x}{dt^2} = -\omega^2 x \qquad (3.1)$$

an equation which we shall recognize later as describing simple harmonic motion.

Equation 3.1 is an example of a differential equation. Since the highest order of differential coefficient is the second, it is called a second order differential equation. If it had contained dx/dt only, we should have called it a first order differential equation.

Another example of a problem requiring the solution of a differential equation is when a body moves in a straight line under a retarding force proportional to the cube of its velocity. Newton's law gives, with the usual notation,

$$-k\left(\frac{dx}{dt}\right)^3 = m\frac{d^2x}{dt^2}$$

another differential equation.

Such equations are met in most sciences. Elementary physics includes Newton's law of cooling, the rate at which a body cools being proportional to the excess of the temperature of the body over the temperature of its surroundings, i.e.

$$\frac{d\theta}{dt} = -k(\theta - \theta_0) \qquad (3.2)$$

where θ is the temperature of the body, θ_0 is the temperature of its surroundings, and k is a constant. Many other examples are given in exercises in this chapter, from chemistry, biology, economics as well as mechanics. The solution of various types of differential equations is included in many pure mathematics textbooks (see, for example, L. Harwood Clarke's *Advanced Level Pure Mathematics*); our task here is to solve two of the commonest types of differential equations, so that we can study the problems which give rise to differential equations.

Separable variables

In the equation derived from Newton's law of cooling,

$$\frac{d\theta}{dt} = -k(\theta - \theta_0)$$

division by $(\theta - \theta_0)$ gives

$$\frac{1}{(\theta - \theta_0)} \frac{d\theta}{dt} = -k$$

Integrating with respect to t,

$$\int \frac{1}{(\theta - \theta_0)} \frac{d\theta}{dt} \, dt = -\int k \, dt$$

i.e.

$$\int \frac{d\theta}{(\theta - \theta_0)} = -\int k \, dt$$

i.e.

$$\log(\theta - \theta_0) = -kt + C$$

If $\theta = \theta_1$ when $t = 0$,

$$C = \log(\theta_1 - \theta_0)$$

$$\Rightarrow \theta - \theta_0 = (\theta_1 - \theta_0)\, e^{-kt}$$

an equation giving us θ at any known time t, and enabling us to find t for any known θ.

Notice how we solved equation 3.2. Division by $(\theta - \theta_0)$ ensured that the only term containing θ, i.e. $(\theta - \theta_0)$, had $d\theta/dt$ as a multiplier. Thus it was possible to integrate.

These equations in which the variables, say θ and t, or x and y, can be *separated* are the easiest type of differential equation to solve, and fortunately the commonest that occur. Many of the integrals are logarithmic, to the base e of course, emphasizing the importance of the exponential function in explaining natural phenomena.

Example 3.1. *If $dy/dx = x(1 + y^2)$ and $y = 0$ when $x = 0$, find y as a function of x.*

Since
$$\frac{dy}{dx} = x(1 + y^2)$$
$$\frac{1}{1 + y^2}\frac{dy}{dx} = x$$
This may be written
$$\int \frac{1}{1 + y^2}\,dy = \int x\,dx$$
$$\Rightarrow \tan^{-1} y = \tfrac{1}{2}x^2 + C$$
But $y = 0$ when $x = 0$, $\Rightarrow C = 0$

$\therefore$
$$\tan^{-1} y = \tfrac{1}{2}x^2$$
i.e.
$$y = \tan(\tfrac{1}{2}x^2)$$

Example 3.2. *If $dy/dx = \sin x/\sin y$ and $y = \pi/2$ when $x = 0$, find y as a function of x.*

If
$$\frac{dy}{dx} = \frac{\sin x}{\sin y}$$
$$\sin y\frac{dy}{dx} = \sin x$$
$$\Rightarrow \int \sin y\,dy = \int \sin x\,dx$$
$$\Rightarrow -\cos y = -\cos x + C$$
But $y = \pi/2$ when $x = 0$, $\therefore C = 1$
$$\Rightarrow \cos y = \cos x - 1$$

In this example it is neater if we do not express y explicitly as a function of x; the form $y = \cos^{-1}(\cos x - 1)$ is not as simple as the form we have obtained.

In a few problems it may be necessary to make a simple substitution to reduce an equation to a form in which the variables can be separated.

Example 3.3. *Solve the differential equation:*

$$xy\frac{dy}{dx} = x^2 + y^2$$

If we divide both sides of the equation by $x(x^2 + y^2)$, as in earlier examples, we have

$$\int \frac{y}{x^2 + y^2}\,dy = \int \frac{1}{x}\,dx$$

As we do not know y in terms of x, we cannot obtain the integral required. Similarly,

$$\int y\,dy = \int \left(x + \frac{y^2}{x}\right)dx$$

is impossible, as are all other forms. However, if we make the substitution $y = zx$, where z is a function of x,

$$\frac{dy}{dx} = z + x\frac{dz}{dx}$$

the equation becomes $$zx^2\left(z + x\frac{dz}{dx}\right) = x^2 + x^2z^2$$

$$\Rightarrow zx^3\frac{dz}{dx} = x^2$$

$$\Rightarrow \text{either } x = 0$$

a trivial solution which may not satisfy the initial conditions,

or $$zx\frac{dz}{dx} = 1$$

Now we can deduce $$z\frac{dz}{dx} = \frac{1}{x}$$

$$\Rightarrow \int z\,dz = \int \frac{1}{x}\,dx$$

$$\Rightarrow \tfrac{1}{2}z^2 = \log_e x + C$$

Substituting back, $$z = \frac{y}{x}$$

$$y^2 = 2x^2(\log_e x + C)$$

In all equations in this book in which a substitution is needed, it will be given. Further examples of less common substitutions can be found in *Advanced Level Pure Mathematics* and specialist books on calculus.

EXERCISE 3(a)

Solve the differential equations:

1. $\dfrac{dy}{dx} = 4y^2$
2. $\dfrac{dy}{dx} = 4 + y$
3. $y\dfrac{dy}{dx} = 4 + y^2$
4. $x\dfrac{dy}{dx} = 4 + y^2$
5. $xy\dfrac{dy}{dx} = 4 + y^2$
6. $\dfrac{y}{x}\dfrac{dy}{dx} = 4 + y^2$
7. $\dfrac{dy}{dx} = y \sin x$
8. $\dfrac{dy}{dx} = \sin x \cos^2 y$
9. $(x + 1)\dfrac{dy}{dx} = y$
10. $(x^2 + a^2)\dfrac{dy}{dx} = y$
11. Use the substitution $y = zx$ to solve

$$2x^2\frac{dy}{dx} = 2xy - y^2$$

12. Use the substitution $y = zx$ to solve

$$x\frac{dy}{dx} = x + y$$

Problems requiring the solution of such equations

We have seen that Newton's law of cooling was first expressed in words, 'the rate at which a body cools is proportional to the excess temperature'. To write this algebraically, the rate of cooling is

$-\mathrm{d}\theta/\mathrm{d}t$, minus since the temperature of the body is falling, and this is a constant multiple of the excess temperature,

i.e.
$$-\frac{\mathrm{d}\theta}{\mathrm{d}t} = k(\theta - \theta_0)$$

$$\Rightarrow \frac{\mathrm{d}\theta}{\mathrm{d}t} = -k(\theta - \theta_0)$$

As another example, suppose that in a certain colony of insects the rate at which they are born is proportional to the number present, and that a constant number die in any one interval of time. If N is the number present

$$\frac{\mathrm{d}N}{\mathrm{d}t} = kN - n$$

the term kN being the rate of natural increase through birth, and n the number dying in a unit interval of time.

Again, in a vessel of a certain shape the rate at which the depth x of the water level in the vessel rises is inversely proportional to the depth of water already in the vessel,

i.e.
$$\frac{\mathrm{d}x}{\mathrm{d}t} = \frac{k}{x}$$

All these statements we have been able to express algebraically and have seen that they result in differential equations.

Returning to the cooling law, suppose a body was heated to 80°C in a room whose temperature may be assumed constant at 10°C, and the body has cooled to 60°C after 5 minutes. We know that

$$\frac{\mathrm{d}\theta}{\mathrm{d}t} = -k(\theta - \theta_0)$$

$$\Rightarrow \int \frac{\mathrm{d}\theta}{\theta - \theta_0} = -\int k\,\mathrm{d}t$$

$$\Rightarrow \log(\theta - \theta_0) = -kt + C$$

But $\qquad \theta_0 = 10 \quad$ and $\quad \theta = 80 \quad$ when $t = 0$,

$$\therefore \qquad C = \log 70$$

$$\Rightarrow \log(\theta - \theta_0) = -kt + \log 70$$

$$\Rightarrow \theta - \theta_0 = 70\,\mathrm{e}^{-kt}$$

The reader will come to recognize solutions of the form $A\,\mathrm{e}^{-kt}$ and will notice that A is the initial value of the unknown which is dependent on t; here, $A = 70$, the value of the excess of the temperature of the body over that of the room at the beginning of the experiment.

We have also recorded that after 5 minutes the temperature of the body is 60°C, i.e. the excess temperature is 50°C,

$$50 = 70\,\mathrm{e}^{-5k}$$

$$\Rightarrow \tfrac{5}{7} = \mathrm{e}^{-5k}$$

$$\Rightarrow k = \tfrac{1}{5}\log_e \tfrac{7}{5}$$

$$= 0.067, \text{ to three decimal places.}$$

For this body under these conditions, the temperature θ°C at time t minutes is given by

$$\theta - 10 = 70\,\mathrm{e}^{-0.067t}$$

To find the temperature after, say, 6 minutes,

$$\theta - 10 = 70\,\mathrm{e}^{-0.402}$$

$$= \frac{70}{1.49}$$

$$\simeq 46.9$$

$$\Rightarrow \theta = 57°\text{C, to the nearest degree.}$$

If we wish to find when the body has cooled to a certain temperature, say 40°C,

$$40 - 10 = 70\,\mathrm{e}^{-0.067t}$$

$$\Rightarrow 30 = 70\,\mathrm{e}^{-0.067t}$$

$$\Rightarrow \tfrac{7}{3} = \mathrm{e}^{0.067t}$$

$$\Rightarrow t = \frac{1}{0.067}\log_e \tfrac{7}{3}$$

i.e. $\qquad t = 12.6$ minutes, to one decimal place.

Example 3.4. *Under certain circumstances, a raindrop falls so that its acceleration is* $(g - \frac{1}{3}v)$ *m* s^{-2}, *where v m* s^{-1} *is the velocity of the raindrop and g m* s^{-2} *the acceleration due to gravity. If the raindrop starts from rest, how long will elapse before the velocity is 2g m* s^{-1}*?*

Since the acceleration of a body is dv/dt, the data give

$$\frac{dv}{dt} = (g - \tfrac{1}{3}v)$$

Separating the variables,

$$\int \frac{dv}{g - \frac{1}{3}v} = \int dt$$

Since $v = 0$ when $t = 0$ and we want the value T of t when $v = 2g$, we can write this as a definite integral

$$\int_0^{2g} \frac{dv}{g - \frac{1}{3}v} = \int_0^T dt$$

$$\Rightarrow [-3 \log (3g - v)]_0^{2g} = [t]_0^T$$

$$\Rightarrow -3 \log g + 3 \log 3g = T$$

$$\Rightarrow T = 3 \log 3$$

$$= 3.30, \text{ to two decimal places,}$$

i.e. about 3.3 s elapse before the velocity is $2g$ m s^{-1}.

Example 3.5. *In a closed community of N persons, n (small compared with N) initially have a certain disease, the rest have not yet caught it. If a person recovers from this disease he becomes immune. Observations show that at any subsequent time t the rate of increase of the number R of persons who have recovered from the disease is proportional to the number I ill with the disease; the rate of increase of the number D dead from the disease is also proportional to I, whereas the rate of decrease of the number S susceptible to the disease is proportional to the product SI. Investigate the variation of I with S and find the greatest number of persons ill at any one time with this disease.*

From the data, $\frac{dR}{dt} = aI$, $\frac{dD}{dt} = bI$ and $\frac{dS}{dt} = -cSI$

Since we are counting those who have died D, and the community is closed, the total population is constant,

i.e. $R + S + D + I = \text{constant}$

Differentiating,

$$\frac{dR}{dt} + \frac{dS}{dt} + \frac{dD}{dt} + \frac{dI}{dt} = 0$$

Substituting the observations,

$$aI - cSI + bI + \frac{dI}{dt} = 0$$

$$\Rightarrow \frac{dI}{dt} = (cS - a - b)I$$

Thus dI/dt is positive if $(cS - a - b) > 0$,
i.e.

$$S > \frac{a + b}{c}$$

so I increases until

$$S = \frac{a + b}{c}$$

and then decreases. This required the restriction that initially n was small compared with N so that,

$$(N - n) > \frac{a + b}{c}$$

Moreover, since

$$\frac{dS}{dt} = -cSI$$

division gives

$$\frac{dI}{dS} = \frac{cS - a - b}{-cS}$$

Separating the variables, $\int dI = \int \left(\frac{a + b}{cS} - 1\right) dS$

i.e. $$I = \left(\frac{a + b}{c}\right) \log_e S - S + A, \text{ say}$$

But initially $(N - n)$ persons are susceptible to the disease and n are ill,

$$\therefore \quad n = \left(\frac{a + b}{c}\right) \log_e (N - n) - (N - n) + A$$

$$\Rightarrow A = N - \left(\frac{a + b}{c}\right) \log_e (N - n)$$

When $\quad S = (a + b)/c,$

$$I = \left(\frac{a+b}{c}\right)\log_e\left(\frac{a+b}{c}\right) - \frac{a+b}{c} + N - \frac{a+b}{c}\log(N-n)$$

$$= N - \left(\frac{a+b}{c}\right)\left[\log_e(N-n) - \log_e\left(\frac{a+b}{c}\right) + 1\right]$$

$$= N - \left(\frac{a+b}{c}\right)\left\{\log_e\left[\frac{ec(N-n)}{a+b}\right]\right\}$$

so the greatest number of persons ill at any one time is

$$N - \left(\frac{a+b}{c}\right)\log_e\left[\frac{ec(N-n)}{a+b}\right]$$

or, of course, the integer next below this.

EXERCISE 3(b)

1. The rate of growth of the number of bacteria in a culture is proportional to the number present. If there were initially 100 bacteria, and 160 bacteria after 10 minutes, find how many there were after 20 minutes.

2. With the data of Question 1, how many will there be after 16 minutes? How long will elapse until there are 300 bacteria?

3. A manufacturer estimates that the rate at which machinery depreciates is proportional to the value of the machinery. If a machine which cost £8000 new is only worth £4000 after 5 years, find its value after
   (a) 10 years,
   (b) 6 years,
   (c) 12 years.

4. Under certain circumstances, the rate of increase of the volume of a spherical raindrop is proportional to the surface area of the raindrop. Show that the radius r at time t is given by

$$r = a + bt$$

where a is the initial radius of the raindrop and b is some constant.

5. A conical vessel, semi-vertical angle α, is being filled with liquid at a constant rate of k cm^3 s^{-1}. Show that the rate at which the water level is rising is

$$\frac{k}{\pi h^2 \tan^2 \alpha}$$

when there is a depth h cm of water in the vessel. Hence show that the depth of water at time t seconds is proportional to $t^{1/3}$, if the vessel initially was empty.
If the water is 0.5 cm deep after 1 s, find the depth after 8 s and after 10 s.

6. For any one kind of glass, the intensity I of light transmitted through glass varies with the thickness x of the glass, the decrease of I with x being proportional to x. If $I = 10$ when $x = 0$, find I as a function of x. If I is reduced from 10 to 7 after passing through glass 5 cm thick, find the intensity of light from the same source after passing through glass 6 cm thick.

7. The rate of decay of a radioactive substance is proportional to the mass of the substance. When the mass is 1.5×10^{-3} gramme, the rate of decay is 0.5×10^{-6} g s^{-1}. Find how long it takes the mass to be reduced from 1.5×10^{-3} g to 0.6×10^{-3} g.

8. When the temperature of a certain body is 65 °C, it is cooling at 1 °C per minute. Assuming Newton's law of cooling, and also that the temperature of the surroundings remains constant at 15 °C, what will be the temperature of the body after 20 minutes, and how long will elapse after the first reading before the temperature is 35 °C?

9. A body is in a room, in which the temperature, assumed constant, is 10 °C. The body is heated to a temperature of 90 °C and is then allowed to cool. If the temperature is 70 °C after 4 minutes, what will be the temperature 20 minutes after cooling has begun, and how long will the body take to cool to 20 °C?

10. A spider is thrown down from the top of a tower with velocity V. The air resistance and air currents are such that the speed of descent is $V\,\mathrm{e}^{-x/h}$, where x is the distance the spider has dropped and h is the height of the tower. Prove that the spider's height y above ground level at time t is given by

$$y = h\left[1 - \log\left(1 + \frac{Vt}{h}\right)\right], \quad t < \frac{h(\mathrm{e}-1)}{V}$$

$$y = 0, \quad t \geqslant \frac{h(\mathrm{e}-1)}{V}$$

(S.M.P.)

11. In a colony of organisms, it is known that the natural growth rate of the colony is λ organisms per organism per minute. Express this fact as a differential equation connecting n and t, where n is the number of organisms present at time t minutes. If, in addition, organisms die at the rate of μ organisms per minute, show that

$$\frac{dn}{dt} = \lambda n - \mu$$

In this latter case, if it is also known that at time t_0 there were n_0 organisms present;

(a) find the time that elapses before the colony is wiped out, given that $n_0 = 200$, $\lambda = 2$ and $\mu = 500$;

(b) find the number of organisms in the colony after $\frac{1}{2}$ minute, given that $n_0 = 200$, $\lambda = 4$ and $\mu = 500$. (C.)

12. A tank with horizontal base and uniform horizontal cross-section is initially full of water. The water leaks out of a small hole in the base at a rate proportional to the square root of the depth of the water. If the tank is half empty after 1 hour, find the further time it will take to be completely empty. (J.M.B.)

13. In a certain process, the rate of production of yeast is kx grammes per minute, where x grammes is the amount already produced and k is a constant. Write down a differential equation relating x and the time t measured in minutes. Show that, if $k = 0.003$, then the amount of yeast is doubled in about 230 minutes.
If, in addition, yeast is removed at a constant rate of m grammes per minute, so that the differential equation becomes

$$\frac{dx}{dt} = kx - m$$

find the amount of yeast at time t minutes, given that at $t = 0$ there were p grammes.
Deduce that if $m \leqslant kp$ the supply of yeast is never exhausted. Find the value of m to three significant figures if $k = 0.003$, $p = 20\,000$ and the supply is exhausted in 100 minutes. (C.)

14. In a certain chemical reaction the quantity Q grammes of a chemical changes so that

$$\frac{dQ}{dt} = 2 - \frac{Q}{30}$$

If there were initially 30 g of chemical present, find how long, to the nearest second, elapses before there are 40 g of the chemical.

15. In an experiment recording the number N of daisies in a given area of garden, it was found that

$$\frac{dN}{dt} = \lambda N \frac{2000 - N}{2000}$$

where λ was constant for certain weather conditions. At the beginning of the experiment there were 1000 daisies in this area of garden. Show that at any subsequent time t

$$N = 2000 \frac{e^{\lambda t}}{1 + e^{\lambda t}}$$

and that the number of daisies present never exceeds 2000.

16 The rate at which electrical charge leaks from a capacitor is proportional to the charge on the capacitor. Show that the charge Q at time t is given by $Q_0 e^{-kt}$, where Q_0 is the charge on the capacitor at the beginning of the experiment.

17. The water in a tank is being heated by an electric heater which supplies a units of heat per second. Heat is lost to the surroundings at the rate of kT units per second, where T is the number of degrees Celsius by which the temperature of the water exceeds that of the surroundings. The amount of heat needed to raise the temperature of water in the tank by one degree is b units, if no heat is lost. When the heater is switched on, $T = 0$. Prove that t seconds later

$$\frac{dT}{dt} = (a - kT)/b$$

and, assuming a, b, k, and the temperature of the surroundings to be constant, find an expression for T in terms of a, b, k, and t. Prove that T is always less than a/k. (O.)

18. A lift of mass m kg falls freely through h metres into a safety device in which the base of the lift compresses air in a cylinder of length a metres. When the lift has fallen x metres down the cylinder, the thrust on the base is known to be

$$\frac{\lambda mga}{a - x} \text{ newtons}$$

Prove that the distance X through which the lift falls before coming first to rest is given by

$$X + h = \lambda a \log \frac{a}{a - X}$$

(O. & C.)

19. The food calories taken in by the human body go partly to increase the mass and partly to fulfil the requirements of the body; these daily requirements are taken to be proportional to the mass M. The rate of increase of mass is proportional to the number of calories available for this. Write down a differential equation connecting M, the time t and the daily intake of calories $f(t)$.
A man's mass is 100 kg: if he took in no calories he would reduce his weight by 10 per cent in 10 days. How long would it take him to reduce by this amount if, instead, he took in exactly half the number of calories needed to keep his mass constant at 100 kg? (M.E.I.)

20. A body of unit mass falls under gravity in a medium in which the resistance is proportional to the velocity of the body. If the body was initially at rest, show that the velocity v after time t is

$$\frac{g}{k}(1 - e^{-kt})$$

21. In a certain electrical circuit, the current i satisfies the differential equation

$$L\frac{di}{dt} + Ri = E$$

Show that, if the current initially is zero, at time t

$$i = \frac{E}{R}(1 - e^{-Rt/L})$$

22. A candidate for parliament estimates that the rate at which support for his party is changing during an election campaign is given by

$$\frac{dx}{dt} = ax(N - x)$$

where x is the number of supporters at time t (measured in days after the start of the campaign), N is the number of electors in that constituency, and a is a constant.
Initially he has 500 supporters out of an electorate of 50 000 and estimates that he is gaining supporters at the rate of ninety-nine a day. If his estimate is correct, find the least number of days he must campaign in order to be certain of winning.

23. Economists define the price elasticity of demand E of a commodity as the ratio

percentage change in demand : percentage change in price

so that

$$E = \frac{P}{D}\frac{dD}{dP}$$

where P is the price and D the demand for the commodity, measured in suitable units.

(a) A publisher estimates that for a certain book $E = -2$, and $D = £20\,000$ when $P = £2$. Find the demand when the price is raised to £2.50. What decrease will this mean in the number of books sold? Why will E usually be negative?

(b) A manufacturer of perfume estimates that in a certain price range for his products $E = +2$, and that $D = £20\,000$ when $P = £2$. Find the value of D when $P = £3$.

24. The price elasticity of supply E^* is similarly defined, so that

$$E^* = \frac{P}{S}\frac{dS}{dP}$$

where S is the supply.
A shirt manufacturer estimates that for a certain range of his goods $E^* = 2$, $P = £2$ and $S = £200\,000$. Find S when P is increased to £2.50.

25. An economic model for the National Debt £D suggests that

$$\frac{dD}{dt} = aI \quad \text{and} \quad \frac{dI}{dt} = bI$$

where £I is the national income. If I_0, D_0 are the initial values of I and D respectively, show that

$$D = \frac{aI_0}{b}(e^{bt} - 1) + D_0$$

Show also that as t becomes large, D/I approaches a/b.

26. An architect estimates that the deflection y of a beam at a distance x from one end is given by

$$\frac{d^4y}{dx^4} = k$$

where k is a constant proportional to w/E, w being the weight per unit length and E the value of Young's modulus for that beam.
For a certain beam of length l, $dy/dx = y = 0$ at each end. Find the deflection half way along the beam.

27. Prove that the circle is the only plane curve for which the tangent at any point P is perpendicular to the radius vector through P.

28. If p is the pressure of the atmosphere and ρ the density at height x above sea level it can be shown that $dp/dx = -g\rho$. Given that p is proportional to ρ, show that

$$p = p_0 \, e^{-\rho_0 g x / p_0},$$

where p_0, ρ_0 are the values of p and ρ at sea level.

29. In a pathological investigation of the spread of infection in a culture, it is found that the time rate at which the area of the infected part spreads is directly proportional to the product of the infected and the uninfected areas. Initially one half of the area is infected and the initial rate of spread is such that, if it remained constant thereafter, the culture would be completely infected in 24 hours. Set up a differential equation relating x, the infected proportion of the total area, to time t, and deduce that after 12 hours about 73 per cent of the culture is infected. (S.M.P.)

30. In a chemical reaction the concentration C of a certain substance is given by the equation

$$\frac{dC}{dt} = k_1 - k_2 C$$

where k_1 and k_2 are constants. Initially the value of the concentration is C_0 and after time t_0 has elapsed it is found to be $2C_0$. By integrating the differential equation obtain an expression for the concentration at any time, and use your solution to show that

$$k_1 = k_2 \frac{C_0(2 - e^{-k_2 t_0})}{(1 - e^{-k_2 t_0})}$$ (M.E.I.)

31. Many chemical reactions obey first order kinetics, i.e. the rate of the reaction is proportional to the concentration of the reacting substance. The isomerization of cyclopropane is one such reaction. In an experiment it was found that the concentration of cyclopropane was 100 per cent initially but had dropped to 79 per cent after 5 hours. Find the percentage concentration of the cyclopropane 10 hours and 2 hours after the experiment began.

32. A uniform chain of length l, mass μl, is initially at rest on a horizontal table. When it is raised by applying a constant force of $\mu l g$ to one end, it is found that the velocity v of that end is related to the length x already raised by the equation

$$\frac{1}{2x}\frac{d}{dx}(v^2 x^2) + gx = lg$$

Show that the velocity of the chain when it has just been lifted from the table is $\sqrt{(\frac{1}{3}gl)}$, and that at time $(3 - \sqrt{3})\sqrt{l/g}$ all the chain has just been brought into motion.

33. A chain, initially in a stationary pile near the edge of a table starts to fall over the edge. At time t a length x of chain is off the table. The equation linking x and t is

$$x\frac{d^2x}{dt^2} + \left(\frac{dx}{dt}\right)^2 = gx$$

Use the substitution $x = z^{1/2}$ to solve this equation, expressing x as a function of t.

34. A flexible cable mass m per unit hangs between two supports a distance $2a$ apart and at the same horizontal level. The length of cable $(2S)$ is greater than $2a$, and the tension in the cable at the bottom is H. Taking the x- and y-directions to be horizontal and vertical respectively, show that

$$\frac{dy}{dx} = \frac{mgs}{H}$$

where s is the length of cable measured from the bottom. By using $\sin\psi = dy/ds$, $\cos\psi = dx/ds$ where $dy/dx = \tan\psi$ or otherwise, prove that

$$S = \frac{H}{mg}\sinh\frac{amg}{H} \qquad \text{(O.S.)}$$

35. The curve in which the chain in Question 34 hangs is called a catenary. Deduce the intrinsic equation $s = c\tan\psi$ of the catenary, and also the equations

$$y = c\sec\psi, \quad x = \log(\sec\psi + \tan\psi)$$

36. A uniform flexible chain is attached to two points A, B, on the same horizontal level, a distance $2a$ apart. The lowest point of the chain is a distance λa below the level of AB. Show that the length of the chain is $2a(1 + \frac{2}{3}\lambda^2)$, neglecting powers of λ above the third.

Second order differential equations

The simplest second order differential equations are of the form

$$\frac{d^2x}{dt^2} + ax = b$$

At the beginning of this chapter we saw that if $x = a \cos \omega t$,

$$\frac{d^2x}{dt^2} + \omega^2 x = 0$$

Thus $x = a \cos \omega t$ is seen to be a solution of

$$\frac{d^2x}{dt^2} + \omega^2 x = 0$$

Is it the only solution, or can we find others?

If we denote dx/dt by v, then

$$\frac{d^2x}{dt^2} = \frac{dv}{dt}$$

$$= \frac{dx}{dt} \cdot \frac{dv}{dx}$$

$$= v \frac{dv}{dx}$$

The equation now reads

$$v \frac{dv}{dx} = -\omega^2 x$$

and integrating we have

$$\int v \, dv = -\int \omega^2 x \, dx$$

$$\Rightarrow \tfrac{1}{2}v^2 = -\tfrac{1}{2}\omega^2 x^2 + C$$

If $v = 0$ and $x = a$ when $t = 0$, $C = \tfrac{1}{2}\omega^2 a^2$

$$\Rightarrow v^2 = \omega^2 (a^2 - x^2)$$

Thus $\quad \dfrac{dx}{dt} = \omega\sqrt{(a^2 - x^2)}$, if x increases with t

and separating the variables

$$\int \frac{dx}{\sqrt{(a^2 - x^2)}} = \int \omega \, dt$$

$$\Rightarrow \sin^{-1} \frac{x}{a} = \omega t + C'$$

But from the initial conditions (or boundary conditions)

$$x = a \quad \text{when } t = 0 \tag{3.3}$$

$$\Rightarrow C' = \frac{\pi}{2}$$

i.e.
$$\sin^{-1}\frac{x}{a} = \omega t + \frac{\pi}{2}$$

$$x = a \sin\left(\omega t + \frac{\pi}{2}\right)$$

i.e.
$$x = a \cos \omega t$$

If instead the initial conditions had been

$$x = 0 \quad \text{and} \quad v = U \quad \text{when } t = 0 \tag{3.4}$$

the reader will easily verify that the solution is

$$x = \frac{U}{\omega} \sin \omega t$$

Either of these can be the correct solution of our equation, depending on the initial conditions.

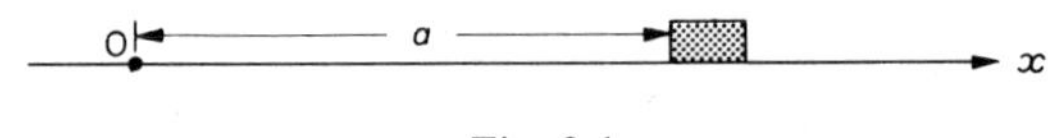

Fig. 3.1

Notice the physical interpretation of these solutions (Fig. 3.1). With data of equation 3.3 the particle whose motion this equation describes is initially at rest a distance a from the origin O. It moves towards O, reaches O when $x = 0$, i.e. after time $\pi/(2\omega)$ moves to $x = -a$ and then returns to its initial position. The particle oscillates about O, the motion being repeated after time $2\pi/\omega$. The constant a is called the amplitude of the motion; the period of the motion is $2\pi/\omega$. Fig. 3.2 uses the cosine curve to illustrate the motion of such a particle.

If instead data of equation 3.4 had been given, choose a now so that $a = U/v$ and the equation of motion is $x = a \sin \omega t$. This time the particle is initially at O with velocity $a\omega$ and moves along the

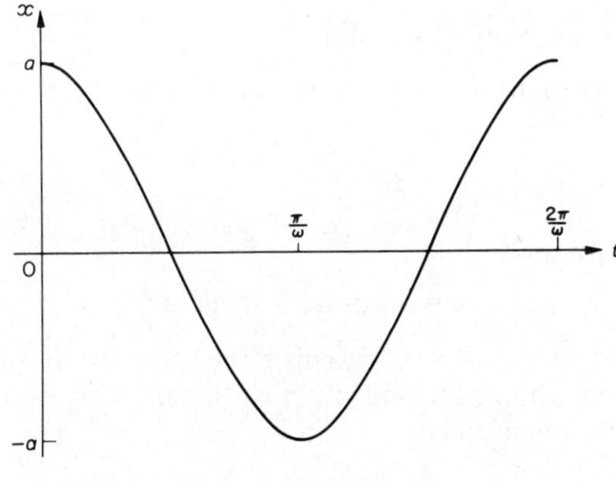

Fig. 3.2

x axis to a point distant a from O (Fig. 3.3). It then returns to O and oscillates as in the first example.

We could, of course, have had different initial conditions, in which case the solution would have been

$$x = A \cos \omega t + B \sin \omega t$$

which can be written

$$x = \sqrt{(A^2 + B^2)} \cos (\omega t + \epsilon), \quad \text{where} \quad \tan \epsilon = -\frac{B}{A}$$

Whatever the initial conditions, the motion of a particle given by this equation is called *simple harmonic motion.* For a fuller solution of these equations, see *Advanced Level Pure Mathematics*. We are now mainly concerned with solutions for which either $x = 0$ or $v = 0$ when $t = 0$.

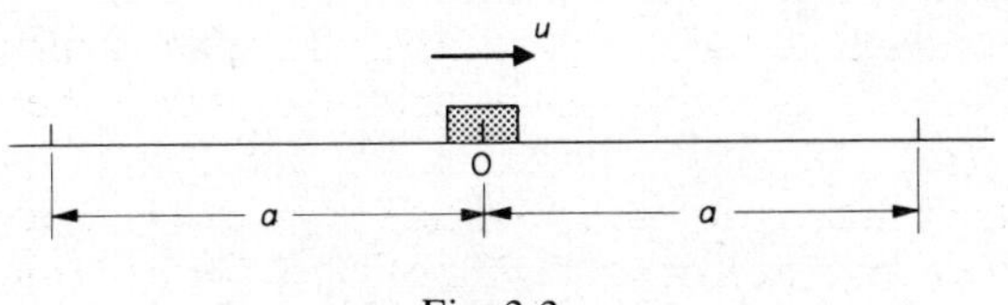

Fig. 3.3

Recognition of required solution

We have seen that the solutions of an equation of the form

$$\frac{d^2x}{dt^2} + \omega^2 x = 0$$

will be of the form

$$x = A \cos \omega t + B \sin \omega t$$

If $x = 0$ when $t = 0$, $A = 0$. If $dx/dt = 0$ when $t = 0$, $B = 0$. Thus if the initial conditions include either of these, we can simplify the possible solution at once.

Example 3.6. *A particle moves along the x axis so that its distance x cm from the origin O at time t seconds is given by $d^2x/dt^2 = -16x$. Initially the particle is at rest 5 cm from O. Express x as a function of t.*

We know the solution must be of the form

$$x = A \cos 4t + B \sin 4t$$

Since $\quad \frac{dx}{dt} = 0 \quad$ when $t = 0$, $B = 0$

Also $\quad x = 5 \quad$ when $t = 0 \Rightarrow A = 5$

The solution is $x = 5 \cos 4t$.

Example 3.7. *If the particle in Example 3.6 had initially been passing through $x = 0$ with velocity 10 cm s^{-1}, express x in terms of t.*

As $x = A \cos 4t + B \sin 4t$ is again the most general form of the solution,

$$x = 0 \quad \text{when } t = 0 \Rightarrow A = 0$$

If $\quad x = B \sin 4t$

$$\frac{dx}{dt} = 4B \cos 4t$$

But $\quad \frac{dx}{dt} = 10 \quad$ when $t = 0 \Rightarrow 4B = 10$

$$\Rightarrow B = 2.5$$

$\therefore$ $x = 2.5 \sin 4t$ is the required solution.

We can usually choose to measure t either from the moment when the particle is at rest at the end of an oscillation, or from when it is passing through the origin, so one or other of the forms above is often suitable. Occasionally this may not be possible.

Example 3.8. *A packet of butter is dropped onto the scale-pan of a spring-balance which oscillates so that its distance x cm above a fixed point is related to the time t seconds after impact by the equation*

$$\frac{d^2x}{dt^2} = -36x$$

Initially x = 1 cm and immediately after impact the velocity of the butter is 9 cm s^{-1} downwards. Find x in terms of t, and also calculate when the butter first comes instantaneously to rest.

Since $x = A \cos 6t + B \sin 6t$ is the form of the solution,

$$x = 1 \quad \text{when } t = 0 \Rightarrow A = 1$$

and
$$\frac{dx}{dt} = -9 \quad \text{when } t = 0 \Rightarrow B = -\tfrac{3}{2}$$

∴ the solution is

$$x = \cos 6t - \tfrac{3}{2} \sin 6t$$

When the butter is at rest,
$$\frac{dx}{dt} = 0,$$

i.e.
$$-6 \sin 6t - 9 \cos 6t = 0$$
$$\tan 6t = -\tfrac{3}{2}$$
$$t = \tfrac{1}{6} \tan^{-1} (-\tfrac{3}{2})$$

Only positive values of t are admissible, and the smallest positive value of t, from tangent and radian tables, is about 0.36. The butter therefore is next instantaneously at rest after 0.36 s.

Equations reducible to this form

If there is also a constant term in the equation, e.g.

$$\frac{d^2x}{dt^2} = -36x + 72$$

the substitution $z = x - 2$ reduces the equation to

$$\frac{d^2z}{dt^2} = -36z$$

and this can be solved as before. The substitution was suggested by

$$\frac{d^2x}{dt^2} = -36(x - 2)$$

Great care must be taken to ensure that the initial conditions are used correctly; either initial values of x must be changed to give initial values of z, or x must be returned by substitution into the equation for z.

Example 3.9. *A particle moves along the x axis so that its distance x cm from the origin at time t seconds is given by*

$$\frac{d^2x}{dt^2} = -25x + 15$$

Initially $x = 0.6$ *and* $dx/dt = 5$. *Express x as a function of t.*

Writing the equation in the form

$$\frac{d^2x}{dt^2} = -25(x - 0.6)$$

suggests that we substitute $z = x - 0.6$. The equation becomes

$$\frac{d^2z}{dt^2} = -25z \qquad (3.5)$$

and initially $z = 0$ and $dz/dt = 5$. Thus since the solution to equation 3.5 is

$$z = A \cos 5t + B \sin 5t$$

$$z = 0 \quad \text{when } t = 0 \Rightarrow A = 0$$

and $$\frac{dz}{dt} = 5 \quad \text{when } t = 0 \Rightarrow B = 1$$

$$\Rightarrow z = \sin 5t$$

$$\Rightarrow x = 0.6 + \sin 5t$$

This particle oscillates about $x = 0.6$, with period $2\pi/5$ seconds, i.e. about 1.26 s.

All the above examples refer to the motion of a particle or of a body in a straight line. Many types of rotatory motion approximate to this form, as do many electrical equations. The analogy between the solutions of electrical problems (e.g. Exercise 3(b), compare Question 16 with Questions 1–3, 6–9), and many other mathematical problems prompted the development of the analogue computer, which solves mathematical problems by setting up an analogous electrical circuit.

EXERCISE 3(c)

Questions 1–10 refer to the motion of a particle executing simple harmonic motion under the law

$$\frac{d^2x}{dt^2} = -\omega^2 x$$

1. Solve the differential equation, given that $\omega^2 = 9$ and $x = 5$, $dx/dt = 0$ when $t = 0$.

2. Solve the differential equation given that $\omega^2 = 25$ and that $x = 0$, $dx/dt = 10$ when $t = 0$.

3. Solve the differential equation given that $\omega^2 = 100$ and that $x = 0$, $dx/dt = 20$ when $t = 0$.

4. Solve the differential equation given that $\omega^2 = 16$ and that $x = 9$, $dx/dt = 0$ when $t = 0$.

5. Solve the differential equation given that $\omega^2 = 25$ and that $x = 16$, $dx/dt = 0$ when $t = \pi/20$.

6. Solve the differential equation given that $\omega^2 = 25$ and that $x = 10$, $dx/dt = 0$ when $t = \pi/10$.

7. If the particle is initially at rest 5 cm from the origin and the acceleration is then 80 cm s^{-2} towards the origin, find the distance x cm of the particle from the origin in terms of t.

8. If the particle is initially at rest 10 cm from the origin, and has a maximum velocity of 50 cm s^{-1}, find ω and hence express x in terms of t.

9. If initially the particle is 5 cm from O and has a velocity of 10 cm s^{-1} away from O, find x in terms of ω and t. Given that $\omega = 1$, find the greatest distance of the particle from O (the amplitude).

10. Given that the particle is initially at O with velocity 10 cm s^{-1} and the amplitude is 5 cm, find x in terms of t. Hence find the period of the motion.

11. The depth of water x metres above a mark in a certain estuary is given approximately by

$$\frac{d^2x}{dt^2} = -\tfrac{1}{4}x$$

when the time t is measured in hours from low water. If the difference between the high and low water marks is 6 m, solve the differential equation to find x in terms of t, the time after low water. How long is there between successive high tides?

12. The depth of water y metres in a tidal creek is given approximately by

$$4\frac{d^2y}{dt^2} + y = 5$$

the time t being measured in hours. Solve the equation to find y in terms of t, the time after any one low tide, given that the water is then 1 m deep and that it will be 9 m deep at high tide.
If low tide one day is at 1.00 p.m., when is the earliest a ship requiring 3 m of water can enter the creek?

13. To a certain passenger on board a ship, the ship appears to be oscillating vertically with simple harmonic motion, the height x metres above the central position at time t seconds being given by

$$\frac{d^2x}{dt^2} = -x$$

The passenger estimates that he travels vertically through 6 metres each time the ship falls. Find the maximum velocity and the maximum acceleration which he thinks he experiences.

14. It used to be thought that simple harmonic motion was a good approximation to the movement of the wing tip of certain small birds, e.g. humming-birds, and some insects, e.g. dragon-flies and locusts. If the period of oscillation of the wing tip of a locust is 1/20 s, and the amplitude is 1.5 cm, find the maximum velocity of the wing-tip.
What is the maximum velocity of the wing-tip of a small fly, whose period is 1/1000 s and whose amplitude is 2 mm?

15. Verify that the equation

$$\frac{d^2x}{dt^2} = 4x$$

is satisfied by solutions of the form $x = A\,e^{2t} + B\,e^{-2t}$ for all values of A and B. Draw two graphs of x against t to show the difference between this motion and simple harmonic motion.

16. Verify that

$$\frac{d^2x}{dt^2} + 3\frac{dx}{dt} + 2x = 0$$

is satisfied by solutions of the form $x = A\,e^{-t} + B\,e^{-2t}$ for all values of A and B. Hence find the solution if initially $x = 1$ and $dx/dt = 1$.

17. A smooth tube XY length $2a$ is free to rotate about X in a horizontal plane. A small bead is placed in the tube at a distance a from X. The tube is then made to rotate with constant angular velocity Ω. The distance r of the bead from X is given by

$$\frac{d^2r}{dt^2} = \Omega^2 r$$

Find r as a function of t, and the velocity of the particle when it leaves the tube.

18. If $A\,e^{nt}$ is a solution of

$$\frac{d^2x}{dt^2} + 2k\frac{dx}{dt} + \omega^2 x = 0$$

show that $n = -k + \sqrt{(k^2 - \omega^2)}$ or $n = -k - \sqrt{(k^2 - \omega^2)}$. Denoting these values of n by n_1 and n_2, show that

$$x = A\,e^{n_1 t} + B\,e^{n_2 t}$$

is also a solution.

19. The angular displacement from the vertical of a simple pendulum in a viscous fluid obeys the differential equation

$$\frac{d^2\theta}{dt^2} + 2k\frac{d\theta}{dt} + \omega^2\theta = 0$$

where k and ω are constants.
If the pendulum is initially held at a small displacement of θ_0 and then released, find expressions for its subsequent motion when $k > \omega$ and when $k < \omega$. Give a rough sketch of θ as a function of t for $k \ll \omega$ and $k \gg \omega$. (C.S.)

20. The deflection θ of a galvanometer satisfies the equation

$$\frac{d^2\theta}{dt^2} + 3\frac{d\theta}{dt} + 2\theta = 0$$

If initially $d\theta/dt = 0$ and $\theta = 1$, find θ as a function of t.

(The remainder of this chapter should be omitted at a first reading.)

Damped harmonic motion

Resistance proportional to the velocity

We have seen that the motion of a particle oscillating with simple harmonic motion is described by an equation of the form

$$\frac{d^2x}{dt^2} = -\omega^2 x.$$

If, for example, this is a body at the end of an elastic spring, the restoring force due to the spring gives the term $-\omega^2 x$. If the motion takes place in a medium in which there is a resistance proportional to the velocity, the equation of motion becomes

$$\frac{d^2x}{dt^2} = -2k\frac{dx}{dt} - \omega^2 x$$

i.e.
$$\frac{d^2x}{dt^2} + 2k\frac{dx}{dt} + \omega^2 x = 0 \qquad (3.6)$$

the factor 2 being introduced to simplify the subsequent algebra.

In Exercise 3(c), we verified that certain functions of x satisfied equations of this form. In general, the solutions are:

(a) if $k^2 > \omega^2$, $\quad x = e^{-kt}(A\,e^{pt} + B\,e^{-pt})$, where $p^2 = k^2 - \omega^2$

i.e. $\quad x = A\,e^{n_1 t} + B\,e^{n_2 t}$

where n_1, n_2 are the roots of $n^2 + 2kn + \omega^2 = 0$,

(b) if $k^2 = \omega^2$, $\quad x = e^{-kt}(A + Bt)$,

(c) if $k^2 < \omega^2$, $\quad x = e^{-kt}(A\cos pt + B\sin pt)$, where $p^2 = \omega^2 - k^2$

and A and B are determined by the initial conditions. (For a fuller discussion of the solution of these differential equations, see *Advanced Level Pure Mathematics,* by L. H. Clarke, chapter 17.)

To verify that $x = e^{-kt}(A + Bt)$ satisfies equation 3.6 when $k^2 = \omega^2$,

$$x = e^{-kt}[A + Bt]$$

$$\Rightarrow \frac{dx}{dt} = e^{-kt}[B - k(A + Bt)]$$

and

$$\frac{d^2x}{dt^2} = e^{-kt}[-2kB + k^2(A + Bt)]$$

$$\therefore \quad \frac{d^2x}{dt^2} + 2k\frac{dx}{dt} + \omega^2 x = e^{-kt}[-2kB + k^2(A + Bt) + 2kB - 2k^2(A + Bt) + \omega^2(A + Bt)]$$

$$= 0 \text{ for all values of } t \text{ if and only if } k^2 = \omega^2$$

The reader can verify likewise that the other functions will satisfy equation 3.6 for $k^2 > \omega^2$ or $k^2 < \omega^2$.

Using these results we see that, for example,

$$\frac{d^2x}{dt^2} + 3\frac{dx}{dt} + 2x = 0$$

has solution $x = A\,e^{-t} + B\,e^{-2t}$, from $n^2 + 3n + 2 = 0$;

$$\frac{d^2x}{dt^2} + 6\frac{dx}{dt} + 4x = 0$$

has solution $x = e^{-3t}(A\,e^{t\sqrt{5}} + B\,e^{-t\sqrt{5}})$, from $n^2 + 6n + 4 = 0$;

$$\frac{d^2x}{dt^2} + 6\frac{dx}{dt} + 9x = 0$$

has solution $x = e^{-3t}(A + Bt)$, from $n^2 + 6n + 9 = 0$;

and

$$\frac{d^2x}{dt^2} + 6\frac{dx}{dt} + 10x = 0$$

has solution $x = e^{-3t}(A \cos t + B \sin t)$, from $n^2 + 6n + 10 = 0$.

Notice the different forms of the solutions, depending on whether the associated quadratic equation has real distinct, equal, or complex roots. In the last example, $k = 3$ and $\omega^2 = 10$, so that $\omega^2 - k^2 = 1$ and the functions $\cos pt$, $\sin pt$, were $\cos t$ and $\sin t$ respectively.

Example 3.10. *A particle executes damped harmonic motion so that its displacement x metres from the origin at time t seconds is given by*

$$\frac{d^2x}{dt^2} + 4\frac{dx}{dt} + 5x = 0$$

Initially, the particle is 1 m from O and is travelling towards O at 1 m s^{-1}. Investigate the subsequent motion

Comparing
$$\frac{d^2x}{dt^2} + 4\frac{dx}{dt} + 5x = 0$$

with
$$\frac{d^2x}{dt^2} + 2k\frac{dx}{dt} + \omega^2 x = 0$$

we see that $k = 2$, $\omega^2 = 5$, so that $\omega^2 - k^2 = 1$. Thus $k^2 < \omega^2$ and the solution is

$$x = e^{-2t}(A \cos t + B \sin t)$$

Initially, $x = 1$ and $dx/dt = -1$. Therefore substituting $t = 0$ in x and in dx/dt,

$$1 = A \quad \text{and} \quad -1 = B - 2A, \quad \text{i.e. } B = 1$$

The solution which satisfies the initial conditions is therefore

$$x = e^{-2t}(\cos t + \sin t)$$

This motion is oscillatory and is illustrated in Fig. 3.4.

Since
$$\cos t + \sin t = \sqrt{2} \sin (t + \pi/4)$$
$$x = \sqrt{2}\, e^{-2t} \sin (t + \pi/4)$$

so that the particle returns to the origin at intervals of π seconds, and the period of the (damped) oscillations is 2π seconds.

To find the extreme values of the amplitude, if

$$x = \sqrt{2}\, e^{-2t} \sin\left(t + \frac{\pi}{4}\right)$$

$$\frac{dx}{dt} = \sqrt{2}\,e^{-2t}\left[\cos\left(t+\frac{\pi}{4}\right) - 2\sin\left(t+\frac{\pi}{4}\right)\right]$$

$$= \sqrt{2}\,e^{-2t}\sqrt{5}\left[\frac{1}{\sqrt{5}}\cos\left(t+\frac{\pi}{4}\right) - \frac{2}{\sqrt{5}}\sin\left(t+\frac{\pi}{4}\right)\right]$$

$$= \sqrt{10}\,e^{-2t}\cos\left(t+\frac{\pi}{4}+\alpha\right)$$

where $\cos\alpha : \sin\alpha : 1 = 1 : 2 : \sqrt{5}$. Thus the greatest values of the amplitude occur when $dx/dt = 0$, i.e. when

$$\cos\left(t+\frac{\pi}{4}+\alpha\right) = 0.$$

Now
$$\cos\alpha = \frac{1}{\sqrt{5}} < \frac{1}{\sqrt{2}}$$

$\therefore$
$$\frac{\pi}{4} < \alpha < \frac{\pi}{2}$$

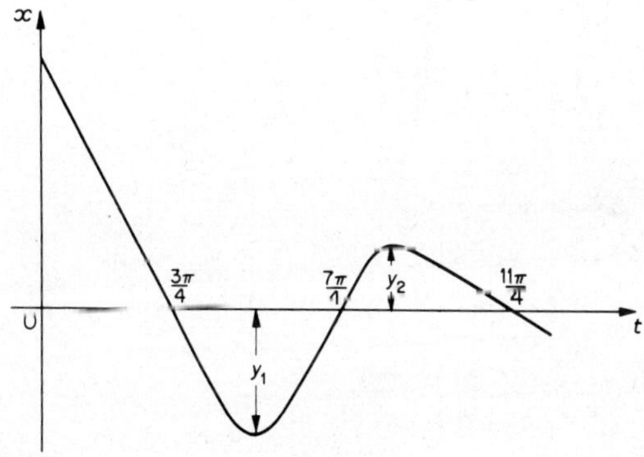

Fig. 3.4

and the first value of t for which $dx/dt = 0$ is when

$$t + \frac{\pi}{4} + \alpha = \frac{3\pi}{2}$$

i.e., $t = (5\pi/4) - \alpha$, which is later than $t = 3\pi/4$ when $x = 0$. The maximum and minimum values y_1, y_2, y_3, occur when

$$t = \frac{5\pi}{4} - \alpha,\quad \frac{9\pi}{4} - \alpha,\quad \frac{13\pi}{4} - \alpha, \ldots \text{etc.}$$

Thus if $y = y_1$ when $t = t_1$, etc.,

$$\frac{y_2}{y_1} = \frac{\sqrt{2}\,e^{-2t_2}\sin(t_2 + \pi/4)}{\sqrt{2}\,e^{-2t_1}\sin(t_1 + \pi/4)}$$

$$= e^{-2(t_2 - t_1)}, \text{ since } \sin(t_2 + \pi/4) = \sin(t_1 + \pi/4),$$

$$= e^{-2\pi}$$

Similarly $$\frac{y_n}{y_{n-1}} = e^{-2\pi}$$

and these oscillations decay very rapidly; y_1, y_2, y_3 had to be very exaggerated in Fig. 3.4 so that they were discernible.

EXERCISE 3(d)

Solve the following differential equations:

1. $\frac{d^2x}{dt^2} + 5\frac{dx}{dt} + 4x = 0$

2. $\frac{d^2x}{dt^2} - 2\frac{dx}{dt} - 8x = 0$

3. $\frac{d^2x}{dt^2} - 4\frac{dx}{dt} + 4x = 0$

4. $\frac{d^2x}{dt^2} - 2\frac{dx}{dt} + x = 0$

5. $\frac{d^2x}{dt^2} - 4\frac{dx}{dt} + 5x = 0$

6. $\frac{d^2x}{dt^2} + 6\frac{dx}{dt} + 10x = 0$

Find the solutions of the following differential equations which satisfy the given initial conditions:

7. $\frac{d^2x}{dt^2} + 3\frac{dx}{dt} - 4x = 0$; $x = 5$ and $\frac{dx}{dt} = 0$

8. $\frac{d^2x}{dt^2} + 2\frac{dx}{dt} + x = 0$; $x = 1$ and $\frac{dx}{dt} = 0$

9. $\dfrac{d^2x}{dt^2} + 2\dfrac{dx}{dt} + 2x = 0$; $x = 1$ and $\dfrac{dx}{dt} = -1$

10. A particle executes damped harmonic motion so that its displacement x metres from the origin at time t seconds is given by the equation

$$\frac{d^2x}{dt^2} + 6\frac{dx}{dt} + 10x = 0$$

Initially the particle is at the origin with velocity 6 m s^{-1}. Find its displacement at any subsequent time t.

11. A particle moves along the x axis so that its displacement x is given by

$$\frac{d^2x}{dt^2} + \frac{dx}{dt} - 2x = 0$$

Show that $x = A\,e^t + B\,e^{-2t}$.

12. A particle is projected from the origin along the x axis with velocity 3 m s^{-1}. The motion of the particle is given by the equation

$$\frac{d^2x}{dt^2} + \frac{dx}{dt} - 2x = 0$$

Find the displacement after t seconds, and the velocity after 1 s

13. A particle is projected along the x axis with velocity 2 m s^{-1} from the origin. The displacement x metres is given by

$$\frac{d^2x}{dt^2} + 6\frac{dx}{dt} + 13x = 0$$

Find the displacement at time t. If the velocity is zero after time T, show that $\tan 2T = \frac{2}{3}$.

14. The displacement x of a particle is given at time t by

$$\frac{d^2x}{dt^2} + 2\frac{dx}{dt} + 5x = 0$$

Show that the particle executes damped oscillatory motion, and find the ratio of the amplitudes of successive half-oscillations.

Additional forces which are functions of time

If the particle is also subject to a force which is a function of time, the differential equation becomes

$$\frac{d^2x}{dt^2} + 2k\frac{dx}{dt} + \omega^2 x = F(t)$$

and we can find other solutions of the equation, called particular integrals. For example,

$$\frac{d^2x}{dt^2} + \omega^2 x = \omega^2 t$$

is obviously satisfied by $x = t$; the equation

$$\frac{d^2x}{dt^2} + 5\frac{dx}{dt} + 4x = 1$$

is obviously satisfied by $x = \frac{1}{4}$; and

$$\frac{d^2x}{dt^2} + 8\frac{dx}{dt} + 20x = 10t$$

is satisfied by $x = \frac{1}{2}t - \frac{1}{5}$.

It can be shown that the complete solution of

$$\frac{d^2x}{dt^2} + 2k\frac{dx}{dt} + \omega^2 x = F(t)$$

is the solution of

$$\frac{d^2x}{dt^2} + 2k\frac{dx}{dt} + \omega^2 x = 0$$

called the complementary function, and any solution of

$$\frac{d^2x}{dt^2} + 2k\frac{dx}{dt} + \omega^2 x = F(t)$$

called the particular integral. Thus since

$$\frac{d^2x}{dt^2} + \omega^2 x = 0$$

is satisfied by $x = A \cos \omega t + B \sin \omega t$, the complete solution of

$$\frac{d^2x}{dt^2} + \omega^2 x = \omega^2 t$$

is

$$x = A \cos \omega t + B \sin \omega t + t$$

Likewise the complete solution of

$$\frac{d^2x}{dt^2} + 5\frac{dx}{dt} + 4x = 1$$

is

$$x = A\,e^{-t} + B\,e^{-4t} + \tfrac{1}{4}$$

and the complete solution of

$$\frac{d^2x}{dt^2} + 8\frac{dx}{dt} + 20x = 10t$$

is

$$x = e^{-4t}(A \cos 2t + B \sin 2t) + \tfrac{1}{2}t - \tfrac{1}{5}$$

Determining the particular integral

The particular integrals are found by inspection, and experience enables us to form certain rules. The ones given here are adequate for all the forms usually found in applied mathematics at this level.

(1) If the term on the right hand side of the equation is a constant, try $x = \alpha$, a constant, as the particular integral.
(2) If $F(t)$ is a polynomial of degree n, try $x = \alpha_0 + \alpha_1 t + \alpha_2 t^2 + \cdots + \alpha_n t^n$, e.g. if $F(t) = at + b$, try $x = \alpha_0 + \alpha_1 t$.
(3) If $F(t)$ contains an exponential, say $k\,e^{\alpha t}$, try $x = \lambda\,e^{\alpha t}$, unless $e^{\alpha t}$ is also in the complementary function; then try $x = \lambda t\,e^{\alpha t}$. If this is also in the complementary function, try $x = \lambda t^2\,e^{\alpha t}$.
(4) If $F(t)$ contains a term in $\cos kt$ or $\sin kt$, try $x = \alpha \cos kt + \beta \sin kt$, unless these appear as part of the complementary function, in which case try $x = t(\alpha \cos kt + \beta \sin kt)$.

These will be found sufficient at this stage, although further forms of $F(t)$ will be encountered in more advanced work. The particular integral is the sum of all the terms corresponding to the terms in $F(t)$.

Example 3.11. *Find the complete solution of*

$$\frac{d^2x}{dt^2} + 4x = 4t + e^t$$

The complementary function is $x = A \sin 2t + B \cos 2t$. Since $F(t)$ contains a term in t, we see by inspection $x = t$ is that particular integral. There is also a term e^t, so we try $x = \alpha e^t$. This satisfies

$$\frac{d^2x}{dt^2} + 4x = e^t$$

if $(\alpha + 4\alpha) e^t = e^t$, i.e. $\alpha = \frac{1}{5}$

so the complete solution is

$$x = A \sin 2t + B \cos 2t + t + \tfrac{1}{5} e^t$$

Spring attached at a moving point

We have considered many examples of a body oscillating at one end of a spring, the other end of which is fixed. Suppose now that the other end can move, as in a lift, or is fixed to a beam which itself oscillates.

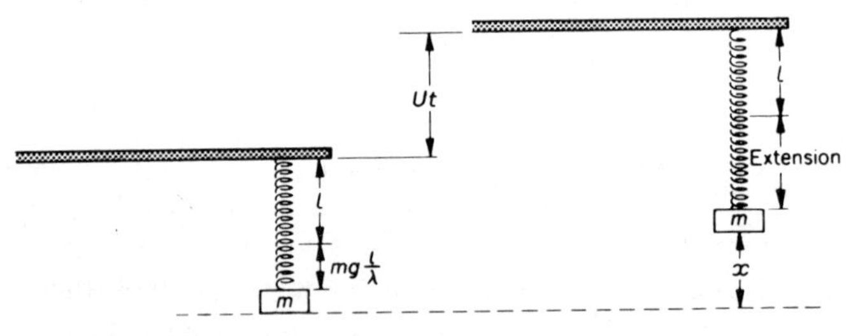

Fig. 3.5

Consider first the spring fixed to the roof of a lift which ascends with constant velocity U. The displacement x of the body must be measured from a fixed position, say the initial position of the body. If the body has mass m, and the spring is of unstretched length l, modulus of elasticity λ, when the lift is at rest the natural extension of the spring will be mgl/λ (Fig. 3.5). If the displacement of the body subsequently is x, the extension of the spring is

$$Ut - x + \frac{mgl}{\lambda}$$

$$\therefore \quad -mg + \frac{\lambda}{l}\left(Ut - x + \frac{mgl}{\lambda}\right) = m\frac{d^2x}{dt^2}, \text{ from Newton's law,}$$

i.e.

$$\frac{d^2x}{dt^2} + \frac{\lambda}{ml}x = \frac{\lambda U}{ml}t$$

The complementary function is the solution of

$$\frac{d^2x}{dt^2} + \frac{\lambda}{ml}x = 0$$

i.e.

$$x = A \sin\left(\sqrt{\frac{\lambda}{ml}}\right)t + B \cos\left(\sqrt{\frac{\lambda}{ml}}\right)t$$

The particular integral must be linear in t and is found to be Ut. Thus the displacement x at time t is given by

$$x = Ut + A \sin\left(\sqrt{\frac{\lambda}{ml}}\right)t + B \cos\left(\sqrt{\frac{\lambda}{ml}}\right)t$$

It is this equation that must satisfy the initial conditions. If the body is initially at rest in equilibrium,

$$x = 0 \quad \text{when } t = 0, \quad \therefore B = 0$$

and $dx/dt = 0$ when $t = 0$, so

$$U + A\sqrt{\left(\frac{\lambda}{ml}\right)} \cos\left(\sqrt{\frac{\lambda}{ml}}\right)t - B\sqrt{\left(\frac{\lambda}{ml}\right)} \sin\left(\sqrt{\frac{\lambda}{ml}}\right)t = 0$$

when $t = 0$

i.e.

$$U + A\sqrt{\frac{\lambda}{ml}} = 0 \text{ since } B = 0,$$

i.e.

$$A = -U\sqrt{\frac{ml}{\lambda}}$$

Thus the motion is described by

$$x = Ut - U\sqrt{\frac{ml}{\lambda}} \sin\left(\sqrt{\frac{\lambda}{ml}}\right)t$$

Notice that if the body is initially in equilibrium and the lift remained at rest, the initial condition would give $A = B = 0$ and the body would remain at rest.

The dimensions of the expressions give a useful check. m has dimensions M, l has dimensions L, and λ, being a force, has dimensions M L T^{-2}. Thus the dimensions of $\sqrt{(ml/\lambda)}$ are T, so that $t\sqrt{\lambda/ml}$ has no dimensions, and $U\sqrt{(ml/\lambda)}$ has dimensions L, as expected.

Oscillating beam

Suppose that instead of being fixed to the roof of the lift, the free end of the spring is attached at a point on a beam which oscillates so that its displacement X from its initial position is given by

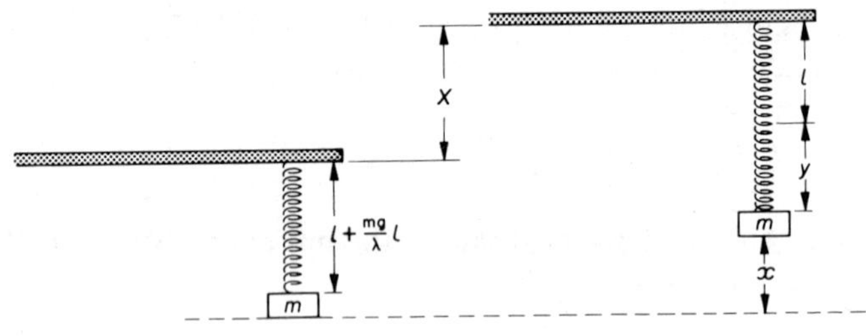

Fig. 3.6

$X = a \sin pt$. From Fig. 3.6, the extension y of the spring when the mass is a distance x from its initial position is given by

$$X + l + \frac{mgl}{\lambda} = x + l + y$$

i.e.

$$y = X + \frac{mgl}{\lambda} - x$$

Thus the equation of motion is

$$T - mg = m\frac{d^2x}{dt^2}$$

i.e.

$$\frac{\lambda}{l}\left(X+\frac{mgl}{\lambda}-x\right)-mg=m\frac{d^2x}{dt^2}$$

$$\frac{d^2x}{dt^2}+\frac{\lambda}{ml}x=\frac{\lambda}{ml}X$$

$$=\frac{\lambda a}{ml}\sin pt \qquad (3.7)$$

since $X = a \sin pt$.

Write $\lambda/ml = n^2$. Then the complementary function is

$$x = A \sin nt + B \cos nt, \text{ as before}$$

If $n^2 \neq p^2$, for the particular integral, try $x = \alpha \sin pt + \beta \cos pt$. This satisfies equation 3.7 if

$$-p^2\alpha \sin pt - p^2\beta \cos pt + n^2(\alpha \sin pt + \beta \cos pt) = n^2 a \sin pt$$

i.e. $\beta = 0$ and $(n^2 - p^2)\alpha = n^2 a$, i.e. $\alpha = \dfrac{n^2 a}{n^2 - p^2}$

Thus the complete solution is

$$x = A \sin nt + B \cos nt + \frac{n^2 a}{n^2 - p^2}\sin pt$$

Again, if initially $x = 0$ and $dx/dt = 0$,

$$B = 0 \quad \text{and} \quad nA + \frac{pn^2 a}{n^2 - p^2} = 0$$

i.e.

$$A = \frac{-pna}{n^2 - p^2}$$

so the solution required is

$$x = \frac{na}{n^2 - p^2}(n \sin pt - p \sin nt)$$

which is oscillatory motion whose amplitude never exceeds a certain value.

Harder form of the particular integral

If however, $p^2 = n^2$, $\sin nt$ is contained in the complementary function, and we must try

$$x = t(\alpha \sin nt + \beta \cos nt)$$

i.e.
$$\frac{d^2x}{dt^2} = (-2n\beta - n^2\alpha t) \sin nt + (2n\alpha - n^2\beta t) \cos nt$$

This will be a particular integral if values α, β can be found so that

$$2n(\alpha \cos nt - \beta \sin nt) = an^2 \sin nt \quad \text{for all } t$$

substituting in equation 3.7,

i.e.
$$\alpha = 0 \quad \text{and} \quad \beta = -\frac{an}{2}$$

Thus the complete solution which satisfies the initial conditions $x = 0$, $dx/dt = 0$ is

$$x = \tfrac{1}{2}a \sin nt - \tfrac{1}{2}ant \cos nt$$

oscillations with steadily increasing amplitude.

This form of solution is of great importance in practice. If the period of the disturbing force is the same as the period of the natural oscillations of the system, the amplitude will increase. Invariably there are physical limits which the system cannot exceed without breaking, so this leads to a disaster. The classic example is of soldiers marching over a bridge who are required to break step so that they do not damage the bridge.

EXERCISE 3(e)

1. A particle of unit mass moves along a straight line which passes through a point A. It is acted on by a force towards A, whose magnitude is proportional to the distance from A. Prove that the motion is oscillatory, and find the period of a complete oscillation when the constant of proportion is p^2.
   An additional force of magnitude K is imposed on the particle. The particle is released from rest at A. Obtain the distance of the particle from A at time t after the instant of release. Find also the maximum speed of the particle in the ensuing motion. (O. & C.)

2. A particle of unit mass moves on the x axis in such a way that its coordinate x at time t satisfies the differential equation

$$\frac{d^2x}{dt^2} + 2k\frac{dx}{dt} + p^2x = A\cos qt, \quad p^2 < k^2$$

Write down the magnitudes and directions of a system of forces which will produce this motion.
Find values of the constants B and α (in terms of p, q, and A) which make $x = B\cos(qt - \alpha)$ a particular solution of the equation.
Determine the general solution of the differential equation and hence find the particular solution for which

$$x = \frac{B}{k}(q\sin\alpha + k\cos\alpha), \quad \frac{dx}{dt} = 0$$

when $t = 0$, giving your answer in terms of B, α, q, k, p, t. (O. & C.)

3. A light elastic spring of natural length l and modulus of elasticity λ hangs in a vertical plane with one end fixed. From the other end is suspended a particle P of mass m. The particle is displaced from its position of equilibrium O and then released. There is a frictional resistance to motion proportional to the velocity at any instant, the factor of proportion being mk. If OP $= x$ at time t, prove that

$$\frac{d^2x}{dt^2} + k\frac{dx}{dt} + n^2x = 0$$

where $n^2 = \lambda/ml$.
Obtain the general solution of this equation when $k^2 < 4n^2$. If $n = 8$ and $k = \frac{1}{4}$ and an additional force $m(\cos 4t + 48\sin 4t)$ is applied vertically downwards to the particle, prove that after a sufficient lapse of time the displacement is approximately $x = \sin 4t$. (O. & C.)

4. A particle of unit mass is moving along a straight line and is attracted to a fixed point O in the line by a force equal to $2x$N, where x metres is the distance of the particle from O at time t seconds. In addition, the particle's motion is resisted by a force $2v$N, where v m s^{-1} is the velocity. Write down a differential equation to determine the motion of the particle and hence show that $x = Ce^{-t}\cos(t + \alpha)$ where C and α are constants.
If initially $x = 3$ and $v = 0$, find the values of C and α and the value of v when $t = \pi/2$. (A.E.B.)

5. An ammeter has a coil and a needle which rotate on a pivot. The moving system has moment of inertia M, and when the deflection is θ,

a spring supplies a restoring couple $-\lambda\theta$. When a current I flows the coil experiences a deflecting couple kI. There is also a resisting couple $-\mu(\mathrm{d}\theta/\mathrm{d}t)$ due to friction and eddy currents whenever the coil is moving. Here M, k, λ, and μ are all constants. Show that the current and deflection are related by

$$M\frac{\mathrm{d}^2\theta}{\mathrm{d}t^2} + \mu\frac{\mathrm{d}\theta}{\mathrm{d}t} + \lambda\theta = kI$$

Find the complementary function for this equation, distinguishing between the cases when μ^2 is greater than, less than, or equal to, $4M\lambda$. Explain how to solve the problem in which θ, $\mathrm{d}\theta/\mathrm{d}t$, and I are initially zero, and a steady current I is switched on at a time $t = 0$.
Why is the choice $\mu^2 = 4M\lambda$ the most convenient in practice? (C.S.)

4. Motion in a Straight Line Under a Variable Force

Most of the problems considered in *Additional Applied Mathematics* concerned bodies moving under the action of constant forces. Since their mass was constant, their acceleration was also constant and so the motion could be discussed using equations such as $v = u + at$, $s = ut + \frac{1}{2}at^2$.

Newton's second law

The second law of motion is 'the applied force on a body is equal to the rate of change of momentum',

i.e. $$\mathbf{F} = \frac{\mathrm{d}}{\mathrm{d}t}(m\mathbf{v})$$

When the mass is constant, this becomes

$$\mathbf{F} = m\frac{\mathrm{d}\mathbf{v}}{\mathrm{d}t}$$

To find the motion of a body when **F** is not constant it is necessary to use the methods of the previous chapter for solving differential equations. Considering first problems in which the direction of the force is constant and the initial motion, if any, is in the direction of that force; we can use the components of **F** and **v** in that direction, thus having the equation

$$\mathrm{F} = m\frac{\mathrm{d}v}{\mathrm{d}t}$$

Force as a function of time

When the driver applies the brakes of a car, he will not in general exert a constant force. Suppose the magnitude of the braking force

F newtons, at time t seconds after he begins to apply it, is given by $F = 1000t$. If the initial mass of the car is 500 kg, Newton's law gives

$$-1000t = 500\frac{dv}{dt}$$

$$\Rightarrow -\int 2t\,dt = \int dv$$

i.e.
$$-t^2 = v + C$$

If the initial velocity of the car is 25 m s^{-1}, $v = 25$ when $t = 0$, so that $C = -25$,

i.e.
$$v = 25 - t^2 \tag{4.1}$$

Thus the car comes to rest in 5 s.

The distance s metres travelled by the car in coming to rest is obtained from equation 4.1, writing v as ds/dt,

$$\frac{ds}{dt} = 25 - t^2$$

giving
$$s = 25t - \tfrac{1}{3}t^3 \tag{4.2}$$

the constant of integration being 0 since $s = 0$ when $t = 0$. When $t = 5$, $s = 83\frac{1}{3}$, so the car comes to rest in $83\frac{1}{3}$ metres.

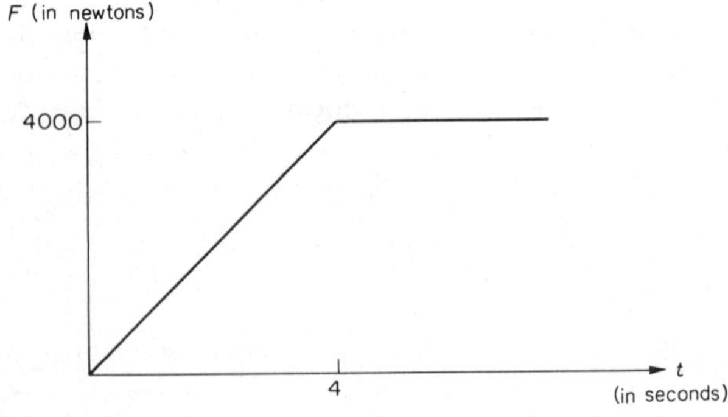

Fig. 4.1

Suppose instead the braking force reaches a maximum after 4 s, being given by

$$F = 1000t, \quad t \leqslant 4$$
$$F = 4000, \quad t > 4$$

illustrated by Fig. 4.1. The motion must now be considered in two parts.

First, when $t \leqslant 4$, we can use equations 4.1 and 4.2 to see that after 4 s the velocity is 9 m s^{-1} and the distance travelled is $78\frac{2}{3}$ metres. When $t \geqslant 4$, the resisting force is constant, 4000 N, so that the acceleration is -8 m s^{-2}, and the car comes to rest after a further $\frac{9}{8}$ s. The distance travelled in this time is $\frac{1}{2}(9 + 0) \times 9/8$, i.e. 81/16 m, so that the total time before the car comes to rest is $5\frac{1}{8}$ s, and the total distance travelled is $78\frac{2}{3} + 5\frac{1}{16}$, about 84 m. Each is slightly greater than the corresponding figures in the first example.

EXERCISE 4(a)

1. A force $(5 - t)$ N acts on a body mass 4 kg initially at rest. Find the velocity of the body 4 s after the force begins to act and the distance travelled in that time.

2. A force $1/(1 + t)$ N acts on a body mass 2 kg. If the body was initially at rest, find its velocity after 5 s, correct to two significant figures.

3. A force $1/(1 + t^2)$ N acts on a body mass 5 kg. If the body was initially at rest, find its velocity after 1 s, correct to two significant figures.

4. A book mass 5 kg is at rest on a horizontal table, the coefficient of friction between the book and the table being 0.2. A force $(5.8 + t)$ N is applied. After how long does the book begin to move? What is its velocity after it has been moving for 2 s? How far has it then travelled?

5. A car of mass 500 kg travelling at 25 m s^{-1} is brought to rest by its brakes, the braking force at time t seconds being λt newtons. Find the value of λ if the car stops in $2\frac{1}{2}$ s.

6. The force acting on a body mass m, initial velocity u, is $\lambda\, e^{-kt}$. Show that its velocity v is given by

$$v = u + \frac{\lambda}{mk}(1 - e^{-kt})$$

and find its displacement s at time t.

7. A book mass 5 kg is at rest on a rough horizontal table, the limiting frictional force exerted by the table on the book being 8 N. A force F newtons is applied to the book, where F at time t seconds is given by

$$F = t, \qquad 0 \leqslant t < 10$$
$$F = 10, \qquad 10 \leqslant t < 20$$
$$F = 30 - t, \qquad 20 \leqslant t < 30$$
$$F = 0, \qquad 30 \leqslant t$$

Find (a) when the book begins to move,
(b) when the book comes to rest,
(c) whether the book stays at rest.

8. The force acting on a body mass 5 kg decreases uniformly from 10 N to 5 N in 10 s. Find the distance travelled by the body in the 10 s, if the body starts from rest.

9. A car mass M starts from rest, the engine exerting a force which decreases uniformly from $2F$ to F in T seconds. Find the velocity of the car after t seconds, $t < T$.

10. The tractive force F newtons exerted by an underground train mass 4×10^5 kg during a certain test is given by the table below:

t (in seconds)	0	20	40	60	80	100	120	140
F (in 10^4 N)	1.0	1.5	2.5	4.0	4.0	4.0	2.1	0

If there is a constant resistance of 6×10^3 N, estimate the maximum speed attained by the train.

Force as a function of the velocity

Many of the forces opposing the motion of a body depend on the velocity at which the body is travelling. The air resistance to a car increases as the speed of the car increases, and the air resistance to a falling body increases likewise with the velocity of the body, its velocity never exceeding a certain limiting value. If a motor exerts constant power, as the velocity increases the tractive force decreases, since the rate of working (i.e. power) is the product of the tractive force and the velocity of the body containing the motor.

Consider a stone mass 0.05 kg, projected vertically upwards with velocity 10 m s^{-1}, the air resistance being $0.01v$ N, where v m s^{-1}

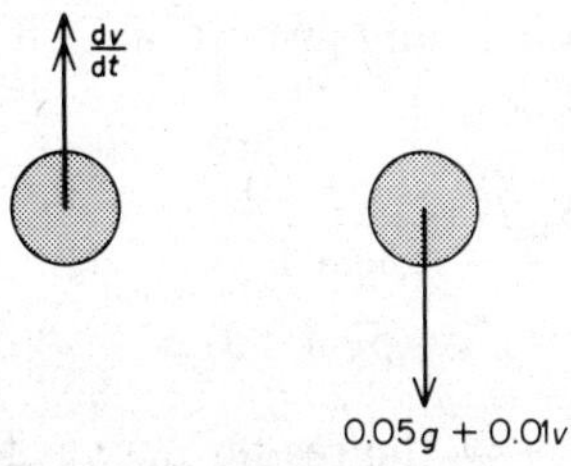

Fig. 4.2

is the velocity of the stone. There are two forces resisting the motion of the stone, its weight $0.05g$ N and the air resistance (Fig. 4.2). The equation of motion is

$$-(0.05g + 0.01v) = 0.05\,\frac{dv}{dt}$$

i.e.
$$5\,\frac{dv}{dt} = -(5g + v)$$

Separating the variables,

$$\int \frac{-5\,dv}{(5g + v)} = \int dt$$

$$t = -5\log_e(5g + v) + C$$

Since $v = 10$ when $t = 0$, $C = 5\log_e(5g + 10)$,

$\therefore$
$$t = 5\log_e\left(\frac{5g + 10}{5g + v}\right) \tag{4.3}$$

Note the numerator of the fraction is the initial value of the denominator, so that the value of the logarithm is zero when $t = 0$. With practice it is possible to proceed directly to the solution given without finding explicitly the arbitrary constant. Note also that the logarithms are natural logarithms, to the base e.

The time that elapses before the stone comes momentarily to rest is

$$5\log_e\left(\frac{5g + 10}{5g}\right)$$

i.e.
$$5\log_e\left(\frac{59}{49}\right),\ \text{about } 0.9\text{ s}$$

To find the velocity v at any given time t, it is necessary to re-arrange equation 4.3 as

$$e^{t/5} = \frac{5g + 10}{5g + v}$$

$$\Rightarrow v = (5g + 10)\, e^{-t/5} - 5g$$

Since $e^{-t/5} \to 0$ as $t \to \infty$, the reader may at first think that $v \to -5g$. But this equation only holds when the stone is travelling upwards, so that t cannot become infinite.

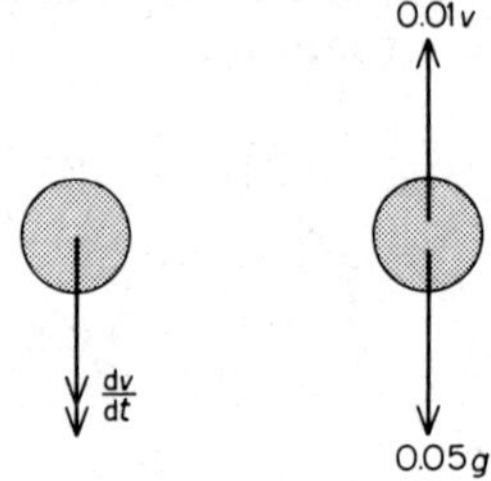

Fig. 4.3

If the stone was released from rest, in the downward motion (Fig. 4.3),

$$0.05g - 0.01v = 0.05\frac{dv}{dt}$$

$$5\frac{dv}{dt} = 5g - v$$

i.e. $$\int \frac{5\, dv}{5g - v} = \int dt$$

i.e. $$t/5 = \log_e\left(\frac{5g}{5g - v}\right), \quad \text{since } v = 0 \text{ when } t = 0$$

Thus $e^{t/5}(5g - v) = 5g$

$$v = 5g(1 - e^{-t/5})$$

As $t \to \infty$, $v \to 5g$, so the terminal (or limiting) velocity is about 49 m s^{-1}.

Example 4.1. *The engine of a bus produces constant power of 60 kW. If the mass of the bus is 5000 kg and the resistance is constant at 5000 N, find the time taken to accelerate from 5 m s^{-1} to 10 m s^{-1}*

The tractive force produced by the engine when the velocity of the bus is v m s^{-1} is

$$\frac{60\,000}{v} \text{ N}$$

so the equation of motion is

$$\frac{60\,000}{v} - 5000 = 5000\frac{dv}{dt}$$

i.e.

$$\frac{dv}{dt} = \frac{12}{v} - 1$$

Thus

$$\int \frac{v\,dv}{12 - v} = \int dt$$

$$\Rightarrow \int \left(\frac{12}{12 - v} - 1\right) dv = t$$

The time T seconds required is given by

$$\begin{aligned} T &= [-12 \log_e (12 - v) - v]_5^{10} \\ &= 12 \log_e 3.5 - 5 \\ &\simeq 10 \text{ s} \end{aligned}$$

The time taken to accelerate from 5 m s^{-1} to 10 m s^{-1} is about 10 s.

Distance as a function of velocity

In the above example, if we wish to find the distance travelled by the bus in accelerating from 5 m s^{-1} to 10 m s^{-1}, we use $v\,dv/ds$ for the acceleration instead of dv/dt. Thus the equation of motion is

$$\frac{60\,000}{v} - 5000 = 5000v\frac{dv}{ds}$$

i.e.

$$\begin{aligned} s &= \int \frac{v^2\,dv}{12 - v} \\ &= \int \left(-v - 12 + \frac{144}{12 - v}\right) dv \end{aligned}$$

The distance S m required is given by

$$S = [-\tfrac{1}{2}v^2 - 12v - 144 \log_e (12 - v)]_5^{10}$$
$$\simeq 83 \text{ m}$$

the distance required to accelerate from 5 m s^{-1} to 10 m s^{-1} is about 83 m.

With the data in this problem, notice that the maximum speed is 12 m s^{-1}, when the tractive force is equal to the resistances, but this is not attained in a finite period of time. The data moreover are only true for some range of values of v, for when $v = 0$ the power produced must also be 0, or the tractive force will be infinite.

EXERCISE 4(b)

1. A body mass 2 kg is projected on a smooth horizontal plane in a medium which exerts a resistance proportional to the velocity of the body. Initially the velocity of the body is 8 m s^{-1} and the resistance is 20 N. Find the time taken before the velocity is reduced to 4 m s^{-1} and the distance travelled in that time.

2. A body mass 50 kg is travelling horizontally in a medium which exerts a resistance of $40\,v$ N, where v m s^{-1} is the velocity of the body. There is also a constant propulsive force of 200 N acting on the body. Find the time taken to reach a velocity of 2 m s^{-1} from rest, and also the time taken to accelerate from 2 m s^{-1} to 4 m s^{-1}.

3. The accelerating force produced by a certain cyclist mass 80 kg is $(64 - v^2)$ N, where v m s^{-1} is the velocity of the cyclist. Find the time taken to reach a velocity of 4 m s^{-1} from rest, and the distance covered by the cyclist in this time.

4. A ball bearing mass 0.01 kg is projected with velocity 2 m s^{-1} horizontally along the floor of a tank containing oil. The friction between the ball bearing and the floor of the tank may be neglected, but the oil exerts a retarding force of $0.1\,v$ N, where v m s^{-1} is the velocity of the ball bearing. Find the time that elapses before the velocity of the ball bearing has fallen to 1 m s^{-1} and the distance travelled in that time. How far from the point of projection will the ball bearing come to rest?

5. A car mass 800 kg is travelling along a road against a constant resistance of 1600 N. The force exerted by the engine is $(40\,000/v)$ N for values

of v from 10 m s^{-1} to 20 m s^{-1}, where v m s^{-1} is the velocity of the car. Find the time taken to accelerate from 10 m s^{-1} to 20 m s^{-1}.

6. The car in Question 5 is travelling in conditions in which the resistance is not constant but is given by 100 v N. Find the time required to accelerate from 10 m s^{-1} to 15 m s^{-1} and the distance travelled in doing so.

7. The force resisting the motion of a lorry, mass 2400 kg is $(324 + v^2)$ N, where v m s^{-1} is the speed of the lorry. The lorry starts from rest with the engine producing a constant force of 900 N until the lorry has a speed of 18 m s^{-1}. How long does the lorry take to accelerate from rest to 9 m s^{-1}? How long does it take to accelerate from rest to 18 m s^{-1}?

8. When the lorry in Question 7 is travelling at 18 m s^{-1}, the power is cut off and the lorry is brought to rest by the resistances. How long elapses before the lorry is brought to rest?

9. The resistance to the motion of a train mass M is $k(u^2 + v^2)$, where v is the velocity of the train and u and k are constants. If the initial velocity is $2u$, prove that the velocity is reduced to u in time

$$\frac{M}{uk} \tan^{-1} (\tfrac{1}{3})$$

How far has the train travelled in this time?

10. A particle leaves a point A at time $t = 0$ with speed u and moves towards a point B with retardation λv, where v is the speed of the particle at time t. The particle is at a distance s from A at time t. Show (a) that $v = u - \lambda s$, (b) that $\log_e (u - \lambda s) = \log_e u - \lambda t$.
At time $t = 0$ a second particle starts from rest at B and moves towards A with acceleration $(2 + 6t)$. The particles collide at the midpoint of AB when $t = 1$. Find the distance AB and the speeds of the particles on impact. (A.E.B.)

11. A steel sphere mass 2.5 kg is placed gently on top of a tank of oil and then released. The oil exerts a retarding force 100 v N, where v m s^{-1} is the velocity of the sphere. How long does the sphere take to acquire a velocity of 0.2 m s^{-1}? How far has it travelled in this time? What is the greatest velocity attained by the sphere?

12. A body is projected vertically upwards with velocity U, the air resistance at speed v being kv^2 per unit mass. Show that the body is instantaneously at rest after time

$$\sqrt{\frac{1}{kg}} \tan^{-1} \left(U\sqrt{\frac{k}{g}} \right)$$

at a height

$$\frac{1}{2k}\log_e(1 + kU^2/g)$$

above the point of projection. Verify that if k is small these are approximately equal to U/g and $U^2/2g$ respectively.

13. If the body in Question 12 is allowed to fall from rest, show that its velocity never exceeds a certain value c. Find the distance the body falls before the velocity is $\frac{1}{2}c$, and the time taken in doing so. Find also the velocity of the body when it has fallen a distance d.

14. A body mass m is projected along a smooth horizontal plane with velocity u. Work is done on the body in the direction of motion at a constant rate of $9mku^2$, where k is a constant. There is a resistance to motion of mkv, where v is the velocity of the body. Find the time taken and the distance travelled by the body in increasing the velocity to $2u$.

15. A particle moves in a straight line against a resistance which varies as the cube of the speed. Prove that the average speed between any two points A and B of the line is equal to the speed at the midpoint of AB. (O. & C.)

16. A body of mass m is entirely immersed beneath the surface of the liquid in a tank. The body has a density twice that of the liquid. The body is released from rest and falls to the bottom of the tank. If the retarding force due to the motion of the body through the liquid at velocity v is kv^2, where k is a constant, show that the relationship between v and the distance h through which the body has fallen is

$$v^2 = \frac{mg}{2k}[1 - \exp(-2kh/m)]$$ (C.S.)

17. The motion of a ship during launching may be considered in three parts:

(a) from rest at O with constant acceleration a to a point P, reaching speed U at P;

(b) from P to Q with acceleration decreasing uniformly with time from a to $(-a)$ at time T;

(c) from Q to the point R at which it comes to rest, with acceleration at each instant given by

$$-\tfrac{1}{2}a\left(1 + \frac{v^2}{U^2}\right)$$

where v is the instantaneous value of the speed. Prove that the speed at Q is U. Find expressions for the distances OP, PQ in terms of a, T, U. Use the expression $v(dv/ds)$ for the instantaneous acceleration of a moving point to prove that

$$QR = \frac{U^2}{a} \log_e 2$$ (M.E.I.)

18. A vehicle of mass m moves in a straight line subject to a resistance $(P + Qv^2)$, where v is the speed and P, Q are constants. Form an equation of motion, using the expression $v(dv/dx)$ for the acceleration. Hence show

(a) that if $P = 0$ the distance required to slow down from speed $\frac{3}{2}U$ to speed U is $(m/Q) \log_e \frac{3}{2}$;

(b) that if $P > 0$ the distance D required to stop from speed U is given by

$$D = \lambda \log_e (1 + \mu U^2)$$

where λ, μ are constants. Express these constants in terms of the data.

Use the above results to estimate the landing run of an aircraft of mass 10^5 kg assuming that the speed falls from 90 m s^{-1} to 60 m s^{-1} under air resistance only, given by $125v^2$ N, and that subsequently the air resistance is supplemented by a constant braking force of 7.5×10^5 N. (M.E.I.)

19. The tractive force F newtons produced by the engine of a car mass 500 kg at time t seconds is given by:

t	0	2	4	6	8	10	12
F	0	150	404	597	895	1257	1401

Estimate the speed of the car 12 s after it starts from rest.

20. A vehicle mass 1500 kg accelerates from rest to 90 km h^{-1} under the action of a constant tractive force 500 N and against a varying resistance. The resistance at different speeds is given by:

Speed (km h^{-1})	0	22.5	45	67.5	90
Resistance (N)	102	105	119	124	131

Estimate the distance the vehicle travels before reaching the speed of 90 km h^{-1}.

Force as a function of displacement

In order to understand the motion of the heavenly bodies, Sir Isaac Newton in about 1665 studied first the motion of the Moon. Since it did not move in a straight line with constant velocity, he concluded that there must be a force acting on it. Moreover, since observations suggested that it moved in a circle with the Earth at the centre, there must be a force towards the Earth. This force is the gravitational force, and is of the same nature as the force exerted by the Sun and planets on each other, and the force which keeps a body on the surface of the Earth. Newton showed that the force F between two bodies, mass m_1 and m_2, a distance r apart, is determined by

$$F \propto \frac{m_1 m_2}{r^2}$$

This is one of the most important examples of a force which is a function of displacement. Examples of others are the restoring force on a body at the end of an elastic string and the upthrust on a body partially immersed in liquid.

To solve problems where the force is of this type, we use $v(\mathrm{d}v/\mathrm{d}s)$ for the acceleration and find v as a function of s. It is then sometimes possible to find s as a function of t, using $v = \mathrm{d}s/\mathrm{d}t$. Often, though, the resulting differential equations at this stage are not soluble by exact methods and are outside the scope of this book.

Example 4.2. *A stone is dropped down a straight tunnel going to the centre of the Earth. Given that the gravitational force acting on a body inside the Earth is proportional to the distance of the body from the centre of the Earth, and is directed towards the centre of the Earth, find the velocity of the stone when it reaches the centre of the Earth. (Assume the Earth is spherical, radius $R = 6.4 \times 10^6$ m.)*

From the data, $F = -\lambda x$, where x is the distance of the body from the centre of the Earth. But on the surface of the Earth, $F = mg$ when $x = R$,

$$\therefore \qquad \lambda = \frac{mg}{R}$$

The equation of motion is

$$-\frac{mg}{R}x = mv\frac{\mathrm{d}v}{\mathrm{d}x}$$

i.e.
$$v\frac{dv}{dx}+\frac{g}{R}x=0$$

Integrating,

$$\frac{1}{2}v^2+\frac{1}{2}\frac{g}{R}x^2=\frac{1}{2}gR$$

since $v = 0$ when $x = R$.

At the centre, $x = 0$, $\therefore$, $v = \sqrt{(gR)}$

$$= \sqrt{(9.8 \times 6.4 \times 10^6)}$$
$$\simeq 7.9 \times 10^3 \text{ m s}^{-1}$$

Example 4.3. *A body mass 5 kg is moving in a straight line under the action of a force (4/s) newtons towards a fixed point O in that straight line, where s metres is the distance of the body from O. If the body is initially at rest 1 m from O, find its velocity when it has travelled 0.5 m.*

The equation of motion is

$$5v\frac{dv}{ds}=-\frac{4}{s}$$

$$\Rightarrow \int v\,dv = -\int \frac{4}{5s}\,ds$$

$$\Rightarrow \tfrac{1}{2}v^2 = -\tfrac{4}{5}\log_e s, \text{ since } s = 1 \text{ when } v = 0$$

$\therefore$ when $s = \frac{1}{2}$,
$$v^2 = \tfrac{8}{5}\log_e 2$$
$$\simeq 1.1 \text{ m s}^{-1}$$

If we try to find the time that has elapsed, we obtain

$$v = \sqrt{(-\tfrac{8}{5}\log_e s)}$$

i.e.
$$t = \sqrt{\tfrac{5}{8}}\int\frac{ds}{\sqrt{(-\log_e s)}}$$

which cannot be integrated exactly, though the integrand is real as $\log_e s$ is negative.

EXERCISE 4(c)

1. A body mass 1 kg is acted on by a force $3s^{1/2}$ N towards a point O, where s metres is the distance of the body from O. The body is initially at rest a distance of 1 m from O. Find the velocity with which it reaches O.

2. A body mass 4 kg is initially at rest 1 m from a point O. It is acted on by a force $1/s^3$ N away from O, where s metres is the distance of the body from O. Find the velocity of the body when it has travelled 0.25 m, and the time taken in doing so.

3. A body mass 4 kg is acted on by a force $9s$ N away from a point O, where s metres is the distance of the body from O. The body is initially at rest at O, then is given a small displacement. Find its velocity when it is 1 m from O and the time taken to travel a further metre.

4. A force $6s^{1/2}\mathbf{i}$ N is applied to a body, mass 2 kg, initially at rest at a point whose position vector is $\mathbf{i}$ m. Find the velocity of the body when it has position vector $4\mathbf{i}$ m.

5. A force $9\,s^{-1/2}\,\mathbf{i}$ N is applied to a body mass 1 kg, initially at rest at a point whose position vector is $\mathbf{i}$ m. Find the velocity of the body when it has position vector $25\,\mathbf{i}$ m.

6. A force $s\,\mathbf{i}$ N is applied to a body mass 1 kg. The body initially is at the origin and has velocity vector $4\,\mathbf{i}$ m s^{-1}. Find the velocity of the body when it has position vector $5\,\mathbf{i}$ m, and the time it has taken to reach this position.

7. A car mass 1500 kg accelerates along a straight road from rest under a net force F N given, at distance s metres from its starting point, by the table below:

s	0	100	200	300	400	500	600
F	250	340	490	650	720	740	750

Estimate the velocity of the car when it has travelled 600 m.

8. A light car mass 500 kg accelerates from rest along a straight road. The resistances may be taken as constant and equal to 400 N. The tractive force T N exerted by the engine is given by the table below:

s (metres)	0	50	100	150	200	250	300
T (newtons)	400	510	630	570	420	420	360

Estimate the velocity of the car when it has travelled 200 m and also the maximum velocity of the car.

9. A remarkable homing device is constructed which accelerates towards its target with an acceleration which is proportional to its distance from the target, the constant of proportion being k. A target is released from a point P and maintains a constant speed u in a straight line away

from P. If the homing device is later released from rest at P, show that it will strike the target in a time less than $\pi/\sqrt{k}$ but greater than $\pi/2\sqrt{k}$. (O.S.)

10. A particle of unit mass is initially at rest at a distance a from each of two equally massive fixed particles, which are separated by a distance $2b$. If the gravitational attraction of each fixed particle on the particle P is k/r^2, where r is the distance between them, what is the maximum speed of the particle? (O.S.)

11. Taking the Earth to be a sphere of radius 6.4×10^6 m, calculate the initial velocity which must be given to a body projected vertically upwards if it is to escape from the Earth's gravitational field.

12. A particle of unit mass is attracted towards a fixed point O by a force μ/r^n, where r is the distance from O, μ a constant, and $n > 1$. Show that the least velocity of projection required (the escape velocity) from a point A so that it may eventually reach an infinite distance is

$$[2\mu/(n-1)a^{n-1}]^{1/2},$$

where a is the distance OA.
A particle is projected from A with escape velocity. Prove that it has escape velocity at every point in its path. (O.S.)

5. Elasticity

Elasticity

The spring balances used in laboratories, and some domestic scales, provide some of the more common applications of a property of many types of materials, that their extension is proportional to the tension in them. We consider at this stage only deformations in a straight line along the axis of the string (or spring), but it is apparent from experience that the stretching of a piece of elastic necessarily involves reducing the area of cross-section, so that a force along the axis produces deformations other than just extension [Fig. 5.1(a)]. Moreover, a force not wholly along the axis nevertheless may have a component along the axis and so may stretch or compress it [Fig. 5.1(b)].

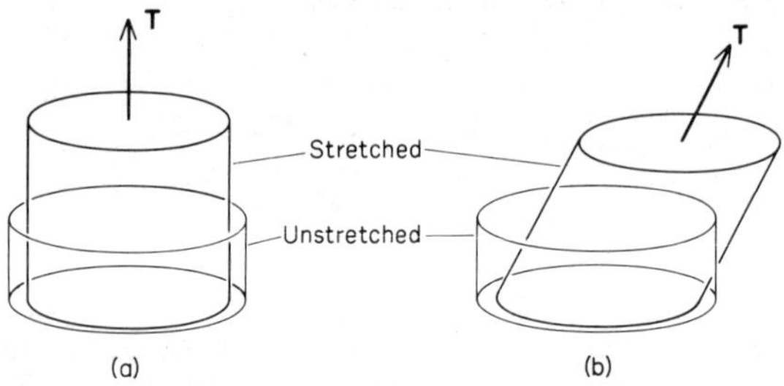

Fig. 5.1

The reader familiar with matrix theory will see that matrices are invaluable for more detailed analysis, for if the force **T** has components T_x, T_y, T_z, the component T_x will produce a translation $(a_{11}x, a_{12}y, a_{13}z)$ of the point (x, y, z). Similarly with T_y, so that the relation needed is

$$\begin{pmatrix} T_x \\ T_y \\ T_z \end{pmatrix} = \begin{pmatrix} a_{11} & a_{12} & a_{13} \\ a_{21} & a_{22} & a_{23} \\ a_{31} & a_{32} & a_{33} \end{pmatrix} \begin{pmatrix} x \\ y \\ z \end{pmatrix}$$

But for our purposes, as stated above, we consider only changes produced in the length of the string, so the law becomes

the tension is proportional to the extension, i.e. $T \propto x$

This is the simplest form of Hooke's law, stated by Robert Hooke, a contemporary of Isaac Newton. It is an experimental law, usually verified by showing that it is possible to draw a straight line graph through points corresponding to readings of T for certain values of x (Fig. 5.2). This law only holds for certain types of materials and over a limited range of values of x. It does not hold for very

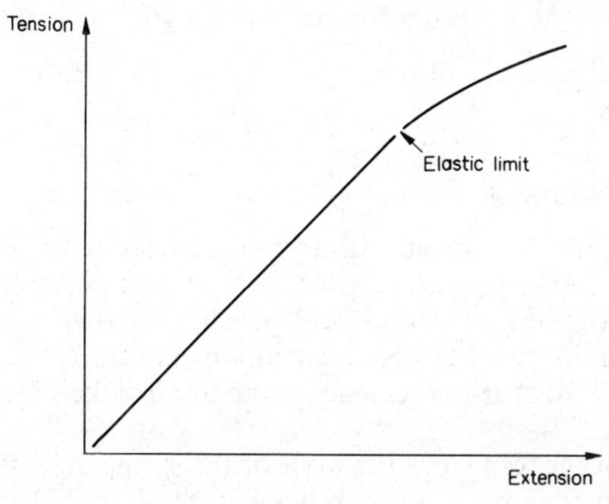

Fig. 5.2

small values of the extension, nor for values above a critical value, called the elastic limit. Materials which regain their original form when the force is removed are called *elastic*; materials which do not regain their original form are called *plastic*. Of course, no body is perfectly elastic when subject to large deformations, and even putty recovers to some extent from very small changes in shape.

By experiment we can also see that if a force F stretches a spring natural length l by k units, the same force F will stretch a spring of the same material but length $2l$ by $2k$ units, i.e. for springs of the same type but of different lengths the law can be expressed as

$$\text{the tension is proportional to } \frac{\text{extension}}{\text{natural length}}$$

This is usually written $T = \lambda(x/l)$, and this is the form of Hooke's law that we shall use.

Modulus of elasticity

The constant λ in the equation above is usually called the *modulus of elasticity*.* Books on the properties of matter define many similar moduli, but these are more usually treated in physics than in applied mathematics. Since λ is the ratio

$$\frac{\text{force}}{\text{extension per unit length}}$$

it has the dimensions of force (M L T^{-2}) and is measured in newtons.

Springs and strings

In mathematics we consider almost exclusively only two types of extensible bodies: springs, for which Hooke's law holds whether they are extended or compressed, the sign of T being determined by the sign of the extension x; strings, by contrast, become slack when $x < 0$, so that the tension is zero and Hooke's law no longer holds.

At this stage we ignore the mass of the springs and strings. In practice, this can be a considerable feature of a problem.

Example 5.1. *Find the extension in a string, modulus of elasticity 5 N, natural length 2.5 m, when a force of 2 N is applied.*

From Hooke's law, if the extension is x metres,

$$2 = \frac{5}{2.5}x$$

i.e.

$$x = 1$$

the extension is 1 metre.

* Physicists and engineers use *elastic modulus* to describe the force per unit area of cross section per unit strain. Thus they measure elastic modulus in newtons per square millimetre, and might say that a steel wire had an elastic modulus of 2×10^5 N mm^{-2}. The dimensions of elastic modulus are M L^{-1} T^{-2}.

Example 5.2. *Find the force needed to stretch by 0.3 m a spring modulus 10 N, natural length 0.2 metres.*

From Hooke's law, if the force is T newtons,

$$T = \frac{10 \times 0.3}{0.2}$$

$$= 15$$

the force is 15 N.

Example 5.3. *In a certain spring balance the distance between readings differing by 1 kg is 0.01 m. If the unstretched length of the spring is 0.1 m, find the modulus of elasticity of the spring.*

The force in the spring is the weight of the body that moves the marker. In this balance, to produce an extra extension of 0.01 m, an extra force of 9.8 N is required. Thus Hooke's law gives

$$9.8 = \frac{\lambda(0.01)}{0.1}$$

$$\lambda = 98$$

the modulus of elasticity is 98 N.

Example 5.4. *Two light springs, each of unstretched length 0.5 m and modulus of elasticity 9.8 N, have one end attached at points A, B at the same horizontal level, 1.6 metres apart. The other end of each string is attached to a heavy body, and the system hangs in equilibrium in a vertical plane with each string stretched to 1 m. Find the mass of the heavy body.*

Considering the vertical forces on the body, supposed of mass m kg (Fig. 5.3),

$$2T \cos \theta - mg = 0$$

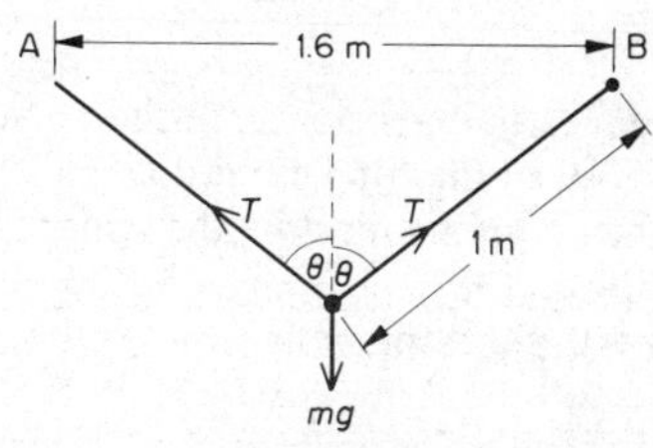

Fig. 5.3

since the body is in equilibrium. But from the geometry of the figure,

$$\sin\theta = 0.8, \quad \text{i.e. } \cos\theta = 0.6$$

and from Hooke's law,

$$T = \frac{9.8(0.5)}{0.5}$$

Whence $$2 \times 9.8 \times 0.6 = mg$$

i.e. $$m = 1.2$$

the mass of the heavy body is 1.2 kg.

Example 5.5. *Two elastic strings each have natural length l. When hanging vertically, a mass m produces an extension of x_1 in one string and x_2 in the other. Find the extension*

(a) when they are joined end to end,
(b) when they are placed side by side, and used to support the mass m.

(a) The tension T is the same throughout the springs, since we ignore the weight of the springs, so $T = mg$.

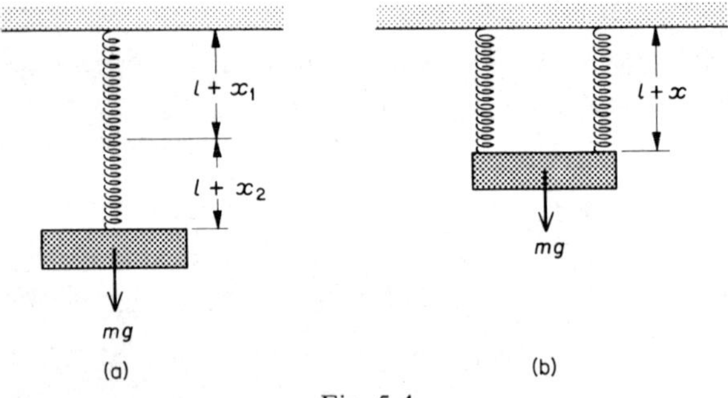

Fig. 5.4

But a force mg produces an extension x_1 in the upper spring and x_2 in the lower spring (Fig. 5.4), so the total extension is $x_1 + x_2$.

(b) The extension x in each spring must be the same. Let T_1 and T_2 denote the tensions in the springs.

Then $T_1 + T_2 - mg = 0$, since the body is in equilibrium.

But $$T_1 = \frac{\lambda_1}{l}x \quad \text{and} \quad T_2 = \frac{\lambda_2}{l}x$$

where $\quad mg = \frac{\lambda_1}{l} x_1$ and $mg = \frac{\lambda_2}{l} x_2$ from the data

$\therefore \quad T_1 = \frac{mgx}{x_1}$ and $T_2 = \frac{mgx}{x_2}$

$$\therefore \quad mg\frac{x}{x_1} + mg\frac{x}{x_2} - mg = 0$$

i.e.

$$\frac{1}{x} = \frac{1}{x_1} + \frac{1}{x_2}$$

$$x = \frac{x_1 x_2}{x_1 + x_2}$$

In the results (a) $x = x_1 + x_2$

and (b) $\frac{1}{x} = \frac{1}{x_1} + \frac{1}{x_2}$

we notice the analogy with electrical resistances in series and in parallel.

EXERCISE 5(a)

Questions 1–5 refer to an elastic spring, modulus of elasticity 100 N, unstretched length 0.1 m.

1. Find the extension produced when a force of 20 N acts along the line of the spring.

2. What force along the line of the spring is needed to produce an extension of 0.05 m?

3. If the spring hangs vertically with one end fixed, what extension will be produced if a body A, mass 10 kg is suspended from the other end?

4. If the spring is hanging vertically, what additional extension will be produced if another body mass 10 kg is placed on A?

5. If two such springs hanging vertically side by side together support a body mass 10 kg, what will be the extension in each?

6. A spring AB modulus of elasticity 50 N, natural length 0.1 m is joined to another spring BC modulus of elasticity 40 N, natural length 0.1 m. They are placed so that ABC is a straight line and a force of 20 N is applied at C in the direction AC, the end A being fixed. Find the total extension in the two springs.

7. Find the force that must be applied to the springs in Question 6 if the total extension is 0.45 m.

8. A small body mass 1 kg is made to describe a circle on a smooth horizontal table at the end of an elastic string, one end of which is fixed. The natural length of the string is 0.3 m and the modulus of elasticity is 45 N. If the angular velocity of the body is 10 rad s^{-1}, find the radius of the circle it describes.

Work done in stretching an elastic string

In order to stretch an elastic string it is necessary to do work. If the tension in the string is T, an equal and opposite force must be exerted to stretch the string, T being of course a multiple of the extension x. Thus the work done in stretching the string from an extension x_1 to an extension x_2 is given by

$$W = \int_{x_1}^{x_2} \mathbf{T} \,.\, \mathbf{dx}$$

$$= \int_{x_1}^{x_2} T \, dx$$

as T and x are in the same direction.

But $$T = \lambda x / a$$

$\therefore$ $$W = \int_{x_1}^{x_2} \frac{\lambda x}{a} \, dx$$

$$= \frac{1}{2} \frac{\lambda x_2^2}{a} - \frac{1}{2} \frac{\lambda x_1^2}{a}$$

The work done is therefore the change in the quantity

$$\frac{1}{2} \frac{\lambda x^2}{a}$$

and this is called the *elastic energy* in the string.

Since $$W = \frac{1}{2} \frac{\lambda}{a} (x_2^2 - x_1^2)$$

$$= \frac{1}{2} \frac{\lambda}{a} (x_2 + x_1)(x_2 - x_1)$$

the relation can be expressed as

work done = average tension x extension.

Conservation of energy

Since the tension in an elastic string is proportional to the extension, the tension cannot suddenly become very large ('infinite'), so that an impulse cannot be applied by an elastic string to a body. Thus energy is conserved throughout all the ensuing motion.

Example 5.6. *A spring natural length 0.2 m, modulus of elasticity 200 N, is extended 0.05 m. Find the work done in extending it a further 0.05 m.*

The elastic energy before it is extended the further 0.05 m is

$$\frac{1}{2}\frac{200 \times (0.05)^2}{0.2}, \quad \text{i.e. } 1.25 \text{ J}$$

When extended a total of 0.1 m, the elastic energy is

$$\frac{1}{2}\frac{200 \times (0.1)^2}{0.2}, \quad \text{i.e. } 5 \text{ J}$$

The work done in stretching it a further 0.05 m is therefore 3.75 J. Note that this is not the same as the work done in stretching it the first 0.05 m, which was merely 1.25 J.

The solution could have been written

$$W = \int_{0.05}^{0.1} \frac{200x}{0.2}\,dx$$

$$= [500x^2]_{0.05}^{0.1}$$

$$= 3.75 \text{ J}$$

Example 5.7. *A catapult consists of two lengths of elastic, modulus of elasticity 20 N, natural length 0.2 m. They are stretched so that the length of each piece is doubled. What velocity will the catapult give to a stone mass 0.02 kg?*

The energy in each length of elastic is $\frac{1}{2}\lambda x^2/a$

i.e. $$\frac{1}{2}\frac{20(0.2)^2}{0.2} = 2 \text{ J}$$

∴ the total energy in the catapult is 4 J

If this is all given to the stone, assumed at a constant height above the ground, suppose the velocity of the stone is v m s^{-1}, where

$$4 = \tfrac{1}{2}(0.02)v^2$$

$$v = 20$$

the velocity given to the stone is 20 m s^{-1}.

Example 5.8. *A body mass 2 kg is attached by an elastic string, length 0.4 m, modulus of elasticity 9.8 N, to a point of a ceiling. The body is released from rest. Find the distance below the ceiling at which the body first comes to rest.*

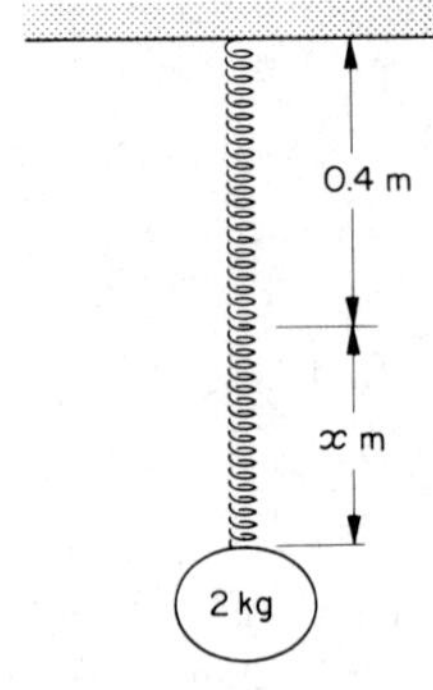

Fig. 5.5

Let the extension in the string be x m when the body is momentarily at rest (Fig. 5.5). Then the potential energy lost in the fall is

$$2g(0.4 + x) \text{ J}$$

and the elastic energy in the string is

$$\frac{1}{2}\frac{9.8x^2}{0.4} \text{ J}$$

Since the body was initially at rest and is now also at rest, there is no change in the kinetic energy, so

$$2g(0.4 + x) = \frac{1}{2}\frac{9.8x^2}{0.4}$$

i.e.

$$x^2 - 1.6x - 0.64 = 0$$

$$x \triangleq 1.93 \text{ or } -0.33$$

so the body first comes to rest 2.33 m below the ceiling, the unstretched length of the string being 0.4 m.

Since the body is attached to a string, Hooke's law does not hold for negative values of x, so the root $x \triangleq -0.33$ is meaningless in this case. The body first comes to rest a distance (0.4 + 1.93), i.e. about 2.33 metres, below the ceiling.

EXERCISE 5(b)

1. Find the work done in each of the following cases:
   (a) An elastic spring, modulus of elasticity 20 N, unstretched length 0.2 m, is stretched a further 0.2 m.
   (b) An elastic spring, modulus of elasticity 50 N, unstretched length 0.5 m, is stretched a further 0.5 m.
   (c) The spring in (b) is stretched so that its length increases from 1 m to 1.5 m.
   (d) The spring in (b) is stretched so that its length increases from 1.5 m to 2 m.
   (e) The spring in (b) is stretched so that its length increases from 2 m to 2.5 m.

   Compare the answers to (b), (c), (d), and (e).

2. An elastic spring AB, length 0.2 m, modulus of elasticity 250 N, is placed on a smooth horizontal table. The end A is fixed at a point on the table and a body mass 0.5 kg is fixed at B. The spring is now stretched so that its total length is 0.7 m, and then released. Considering the conservation of energy, find the velocity of B when (a) the spring is extended 0.48 m, (b) the spring is just slack.

3. An elastic spring AB length 0.25 m, modulus of elasticity 100 N is placed on a smooth horizontal table. The end A is fixed and a body mass 1 kg is fixed to the spring at B. This body is then projected along the table with velocity 10 m s^{-1}. Find (a) the velocity of B when the spring is stretched 0.4 m, (b) the extension of the spring when B is instantaneously at rest.

4. An elastic spring AB, length l, modulus of elasticity $4mg$, is placed on a smooth horizontal table, with a body mass m fixed at B, the other end A being fixed at a point on the table. The body is projected with velocity U along the table in the direction AB. Show that the body is instantaneously at rest when a distance $l + \frac{1}{2}U\sqrt{(l/g)}$ from A, and find its velocity when the spring has been stretched a distance $\frac{1}{4}U\sqrt{(l/g)}$.

5. One end of an elastic string of natural length l is attached at a fixed point X. When a body mass m is attached to the other end and hangs freely in equilibrium, the extension in the string is a. Find the vertical velocity which must then be given to the body if it is just to reach the point X. Find also the distance the body must be pulled down below the equilibrium position if, when released, it is to rise just to the level of X.

6. A uniform heavy rod AB, length l and mass m, is freely pivoted about the end A. An elastic string of unstretched length l and modulus of elasticity $\frac{1}{4}mg$ joins B to a fixed point C, on the same horizontal level as A and a distance l away. By taking moments about a horizontal axis through A, show that in equilibrium the angle BAC, equal to 2θ, is given by $2 \cos 2\theta - \sin 2\theta + \cos \theta = 0$.

7. A body mass 1 kg is attached by an elastic string modulus of elasticity 98 N, natural length 0.5 m, to a point X of a ceiling. The body is released from rest at X. Find the extension of the string when the body first comes to rest.

8. A body mass 1 kg is attached to one end of an elastic string, modulus 196 N, natural length 0.5 m. The other end of the string is attached at a point X in a ceiling. The body is projected vertically downwards from X with velocity 7 m s^{-1}. Find the velocity of the body when the string is just taut, and how far below the level of the ceiling the body first comes to rest. With what velocity will the body strike the ceiling on its return to X?

9. One end of a light elastic string of natural length a and modulus of elasticity mg is attached at a fixed point O, and the other end is attached to a particle of mass m. The particle is held at a depth x vertically below O and then released. Find the height above O to which the particle rises in the cases

   (a) $x = 4a$, (b) $x = 9a/2$ (O. & C.)

10. A scale pan of mass m hangs in equilibrium supported by an elastic spring of modulus kmg, natural length a. A body mass m is placed gently in the scale pan. Find the extension of the spring when the scale pan comes to rest for the first time.

11. Two bodies masses m, $2m$, are hanging in equilibrium supported by a light elastic string, modulus $3mg$, natural length a. The body mass m falls off. How high will the other body rise before coming instantaneously to rest? If the heavier body had fallen off instead, how far would the other rise before first coming to rest?

12. A body mass 5 kg is attached to the end B of a light elastic string AB of natural length 2 m and modulus 98 N, and is suspended vertically in equilibrium by the string whose other end A is attached at a fixed point.
    (a) Find the depth of B below A when the body is in equilibrium,
    (b) Use energy principles to find the distance through which the body must be pulled down vertically from its equilibrium position so that it will just reach A after release. (S.U.)

13. One end of an elastic string natural length a is fastened at a fixed point X and a particle mass m is attached at the other end. The particle is released from rest at X and first comes to rest when it is a distance $3a$ below X. Find the greatest tension in the string during this motion.

14. A body mass m is attached at one end of a light elastic string of modulus of elasticity $2mg$ and the other end of the string is fixed at a point A. The body hangs at rest a distance h below A. Find the natural length of the string.
    A small smooth ring of mass m is threaded on the string and is held at A. It is then released to fall and strike the body. Find the depth below A at which the body next comes momentarily to rest (a) if the ring adheres to the body, (b) if the ring rebounds, the coefficient of restitution between the ring and the body being $\frac{1}{3}$. (A.E.B.)

15. A small ring of mass m is threaded on a smooth wire bent in the form of a circle of radius a and fixed in a vertical plane. The ring is connected to the highest point of the wire by a light elastic string of natural length $\frac{1}{4}a\sqrt{3}$ and modulus of elasticity $\frac{1}{3}mg$. The ring is held at rest at a height $\frac{1}{2}a$ above the lowest point of the wire and then released. Show that the ring will come to instantaneous rest before reaching a height a above the lowest point of the wire. (A.E.B.)

Nature of the oscillations

Period of oscillation

Suppose one end of an elastic string, modulus of elasticity λ and natural length l, is fastened at a fixed point and the string hangs vertically supporting a body mass m (Fig. 5.6). In equilibrium, since the acceleration of the body is zero,

$T - mg = 0,$ where T is the tension in the string

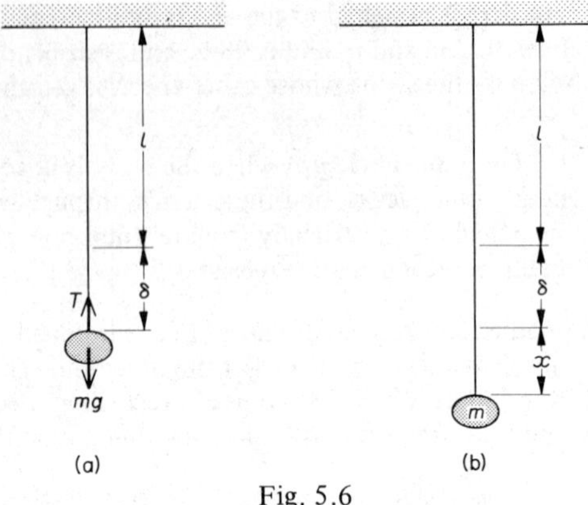

Fig. 5.6

but $\qquad T = \dfrac{\lambda}{l}\,\delta,\quad$ where δ is the extension of the string

$\therefore \qquad \dfrac{\lambda\delta}{l} = mg$

i.e. $\qquad \delta = \dfrac{mgl}{\lambda}$

If the body is now displaced so that it is a distance x below this equilibrium position,

$$mg - T = m\,\frac{\mathrm{d}^2x}{\mathrm{d}t^2}$$

the direction of the forces being that in which x is increasing.

But $$T = \frac{\lambda}{l}\left(x + \frac{mgl}{\lambda}\right)$$

$\therefore$ $$mg - \frac{\lambda}{l}\left(x + \frac{mgl}{\lambda}\right) = m\,\frac{\mathrm{d}^2x}{\mathrm{d}t^2}$$

i.e. $$\frac{\mathrm{d}^2x}{\mathrm{d}t^2} + \frac{\lambda}{ml}\,x = 0 \qquad (5.1)$$

As our observations confirm, the body oscillates with simple harmonic motion, (page 85) period $2\pi\sqrt{(ml/\lambda)}$, however the motion was caused. The *amplitude* depends on the manner in which the motion was started; obviously unless the body had been moved from its equilibrium position it would have remained at rest.

Conservation of energy

From equation 5.1, multiplying both sides by $\mathrm{d}x/\mathrm{d}t$

$$m\frac{\mathrm{d}x}{\mathrm{d}t}\frac{\mathrm{d}^2x}{\mathrm{d}t^2}+\frac{\lambda}{l}x\left(\frac{\mathrm{d}x}{\mathrm{d}t}\right)=0$$

Integrating $\quad \dfrac{1}{2}m\left(\dfrac{\mathrm{d}x}{\mathrm{d}t}\right)^2+\dfrac{1}{2}\dfrac{\lambda}{l}x^2=\text{constant}$

Now the elastic energy E in the spring is

$$\frac{1}{2}\frac{\lambda}{l}\left(x+\frac{mgl}{\lambda}\right)^2$$

since the total extension is

$$x+\frac{mgl}{\lambda}$$

$$\therefore \qquad \frac{1}{2}m\left(\frac{\mathrm{d}x}{\mathrm{d}t}\right)^2+E-mgx+\frac{1}{2}\frac{m^2g^2l}{\lambda}=\text{constant}$$

But $\frac{1}{2}m(\mathrm{d}x/\mathrm{d}t)^2$ is the kinetic energy, and $-mgx$ is the (gravitational) potential energy, which is negative since this decreases as x increases, so we have

kinetic energy + elastic energy + potential energy = constant

As an introduction to the different types of oscillatory motion, it is helpful to consider the following example.

Example 5.9. *A body mass 2 kg is suspended by an elastic string, and stretches it 0.04 m. Discuss the ensuing motion in the following cases:*
1. A small body mass 0.5 kg is placed gently on top of the 2 kg mass, and the system is allowed to move freely.

In Fig. 5.7, X is the position of the lower end of the string when unstretched, Y the equilibrium position when only the 2 kg mass is suspended, and Z the equilibrium position when both masses are hanging in equilibrium. The total

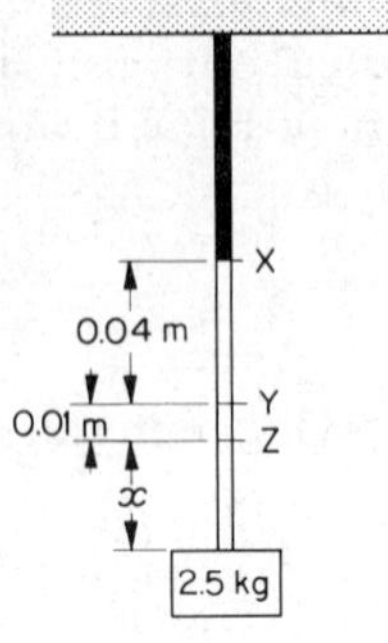

Fig. 5.7

extension then is 0.05 m, as the 0.5 kg mass has caused a further extension of 0.01 m. The displacement x metres must be measured from Z, otherwise an additional constant appears in the equation of motion, and the downwards direction will be taken as positive since x increases in that direction.

Considering the extension produced by the 2 kg mass,

$$2 \times 9.8 = \frac{\lambda}{l}(0.04)$$

i.e.

$$\frac{\lambda}{l} = 490 \text{ N m}^{-1}$$

where λ is the modulus of elasticity and l the unstretched length of the string.

In the subsequent motion, by Newton's law,

$$2.5 \times 9.8 - T = 2.5\frac{d^2x}{dt^2}$$

i.e.

$$2.5 \times 9.8 - 490(x + 0.05) = 2.5\frac{d^2x}{dt^2}$$

i.e.

$$\frac{d^2x}{dt^2} + 196x = 0$$

This is simple harmonic motion, period $\pi/7$ seconds. But in this example, initially $x = -0.01$ (negative as x is the distance *below* Z) and $dx/dt = 0$; since the 0.5 kg mass was placed *gently* onto the 2 kg mass, there was no initial momentum.

Thus the solution required is

$$x = -0.01 \cos 14t$$

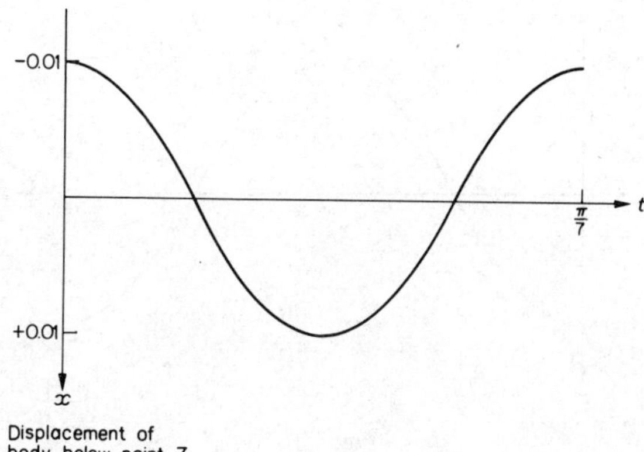

Fig. 5.8

illustrated in Fig. 5.8. We see that the bodies describe simple harmonic motion together, amplitude 0.01 m, period $\pi/7$ s.

2. *After the smaller body has been placed gently on top of the larger, they are both pulled down to a point W, 0.025 m below the equilibrium position Z, and then released from rest (Fig. 5.9).*

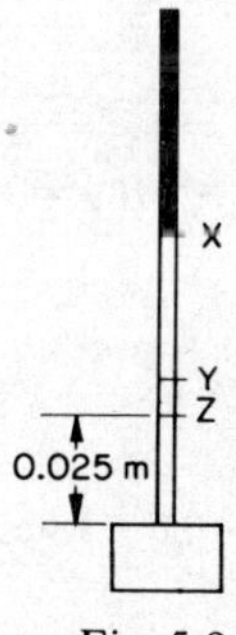

Fig. 5.9

Proceeding as before, the same differential equation

$$\frac{d^2x}{dt^2} + 196x = 0$$

describes the motion, but we have a different initial value of x, 0.025, so the solution required is (Fig. 5.10):

$$x = 0.025 \cos 14t$$

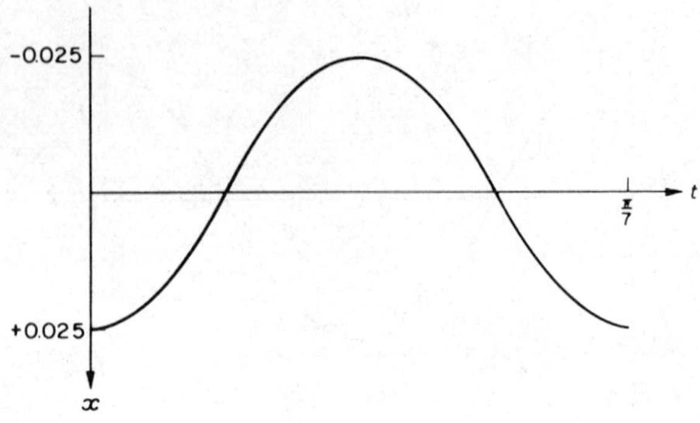

Fig. 5.10

Notice that the amplitude is less than 0.05 so the string never becomes slack. Simple harmonic motion, period $\pi/7$ seconds again, but amplitude 0.025 and $\pi/14$ seconds out of phase with the first motion.

3. The bodies are moved to the point Z, then projected vertically upwards with velocity 0.7 m s⁻¹.

The equation of motion is still

$$\frac{d^2x}{dt^2} + 196x = 0$$

but the initial conditions now are $x = 0$, $dx/dt = -0.7$, so we require a solution of the form $x = A \sin 14t$.

Since $$\frac{dx}{dt} = -0.7 \quad \text{when } t = 0$$

$$14A = -0.7$$

i.e. $$A = -0.05$$

The motion therefore is described by $x = -0.05 \sin 14t$, negative because x is initially decreasing.

As the extension of the string in equilibrium is 0.05 m, the string does not become slack, so the bodies describe simple harmonic motion, period $\pi/7$ s, amplitude 0.05 m, differing by a quarter of a cycle from each of the two considered in cases (1) and (2).

4. *The bodies are pulled down a distance 0.1 m below Z, then released.*

Measuring x positive downwards, the required solution to the equation of motion is

$$x = +0.1 \cos 14t$$

But the string becomes slack when $x = -0.05$, so that the bodies do not describe a complete oscillation of simple harmonic motion. The string becomes slack when

$$-0.05 = +0.1 \cos 14t$$

of which $t = \pi/21$ is the smallest positive solution. The bodies then travel under gravity, the velocity of projection v being given by

$$v = \frac{\mathrm{d}x}{\mathrm{d}t} = -1.4 \sin 14t$$

$$= -1.4 \sin\left(14 \times \frac{\pi}{21}\right)$$

$$= -\frac{7}{10}\sqrt{3} \text{ m s}^{-1}$$

so the time of flight is

$$\frac{2}{g} \times \frac{7}{10}\sqrt{3} \text{ s}$$

about 0.25 s. From the graph we see that if the bodies had described simple harmonic motion, they would have returned to Z after $\pi/21$ s, about 0.15 s. In this example (Fig. 5.11) in which the string becomes slack, the displacement-time graph is partly sinusoidal, partly parabolic. The period is

$$\left(\frac{2\pi}{21} + \frac{\sqrt{3}}{7}\right) \text{s.}$$

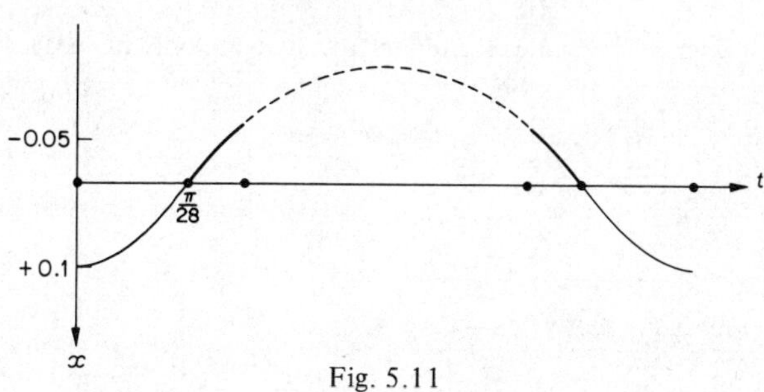

Fig. 5.11

5. The elastic string is now replaced by a spring, of the same length and same modulus of elasticity. The bodies are pulled down 0.1 m below Z, as in part (4).

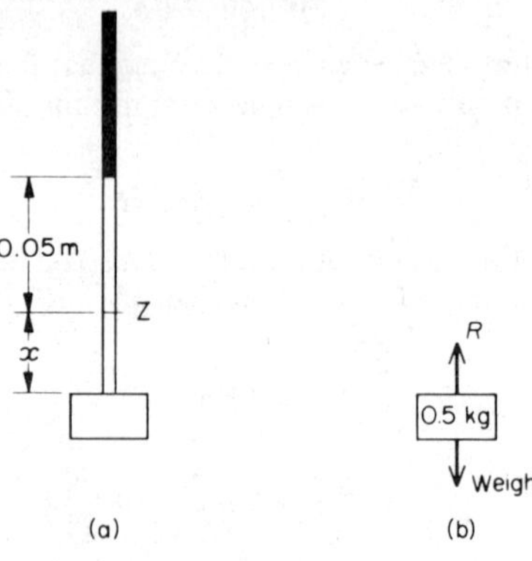

Fig. 5.12

From Newton's law, as before (Fig. 5.12)

$$2.5g - 490(0.05 + x) = 2.5 \frac{d^2x}{dt^2}$$

i.e.

$$\frac{d^2x}{dt^2} + 196x = 0$$

But considering the forces on the smaller mass, if R N is the force between the masses,

$$0.5g - R = 0.5 \frac{d^2x}{dt^2}$$

Since $R \geqslant 0$ when the bodies are in contact, they are only in contact when

$$\frac{d^2x}{dt^2} \leqslant g$$

But since

$$\frac{d^2x}{dt^2} = -196x$$

they are only in contact when $-196x \leqslant g$

i.e.

$$x \geqslant -0.05$$

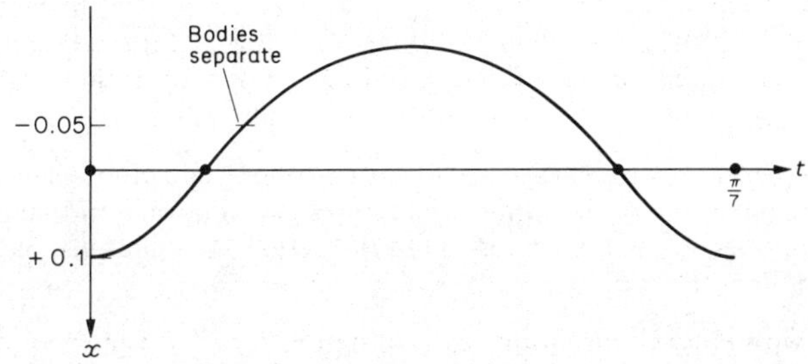

Fig. 5.13

From the graph (Fig. 5.13), we see that the larger body, attached to the end of the spring, executes simple harmonic motion, while the smaller one separates from it when 0.05 m above the equilibrium position.

EXERCISE 5(c)

1. A body stretches a light vertical string, natural length 1 m, by 0.2 m when suspended from one end of the string. The body is pulled down a further 0.01 m and then released from rest. Find the period of the resulting oscillations. If, instead, the body had been pulled down 0.005 m, what would have been the period of the oscillations? What is the amplitude of the motion in each case?

2. A body mass 4 kg is suspended by a vertical string, one end of which is fixed. When displaced from the equilibrium position, the body makes two complete oscillations a second. Find the extension in the string produced by the body when hanging in equilibrium, if the string remains taut.

3. When the body in Question 2 is hanging at rest supported by the string it receives an impulse of 0.4 N s along the line of the string so as to increase the extension in the string. Find the amplitude of the resulting oscillations. If the impulse had been in the opposite direction, what difference, if any, would it have made to the amplitude of the oscillations?

4. A body mass 4 kg stretches a light vertical string by 0.02 m when suspended from one end of the string. A mass of 2 kg is placed gently onto the heavier body, and the system is allowed to oscillate. Find the amplitude and period of the resulting motion.

5. A certain body extends a spring by 0.8 m when hanging in equilibrium. Find the time of oscillation if it is pulled down a further 0.2 m and then released. Find also the velocity and acceleration of the body when 0.1 m below and 0.1 m above the equilibrium position.

6. A mass M kg stretches a light vertical spring by b metres when suspended from one end of the spring. The mass is pulled down a further c metres and then released from rest. Find the period and amplitude of the motion, if $c < b$.

7. Two similar elastic strings, each of natural length 0.5 m and modulus 64 N, are fastened at one end to a particle of mass 4 kg. Their other ends are fastened to two fixed points A and B, 2 m apart, on a smooth horizontal table. Initially the system is at rest with the particle at a point O midway between A and B. The particle is then displaced 0.25 m towards B and is there released. Show that the particle performs simple harmonic motion with period $\pi/4$ seconds, and that it passes through O with velocity of 2 m s^{-1}. (C.)

8. One end of a light elastic string AB, of natural length 1 m, is fixed; when a body of mass 1 kg is attached to the string at B and hangs freely under gravity, the extension of the string in equilibrium is 0.05 m. Calculate the modulus of elasticity of the string.
The body is now displaced a further 0.06 m and then released. Show that, until the string becomes slack, the particle performs simple harmonic motion and find the period. Find also the distance from A at which the particle first comes to instantaneous rest. (A.E.B.)

9. A point A is at a height $6a$ vertically above a point B. To a particle of mass m are fastened two similar elastic strings, each of modulus mg and natural length a. The other ends of the strings are fixed, one at A and the other at B. Find the distance below A of the point P at which the particle will rest in equilibrium.
The particle is now lifted to the middle point of AB and is there released. By considering the forces on the particle when it is at a distance x below P, or otherwise, show that the particle performs simple harmonic motion. State the amplitude and period of the motion. (C.)

10. A vertical light spring has two equal masses fixed to its ends, as shown in Fig. 5.14. When the lower mass lies on a table, the spring is compressed a distance d by the weight of the upper mass. If the upper mass is now pushed down a further distance 2.5 d and then released, examine whether the lower mass will at some time leave the table. (You may assume that if the lower mass were fixed, the upper mass would oscillate symmetrically about its equilibrium position.) (S.M.P.)

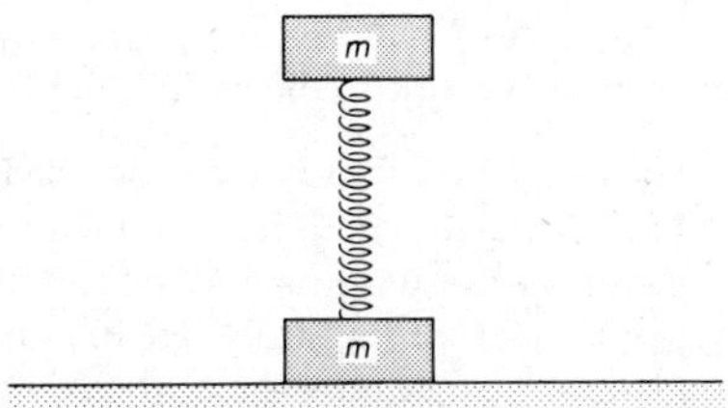

Fig. 5.14

11. Beads of mass m and $3m$ are threaded on a smooth fixed horizontal circular wire of radius a and are joined by a light elastic spring of natural length a and spring constant k. (*The spring constant is equal to the ratio tension : extension.*) Initially the beads are at the opposite ends of a diameter and are given a slight displacement. Find the ratio of their tangential accelerations at any time before the string slackens and hence the location of the point where they collide in relation to their initial positions. Show that the speed of the larger mass, when the string becomes slack, is $\frac{1}{2}a\sqrt{(k/3m)}$. (S.M.P.)

12. A particle mass m is suspended by two elastic strings each of natural length a and modulus of elasticity mg, the other ends being attached at two fixed points A and B distant $2a$ apart in the same horizontal line. If θ is the angle made with the horizontal by each string, show that in the equilibrium position θ satisfies

$$\tan\theta - \sin\theta = \tfrac{1}{2}$$

If the particle is dropped from rest at the middle point of AB, show that (*a*) when $\theta = 60°$, the acceleration of the particle is $(\sqrt{3} - 1)g$ vertically upwards, (b) the value of θ when the particle first comes to instantaneous rest satisfies the equation

$$\sec^3\theta - 3\sec^2\theta + 2\sec\theta - 2 = 0$$ (W.J.E.C.)

13. A particle of weight W is attached by a light elastic string of natural length l to a fixed point A, from which it is allowed to fall freely. When the particle is at its lowest point the length of the string is $2l$. Prove that the modulus of the string is $4W$ and that the speed is a maximum when the particle is at a distance $\frac{5}{4}l$ below A.
Prove that the time between the string becoming taut and becoming slack again is $(\pi - \cos^{-1}\frac{1}{3})\sqrt{(l/g)}$. (O. & C.)

14. A flat plate is oscillating in a horizontal plane about a fixed point O with period $2\pi/\omega$. A small body is placed on the plate a distance k

from O. If the body does not slip on the plate, show that the coefficient of friction between the body and the plate is not less than $k\omega^2/g$.

15. Three equal particles each of mass m are connected in pairs by three elastic strings. Each string has modulus λ and natural length l. The system is rotating on a smooth horizontal table with constant angular velocity ω in such a way that the strings are of constant length r forming an equilateral triangle, and the centre of rotation is the centroid of the triangle. Find an expression for r in terms of λ, ω, m, and l and show that such a motion is impossible if

$$\omega^2 \geqslant \frac{3\lambda}{ml}$$ (O. & C.)

16. A light helical spring of natural length l surrounds a long cylindrical rod without touching it, and one end of the spring is fixed to a point A of the rod. A symmetrical ring of mass m slides on the rod and is attached to the other end of the spring. When the rod is held vertically, the ring can remain at rest at a distance $l + b$ below A.
The rod is placed horizontally and the ring is released from rest at a distance a from A. If μ is the coefficient of friction between the ring and the rod, show that, provided $a > l + \mu b$, the ring comes to rest at a distance $2(l + \mu b) - a$ from A, and find the time elapsed before it does so.
If $a > l + 3\mu b$, find the distance of the ring from A when it comes to rest a second time. What happens if $a \leqslant l + 3\mu b$?
What can you say about the final distance of the ring from A irrespective of the value of a? (C.S.)

17. A light smooth elastic string AB is of modulus λ and natural length l. A particle of mass m is attached at A, and lies on a rough horizontal table, the coefficient of friction being μ. A similar particle is attached at B. Initially, at time $t = 0$, the particle A is at a distance l from the edge of the table, and B is at a vertical depth l below the edge, the length of the string being $2l$. If the particles are released show that A starts to move immediately, provided $\lambda > \mu mg$.
Assuming this to be the case, find the distances x (supposed $< l$) and y of A and B from the edge of the table at time t.
Show that the length of the string is $a + (2l - a)\cos nt$, where

$$a = l\left[1 + \frac{mg(1 + \mu)}{2\lambda}\right]$$

and $n^2 = \dfrac{2\lambda}{ml}$ (C.S.)

6. Velocity and Acceleration

Velocity

One of the first problems when investigating the motion of a particle was to distinguish between speed and velocity (*Additional Applied Mathematics*, page 1). Velocity we defined as the rate of change of the displacement of a particle from an initial point, the particle moving in a straight line through that point. When a particle is moving in two or three dimensions, we need to extend our definition of velocity.

The position of a point P relative to a fixed point O is uniquely determined by the position vector $\overrightarrow{OP}$, invariably denoted by $\mathbf{r}$. The velocity of a particle at the point we can define as $d\mathbf{r}/dt$, and the acceleration as $d^2\mathbf{r}/dt^2$. If the velocity is denoted by $\mathbf{v}$, the acceleration thus is $d\mathbf{v}/dt$.

Differentiation of a vector

Suppose a particle moving in a curve, not necessarily a plane curve, is at a point P, position vector $\mathbf{r}$ at time t, and has reached another point P$'$, position vector $\mathbf{r} + \delta\mathbf{r}$ after time $t + \delta t$, by travelling along an arc length δs of the curve (Fig. 6.1). The arc length of the curve

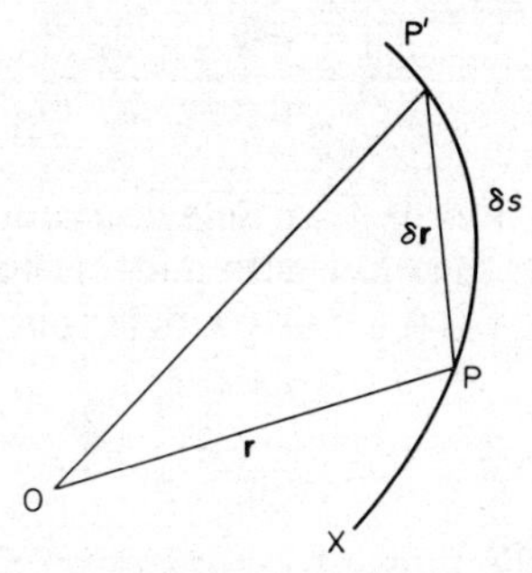

Fig. 6.1

is measured from some fixed point X on the curve. Then the change in the position vector is $\delta\mathbf{r}$, and the rate of change of $\mathbf{r}$ is $\mathrm{d}\mathbf{r}/\mathrm{d}t$,

where
$$\frac{\mathrm{d}\mathbf{r}}{\mathrm{d}t} \equiv \underset{\delta t \to 0}{\mathrm{Lt}} \frac{\delta \mathbf{r}}{\delta t}$$

But
$$\frac{\delta \mathbf{r}}{\delta t} = \frac{\delta \mathbf{r}}{\delta s} \cdot \frac{\delta s}{\delta t}$$

$\therefore$
$$\frac{\mathrm{d}\mathbf{r}}{\mathrm{d}t} = \underset{\delta t \to 0}{\mathrm{Lt}} \frac{\delta \mathbf{r}}{\delta s} \cdot \frac{\delta s}{\delta t}$$

Now as $\delta t \to 0$, $\delta s/\delta t \to \mathrm{d}s/\mathrm{d}t$. which is the rate of change of the arc length from a fixed point, and so is the *speed* of the particle. As $\delta t \to 0$, $\delta\mathbf{r}/\delta s$ approaches a unit vector, and as P′ approaches P along the curve, the direction of this unit vector is along the tangent to the curve at P. Thus the velocity of P is $(\mathrm{d}s/\mathrm{d}t)\hat{\mathbf{s}}$, where $\hat{\mathbf{s}}$ is a unit vector along the tangent at P.

Acceleration

Since acceleration is defined as $\mathrm{d}^2\mathbf{r}/\mathrm{d}t^2$, this is

$$\frac{\mathrm{d}}{\mathrm{d}t}\left(\frac{\mathrm{d}s}{\mathrm{d}t}\,\hat{\mathbf{s}}\right)$$

As both these terms may vary, we need to differentiate a product. Assuming that the method of differentiating a product, one term of which is a scalar, is the same as when both terms are scalars, we have

$$\frac{\mathrm{d}^2\mathbf{r}}{\mathrm{d}t^2} = \frac{\mathrm{d}^2 s}{\mathrm{d}t^2}\,\hat{\mathbf{s}} + \frac{\mathrm{d}s}{\mathrm{d}t}\frac{\mathrm{d}}{\mathrm{d}t}(\hat{\mathbf{s}})$$

Thus the acceleration of a particle contains a component $\mathrm{d}^2 s/\mathrm{d}t^2$ along the tangent, together with another term. The second term is only zero if $\mathrm{d}s/\mathrm{d}t = 0$ (i.e. the particle is at rest), or

$$\frac{\mathrm{d}}{\mathrm{d}t}(\hat{\mathbf{s}}) = 0$$

the direction of the tangent is constant, i.e. the particle is moving along a straight line.

Differentiation of a unit vector

Suppose a particle is describing a circle centre O, unit radius. If the particle is initially at the point P, position vector $\hat{\mathbf{r}}$, and at P′,

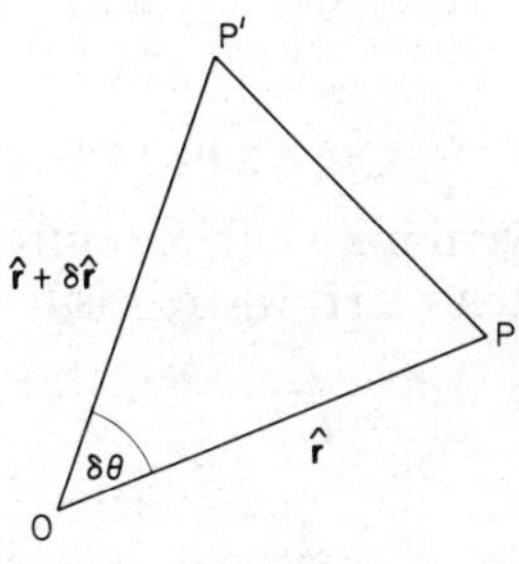

Fig. 6.2

position vector $\hat{\mathbf{r}} + \delta\hat{\mathbf{r}}$ after further time δt, where angle POP′ = $\delta\theta$, then from Fig. 6.2,

$$\delta\hat{\mathbf{r}} = \overrightarrow{PP'},$$

i.e.
$$\frac{\delta\hat{\mathbf{r}}}{\delta t} = \frac{\overrightarrow{PP'}}{\delta t}$$

Now since $\overrightarrow{OP}$ and $\overrightarrow{OP'}$ are both unit vectors, their magnitudes are both equal to 1, so PP′ = 2 sin ($\delta\theta/2$)

$$\therefore \qquad \frac{PP'}{\delta t} = \frac{2\sin(\delta\theta/2)}{\delta t}$$

i.e.
$$\underset{\delta t \to 0}{\text{Lt}} \frac{PP'}{\delta t} = \underset{\delta t \to 0}{\text{Lt}} \frac{2\sin(\delta\theta/2)}{\delta t}$$

$$= \underset{\delta t \to 0}{\text{Lt}} \left(\frac{\sin(\delta\theta/2)}{\delta\theta/2}\right) \cdot \frac{\delta\theta}{\delta t}$$

$$= \frac{d\theta}{dt}$$

But the direction of the velocity of a particle travelling along a curve is along the tangent to that curve, therefore

$$\frac{d\mathbf{r}}{dt} = \frac{d\theta}{dt}\,\hat{\mathbf{s}}$$

$\hat{\mathbf{s}}$ being again a unit vector along the tangent to the curve at P.

Acceleration of a particle moving in a circle

When a particle is describing a circle, centre the origin, its position vector $\mathbf{r}$ may be written $\mathbf{r} = r\hat{\mathbf{r}}$, where r is the radius of the circle.

Now $$\frac{d\hat{\mathbf{r}}}{dt} = \omega\hat{\mathbf{s}}$$

$\therefore$ $$\frac{d\mathbf{r}}{dt} = \frac{d}{dt}(r\hat{\mathbf{r}}) = r\omega\hat{\mathbf{s}}$$

$\therefore$ $$\frac{d^2\mathbf{r}}{dt^2} = r\frac{d\omega}{dt}\,\hat{\mathbf{s}} + r\omega\frac{d\hat{\mathbf{s}}}{dt}$$

But $\hat{\mathbf{s}}$ is a unit vector perpendicular to $\hat{\mathbf{r}}$, so $\hat{\mathbf{s}}$ rotates at the same angular speed as $\hat{\mathbf{r}}$ (Fig. 6.3).

Since $$\frac{d\hat{\mathbf{r}}}{dt} = \omega\hat{\mathbf{s}} \text{ in the direction } \left(\theta + \frac{\pi}{2}\right)$$

$$\frac{d\hat{\mathbf{s}}}{dt} = \omega\hat{\mathbf{r}} \text{ in the direction } (\theta + \pi)$$

i.e. $$= -\omega\hat{\mathbf{r}}$$

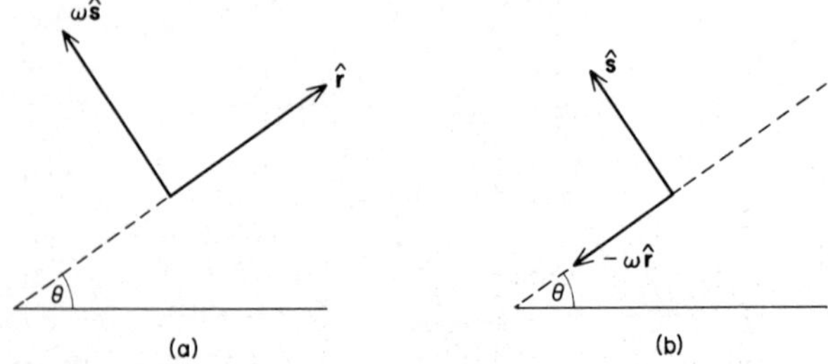

Fig. 6.3

Thus $$\frac{d^2\mathbf{r}}{dt^2} = \left(r\frac{d\omega}{dt}\right)\hat{\mathbf{s}} - (r\omega^2)\hat{\mathbf{r}}$$

When the particle is travelling with constant angular speed, $d\omega/dt = 0$, and

$$\frac{d^2\mathbf{r}}{dt^2} = -r\omega^2\hat{\mathbf{r}}$$

an expression with which we are already familiar.

Example 6.1. *The position vector* $\mathbf{r}$ *of a particle at time* t *is given by* $\mathbf{r} = t^2\mathbf{i} + t^3\mathbf{j}$. *Find the velocity* $\mathbf{v}$ *and acceleration* $\mathbf{a}$ *of the particle.*

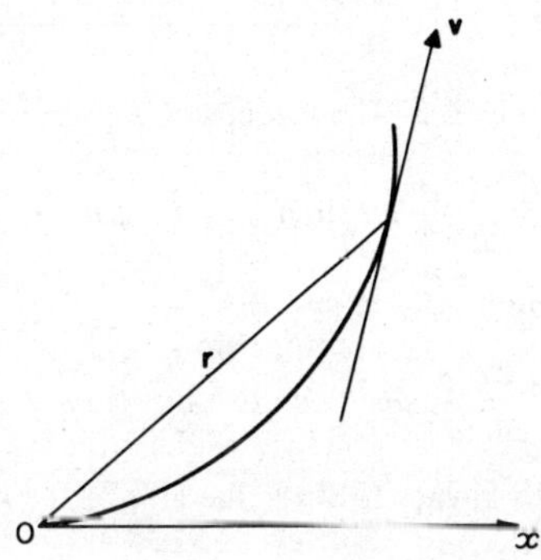

Fig. 6.4

Differentiating,

$$\mathbf{v} \equiv \frac{d\mathbf{r}}{dt} = 2t\mathbf{i} + 3t^2\mathbf{j}$$

and $$\mathbf{a} \equiv \frac{d\mathbf{v}}{dt} = 2\mathbf{i} + 6t\mathbf{j}$$

The path of the particle is a semi-cubical parabola, $y^2 = x^3$. Since t is positive, only one half of the semi-cubical parabola is described (Fig. 6.4). The figure illustrates that the rate of change of the velocity parallel to $\mathbf{j}$ is increasing, whereas parallel to $\mathbf{i}$ there is no change in the acceleration.

Example 6.2. *Find the velocity and acceleration of a particle moving in a helix, position vector* $\mathbf{r} = a\cos nt\mathbf{i} + a\sin nt\mathbf{j} + ct\mathbf{k}$.

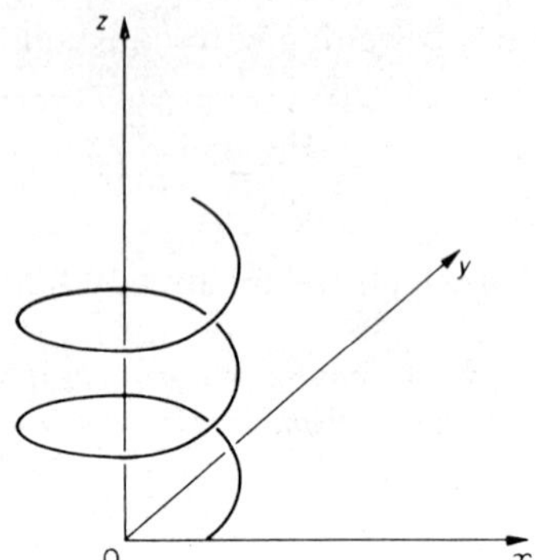

Fig. 6.5

The helix is shown in Fig. 6.5. The velocity $\mathbf{v}$ is given by

$$\mathbf{v} \equiv \frac{d\mathbf{r}}{dt} = -an\sin nt\mathbf{i} + an\cos nt\mathbf{j} + c\mathbf{k}$$

and the acceleration by

$$\frac{d\mathbf{v}}{dt} = -an^2\cos nt\mathbf{i} - an^2\sin nt\mathbf{j}$$

Thus the acceleration is always towards the axis of the helix and is of constant magnitude an^2.

EXERCISE 6(a)

1. The position vector $\mathbf{r}$ of a particle at time t is given by

$$\mathbf{r} = a\cos nt\mathbf{i} + b\sin nt\mathbf{j}.$$

Show that the acceleration $\mathbf{a} = \lambda\mathbf{r}$, where λ is a scalar.

2. The position vector $\mathbf{r}$ of a particle at time t is given by $\mathbf{r} = at\mathbf{i} + (a/t)\mathbf{j}$. Show that the acceleration of the particle is parallel to $\mathbf{j}$.

3. The position vector $\mathbf{r}$ of a particle at time t is given by $\mathbf{r} = at^2\mathbf{i} + 2at\mathbf{j}$. Show that the acceleration $\mathbf{a}$ is such that $\mathbf{a} = \lambda\mathbf{i}$, where λ is a constant scalar.

4. The position vector $\mathbf{r}$ of a particle at time t is given by $\mathbf{r} = (at + b)\mathbf{i} + (ct + d)\mathbf{j}$. Show that the particle is moving in a straight line with constant velocity.

5. The position vector $\mathbf{r}$ of a particle at time t is given by $\mathbf{r} = (at^2 + b)\mathbf{i} + (ct^2 + d)\mathbf{j}$. Show that the particle is moving in a straight line with constant acceleration.

6. The position vector $\mathbf{r}$ of a particle at time t is given by $\mathbf{r} = at\mathbf{i} + bt\mathbf{j} + c\,e^{-t}\mathbf{k}$. Show that the acceleration of the particle has fixed direction.

7. The position vector $\mathbf{r}$ of a particle at time t is $\mathbf{r} = a \sin t\mathbf{i} + a \cos t\mathbf{j} + at\mathbf{k}$. Find the position vector and the velocity vector of the particle at times $t = 0$ and $t = \frac{1}{2}\pi$. Find also the angle between the paths of the particle at $t = 0$ and $t = \frac{1}{2}\pi$. (A.E.B.)

8. The position vector $\mathbf{r}$ of a particle is given by $\mathbf{r} = \cos nt\mathbf{i} + \sin nt\mathbf{j}$. Find the speed of the particle at time t. Show that the acceleration at time t is given by the vector $-n^2\mathbf{r}$. (S.M.P.)

9. $\mathbf{u}$ is the unit vector $\cos\theta\mathbf{i} + \sin\theta\mathbf{j}$, and $\mathbf{v}$ is obtained from $\mathbf{u}$ by an anti-clockwise rotation through $\frac{1}{2}\pi$. Find $\mathbf{v}$ in terms of $\mathbf{i}$, $\mathbf{j}$, and θ. If $\mathbf{u}$ and $\mathbf{v}$ now rotate, so that θ varies with time, show that

$$\frac{d\mathbf{u}}{dt} = \mathbf{v}\frac{d\theta}{dt}$$

P has polar coordinates (r, θ) and position vector $\mathbf{r}$. Show that $\mathbf{r} = r\mathbf{u}$ and deduce that

$$\frac{d\mathbf{r}}{dt} = \frac{dr}{dt}\mathbf{u} + r\frac{d\theta}{dt}\mathbf{v}$$

Hence or otherwise show that if P is moving on the spiral $r = a\,e^{\theta}$, the velocity of P makes an angle $\frac{1}{4}\pi$ with $\mathbf{r}$ and has magnitude

$$\frac{dr}{dt}\sqrt{2}$$

(S.M.P.)

10. $\overrightarrow{OP}$ is a vector of length r making an angle θ with OX. P moves so that (a) θ increases at a constant rate ω, and (b) the velocity of P makes a constant angle α with the vector $\overrightarrow{OP}$. Show that t units of time after r takes the value a, $r = a\,e^{bt}$ where $b = \omega \cot \alpha$.
Show also that the direction of the acceleration makes an angle 2α with the direction of $\overrightarrow{OP}$ and find its value in terms of r, ω and α. (M.E.I.)

11. Two particles, P and Q, start at the same point O and move in a plane with velocities $\mathbf{v}_P$, $\mathbf{v}_Q$ given at time t by the equations

$$\mathbf{v}_P = u \cos mt\mathbf{i} + u \sin mt\mathbf{j}$$
$$\mathbf{v}_Q = u \sin nt\mathbf{i} - u \cos nt\mathbf{j}$$

where u, m, n are constants. Prove that, if $m \neq n$, the directions of the particles are infinitely often perpendicular to one another. What is the corresponding result if $m = n$? Sketch on the same diagram the paths followed by P and Q. Prove that, if $m = n$, the acceleration of P is always parallel to the velocity of Q but in the opposite sense. (M.E.I.)

12. A ball mass m is thrown into the air with initial velocity $\mathbf{u}$, and during its flight experiences a resistance given by the vector $-mc\mathbf{v}$, where $\mathbf{v}$ is the velocity of the ball at that instant. Write down a differential equation for the velocity as a function of time, and verify that this equation and the initial conditions are both satisfied by

$$\mathbf{v} = \frac{1 - e^{-ct}}{c}\mathbf{g} + e^{-ct}\mathbf{u}$$

where $\mathbf{g}$ is the vector acceleration due to gravity.
Find an expression for $\mathbf{r}$, the displacement of the ball from its initial position, at time t; and show that, if c is small, this is approximately equal to

$$\mathbf{r}^* - c(\tfrac{1}{6}t^3\mathbf{g} + \tfrac{1}{2}t^2\mathbf{u})$$

where $\mathbf{r}^*$ is the position that it would occupy in the absence of air resistance. (S.M.P.)

13. The position vector $\mathbf{p}$ of a passenger in a roundabout at a fairground is given by

$$\mathbf{p} = 9\mathbf{i}\cos\tfrac{2}{3}t + 9\mathbf{j}\sin\tfrac{2}{3}t + \tfrac{9}{2}\mathbf{k}\left(1 - \cos\frac{4t}{3}\right)$$

where $\mathbf{i}, \mathbf{j}, \mathbf{k}$ are mutually perpendicular vectors each of length 1 metre $\mathbf{k}$ being vertical, t is the time measured in seconds and the angles are measured in radians.
How long does it take to perform a complete revolution, and what happens in the vertical direction while this is taking place?
Find the acceleration of the passenger at time t. What is the magnitude of the greatest acceleration he experiences? (S.M.P.)

14. A cycloid is traced out by a point K on the circumference of a circle of radius c which rolls along a line (Fig. 6.6). Initially K coincides with a point O on the line. If $\mathbf{i}$ and $\mathbf{j}$ denote unit vectors along and perpendicular to the line, and $\hat{\mathbf{u}}$ and $\hat{\mathbf{n}}$ denote unit vectors along and perpendicular to the radius through K when the circle has rotated through an

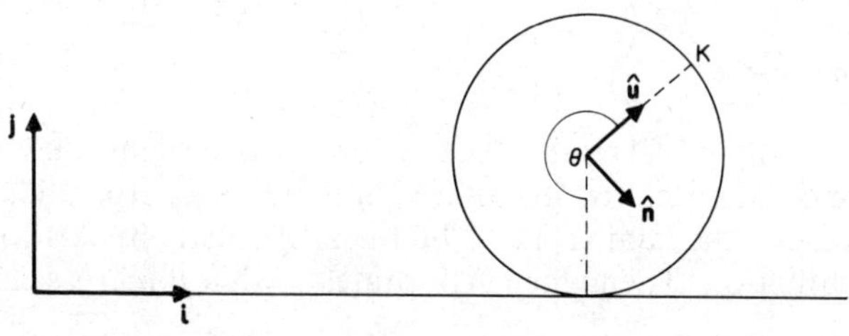

Fig. 6.6

angle θ, $0 < \theta < 2\pi$, find an expression for the vector $\mathbf{r} = \text{OK}$ and deduce that

$$\frac{d\mathbf{r}}{d\theta} = c(\mathbf{i} + \hat{\mathbf{n}})$$

Give the direction of this vector. (S.M.P.)

15. Fig. 6.7 shows a particle on the end of a string which is unwinding in a horizontal plane from a cylindrical reel of radius b whose axis is vertical. Initially the particle is in contact with the reel and is given a velocity away from the axis of the reel; after a time t the radius to the point where the string leaves the reel has rotated through an angle θ. $\hat{\mathbf{u}}$ and $\hat{\mathbf{n}}$ are unit vectors along and perpendicular to this radius. Express the position vector of the particle, relative to the point in the plane of motion on the axis of the reel, in terms of b, θ, $\hat{\mathbf{u}}$, and $\hat{\mathbf{n}}$, and deduce its velocity and acceleration.
Supposing that the only force in the plane acting on the particle is the tension in the string, prove that θ is proportional to $\sqrt{t}$, and that the magnitude of the acceleration is inversely proportional to θ. (S.M.P.)

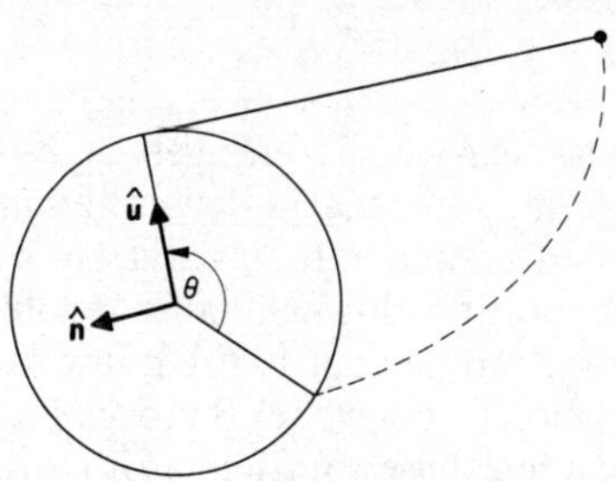

Fig. 6.7

(The remainder of this chapter may be left for a second reading.)

Angular speed

Suppose AB and CD in Fig. 6.8 are any two straight lines in the surface of a lamina free to rotate about an axis perpendicular to the plane of the lamina. Let θ be the angle made by AB with any fixed direction. Then when AB rotates so that θ increases to

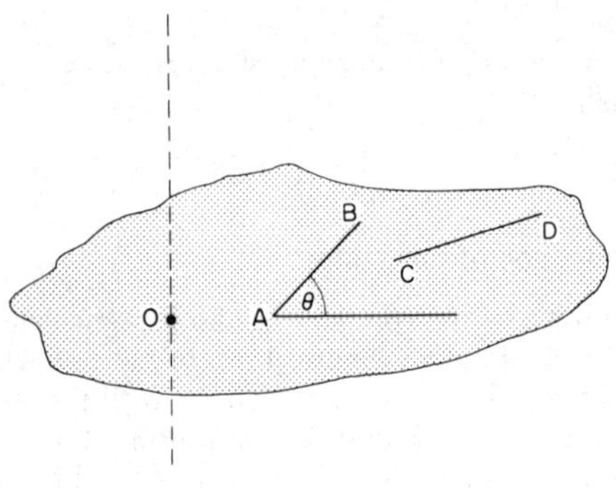

Fig. 6.8

$\theta + \phi$, the angle made by CD also increases by ϕ, so that both AB and CD rotate at the same rate. This we have called the *angular speed*. (It is sometimes loosely called the angular velocity.)

Angular velocity

Consider two identical gear wheels, engaged as in Fig. 6.9. They clearly rotate at the same rate, that is, have the same angular speed. Yet there is a difference in their rotation, because their axes are perpendicular. A rotation through half a revolution of cogwheel A moves a point which had been at P, the point of contact, to Q, whereas half a revolution of cogwheel B moves P to R.

To distinguish between these rotations it is convenient to define angular velocity more exactly.

When a lamina is rotating about an axis Oz (Fig. 6.10) perpendicular to the lamina, in the sense of rotating from Ox to Oy, with angular speed ω, we define the angular velocity as the vector $\omega\hat{\mathbf{k}}$, where $\hat{\mathbf{k}}$ as usual is a unit vector along Oz. The direction of $\hat{\mathbf{k}}$ is that which we invariably take when using three mutually perpendicular vectors.

Thus the angular velocity vectors of cogwheels A and B are different and can be expressed as $\omega\mathbf{i}$ and $\omega\mathbf{j}$ respectively, taking suitable axes.

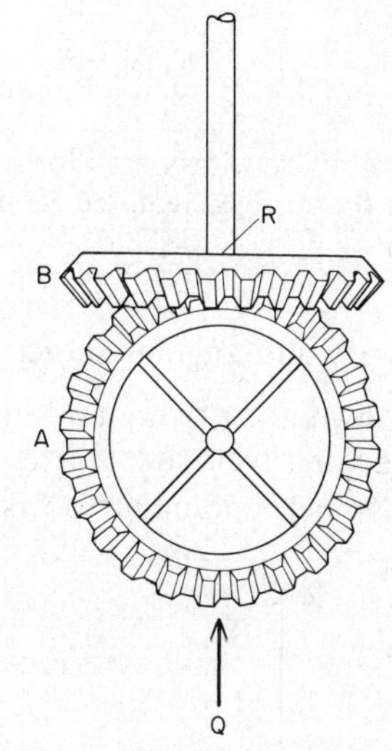

Fig. 6.9

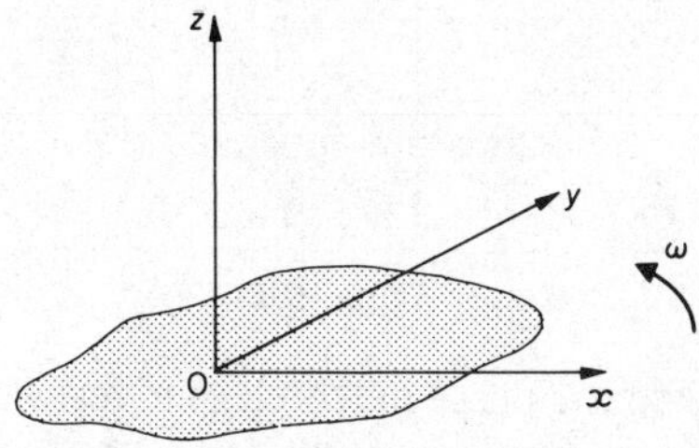

Fig. 6.10

Example 6.3. *A gear wheel is rotating with angular speed 2 rad* s^{-1} *about an axis along OP, where P has position vector relative to O of* **i** + **j** + **k**. *Find the angular velocity of the gear wheel.*

A *unit* vector along the axis is

$$\frac{1}{\sqrt{3}}(\mathbf{i}+\mathbf{j}+\mathbf{k})$$

Thus the angular velocity of the gear wheel is

$$\frac{2}{\sqrt{3}}(\mathbf{i}+\mathbf{j}+\mathbf{k}) \text{ rad s}^{-1}$$

The term angular velocity is still so widely used for angular speed that when we wish to emphasize that the vector is required we shall say angular velocity vector.

Relation of linear velocity and angular velocity

When a point P position vector **r** from a point on the axis (Fig. 6.11) is rotating with angular velocity $\boldsymbol{\omega}$, the velocity of P is perpendicular to $\boldsymbol{\omega}$ and also perpendicular to **r**, since $\boldsymbol{\omega}$ by definition

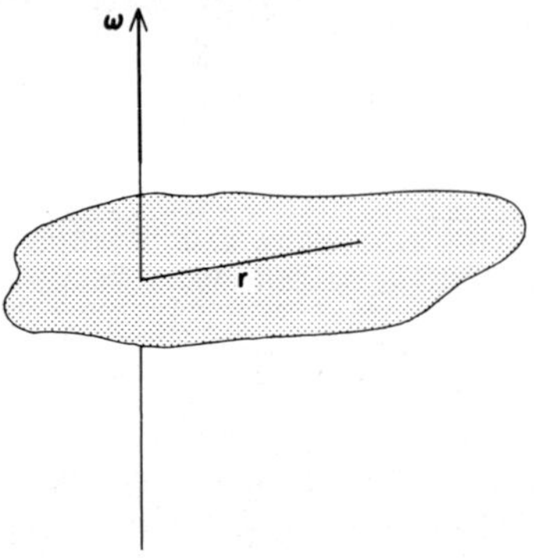

Fig. 6.11

is perpendicular to the plane in which **r** moves. Therefore **v** is parallel to $\boldsymbol{\omega} \times \mathbf{r}$. Since **v** is proportional to $\boldsymbol{\omega}$ and to **r**, we have (Fig. 6.12)

$$\mathbf{v} = \boldsymbol{\omega} \times \mathbf{r}$$

To show that the velocity of P is not dependent on which point on the axis of rotation is taken as the origin of the position vector, any other point Q on the axis has position vector $\lambda \boldsymbol{\omega}$ relative to O,

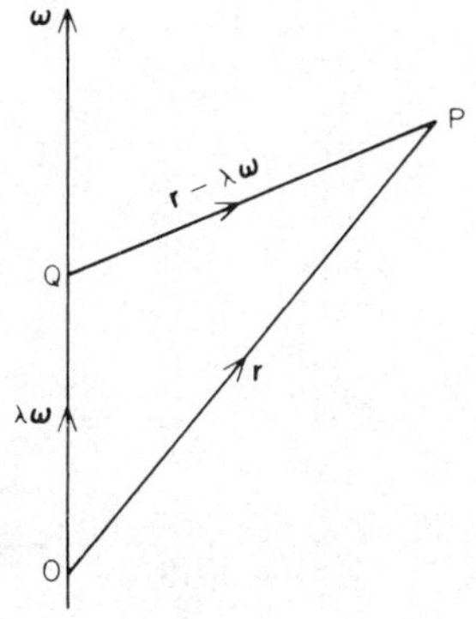

Fig. 6.12

so the position vector of P relative to Q is $\mathbf{r} - \lambda\boldsymbol{\omega}$. By the above, the velocity of P is

$$\boldsymbol{\omega} \times (\mathbf{r} - \lambda \boldsymbol{\omega})$$

which is equal to $\boldsymbol{\omega} \times \mathbf{r}$, since $\boldsymbol{\omega} \times \boldsymbol{\omega} = 0$.

Example 6.4. *A point P position vector* $\mathbf{i} + 2\mathbf{j} + \mathbf{k}$ *is rotating about an axis through the origin with angular velocity vector* $\mathbf{i} - 2\mathbf{j} - 2\mathbf{k}$. *Find the velocity of P.*

As above, the velocity $\mathbf{v}$ is given by

$$\begin{aligned} \mathbf{v} &= (\mathbf{i} - 2\mathbf{j} - 2\mathbf{k}) \times (\mathbf{i} + 2\mathbf{j} + \mathbf{k}) \\ &= 2\mathbf{i} - 3\mathbf{j} + 4\mathbf{k} \end{aligned}$$

Notice that the point Q position vector $\mathbf{i} - 2\mathbf{j} - 2\mathbf{k}$ lies on the axis. The position vector of P relative to Q is $4\mathbf{j} + 3\mathbf{k}$. Thus the velocity of P is
$(\mathbf{i} - 2\mathbf{j} - 2\mathbf{k}) \times (4\mathbf{j} + 3\mathbf{k})$

$$= 2\mathbf{i} - 3\mathbf{j} + 4\mathbf{k}$$

This illustrates the general result proved above that the velocity of P is independent of the point on the axis of rotation from which the position vector of P is measured.

Example 6.5. *A body is rotating with angular velocity vector* $\mathbf{i} + \mathbf{j} + \mathbf{k}$ *about an axis through the point Q whose position vector is* $2\mathbf{i} + \mathbf{j} + 3\mathbf{k}$. *Find the velocity of a point P of this body, position vector* $3\mathbf{i} - \mathbf{j} + \mathbf{k}$ *(Fig. 6.13).*

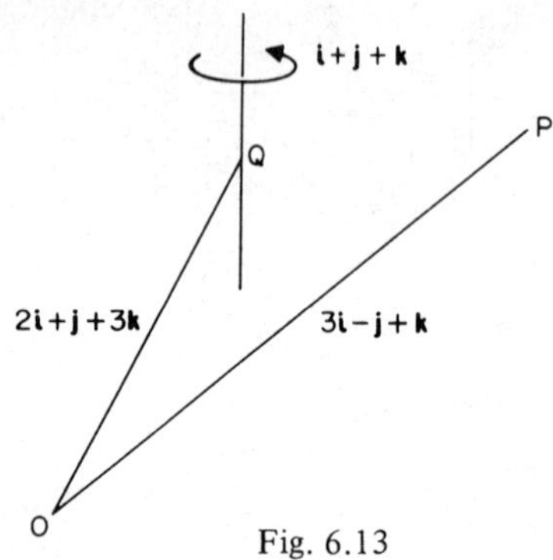

Fig. 6.13

The position vector of P relative to Q is

$$(3\mathbf{i} - \mathbf{j} + \mathbf{k}) - (2\mathbf{i} + \mathbf{j} + 3\mathbf{k}), \quad \text{i.e. } \mathbf{i} - 2\mathbf{j} - 2\mathbf{k}$$

Q is a point on the axis of rotation, so the velocity of P is

$$(\mathbf{i} + \mathbf{j} + \mathbf{k}) \times (\mathbf{i} - 2\mathbf{j} - 2\mathbf{k}) = 3\mathbf{j} - 3\mathbf{k}$$

EXERCISE 6(b)

1. A rigid body is rotating with angular speed of 4 rad s^{-1} about an axis through the origin parallel to the vector $\mathbf{i} + 2\mathbf{j} + 3\mathbf{k}$. Find the angular velocity vector of the body.

2. A rigid body has angular velocity vector $\mathbf{i} - 2\mathbf{j} - \mathbf{k}$. Find the angular speed of the body.

3. A rigid body has angular speed 2 rad s^{-1} about an axis parallel to $\mathbf{i} + \mathbf{j} + 2\mathbf{k}$ through the point position vector $\mathbf{i} + \mathbf{j} + \mathbf{k}$. Find the velocity of the point on the body whose position vector is $2\mathbf{i} - \mathbf{j} - 2\mathbf{k}$.

4. A rigid body is spinning with an angular velocity of 4 rad s^{-1} about an axis of direction $(0, 3, -1)$ passing through the point $(1, 3, -1)$. Find the magnitude and direction of the velocity of a particle at the point $(4, -2, 1)$. (*The notation $(4, -2, 1)$ is used instead of* $4\mathbf{i} - 2\mathbf{j} + \mathbf{k}$.) (M.E.I.)

5. A spaceship is rotating with angular velocity vector $2\mathbf{j} + \mathbf{k}$ about an axis through the origin. A Martian on the space ship has position vector

$2\mathbf{i} + 2\mathbf{j} - \mathbf{k}$. Find the velocity of the Martian. A second space ship is rotating with angular velocity $\mathbf{i} - 2\mathbf{k}$ about an axis through the origin. Another Martian, on the second space ship, has position vector $\mathbf{i} + \mathbf{j}$. Find the velocity of the second Martian relative to the first.

6. A satellite is moving with constant angular velocity $\boldsymbol{\omega}$ and in such a way that a certain point P of it has the constant velocity $\mathbf{v}, \neq 0$. Prove that the velocity $\mathbf{V}$ of a point Q of the body is given by

$$\mathbf{V} = \mathbf{v} + \boldsymbol{\omega} \times (\mathbf{r}_Q - \mathbf{r}_P),$$

where $\mathbf{r}_P$ and $\mathbf{r}_Q$ are the position vectors of P and Q respectively. Prove that

$$\mathbf{v} \times \boldsymbol{\omega}.(\mathbf{r}_Q - \mathbf{r}_P) = -v^2$$

is a necessary and sufficient condition that $\mathbf{V}$ is perpendicular to $\mathbf{v}$. Show that this condition cannot be satisfied if $\mathbf{v}$ is parallel to $\boldsymbol{\omega}$, and draw a diagram to illustrate why this is so. (S.M.P.)

More general motion in a plane

So far we have referred the velocity and acceleration either to mutually perpendicular axes, with unit vectors $\mathbf{i}, \mathbf{j}, \mathbf{k}$, or to unit vectors along and at right angles to the radius vector $\mathbf{r}$. It was convenient to use $\hat{\mathbf{s}}$ to denote a unit vector along the tangent at a point, and in the case of the circle $\hat{\mathbf{s}}$ was perpendicular to $\hat{\mathbf{r}}$. However, in general that is not so, and we introduce $\hat{\boldsymbol{\theta}}$ as a vector perpendicular to $\hat{\mathbf{r}}$. There is at present not a standard notation, but this causes less confusion than if we were to use $\hat{\mathbf{s}}$, since s is invariably used for arc length. We use $\hat{\mathbf{t}}$ as a unit vector along the tangent, and $\hat{\mathbf{n}}$ as a unit vector along the *inward* normal (Fig. 6.14).

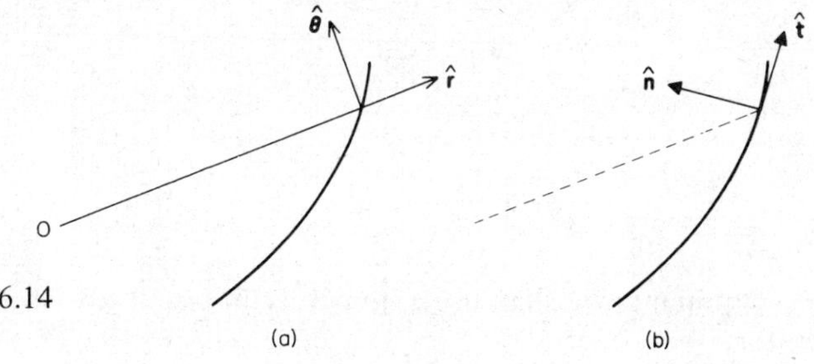

Fig. 6.14

Radial and transverse components of acceleration

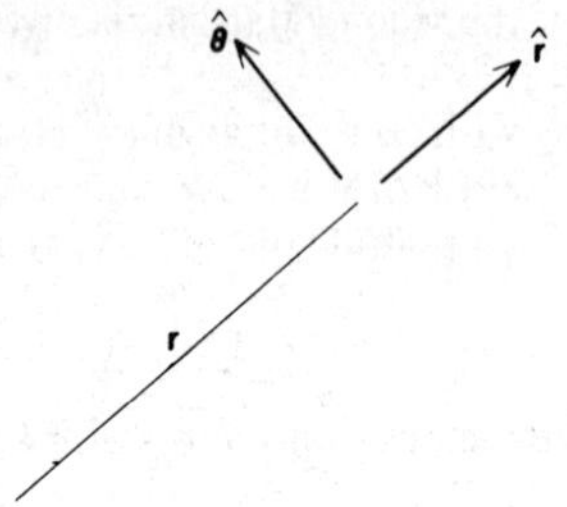

Fig. 6.15

In Fig. 6.15, since $\mathbf{r} = r\hat{\mathbf{r}}$

$$\mathbf{v} = \frac{d\mathbf{r}}{dt}$$

$$= \frac{dr}{dt}\,\hat{\mathbf{r}} + r\,\frac{d}{dt}\,(\hat{\mathbf{r}})$$

$$= \frac{dr}{dt}\,\hat{\mathbf{r}} + r\omega\,\hat{\boldsymbol{\theta}}$$

Then the acceleration $\mathbf{a} = \dfrac{d\mathbf{v}}{dt}$

$$= \frac{d^2r}{dt^2}\,\hat{\mathbf{r}} + 2\,\frac{dr}{dt}\,\omega\hat{\boldsymbol{\theta}} + r\,\frac{d\omega}{dt}\,\hat{\boldsymbol{\theta}} - r\omega^2\hat{\mathbf{r}}.$$

as $\dfrac{d\hat{\boldsymbol{\theta}}}{dt} = -\,\omega\hat{\mathbf{r}}$

$$\therefore \qquad \mathbf{a} = \left(\frac{d^2r}{dt^2} - r\omega^2\right)\hat{\mathbf{r}} + \frac{1}{r}\,\frac{d}{dt}\,(r^2\omega)\hat{\boldsymbol{\theta}}$$

These components we shall use extensively in our study of orbits in Chapter 7.

Tangential and normal components of acceleration

Let $\hat{\mathbf{t}}$ denote a unit vector along the tangent, and $\hat{\mathbf{n}}$ a unit vector along the inward normal (Fig. 6.16). Let ψ denote the angle made

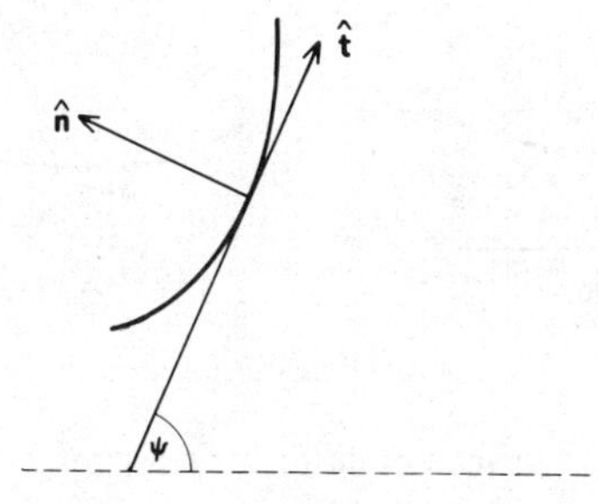

Fig. 6.16

by the tangent at P with a fixed direction. Then

$$\mathbf{v} = v\hat{\mathbf{t}}$$

so the acceleration **a** is given by

$$\mathbf{a} = \frac{\mathrm{d}\mathbf{v}}{\mathrm{d}t} = \frac{\mathrm{d}v}{\mathrm{d}t}\hat{\mathbf{t}} + v\frac{\mathrm{d}\hat{\mathbf{t}}}{\mathrm{d}t}$$

But
$$\frac{\mathrm{d}\hat{\mathbf{t}}}{\mathrm{d}t} = \frac{\mathrm{d}\psi}{\mathrm{d}t}\hat{\mathbf{n}}$$

$\therefore$
$$\frac{\mathrm{d}\mathbf{v}}{\mathrm{d}t} = \frac{\mathrm{d}v}{\mathrm{d}t}\hat{\mathbf{t}} + v\frac{\mathrm{d}\psi}{\mathrm{d}t}\hat{\mathbf{n}}$$

$$= \frac{\mathrm{d}v}{\mathrm{d}t}\hat{\mathbf{t}} + v\frac{\mathrm{d}\psi}{\mathrm{d}s}\frac{\mathrm{d}s}{\mathrm{d}t}\hat{\mathbf{n}}$$

$$= \frac{\mathrm{d}v}{\mathrm{d}t}\hat{\mathbf{t}} + \frac{v^2}{\rho}\hat{\mathbf{n}}$$

where ρ is the radius of curvature of the curve at P.

When the particle is travelling in a circle, $\hat{\mathbf{n}}$ is along the inward radius, giving the central acceleration v^2/r with which we are already familiar.

Example 6.6. *A bead mass m moves (Fig. 6.17) in a vertical plane on a smooth wire in the shape of an arch of a cycloid, equation* $s = 4a \sin \psi$. *Show that the motion is simple harmonic when the bead is disturbed from its position of equilibrium at the point (0, 0).*

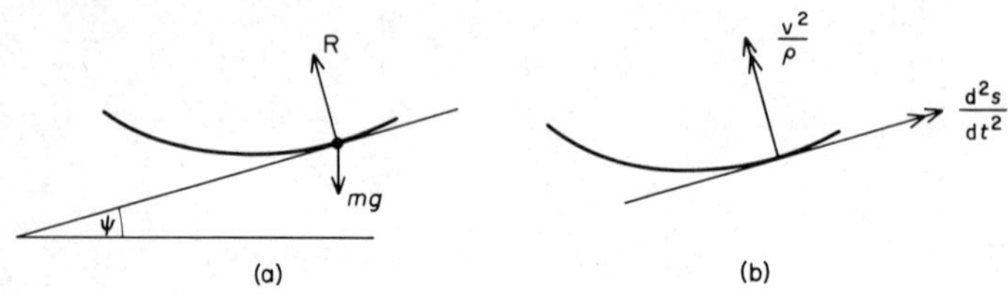

Fig. 6.17

Using the form $\mathrm{d}^2s/\mathrm{d}t^2$ instead of $\mathrm{d}v/\mathrm{d}t$ for the component of acceleration along the tangent,

$$-mg \sin \psi = m \frac{\mathrm{d}^2s}{\mathrm{d}t^2}$$

from Newton's law.

But $$\sin \psi = s/4a$$

being the equation of the cycloid,

$$\therefore \quad -mgs/4a = m \frac{\mathrm{d}^2s}{\mathrm{d}t^2}$$

i.e. $$\frac{\mathrm{d}^2s}{\mathrm{d}t^2} + \frac{g}{4a} s = 0$$

This is simple harmonic motion (s.h.m.), period $2\pi\sqrt{(4a/g)}$. This motion is an example of motion which is exactly s.h.m., not merely approximately simple harmonic for small displacements, as so many are.

Isochronous property of the cycloid

The period of this motion is independent of the velocity given to the bead to disturb it from the position of equilibrium. Thus we can see that, if the bead is released from rest at any point on the cycloid, it will describe one quarter of an oscillation before reaching the lowest point O, taking $\pi\sqrt{(a/g)}$ seconds, which is independent of the position on the cycloid from which the bead is released. This is known as the isochronous property of the cycloid.

Example 6.7. *A parachutist mass m steps from an aircraft flying horizontally with speed U. The parachute exerts a force $-mg\hat{\mathbf{v}}$, where* **v** *is the velocity of the parachutist at any instant. Show that the vertical component of the velocity of the parachutist cannot exceed $\frac{1}{2}U$ (Fig. 6.18).*

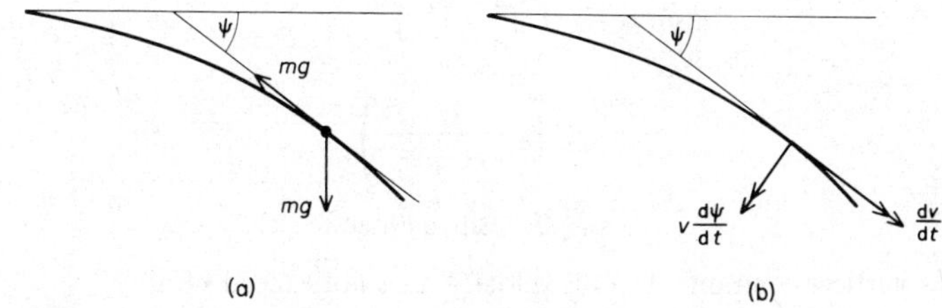

Fig. 6.18

Take the acceleration of the parachutist as

$$\frac{dv}{dt}\hat{\mathbf{t}} + v\frac{d\psi}{dt}\hat{\mathbf{n}}$$

since we require a differential equation in v and ψ. Care must be taken that $v(d\psi/dt)$ is along the inward normal, in the direction of ψ increasing. Then from Newton's law,

$$(mg \sin \psi - mg)\hat{\mathbf{t}} + mg \cos \psi\hat{\mathbf{n}} = m\left(\frac{dv}{dt}\hat{\mathbf{t}} + v\frac{d\psi}{dt}\hat{\mathbf{n}}\right)$$

i.e. $$\frac{dv}{dt} = g \sin \psi - g$$

and $$v\frac{d\psi}{dt} = g \cos \psi$$

$\therefore$ $$\frac{1}{v}\frac{dv}{d\psi} = \tan \psi - \sec \psi$$

$$\log v = \log \sec \psi - \log (\sec \psi + \tan \psi) + C$$

$$= \log\left(\frac{1}{1 + \sin \psi}\right) + C$$

But initially $v = U$ and $\psi = 0$, as the man has the velocity of the aircraft when he steps out,

$\therefore$ $$\log\left(\frac{v}{U}\right) = \log\left(\frac{1}{1 + \sin \psi}\right)$$

i.e.
$$v = U\left(\frac{1}{1 + \sin\psi}\right)$$

The vertical component of the man's velocity is $v \sin\psi$. But

$$\begin{aligned} v \sin\psi &= U\left(\frac{\sin\psi}{1 + \sin\psi}\right) \\ &= U\left(\frac{1}{\operatorname{cosec}\psi + 1}\right) \\ &\leqslant \tfrac{1}{2}U, \quad \text{since } \operatorname{cosec}\psi \geqslant 1 \end{aligned}$$

so the vertical component of his velocity does not exceed $\frac{1}{2}U$.

Curve of pursuit

The following example illustrates a family of curves encountered in many and various contexts.

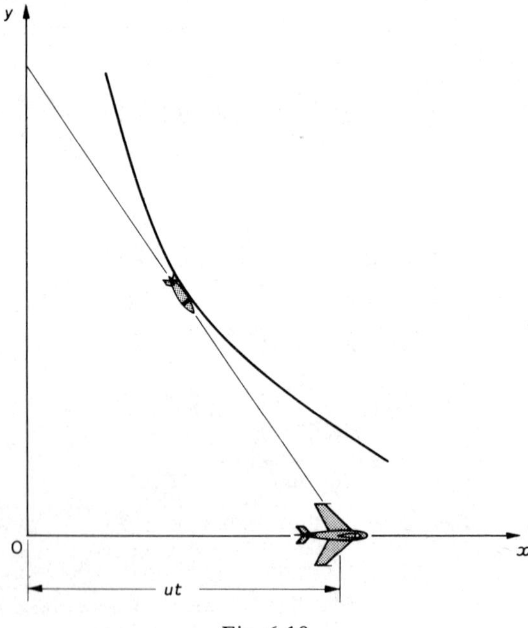

Fig. 6.19

Example 6.8. *An aircraft is flying with constant velocity* **u**i. *An enemy aircraft, relative position vector* **b**j, *launches a rocket whose speed is 2u. The rocket is designed to 'home' onto the first aircraft. Find the equation of the path of the rocket, and the time that elapses before the rocket hits the aircraft (Fig. 6.19).*

The rocket is designed so that the direction of its flight is always towards the aircraft. If the rocket has position vector $x\mathbf{i} + y\mathbf{j}$ at time t,

$$\frac{dy}{dx} = \tan\psi = \frac{-y}{ut - x}$$

But $s = 2ut$, where s is the distance travelled by the rocket, so that

$$\tfrac{1}{2}s - x = -y\frac{dx}{dy}$$

Now the only relations between s, x, and y are between their differentials,

$$\therefore \quad \frac{1}{2}\frac{ds}{dy} - \frac{dx}{dy} = -\frac{dx}{dy} - y\frac{d^2x}{dy^2}$$

i.e.
$$\frac{1}{2}\frac{ds}{dy} = -y\frac{d^2x}{dy^2} \tag{6.1}$$

Since
$$\left(\frac{ds}{dy}\right)^2 = 1 + \left(\frac{dx}{dy}\right)^2$$

$$\left(\frac{ds}{dy}\right) = -\sqrt{\left[1 + \left(\frac{dx}{dy}\right)^2\right]}$$

negative since s decreases as y increases.

$$\therefore \quad -\frac{1}{2}\sqrt{\left[1 + \left(\frac{dx}{dy}\right)^2\right]} = -y\frac{d^2x}{dy^2} \quad \text{from equation 6.1.}$$

Put
$$z = \frac{dx}{dy}, \quad \text{i.e.}\ \frac{d^2x}{dy^2} = \frac{dz}{dy}$$

Then
$$\sqrt{(1 + z^2)} = 2y\frac{dz}{dy}$$

i.e.
$$\tfrac{1}{2}\log y + \log C = \sinh^{-1}(z)$$

But $y = b$ when z, i.e., dx/dy, $= 0$, since the rocket is launched at right angles to the path of the aircraft,

$$\therefore \qquad \log\left(\frac{y}{b}\right)^{1/2} = \sinh^{-1} z$$

i.e.

$$z = \frac{1}{2}\left[\left(\frac{y}{b}\right)^{1/2} - \left(\frac{y}{b}\right)^{-1/2}\right]$$

$$\therefore \qquad 2\frac{dx}{dy} = \left(\frac{y}{b}\right)^{1/2} - \left(\frac{y}{b}\right)^{-1/2}$$

i.e.

$$2x + C = \tfrac{2}{3}y^{3/2}b^{-1/2} - 2y^{1/2}b^{1/2}$$

But when $x = 0$, $y = b$, therefore $C = -\frac{4}{3}b$, so the equation of the path of the rocket is

$$x = \tfrac{1}{3}y^{3/2}b^{-1/2} - y^{1/2}b^{1/2} + \tfrac{2}{3}b$$

The rocket hits the aircraft when $y = 0$, i.e. $x = \frac{2}{3}b$. The aircraft has taken $2b/3u$ to fly this distance, so the time that elapses before the rocket hits the aircraft is $2b/3u$. Notice if the aircraft had remained at rest, the rocket would have hit it sooner, in time $b/2u$.

EXERCISE 6(c)

1. A particle moves so that the tangential and normal components of acceleration are constant. Prove that the path of the particle is in general a spiral of the form $s = A\,e^{k\psi}$. Investigate any special cases.

2. Prove that, when a particle moves in a plane, the radius of curvature ρ of its path is given by $\rho = v^3/|\mathbf{v} \times \mathbf{a}|$, where **a**, **v** are the acceleration and velocity vectors and v is the magnitude of **v**.
Given that at a certain instant $\mathbf{v} = 4\mathbf{i} - 3\mathbf{j}$ and $\mathbf{a} = 3\mathbf{i} + 4\mathbf{j}$, find the value of ρ. (J.M.B.)

3. A particle mass m has position vector **r** relative to a fixed point O. It is acted upon by a force

$$\lambda\mathbf{k} \times \frac{d\mathbf{r}}{dt} - \mu\mathbf{r}$$

where λ and μ are positive constants, and **k** is one of a right handed set **i**, **j**, **k** of mutually orthogonal unit vectors. Write down the equation of motion of the particle.

Show that if $\mathbf{r} = x\mathbf{i} + y\mathbf{j} + z\mathbf{k}$, then z satisfies the equation

$$m \frac{\mathrm{d}^2 z}{\mathrm{d}t^2} + \mu z = 0$$

Deduce that if $\mathbf{r}$ and $\mathrm{d}\mathbf{r}/\mathrm{d}t$ are initially perpendicular to $\mathbf{k}$, the particle moves in a plane.
Show also that the vector equation of motion is satisfied by $\mathbf{r} = a(\mathbf{i} \cos \omega t + \mathbf{j} \sin \omega t)$ where a is an arbitrary constant, and ω is either of the two real roots of a certain quadratic equation. Deduce that the particle can describe a circle about O under this force with either of two constant angular speeds. (J.M.B.)

4. Three point-elements A, B, C of a lamina moving in its own plane are such that their position vectors are given, as functions of time t, by $\mathbf{r}_A = \mathbf{R}(t)$, $\mathbf{r}_B = \mathbf{R}(t) + a\mathbf{S}(t)$, $\mathbf{r}_C = \mathbf{R}(t) + b\, \mathrm{d}\mathbf{S}/\mathrm{d}t$ where $\mathbf{S}(t)$ is a unit vector and $\mathrm{d}\mathbf{S}/\mathrm{d}t$ is its derivative with respect to time, and a and b are constants. Prove that,
(a) the angle subtended by BC at A is a right angle,
(b) the magnitude of the body's angular velocity is constant. (S.M.P.)

5. A particle is projected in a medium which offers a resistance to motion equal to $k\mathbf{v}$ per unit mass, k being a constant. Prove that in the subsequent motion

$$\frac{\mathrm{d}v}{\mathrm{d}\psi} = v \tan \psi + \frac{k}{g} v^2 \sec \psi$$

By means of the integrating factor $\sec \psi / v^2$, solve this differential equation to obtain a relation between v and ψ. If the particle is projected with velocity $10\sqrt{3}g/k$ at an angle of elevation 60°, prove that the velocity at the highest point of its path is $5\sqrt{3}g/16k$. (O. & C.)

6. A particle lies on a rough plane which is inclined at an angle α to the horizontal, and the coefficient of friction between the particle and the plane is $2 \tan \alpha$. The particle is projected along the plane in a direction perpendicular to the line of greatest slope with velocity V. Prove that, if v is the velocity of the particle and ψ the inclination of its path to the initial direction after time t,

$$\frac{\mathrm{d}v}{\mathrm{d}t} = g \sin \alpha \sin \psi - 2g \sin \alpha$$

$$v \frac{\mathrm{d}\psi}{\mathrm{d}t} = g \sin \alpha \cos \psi$$

Deduce an expression for $\mathrm{d}v/\mathrm{d}\psi$ and prove that

$$v = \frac{V \sec \psi}{(\sec \psi + \tan \psi)^2}$$

$$\frac{\mathrm{d}\psi}{\mathrm{d}t} = \frac{g \sin \alpha \cos^2 \psi}{V(\sec \psi - \tan \psi)^2}$$

Prove that the direction of motion is inclined at 45° to the initial direction after time $V(7 - 4\sqrt{2})/3g \sin \alpha$. (O. & C.)

7. A bomb is released from an aeroplane travelling horizontally at a speed U, and the air resistance per unit mass on the bomb is k times its speed. Prove that at time t after its release the bomb has travelled a horizontal distance $U(1 - e^{-kt})/k$.
Find the downward velocity of the bomb at this instant and prove that its path is inclined to the horizontal at an angle $\tan^{-1} [g(e^{kt} - 1)/kU]$. (O. & C.)

8. A smooth wire is bent into the form $y = \sin x$ and placed in a vertical plane with the x axis horizontal. A bead of mass m slides down the wire starting from rest at $x = \frac{1}{4}\pi$. Show that the force on the wire as the bead passes through the origin is $mg/\sqrt{2}$, and find the force as it passes through $x = -\frac{1}{2}\pi$. (C.S.)

9. A switchback railway consists of straight stretches smoothly joined by circular arcs, the whole lying in a vertical plane. Show that a car started on a level stretch and running freely will leave the track if the downward gradient exceeds $\cos^{-1} (\frac{2}{3})$ at any point; but that if braking up to half the weight of the car is available, gradients of about 70° are admissible.
A level and a straight descending stretch are smoothly joined by an arc of radius a. Two equal cars without brakes are joined by a cable of length $2a$. Show that the greatest admissible gradient such that the second car does not leave the track is $\cos^{-1} (11/12)$. (C.S.)

10. The motion of a boomerang is illustrated by a particle of mass m moving in a horizontal plane with instantaneous speed v under the action of a tangential resistive force $mkv^2 \cos \alpha$ and a normal force $mkv^2 \sin \alpha$ tending to deflect the particle to the right, where α is a constant acute angle. If it is projected with speed U, show that it returns to the point of projection after a time

$$\frac{\exp (2\pi \cot \alpha) - 1}{kU \cos \alpha}$$

where $\exp (z) \equiv e^z$. (C.S.)

7. Dynamics of a Particle Moving in a Plane

Motion of a particle under gravity

We have seen that Newton's second law of motion is fundamental to our study of dynamics. If we consider only the force due to gravity $m\mathbf{g}$ acting on a body mass m, and consider only motion over distances such that $\mathbf{g}$ may be regarded as constant,

$$\mathbf{F} = m\mathbf{a} \Rightarrow m\mathbf{g} = m\mathbf{a}$$

i.e.

$$\mathbf{a} = \mathbf{g}$$

Integrating,

$$\mathbf{v} = \mathbf{u} + t\mathbf{g} \tag{7.1}$$

where u is the initial velocity. This is illustrated in Fig. 7.1. Considering the velocity of the particle after subsequent intervals $t_1, t_2, t_3, \ldots$ we see in Fig. 7.2 that since the direction of $\mathbf{g}$ is constant, i.e. vertical, there is no change in the horizontal component of the velocity.

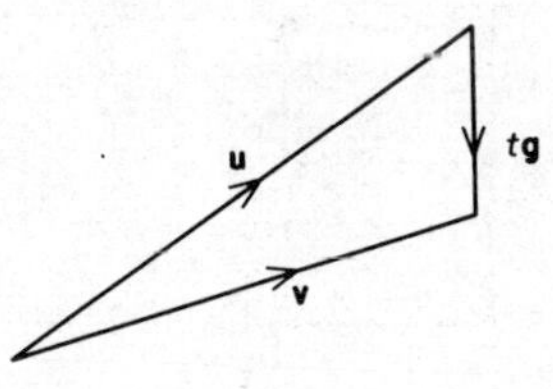

Fig. 7.1

Thus the horizontal component of the velocity remains unchanged throughout the motion, while the vertical component changes by $\mathbf{g}$ per unit interval of time.

Integrating equation 7.1,

$$\mathbf{s} = t\mathbf{u} + \tfrac{1}{2}t^2\mathbf{g}$$

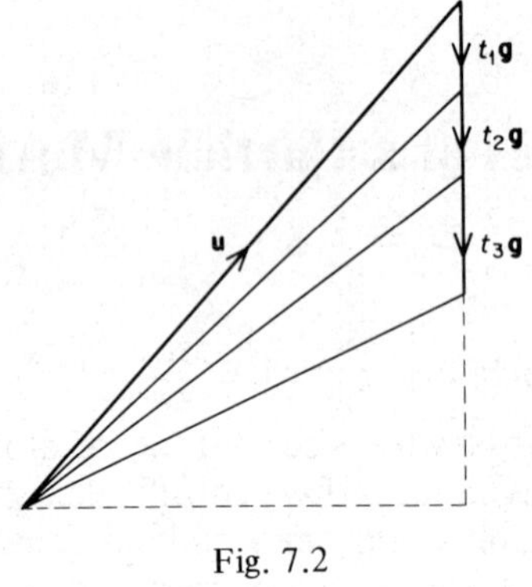

Fig. 7.2

taking s = 0 when $t = 0$, where s is the position vector of the particle at time t.

Use of rectangular coordinate axes

It is often convenient to refer the data of a problem to horizontal and vertical axes, and to use **i** to denote a unit horizontal vector and **k** unit vertical vector, upwards being taken as the positive

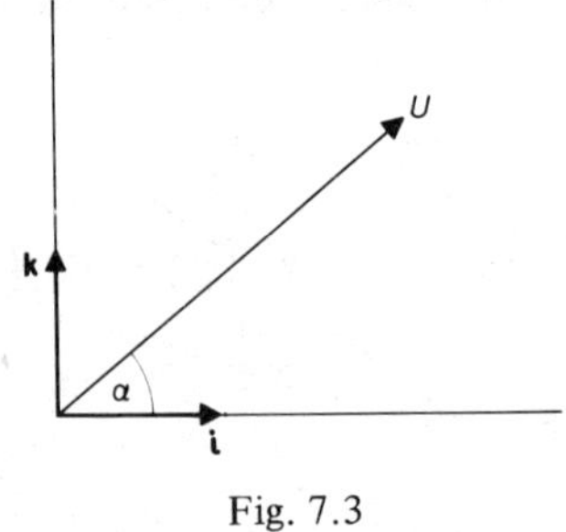

Fig. 7.3

direction (Fig. 7.3). Thus for a particle projected with velocity U at an angle α above the horizontal,

$$x\mathbf{i} + y\mathbf{k} = t(U\cos\alpha\mathbf{i} + U\sin\alpha\mathbf{k}) - \tfrac{1}{2}gt^2\mathbf{k}$$

since $\mathbf{g} = -g\mathbf{k}$.

Equating components,

$$x = U \cos \alpha t$$
$$y = U \sin \alpha t - \tfrac{1}{2}gt^2$$

Eliminating t,

$$y = U \sin \alpha \left(\frac{x}{U \cos \alpha}\right) - \tfrac{1}{2}g\left(\frac{x}{U \cos \alpha}\right)^2$$

i.e. $$y = x \tan \alpha - \frac{gx^2 \sec^2 \alpha}{2U^2}$$

This is the Cartesian equation of the trajectory and is recognized as that of a parabola with axis vertical.

Example 7.1. *A ball is thrown with velocity 7 m s^{-1} from a point at the top of a quarry so as to hit the floor 40 m below the level of the point of projection and at a horizontal distance of 20 m from that point. Show there are two possible paths and find the angle of elevation of each of them.*

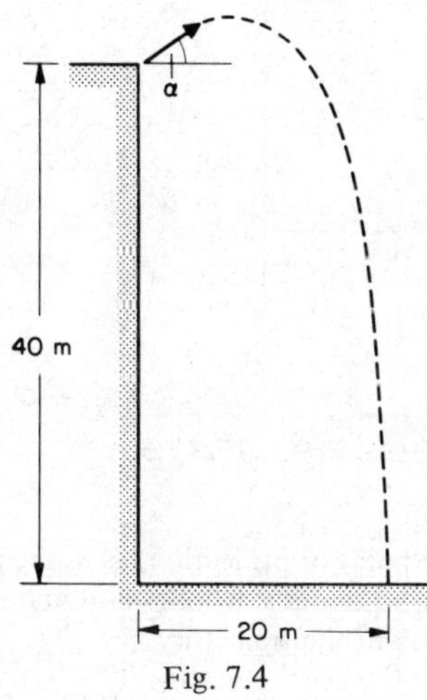

Fig. 7.4

Denote the angle of elevation by α (Fig. 7.4). The coordinates of the point at which the ball strikes the floor of the quarry are (20, –40), so substituting in the equation of the trajectory,

$$-40 = 20 \tan \alpha - \tfrac{1}{2}(9.8)\frac{400}{49} \sec^2 \alpha$$

i.e. $$-2 = \tan\alpha - 2\sec^2\alpha$$

i.e. $$2\tan^2\alpha - \tan\alpha = 0, \quad \text{since } \sec^2\alpha = 1 + \tan^2\alpha$$

i.e. $$\tan\alpha = 0 \quad \text{or} \quad \tfrac{1}{2}$$

The ball can thus be thrown horizontally or at an angle $\tan^{-1}\frac{1}{2}$ above the horizontal.

Example 7.2. *A stone is thrown from the top of a tower, height 40 m, reaches a maximum height 49 m above the ground, and then strikes the ground at a distance 10 m from the foot of the tower at a point on the same horizontal level as the foot of the tower. Find the angle of elevation at which the stone is projected (Fig. 7.5).*

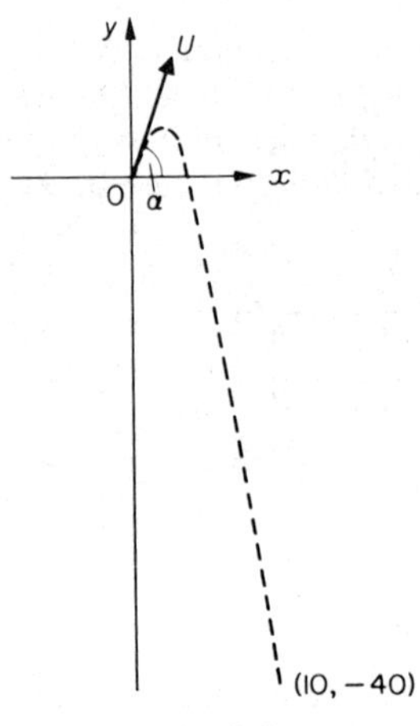

Fig. 7.5

Take axes through the point of projection, as in the previous example. Since the stone passes through the point whose coordinates are (10, –40), substituting in the equation of the trajectory,

$$-40 = 10\tan\alpha - \frac{1}{2}\frac{g(100)}{U^2}\sec^2\alpha \tag{7.2}$$

But the greatest height the stone rises above the point of projection is 9 m,

$$\therefore \quad \frac{U^2}{2g}\sin^2\alpha = 9$$

from $v^2 = u^2 + 2as$, v being zero at the highest point, $a = -g$, $u = U \sin \alpha$ and $s = 9$,

i.e.
$$\frac{g}{U^2} = \frac{1}{18} \sin^2 \alpha$$

Substituting in equation 7.2,

$$-40 = 10 \tan \alpha - \frac{50}{18} \tan^2 \alpha$$

i.e.
$$5 \tan^2 \alpha - 18 \tan \alpha - 72 = 0$$
$$(\tan \alpha - 6)(5 \tan \alpha + 12) = 0$$
$$\tan \alpha = 6 \quad \text{or } -12/5$$

Since the stone must be projected upwards, the only possible value of $\tan \alpha$ is 6.

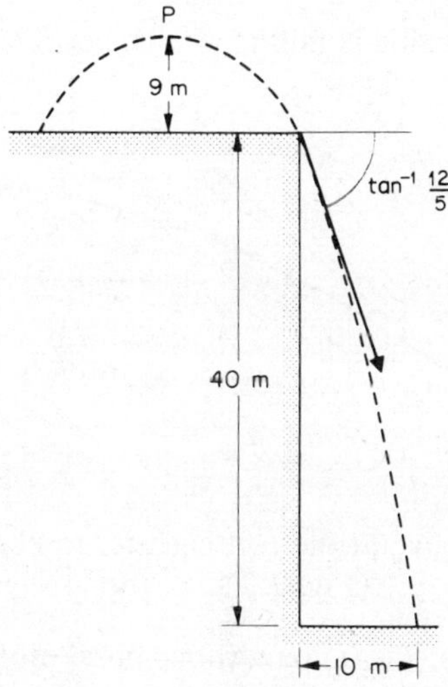

Fig. 7.6

The existence of the other root illustrates that a projectile only travels along *part* of the trajectory; a parabola is unending, whereas the motion of the projectile begins at a particular point on the trajectory. Fig. 7.6 shows the geometrical significance of the value $\tan^{-1}(12/5)$. There is a point P on this path 9 m above the top of the tower, and the path goes through both the point of projection and the point at which the stone strikes the ground.

Direction of motion

At any moment in flight, a projectile is travelling along the tangent to its path (page 146). If this tangent is inclined to the horizontal at an angle ψ, $\tan \psi = dy/dx$,

i.e.
$$\tan \psi = \tan \alpha - \frac{gx}{U^2} \sec^2 \alpha$$

whence ψ can be found for any x. (Notice that $\tan \psi < \tan \alpha$ for all ψ.) Thus in Example 7.2 above, the stone strikes the ground at an angle ψ to the horizontal where

$$\begin{aligned}\tan \psi &= 6 - \frac{10}{18} \times 36 \\ &= -14\end{aligned}$$

As expected, the stone is falling almost vertically when it strikes the ground.

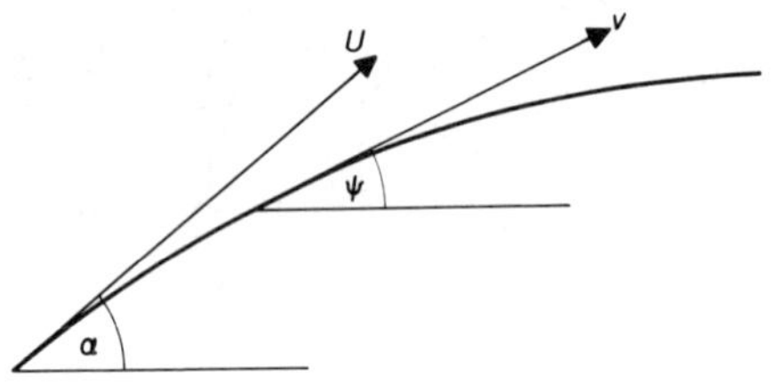

Fig. 7.7

To find ψ at a given time t, it is easier to consider the resolved parts of the velocity v (Fig. 7.7),

$$v \cos \psi = U \cos \alpha \text{ (horizontal motion)}$$
$$v \sin \psi = U \sin \alpha - gt \text{ (vertical motion)}$$

whence

$$\tan \psi = \tan \alpha - (gt/U) \sec \alpha$$

Example 7.3. *A shell is fired at 100 m s^{-1} at an angle $\tan^{-1} 2$ above the horizontal. Find the angle made by the shell with the horizontal two seconds later.*

Since the horizontal velocity is unaltered,

$$v \cos \psi = 100 \cos \alpha, \quad \text{where } \tan \alpha = 2$$

From the vertical motion,

$$v \sin \psi = 100 \sin \alpha - 2g$$

$$\therefore \qquad \tan \psi = \tan \alpha - (g/50) \sec \alpha$$

$$\text{i.e.} \qquad \tan \psi \simeq 1.56$$

$$\psi \simeq \tan^{-1} (1.56)$$

Range on an inclined plane

We have seen (*Additional Applied Mathematics*, Chapter 14) that the range on a horizontal plane through the point of projection is $V^2 \sin 2\alpha/g$, which has a maximum value of V^2/g when $\alpha = \pi/4$, and also that the greatest height attained by a projectile is $V^2 \sin^2 \alpha/2g$, the maximum value of which is $V^2/2g$. These results are easy to use and should be committed to memory.

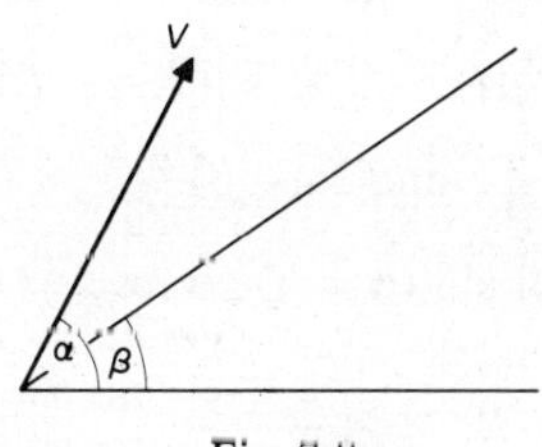

Fig. 7.8

If a particle is projected onto a plane inclined at β to the horizontal, through the point of projection, suppose the range on this plane is denoted by R. Then the position vector of the point at which the projectile meets the plane is $R \cos \beta\mathbf{i} + R \sin \beta\mathbf{k}$. The position vector of the projectile at time t is

$$Vt \cos \alpha\mathbf{i} + (Vt \sin \alpha - \tfrac{1}{2}gt^2)\mathbf{k},$$

so equating components,

$$R \cos \beta = V \cos \alpha t$$

$$\text{and} \qquad R \sin \beta = V \sin \alpha t - \tfrac{1}{2}gt^2$$

whence $$R \sin \beta = R \sin \alpha \frac{\cos \beta}{\cos \alpha} - \frac{gR^2 \cos^2 \beta}{2V^2 \cos^2 \alpha}$$

Alternatively, this could have been obtained by substituting ($R \cos \beta, R \sin \beta$) in the equation of the trajectory.

From this equation we have

$$R = 0 \quad \text{or} \quad R = \frac{2V^2(\sin \alpha \cos \beta - \cos \alpha \sin \beta)}{g \cos^2 \beta} \cos \alpha$$

The root $R = 0$ corresponds to the trivial solution that the line of the plane and the trajectory intersect at the point of projection. The other root gives the range R, where

$$R = \frac{2V^2 \sin (\alpha - \beta) \cos \alpha}{g \cos^2 \beta}$$

since $$\sin (\alpha - \beta) = \sin \alpha \cos \beta - \cos \alpha \sin \beta.$$

To find the maximum range R_{max}, since

$$2 \sin (\alpha - \beta) \cos \alpha = [\sin (2\alpha - \beta) - \sin \beta]$$

and $$\sin (2\alpha - \beta) \leqslant 1$$

the maximum value of $\sin (\alpha - \beta) \cos \alpha$ is $\frac{1}{2}(1 - \sin \beta)$,

i.e. $$R_{max} = \frac{V^2(1 - \sin \beta)}{g \cos^2 \beta}$$

This occurs when $2\alpha - \beta = \pi/2$, i.e. $\alpha = \frac{1}{2}[(\pi/2) + \beta]$. At this angle, the direction of the initial motion bisects the angle between the plane and the vertical (Fig. 7.9).

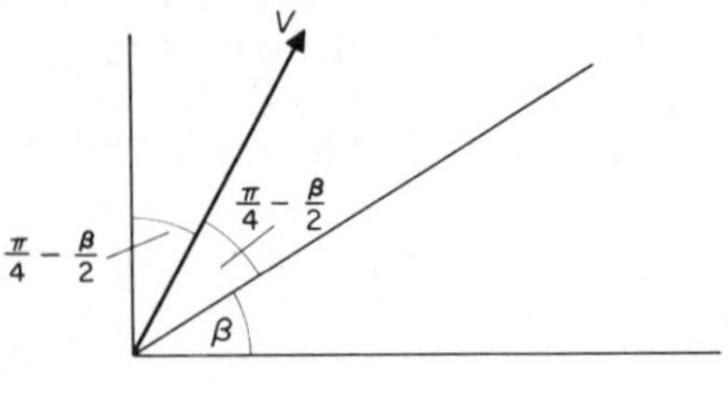

Fig. 7.9

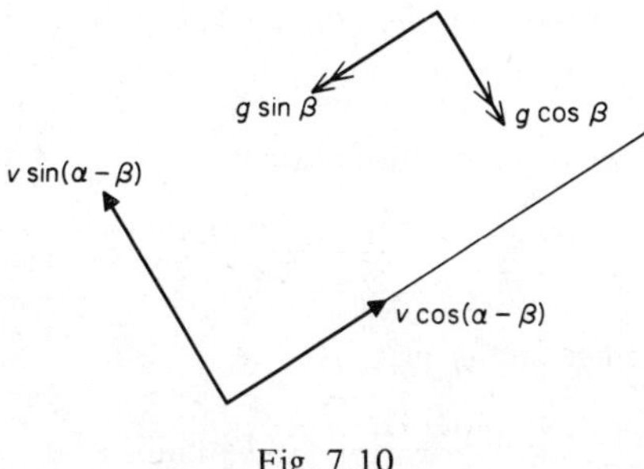

Fig. 7.10

Instead of the horizontal and vertical components we could have considered the motion along the perpendicular to the inclined plane (Fig. 7.10). Using the components of velocity and of acceleration shown in Fig. 7.10, we see that the time of flight T is given by

$$2V \sin (\alpha - \beta) = T(g \cos \beta)$$

i.e.

$$T = \frac{2V \sin (\alpha - \beta)}{g \cos \beta}$$

It is, however, almost invariably better to consider the horizontal and vertical components of the vectors. The commonest exceptions are problems concerning bodies bouncing on inclined planes (see page 193).

Example 7.4. *The greatest range of a certain gun on a horizontal plane is 10 km. Find its greatest range (a) up a plane inclined at 30° above the horizontal, (b) down the same plane (Fig. 7.11).*

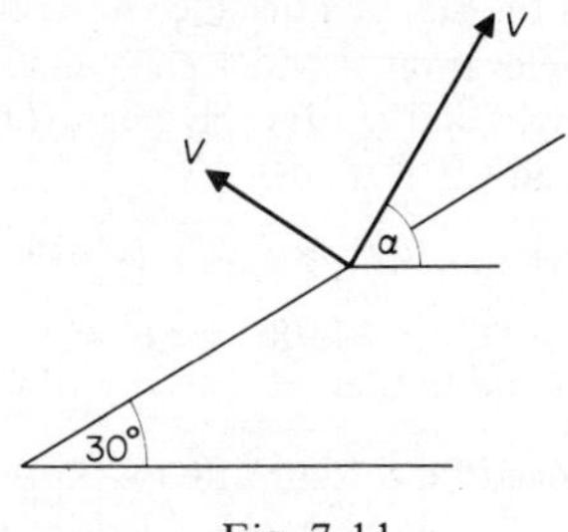

Fig. 7.11

Since the maximum range on a horizontal plane is V^2/g,

$$V^2/g = 10$$

The maximum range on an inclined plane is

$$\frac{V^2(1 - \sin\beta)}{g\cos^2\beta}$$

$\therefore$ the maximum range on this plane is

$$\frac{10(1 - \frac{1}{2})}{\frac{3}{4}} = 6\tfrac{2}{3}\text{ km}$$

The greatest range down the plane is found by putting $\beta = -30°$,

i.e.
$$R_{max} = \frac{10}{\frac{3}{4}}(1 + \tfrac{1}{2})$$
$$= 20\text{ km}$$

The greatest range up the plane is $6\frac{2}{3}$ km and down the plane is 20 km.

EXERCISE 7(a)

1. A ball is thrown at such an angle that the range on a horizontal plane is three times the greatest height attained by the ball. Find the angle to the horizontal at which the ball was thrown.

2. The maximum range of a certain gun on a horizontal plane is R. Find the two possible angles α at which the gun can be fired to give a range of $\frac{1}{2}R$. If T_1, T_2 are the corresponding times of flight, find $T_1 : T_2$.

3. With the data of Question 2, if H_1 and H_2 are the greatest heights attained on the two paths, find $H_1 : H_2$.

4. A shell is fired with velocity 70 m s^{-1} and strikes a target on the same horizontal level as the gun at a distance of 480 m. Show there are two possible angles of elevation at which the gun could be fired. If T_1, T_2 are the times of flight and H_1, H_2 the greatest heights attained on each path, find $T_1 : T_2$ and $H_1 : H_2$.

5. A shell is fired with velocity 147 m s^{-1} at 45° above the horizontal. How far does it pass above a target 2 km away on the same horizontal level? How far beyond the target does it strike the ground?

6. The maximum range of a certain rifle is 2 km. Show that the range is increased by about 560 m when the rifle is mounted in a car travelling

at 100 km h^{-1} towards the target, the angle of elevation being unaltered.

7. Two particles are projected simultaneously from the same point with the same initial speed, but at angles α_1, α_2 above the horizontal. Show that the line joining them is always inclined at an angle $\frac{1}{2}(\alpha_1 + \alpha_2)$ to the vertical.

8. A stone thrown with velocity 28 m s^{-1} just clears a wall 5.1 m high which is 20 m from the point of projection. Assuming the stone is thrown from a point at the same horizontal level as the foot of the wall, find the angle above the horizontal at which the stone is thrown.

9. A ball is thrown from a point on the ground 10 m from a vertical garden wall and just clears this wall and another parallel wall. The distance between the walls is 20 m, and the height of each wall is 2 m. The plane in which the ball travels is perpendicular to the planes of the walls. Find the angle above the horizontal at which the ball was projected, and the greatest height above the top of the walls attained by the ball.

10. A boy throws a stone with a velocity of 7 m s^{-1} and shortly afterwards throws another stone from the same point with the same speed but at a different angle of elevation. The stones collide at a point 1 m horizontally from and 1.5 m vertically above the point of projection. Find the time that elapsed between the throwing of the stones.

11. A body is projected from a point O on horizontal ground with a velocity of 70 m s^{-1} and passes through a point P 45 m above the ground and at a horizontal distance of 50 m from O. Find the tangents of the two possible angles of elevation at which the body could have been projected. Find also the gradients at P to the two paths.

12. A cricketer bowls the ball at the wicket which is at a horizontal distance of 20 m from him. The ball strikes the wicket 2 m below the level of the point at which it was released by the bowler, without hitting the ground. The greatest height above the bowler's hand, reached by the ball was 1.6 m. Find the angle of elevation at which the ball was projected and the angle made with the horizontal by the direction of motion of the ball as it strikes the stumps.

13. A vertical wall of height h stands on horizontal ground. When a particle is projected in a vertical plane at right angles to the wall from a point on the ground distant a from the wall, it just clears the wall at the highest point of its trajectory. Find the speed of projection and the angle of projection.

The particle is next projected from the same point with the same speed and the same angle of projection in a vertical plane making an angle of 45° with the wall. Show that the distance below the top of the wall at which it strikes the wall is

$$h(3 - 2\sqrt{2}) \qquad \text{(C.)}$$

14. A particle is projected from a point O on horizontal ground with velocity V at angle of elevation θ. Prove that the range R and the greatest height reached H are given by

$$R = \frac{V^2}{g}\sin 2\theta, \quad H = \frac{V^2}{2g}\sin^2\theta$$

(a) Find the value of θ if $R = H$. (b) A particle is projected from O with velocity V and angle of elevation α. A second particle is projected from O with the same velocity but angle of elevation β, where $\tan\beta = 2\tan\alpha$. The ranges and greatest heights are R_1, H_1, and R_2, H_2 respectively. If $R_1 : R_2 = 13 : 20$, find the ratio $H_1 : H_2$. (C.)

15. A particle is projected with velocity V at an angle α to the horizontal from a point on a plane of inclination β ($\beta < \alpha$). Find the condition that it strikes the plane at right angles.

16. A ball is projected with velocity V at an angle α to the horizontal so that it just clears two walls of equal height b which are a distance b apart. Show that

$$2V\cos\alpha\sqrt{(V^2\sin^2\alpha - 2bg)} = bg$$

17. A ball is projected from a point O at an angle of elevation α. Prove that, if $\tan\alpha > 2\sqrt{2}$, there are two points P and Q on its trajectory such that the directions of motion at P and Q are perpendicular to OP and OQ respectively. Prove also, that, if $\tan\alpha = 3$ and p and q are the x coordinates of P and Q, then $5p = 4q$. (O. & C.)

18. The speed at which a boy can throw a cricket ball is $v\sqrt{(\cos\theta)}$, where θ is the angle of elevation at which he throws the ball. Find the greatest height to which he can throw the ball, and the greatest range on a horizontal plane.

19. A long jumper at the instant of leaving the ground has a horizontal velocity u (due to his run), together with a velocity λu inclined at θ to the horizontal, due to his jump. Find an expression for the horizontal length l of his jump, and show that if $\lambda = 1$ and θ is chosen to make l a maximum then his greatest height during the jump is about equal to $\frac{1}{7}l$. (M.E.I.)

20. A ship is sailing ahead with velocity V. A gun on the ship points backwards and is fixed at an angle of elevation α. If the velocity of projection of the shell relative to the gun is v, show that the range of the gun is

$$\frac{2v}{g}\sin\alpha\,(v\cos\alpha - V)$$

and find the angle of elevation for maximum range.

21. The maximum range of a certain rifle is 2 km. Find the maximum range of this rifle if mounted in a car travelling at 49 m s^{-1} towards the target, and the angle of elevation required to give this maximum range.

22. A stone, projected with velocity V at an angle of elevation $\alpha°$ from a point O on the top of a cliff, hits a small object A at a horizontal distance a from O and at a vertical distance h below the level of O. A hit is also made if the stone is projected from O with velocity V at an angle of depression of $(90 - \alpha)°$. Prove that

$$V^2 + ga\cot 2\alpha° = 0 \quad \text{and} \quad h + a\tan 2\alpha° = 0$$

Find also, when $\alpha = 60$, the tangent of the angle between the two trajectories at impact with the object A. (O. & C.)

23. Points A, B lie on the same horizontal plane at a distance d metres apart. A projectile is fired from A in the vertical plane through AB towards B with speed v m s^{-1} at an angle of elevation θ. Simultaneously a particle is fired from B in the same vertical plane towards A with a speed $2v$ m s^{-1} at an angle of elevation ϕ. Find an expression for the distance between the two particles when one is vertically above the other, and hence prove that they collide if $\sin\phi = \frac{1}{2}\sin\theta$. If $\theta = \frac{1}{3}\pi$, prove that they collide at a point above the level of AB if

$$v^2 > \frac{gd(\sqrt{13} - 1)}{6\sqrt{3}}$$ (O. & C.)

24. A ball is thrown with velocity V at an angle of elevation α by a boy standing a distance a from a smooth vertical wall. The ball is caught by the boy with his hand in the same position. Show that

$$\sin 2\alpha = \frac{ga(1 + 1/e)}{V^2}$$

where e is the coefficient of restitution between the ball and the wall.

Motion in a circle in a vertical plane

Since a particle when projected will move in a parabola if its weight is the only force acting on it, if the particle is to be made to move in a circle there must be at least one other force acting. This force may be the tension in a string, or the force exerted by a circular wire on a ring free to slide on that wire, or the force exerted by the road on a car when it is travelling over a hump-backed bridge. Unless there is such a force, the body will not move in a circle. The string may break and the body will become a projectile and travel in a parabola; the car leaves the surface of the road if it is travelling so fast that there is not sufficient force to provide the necessary central acceleration--though in practice this is mitigated by the springing of the car!

When a particle is describing a circle radius a with speed v, we have seen (page 161) that its acceleration is

$$\frac{\mathrm{d}v}{\mathrm{d}t}\,\hat{\mathbf{s}} + \frac{v^2}{a}\,\hat{\mathbf{n}}$$

where $\mathrm{d}v/\mathrm{d}t = 0$ if v is a constant. To solve problems in circular motion we usually just apply Newton's law, $\mathbf{F} = m\mathbf{a}$.

Example 7.5. *A stone mass 0.5 kg is suspended by an inelastic string, length 0.4 m, one end of which is fixed. When the stone is at rest with the string vertical, it receives an impulse of 4 N s. Find the tension in the string before and immediately after the impulse.*

When the stone is in equilibrium (Fig. 7.12), $T - 0.5g = 0$,

i.e. $$T = 4.9 \text{ N}$$

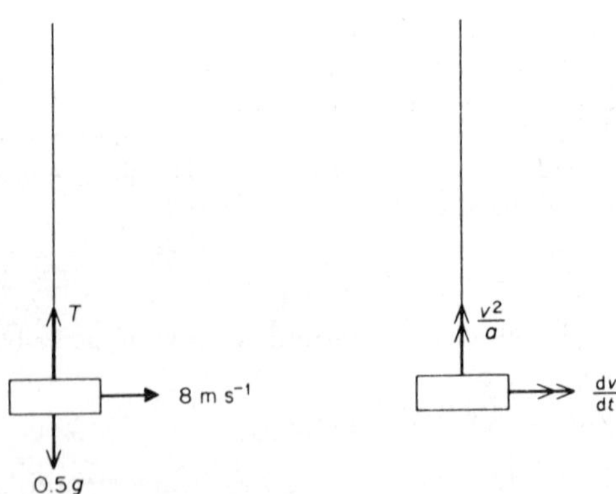

Fig. 7.12

After the impulse the stone has velocity 8 m s^{-1} in a circle radius 0.4 m, so there is an acceleration towards the centre of $8^2/(0.4)$ m s^{-2}, i.e. 160 m s^{-2}.

$$\therefore \qquad T - 0.5g = 0.5 \times 160$$

$$T = 84.9 \text{ N}$$

Thus the tension before the impulse was 4.9 N, then increased to 84.9 N.

The centrifuge

A centrifuge is a vessel that can be rotated at a high speed. Liquids placed in this vessel are subject to very large forces, for if a body is to describe a circle at a fairly high speed, it will have to have a large central acceleration. If the forces acting on the body cannot produce that acceleration, then the body will not move in a circle, as emphasized above. Centrifuges made at present can rotate at nearly 250 000 r.p.m., and even though the radius of this model is only $\frac{1}{4}$ cm, to rotate in a circle at this speed would require a force nearly 200 000 times the weight of the particle. They are used extensively in chemistry, in work on plastics, and even in refining sugar.

Critical values of greatest speed

Consider now a small stone, mass m, being whirled in a vertical circle on the end of a string length a, one end of which is fixed. Suppose the motion is started by giving the stone a velocity U when the string is hanging vertically. For what values of U will the stone make complete circles?

The forces on the stone must be sufficient to produce the necessary accelerations, Fig. 7.13, so that

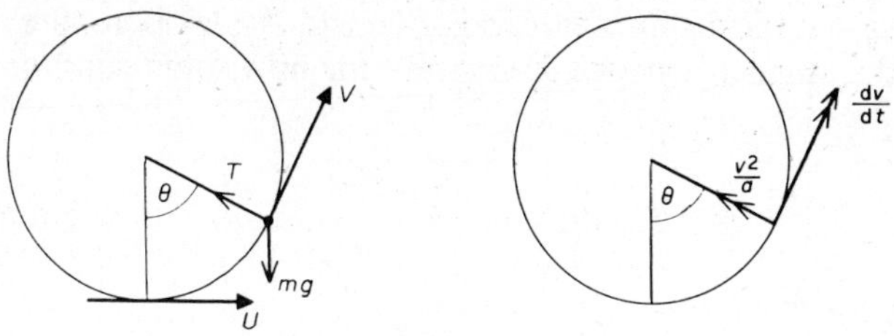

Fig. 7.13

$$\mathbf{T} + m\mathbf{g} = m\left(\frac{\mathrm{d}v}{\mathrm{d}t}\,\hat{\mathbf{s}} + \frac{v^2}{a}\,\hat{\mathbf{n}}\right)$$

If the radius vector through the stone is inclined at an angle θ to the vertical, we have

$$\mathbf{T} = T\hat{\mathbf{n}}$$

and
$$m\mathbf{g} = -mg\sin\theta\,\hat{\mathbf{s}} - mg\cos\theta\,\hat{\mathbf{n}}$$

i.e. $-\,mg\sin\theta\,\hat{\mathbf{s}} + (T - mg\cos\theta)\hat{\mathbf{n}} = m\left(\dfrac{\mathrm{d}v}{\mathrm{d}t}\,\hat{\mathbf{s}} + \dfrac{v^2}{a}\,\mathbf{n}\right)$

Considering the $\hat{\mathbf{s}}$ components,

$$-mg\sin\theta = ma\,\frac{\mathrm{d}^2\theta}{\mathrm{d}t^2}$$

since
$$\frac{\mathrm{d}v}{\mathrm{d}t} = \frac{\mathrm{d}}{\mathrm{d}t}\left(a\,\frac{\mathrm{d}\theta}{\mathrm{d}t}\right) = a\,\frac{\mathrm{d}^2\theta}{\mathrm{d}t^2}$$

$\therefore \quad ma\,\dfrac{\mathrm{d}\theta}{\mathrm{d}t}\,\dfrac{\mathrm{d}^2\theta}{\mathrm{d}t^2} + mg\sin\theta\,\dfrac{\mathrm{d}\theta}{\mathrm{d}t} = 0,\quad$ multiplying by $\dfrac{\mathrm{d}\theta}{\mathrm{d}t}$

Integrating, $\tfrac{1}{2}ma\left(\dfrac{\mathrm{d}\theta}{\mathrm{d}t}\right)^2 - mg\cos\theta = \tfrac{1}{2}ma\,\dfrac{U^2}{a^2} - mg$

since
$$\frac{\mathrm{d}\theta}{\mathrm{d}t} = \frac{U}{a}\quad\text{when } \theta = 0$$

This equation could of course have been obtained from the conservation of energy, and in general it is easier to do so,

i.e.
$$\tfrac{1}{2}mU^2 - mga = \tfrac{1}{2}mv^2 - mga\cos\theta \qquad (7.3)$$

Newton's law was used in this example to illustrate that the energy equation is the distance integral of Newton's law. Here, the distance was the angular distance θ. Considering now the $\hat{\mathbf{n}}$ components,

$$T - mg\cos\theta = mv^2/a$$

$$\therefore \quad T = mg\cos\theta + m\,\frac{U^2}{a} - 2mg + 2mg\cos\theta$$

from equation 7.3,

$$= \frac{m}{a}\,(U^2 - 2ga + 3ga\cos\theta)$$

If the stone is to describe a complete circle, $T \geqslant 0$ for all θ,

$$\therefore \qquad U^2 - 2ga + 3ga \cos \theta \geqslant 0$$

i.e. $U^2 \geqslant 5ga$, since the least value of $\cos \theta = -1$.

Thus if the initial velocity U is not less than $\sqrt{(5ga)}$, the stone will describe a complete circle.

We know also from experience that if the initial velocity is small the stone will oscillate about $\theta = 0$, coming to rest at positions say $\theta = \pm\alpha$.

From equation 7.3, since $v = 0$ when $\theta = \pm\alpha$,

$$\tfrac{1}{2}mU^2 - mga = -mga \cos \alpha$$

$$\cos \alpha = \frac{2ga - U^2}{2ga}$$

This has real solutions $\alpha < \pi/2$ if and only if $U^2 < 2ga$, so that if $U < \sqrt{(2ga)}$, the stone oscillates about $\theta = 0$.

For values of U^2 such that $2ga < U^2 < 5ga$, $T = 0$ at an angular position β where

$$U^2 - 2ga + 3ga \cos \beta = 0,$$

i.e.
$$\cos \beta = \frac{2ga - U^2}{3ga}$$

so that at this position the string becomes slack and the stone moves in a parabola. Since $U^2 > 2ga$, $\cos \beta$ is negative and $\beta > \pi/2$. But could the stone have first come to rest so that this position is not attained?

We have found that the stone comes to rest when $\theta = \alpha$ where $\cos \alpha = (2ga - U^2)/2ga$; that the string becomes slack when $\theta = \beta$ where $\cos \beta = (2ga - U^2)/3ga$. Since both expressions are negative, θ attains the value β, before it attains the value α, as $\cos \beta = \frac{2}{3} \cos \alpha$, so that the string becomes slack before the stone comes to rest (Fig. 7.14). For example, if $U^2 = (5/2)ga$, the string becomes slack when $\cos \theta = -\frac{1}{6}$, whereas the body comes to rest if it continues in circular motion when $\cos \theta = -\frac{1}{4}$. Thus a ring threaded on a smooth circular wire in a vertical plane and projected from the lowest point with velocity $\sqrt{[(5/2)ga]}$ would have no force acting between the wire and the ring when $\cos \theta = -\frac{1}{6}$, and would come

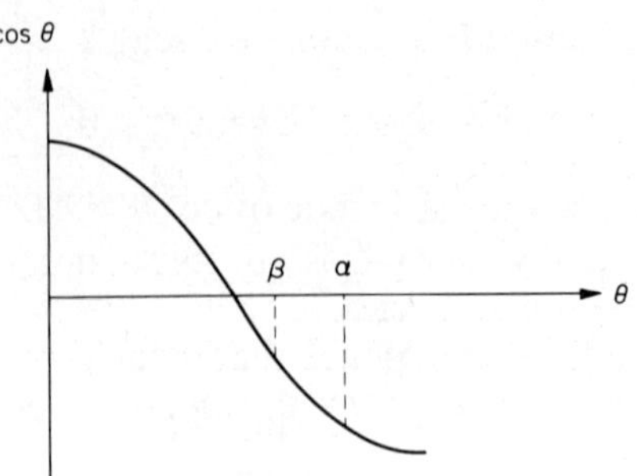

Fig. 7.14

to rest when $\cos\theta = -\frac{1}{4}$. For the last part of the upward motion the force exerted by the wire on the bead would be outwards.

Thus we have three possibilities.

(a) if $U^2 \leqslant 2ga$, the stone oscillates about $\theta = 0$. Note that when $U^2 = 2ga$ the stone comes to rest when $\theta = \pi/2$ and the tension is also zero at that point;
(b) if $2ga < U^2 < 5ga$, the stone leaves the circular path and travels in a parabola (Fig. 7.15);
(c) if $U^2 \geqslant 5ga$, the stone describes complete circles.

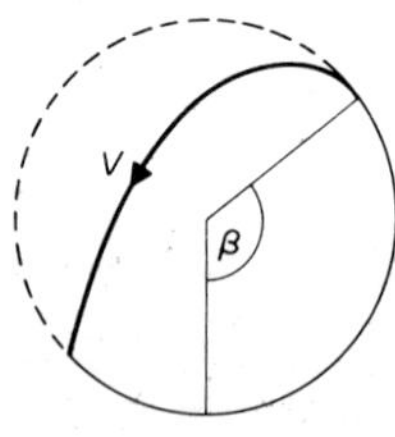

Fig. 7.15

Period of oscillations

Since we have found the period of so many oscillatory motions it is interesting to try to find the period when $U^2 < 2ga$.

From the energy equation, we obtained

$$\tfrac{1}{2}ma\left(\frac{d\theta}{dt}\right)^2 - mga\cos\theta = k, \quad \text{a constant}$$

i.e.
$$\frac{d\theta}{dt} = \sqrt{\left[\frac{2}{ma}(k + mga\cos\theta)\right]}$$
$$= \lambda\sqrt{(1 + A\cos\theta)}, \quad \text{say}$$

Separating the variables,

$$t = \frac{1}{\lambda}\int \frac{d\theta}{\sqrt{(1 + A\cos\theta)}}$$

There is not, however, an expression whose differential is $1/\sqrt{(1 + A\cos\theta)}$, so the right hand side of the equation is non-integrable, and is one of a family of elliptic integrals. If A is small, $(1 + A\cos\theta)^{-1/2}$ can of course be expanded by the Binomial Theorem to enable us to find a numerical approximation, and for all values of A we can obtain approximations by numerical methods. These elliptic integrals are of great importance in investigating more advanced problems on oscillations.

EXERCISE 7(b)

1. A stone mass 0.2 kg is suspended by a string so that it can describe a vertical circle radius 0.5 m. It is projected from the lowest point in its path with velocity 7 m s^{-1}. Find the tension in the string in the positions when
   (a) the string is vertical,
   (b) the string is inclined at 60° to the vertical,
   (c) the string is horizontal.

2. Explain why the five answers to Question 1 can be arranged to be consecutive terms in an arithmetic progression.

3. A small stone mass 0.02 kg is placed on top of a smooth sphere radius 0.1 m. The stone receives an impulse of 0.014 N s. Find where the stone leaves the sphere.

4. A small stone attached to an inextensible string is made to describe a vertical circle radius 0.5 m. If the ratio of the greatest tension in the string to the least tension is 11:5, find the greatest speed of the stone during its motion.

5. A smooth circular tube is held fixed in a vertical plane. A bead, mass m, which can slide in the tube, is released from rest at the highest point in the tube. Find the force exerted by the tube on the bead when the bead is at the lowest point in the tube.

6. A particle is at rest at the lowest point of the smooth inside surface of a cylinder of radius a which is fixed with its axis horizontal. The particle is given a velocity $\sqrt{(3ag)}$ so that it starts to move in a vertical circle on the inside surface of the cylinder. Find the force exerted by the cylinder on the particle when the particle is at the same horizontal level as the axis of the cylinder, and also at what vertical height above the lowest generator of the cylinder the particle leaves the cylinder.

7. A particle is attached to one end of a light inextensible string, the other end of which is fixed. The particle is held with the string making an angle α with the downward vertical. It is then released, and as it passes through the lowest point in its path the midpoint of the string strikes a fixed horizontal bar, so that the particle starts to describe a vertical circle whose radius is half the length of the string. If the particle comes instantaneously to rest when the string is inclined at an angle β with the vertical, show that $2 \cos \alpha = 1 + \cos \beta$.

8. A smooth circular band, of centre O and radius a, is fixed in a vertical plane. A particle is projected from the lowest point along the inside of the band with velocity $\sqrt{[ga(2 + 3 \cos \alpha)]}$. Prove that the velocity v of the particle when it is at a height $a \cos \alpha$ above the centre is given by $v^2 = ga \cos \alpha$, and show that the particle leaves the band at this instant. Prove further that, if $\alpha = 30°$, the particle hits the band again at the end of its horizontal diameter. (O. & C.)

9. If the particle in Question 8 is projected from the lowest point on the band with velocity $\sqrt{(7ga/2)}$, show that the particle leaves the band in the subsequent motion and returns to the original circular path, meeting it at the lowest point of the band.

10. A particle weight $4W$ lies on a rough horizontal table, the coefficient of friction being $\frac{1}{2}$. A light string attached to the particle passes through a smooth-rimmed hole in the table and has a particle weight W attached to the other end. Find the greatest angle through which the second particle can oscillate on either side of the vertical without moving the first particle.
Show that this angle is also the greatest angle which the part of the string below the table can make with the vertical if the second particle moves in a horizontal circle without disturbing the first particle. (O. & C.)

11. Show that the acceleration of a particle, position vector $\mathbf{r}$ moving in a circle can be written

$$\frac{d\omega}{dt}\hat{\mathbf{n}} \times \mathbf{r} - \omega^2\mathbf{r}$$

where ω is the angular speed at that instant and $\hat{\mathbf{n}}$ is a unit vector perpendicular to the plane of the circle.

12. A commando swings on a rope fixed at its upper end A. The rope, initially inclined at $60°$ to the downward vertical, remains taut and may be considered as inextensible and of negligible mass. The commando can be idealized as a particle at the end of the rope. If (a) his mass is 70 kg; (b) the rope is 10 m long; (c) he lets go when the rope is vertical; (d) A is 12 m above the ground; find his landing speed. (Neglect air resistance and take $g = 10 \text{ m s}^{-2}$.)
Which of (a), (b), (c), (d) can be varied, one at a time, without affecting this speed? (S.M.P.)

(The next section may be omitted at a first reading.)

Accessible points: the bounding parabola

In many of the previous problems we found possible paths for projectiles, with known velocity of projection, so that they passed through given points. There were usually two paths, one corresponding to each root of a certain quadratic equation.

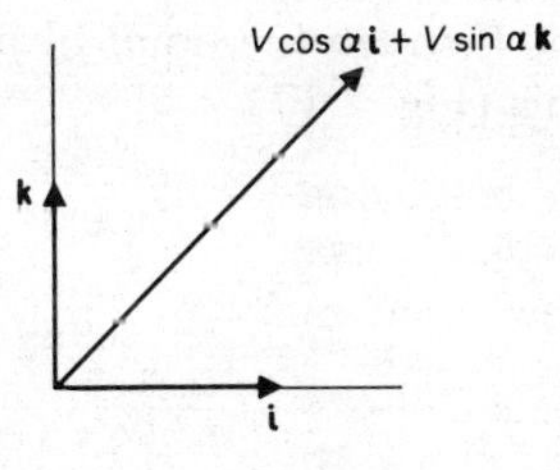

Fig. 7.16

More generally, if a particle is projected (Fig. 7.16) with velocity $V \cos \alpha\mathbf{i} + V \sin \alpha\mathbf{k}$, to pass through a point position vector $X\mathbf{i} + Y\mathbf{k}$,

$$X\mathbf{i} + Y\mathbf{k} = (V \cos \alpha\mathbf{i} + V \sin \alpha\mathbf{k})t - \tfrac{1}{2}(g\mathbf{k})t^2$$

$$\Rightarrow X = V \cos \alpha t \quad \text{and} \quad Y = V \sin \alpha t - \tfrac{1}{2}gt^2$$

i.e.
$$Y = X \tan \alpha - \frac{gX^2}{2V^2} \sec^2 \alpha$$

As a quadratic equation in tan α, this becomes

$$Y = X \tan\alpha - \frac{gX^2}{2V^2}(1 + \tan^2\alpha)$$

i.e.
$$gX^2 \tan^2\alpha - 2V^2X\tan\alpha + 2YV^2 + gX^2 = 0$$

From this,

$$\tan\alpha = \frac{2V^2X \pm \sqrt{[4V^4X^2 - 4gX^2(2YV^2 + gX^2)]}}{2gX^2}$$

Thus the equation has two real distinct roots, two equal roots, or no real roots according as

$$V^4 \gtreqless g(2YV^2 + gX^2)$$

Points which can be reached lie on or inside the curve whose equation is

$$V^4 = g(2yV^2 + gx^2)$$

i.e.
$$y = \frac{1}{2gV^2}(V^4 - g^2x^2), \quad \text{for all values of } X,\ Y$$

This is a parabola, concave vertically downwards, symmetrical about the vertical line through the point of projection, and is called the bounding parabola (Fig. 7.17).

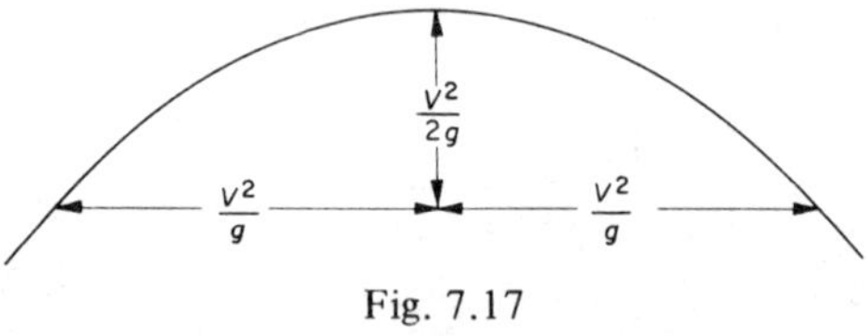

Fig. 7.17

The highest accessible point is $(0, V^2/2g)$, as expected, and when $y = 0$, $x = \pm V^2/g$, giving the maximum range on a horizontal plane. The maximum range on an inclined plane through the point of projection can also be found by considering the points of intersection of the bounding parabola (Fig. 7.18) and the line $y = x$ tan the line of section of the plane. For when $x = R\cos\beta$, $y = R\sin\beta$,

$$R\sin\beta = \frac{1}{2gV^2}(V^4 - g^2R^2\cos^2\beta)$$

i.e.
$$g^2R^2 \cos^2 \beta + 2gV^2R \sin \beta - V^4 = 0$$
$$\Rightarrow [gR(1 - \sin \beta) - V^2][gR(1 + \sin \beta) - V^2] = 0,$$

using $\cos^2 \beta = 1 - \sin^2 \beta$,

$$\Rightarrow R = \frac{V^2}{g(1 - \sin \beta)} \quad \text{or} \quad \frac{V^2}{g(1 + \sin \beta)}$$

giving the maximum range up or down an inclined plane.

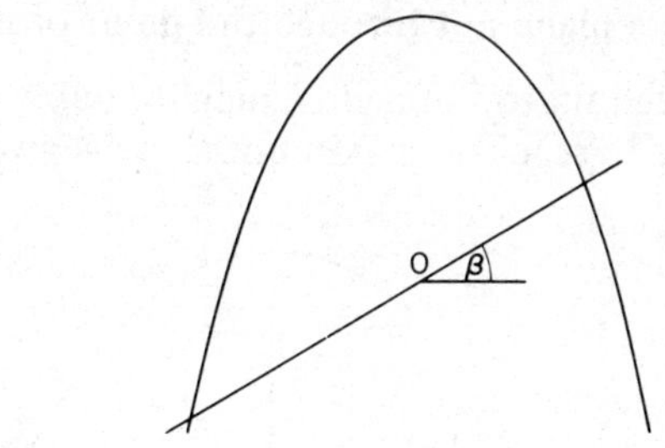

Fig. 7.18

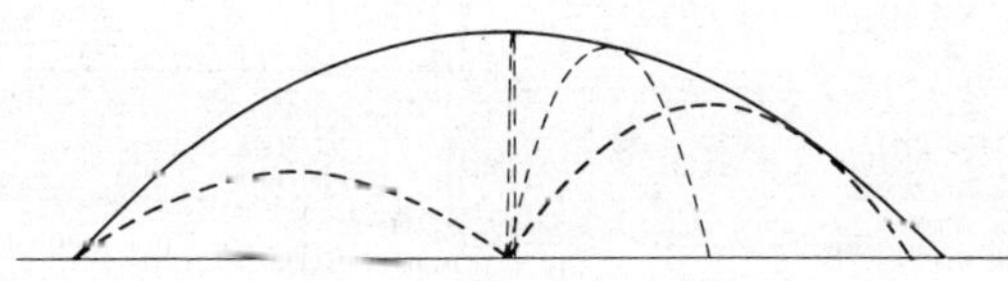

Fig. 7.19

The bounding parabola may also be thought of as the envelope (Fig. 7.19) of all possible trajectories with a given speed V from O, as the reader familiar with partial differentiation will see. For the envelope of

$$y = x \tan \theta - \frac{gx^2}{2V^2} \sec^2 \theta$$

is obtained by differentiating partially with respect to θ,

i.e.
$$0 = x \sec^2 \theta - \frac{gx^2}{V^2} \sec^2 \theta \tan \theta$$

$\Rightarrow$
$$\tan \theta = V^2/gx$$

$$\therefore \qquad y = \frac{V^2}{g} - \frac{gx^2}{2V^2}\left(1 + \frac{V^4}{g^2x^2}\right)$$

$$y = \frac{1}{2gV^2}(V^4 - g^2x^2)$$

Notice that the dimensions of this equation are consistent. g has dimensions L T^{-2}, V has dimensions L T^{-1}, so that the dimension of the right hand side of the equation is L.

Maximum range on a plane not through the point of projection

Consider a gun placed on top of a cliff, height h, able to fire shells with velocity V out to sea. The maximum range is given by the

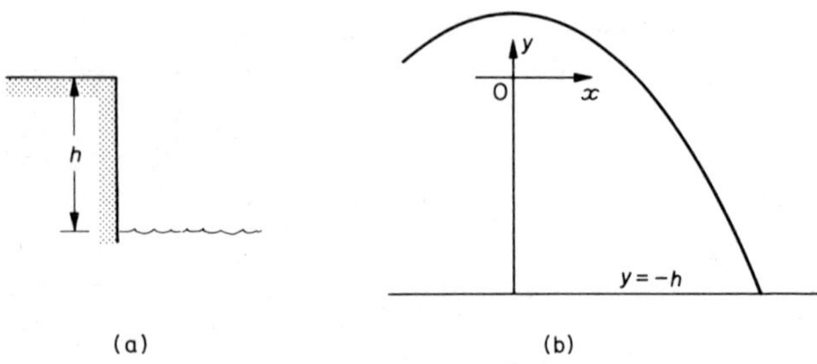

Fig. 7.20

intersection of the bounding parabola and the equation of the section of the surface of the sea, $y = -h$ (Fig. 7.20).

When $\qquad y = -h, \quad x^2 = \dfrac{1}{g^2}(V^4 + 2ghV^2)$

$\therefore \qquad$ the maximum range of the gun is $\dfrac{V}{g}\sqrt{(V^2 + 2gh)}$

Similarly, a ship armed with the same guns would need to be within

$$\frac{V}{g}\sqrt{(V^2 - 2gh)}$$

of the foot of the cliff to be able to hit the gun on the top, since we must take coordinate axes through the point of projection in

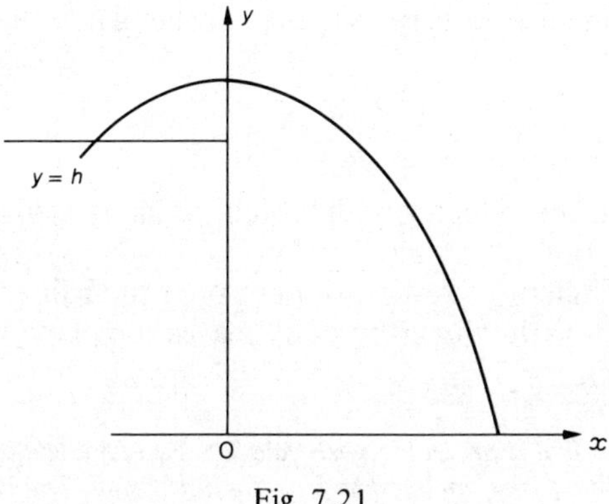

Fig. 7.21

each case and the section of the cliff top has equation $y = +h$, relative to axes through the ship (Fig. 7.21).

Motion of elastic bodies projected onto an inclined plane

The velocity of a body striking a fixed surface can be expressed in terms of components u, v, along and perpendicular to the surface. At impact, since the surface is smooth, u is unaltered but v is reversed in direction and reduced to ev. Since these components of velocity are along and perpendicular to the plane, we must choose coordinate axes and, where appropriate, unit vectors, in these directions. Thus the velocity and acceleration shown in Fig. 7.22(a) have components as in Fig. 7.22(b).

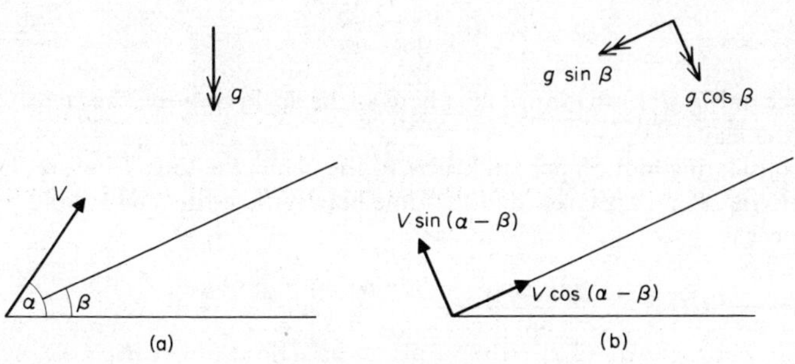

Fig. 7.22

Considering motion perpendicular to the plane, the time of flight is

$$\frac{2V \sin (\alpha - \beta)}{g \cos \beta}$$

as before, and the velocity with which the body strikes the plane is $V \sin (\alpha - \beta)$.

If the coefficient of restitution between the ball and the plane is e, the velocity with which the body leaves the plane will be $eV \sin (\alpha - \beta)$.

Example 7.6. *A ball is projected with velocity V at an angle α to the line of greatest slope of a plane, inclined at β to the horizontal. The coefficient of restitution between the ball and the plane is $\frac{1}{2}$. Prove that the point of second impact of the ball with the plane will be higher than the point of first impact if $\tan \alpha \tan \beta < 2/5$.*

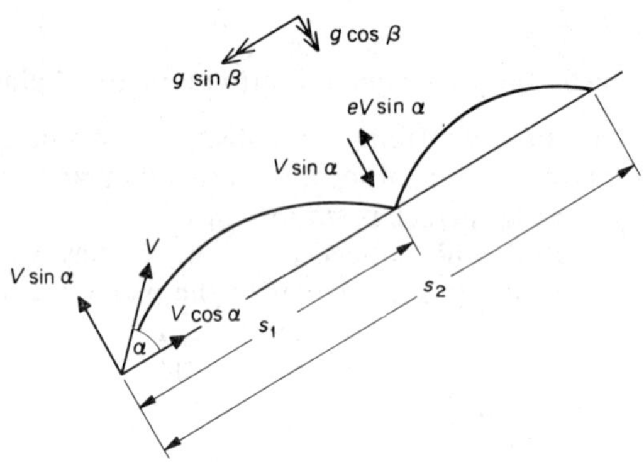

Fig. 7.23

Notice in Fig. 7.23 that α is taken here as the angle between the trajectory and the plane.

Considering motion perpendicular to the plane, the time T before the first bounce is $2V \sin \alpha/g \cos \beta$, and the time between the first and second bounces is

$$\frac{2eV \sin \alpha}{g \cos \beta} = \frac{V \sin \alpha}{g \cos \beta}, \quad \text{since } e = \tfrac{1}{2}$$

$$= \tfrac{1}{2}T$$

The distance S_1 along the plane is $V \cos \alpha T - \frac{1}{2}g \sin \beta T^2$, and if the ball strikes the plane a second time a distance S_2 from the point of projection,

$$S_2 = V \cos \alpha(\tfrac{3}{2}T) - \tfrac{1}{2}g \sin \beta(\tfrac{3}{2}T)^2$$

since the total time that has elapsed since projection is $\frac{3}{2}T$, and motion along the plane is not affected by the impacts.

The second point will be above the first if $S_2 > S_1$,

i.e. $$V \cos \alpha(\tfrac{3}{2}T) - \tfrac{1}{2}g \sin \beta(\tfrac{3}{2}T)^2 > V \cos \alpha T - \tfrac{1}{2}g \sin \beta T^2$$

i.e. $$\tfrac{1}{2} V \cos \alpha > \tfrac{5}{8}g \sin \beta T$$

i.e. $$\tan \alpha \tan \beta < 2/5, \quad \text{since } T = \frac{2V \sin \alpha}{g \cos \beta}$$

These later examples illustrate suitable methods for solving more difficult problems on projectiles.

Example 7.7. *A shell is fired from a gun with velocity V at a target in the same horizontal plane as the gun. Show that if there are small errors ϵ in the angle of elevation and 2ϵ in the direction, the shell will hit the plane a distance $2(V^2/g)\epsilon$ from the target T.*

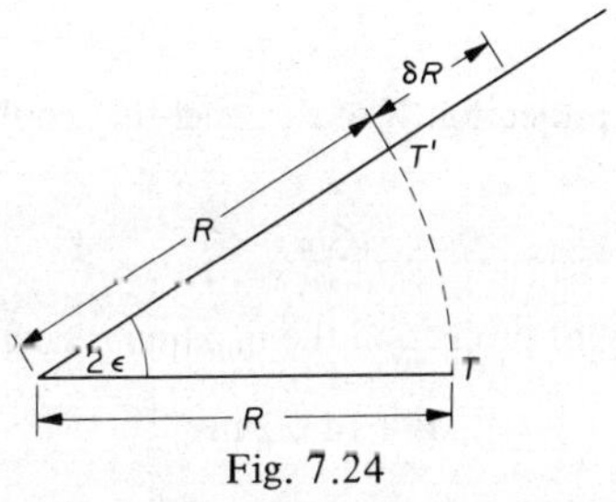

Fig. 7.24

The range R on a horizontal plane is given by

$$R = \frac{V^2}{g} \sin 2\theta$$

By the calculus of small errors,

$$\delta R \simeq \frac{V^2}{g} \cos 2\theta \delta(2\theta)$$
$$= \frac{2V^2\epsilon}{g} \cos 2\theta$$

From Fig. 7.24, the effect of the error in direction is $2R\epsilon$, since T T′ is the arc of a circle. By Pythagoras' theorem, the distance from the target at which the shell strikes the plane is $\sqrt{[(2R\epsilon)^2 + (\delta R)^2]}$, approximately,

i.e. $$\frac{2V^2}{g}\epsilon\sqrt{(\sin^2 2\theta + \cos^2 2\theta)}$$

i.e. $$\frac{2V^2}{g}\epsilon$$

Example 7.8. *A shell bursts on striking some level ground and pieces of shrapnel fly in all directions with all velocities up to 28 m s^{-1}. Show that a small insect 40 m away (Fig. 7.25) is in danger of being hit for $(20/7)\sqrt{2}$ s.*

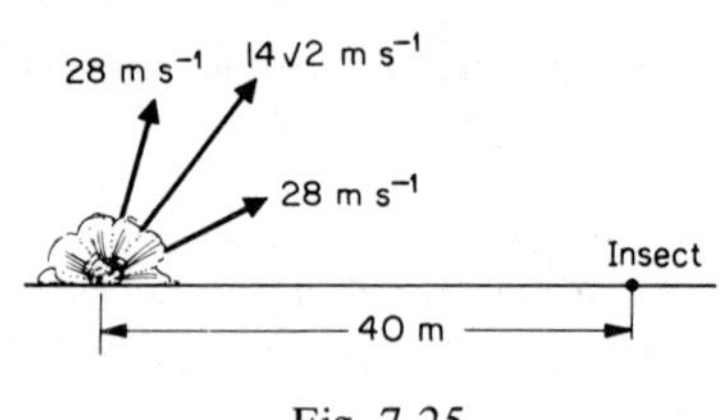

Fig. 7.25

The least velocity of projection V of shrapnel that could hit the insect is given by

$$V^2/g = 40$$

since for this velocity of projection the maximum range is 40 m, i.e.

$$V = 14\sqrt{2} \text{ m s}^{-1}$$

The first pieces of shrapnel that could hit it, however, are those projected with velocity 28 m s^{-1} on the lower of the two possible trajectories, since the horizontal component of their velocity is greater than that of any others that could hit it. Pieces of shrapnel with smaller velocities, down to $14\sqrt{2}$ m s^{-1}, projected on suitable paths, could then arrive, followed by pieces projected at 28 m s^{-1} on the higher of the two paths.

For the extreme paths, since $(V^2/g)\sin 2\theta$ is the range on a horizontal plane,

$$\frac{(28)^2}{9.8}\sin 2\theta = 40$$

i.e. $$\sin 2\theta = \tfrac{1}{2}$$

$$\theta = 15° \text{ or } 75°$$

The times of flight are $(2V/g) \sin 15°$ and $(2V/g) \sin 75°$, so the insect is in danger for

$$\frac{2 \times 28}{9.8}(\sin 75° - \sin 15°) \text{ seconds}$$

This could be evaluated approximately using tables, but in this case an exact value can be found, since

$$\sin 75° - \sin 15° = 2 \sin 30° \cos 45°$$
$$= \frac{1}{\sqrt{2}}$$

so the insect is in danger for $\dfrac{2 \times 28}{9.8} \times \dfrac{1}{\sqrt{2}}$

i.e. $\dfrac{20\sqrt{2}}{7}$ seconds

Example 7.9. *O is a point on a plane P inclined at 30° to the horizontal. A ball is projected from O in a vertical plane through the line of greatest slope of P with speed V at an angle of 60° above the horizontal. The coefficient of restitution between the ball and the plane is $\frac{2}{3}$. Find the distance from O up the plane P to the point where the ball strikes P a second time.*

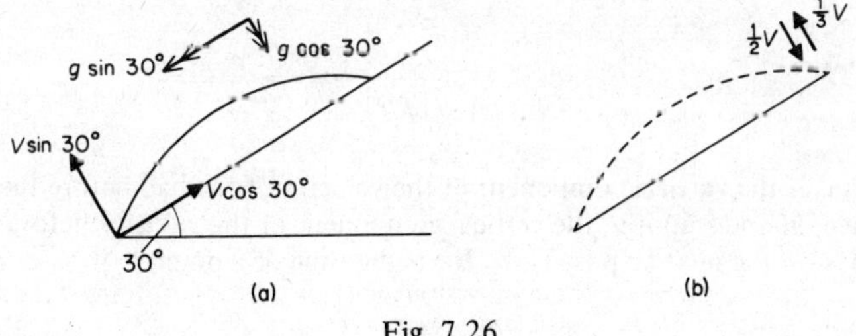

Fig. 7.26

The resolved parts of the initial velocity and the acceleration are shown in Fig. 7.26(a). The time of flight of the first bounce is therefore $2V/g\sqrt{3}$.

The resolved parts of the velocity before and after the first bounce are in Fig. 7.26(b). (The component perpendicular to the plane, of the velocity after the bounce, is two thirds of the component before the bounce.) The time of flight of the second bounce is $4V/3g\sqrt{3}$.

But the velocity along the plane is unaffected by the bounce so we can consider motion over the whole total time so far, i.e. $10V/3g\sqrt{3}$.

$\therefore$ the distance s travelled up the plane is given by

$$S = \frac{V\sqrt{3}}{2}\left(\frac{10V}{3g\sqrt{3}}\right) - \frac{1}{2}\left(\frac{g}{2}\right)\left(\frac{10V}{3g\sqrt{3}}\right)^2$$

i.e.
$$S = \frac{20}{27}\frac{V^2}{g}$$

Example 7.10. *A stairway has uniformly spaced equal horizontal treads. A ball bounces down the stairs, hitting each tread at its midpoint. Show that the coefficient of restitution between the ball and the stairs is greater than* $\frac{1}{3}$ *(Fig. 7.27).*

Let e be the coefficient of restitution. Since the acceleration due to gravity of the ball is vertical, and the impacts are vertical, there is no change in the horizontal velocity of the ball. As moreover, the ball strikes each step in the middle, the time of flight of each bounce is the same, and so the motion is repeated exactly between each bounce.

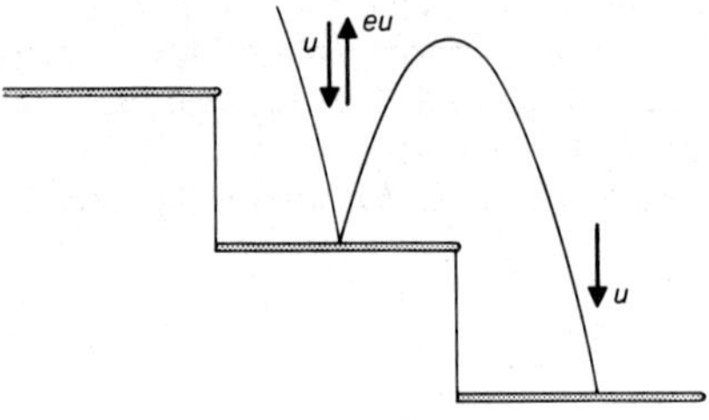

Fig. 7.27

Thus if the vertical component of the velocity of the ball before the bounce on one step is u, the vertical component of the velocity before the bounce on the next step is also u. If t is the time of a bounce,

$$u = -eu + gt$$

i.e.
$$t = \frac{u}{g}(1 + e)$$

The motion, however, will not be possible if the ball leaves a step with such a small vertical component of velocity that it strikes that step again. So since the ball strikes each step at its midpoint, after time $\frac{1}{2}t$, the ball must still be above the level of the first step. But the velocity of the ball has a vertical component eu when the ball is at the level of the step, so when it is above the level of the step the vertical velocity must be less than eu;

i.e.
$$-eu + g(\tfrac{1}{2}t) < eu$$

Since
$$t = (1 + e)\frac{u}{g}$$

$$u(1 + e) < 4eu$$

i.e.
$$e > \tfrac{1}{3}$$

Example 7.11. *A goal is scored in rugby football by placing the ball on the ground in the field of play and then kicking it over a horizontal crossbar placed at a height h between two goal posts. A certain player can kick the ball with a velocity V at an angle of elevation α. If the plane in which the ball travels is the perpendicular bisector of the crossbar, show he can only kick a goal if $h < (V^2/2g)\sin^2\alpha$, and that he must place the ball at some point along a line of length*

$$\frac{2V\cos\alpha}{g}\sqrt{(V^2\sin^2\alpha - 2gh)}$$

The maximum height attained by the ball is $(V^2/2g)\sin^2\alpha$, so the player can only kick a goal if $(V^2/2g)\sin^2\alpha > h$, as required.

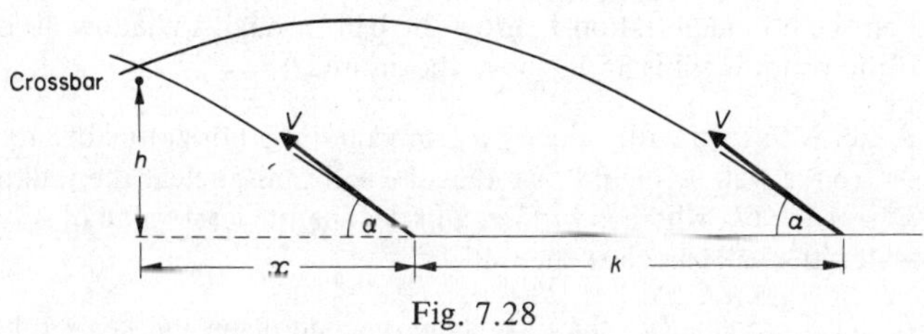

Fig. 7.28

Suppose that the closest he can place the ball to the goal line is x, and the furthest is $x + k$. The extreme paths are shown in Fig. 7.28. If t is the time of flight, the roots of the equation

$$h = V\sin\alpha t - \tfrac{1}{2}gt^2$$

give the two values of t, one corresponding to each path. This equation can be expressed as

$$gt^2 - 2V\sin\alpha t + 2h = 0$$

Denoting the roots by t_1, t_2, where $t_1 > t_2$, and considering the horizontal motion of the ball

$$V\cos\alpha t_2 = x \quad \text{and} \quad V\cos\alpha t_1 = x + k$$

$\therefore$
$$k = V(t_1 - t_2)\cos\alpha$$

But $$t_1 + t_2 = \frac{2V \sin \alpha}{g} \quad \text{and} \quad t_1 t_2 = \frac{2h}{g}$$

(sum and product of the roots of a quadratic equation),

$$\therefore \qquad (t_1 - t_2)^2 = \left(\frac{2V \sin \alpha}{g}\right)^2 - 4\left(\frac{2h}{g}\right)$$

$$\therefore \qquad k = V \cos \alpha \sqrt{\left(\frac{4V^2 \sin^2 \alpha}{g^2} - \frac{8h}{g}\right)}$$

$$= \frac{2V \cos \alpha}{g} \sqrt{(V^2 \sin^2 \alpha - 2gh)}$$

Notice that k is only real if $V^2 \sin^2 \alpha \geqslant 2gh$, the condition already obtained.

EXERCISE 7(c)

1. A boy can throw a ball with velocity 28 m s^{-1}. Find the greatest height he can attain on a vertical cliff 20 m away.

2. Can the boy in Question 1 throw the ball through a window 30 m away, if the window sill is 35 m above the ground?

3. A ball is thrown with velocity u from a point a horizontal distance of $4a$ from a wall $3a$ high. Prove that the ball cannot clear the wall unless $k^2 - 16 > 6k$, where $k = u^2/ag$, and deduce the least value of u for which the ball can clear the wall.

4. A ball is projected so that it hits an inclined plane and keeps rebounding from it. Show that the times between successive impacts form a geometric progression, and that the common ratio of this progression is equal to the coefficient of restitution between the ball and the plane.

5. A particle is projected from the ground (assumed smooth and horizontal) towards a smooth vertical wall, distant d from the point of projection. Show that if it returns to the point of projection after rebounding from the wall and then bouncing once on the ground, its speed of projection must have been at least $\sqrt{(dg/e)}$, where e is the coefficient of restitution for impact between the particle and either the wall or the ground. (C.S.)

6. O is a point on a smooth plane inclined at an angle α to the horizontal. A ball is projected from O with speed V in a direction inclined at β to the plane and $\alpha + \beta$ to the horizontal. The ball arrives at O again on the

nth bounce. Prove, by treating the motions along and perpendicular to the plane separately, that

$$\cot \alpha \cot \beta = \frac{1 - e^n}{1 - e}$$

where e is the coefficient of restitution. (O. & C.)

7. A smooth ball of mass m moves in a vertical line between two fixed horizontal planes a distance h apart. The coefficient of restitution between the ball and either plane is e. Initially the ball is projected vertically downwards so that its velocity before hitting the lower plane is u_0. If the ball hits the lower plane for the nth time with velocity u_n, show by considering energy that

$$u_{n+1}^2 = e^4 u_n^2 + (1 - e^2)2gh$$

providing $$e^2 u_n^2 \geqslant 2gh$$

If $$u_0 = [(gh/e^6)(1 - e^2 + 2e^4)]^{1/2}$$

describe the whole motion and show that the total distance travelled by the ball, from its first impact with the lower plane until it finally comes to rest, is

$$\left(\frac{3 - e^2}{1 - e^2}\right) h$$

(O. S.)

8. A small ball of mass m is dropped from a point at height H above a horizontal table. After falling a distance h the ball strikes an inclined plate and leaves it horizontally with its speed reduced to a fraction f of its value just before the impact. Show that the impulse on the ball due to the plate is inclined at an angle $\tan^{-1}(f)$ to the vertical. Determine the magnitude of the impulse and show its direction clearly on a diagram. (Air resistance may be neglected.)
The ball strikes the table after moving through a horizontal distance d. Find an expression for d in terms of H, h, f and g and show that for given f and variable h the maximum value of d is fH. (M.E.I.)

9. If an elastic ball moving vertically downwards strikes a smooth fixed plane inclined at an angle α, and rebounds horizontally, show that the coefficient of restitution is $\tan^2 \alpha$.
If a ball moving with speed v strikes the plane so that it first rebounds vertically and then rebounds horizontally, show that its speed after the second bounce is

$$v \tan^3 \alpha / \sqrt{(1 - \tan^2 \alpha + \tan^4 \alpha)}$$

(O. & C.)

10. A particle is projected from a point O on horizontal ground with horizontal and vertical velocity components 100 m s^{-1} and 196 m s^{-1} respectively. When the particle strikes the ground the impact has the effect of reducing both the horizontal and vertical components of velocity to half their original values, and these reductions in velocity continue each time the particle bounces in the same vertical plane across the ground. Show that the particle is moving for a time not greater than 80 seconds and calculate the limiting horizontal distance it could travel. (A.E.B.)

11. A circular flywheel is rotating with angular speed ω about a horizontal axis when it disintegrates into small pieces. Find the maximum possible height a piece could rise above the axis. (O.S.)

12. A stone is thrown with speed u from the top of a vertical wall which is of height h and stands on level ground. Find the maximum distance from the wall which can be reached by the stone. Find also the tangent of the angle of elevation at which the stone must be thrown to achieve this maximum range.
If $u = \sqrt{(2gh)}$, show that this maximum distance is $h\sqrt{8}$. (A.E.B.)

13. A shell is fired from a gun with muzzle velocity V so as to hit a helicopter hovering at a height b ($< V^2/2g$) and at a horizontal distance a from the gun. If the angle of projection of the shell to the horizontal is θ show that

$$ga^2 \tan^2 \theta - 2V^2 a \tan \theta + ga^2 + 2V^2 b = 0$$

By considering this equation as a quadratic for $\tan \theta$ deduce the farthest horizontal distance at which the helicopter can be hit if the height b and the muzzle velocity V are given. (J.M.B.)

14. A gun crew at O observes, at elevation 45° above the horizontal, an unpowered rocket R, at oblique range OR determined by radar as equal to r. The rocket is moving under gravity in the vertical plane through O and R with an instantaneous velocity V in a direction 30° below the horizontal and at 15° to the line RO. A shell is fired from O at that instant with initial speed V at a certain angle of projection α so as to hit the rocket above the horizontal plane through O. Find the required value of α, and show that r must be less than

$$\frac{3+\sqrt{3}}{\sqrt{2}}\left(\frac{V^2}{g}\right)$$

(C.)

15. A smooth plane is inclined at an angle α to the horizontal. A ball is projected from a point on the plane so that it bounces up the line of greatest slope. The velocity of projection is V and makes an angle θ with the line of greatest slope, and the coefficient of restitution between the ball and the plane is e. Find the time which elapses between the instant of projection and the instant at which bouncing stops and rolling starts. Prove that, if

$$\tan\theta = \tfrac{1}{2}(1-e)\cot\alpha$$

the ball stops bouncing at the instant when the component of its velocity parallel to the plane vanishes. Prove also, that at this instant, the ball is at a distance

$$\frac{V^2}{2g\sin\alpha}\left[1+\tfrac{1}{4}(1-\mathrm{e})^2\cot^2\alpha\right]^{-1}$$

from its starting point. (O. & C.)

Further examples on the motion of a particle in a plane

Components of acceleration along and perpendicular to the radius vector

We have seen (page 160) that if **r** is the position vector of a particle P relative to a fixed origin O, the acceleration of P is

$$\left[\frac{\mathrm{d}^2 r}{\mathrm{d}t^2} - r\left(\frac{\mathrm{d}\theta}{\mathrm{d}t}\right)^2\right]\hat{\mathbf{r}} + \frac{1}{r}\frac{\mathrm{d}}{\mathrm{d}t}\left(r^2\frac{\mathrm{d}\theta}{\mathrm{d}t}\right)\hat{\boldsymbol{\theta}},$$

where $\hat{\mathbf{r}}$ is a unit vector along OP and $\hat{\boldsymbol{\theta}}$ is a unit vector perpendicular to OP. If the forces acting on the particle can be resolved into components in these directions, we can often investigate the motion of P. More especially, if the component in one direction is zero, we have an easy differential equation for solving the motion in the other direction. The first, and best known, case, in which this was used was in the motion of celestial bodies, for the force acting on each body was supposed to be k/r^2 along the radius vector, and there was no component at right angles to the radius vector.

Conservation of moment of momentum

If there is not a force perpendicular to the radius vector,

$$\frac{1}{r}\frac{\mathrm{d}}{\mathrm{d}t}\left(r^2\frac{\mathrm{d}\theta}{\mathrm{d}t}\right) = 0 \qquad (7.4)$$

But if a body mass m is moving with velocity $\mathbf{v}$, and the perpendicular distance from a point O to the line of motion of the body is p, the quantity $mp\mathbf{v}$ is called the moment of momentum [Fig. 7.29(a)] (and see page 320), or angular momentum.

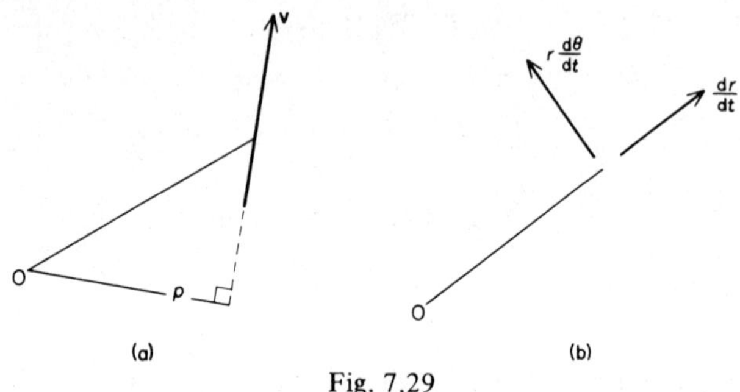

Fig. 7.29

Resolving $\mathbf{v}$ [Fig. 7.29(b)], the moment of momentum can also be written

$$mr\left(r\frac{\mathrm{d}\theta}{\mathrm{d}t}\right)\hat{\boldsymbol{\theta}}, \quad \text{i.e. } mr^2\frac{\mathrm{d}\theta}{\mathrm{d}t}\hat{\boldsymbol{\theta}}$$

But from equation 7.4, this quantity is constant, so that for a body moving only under the action of forces whose lines of action pass through O, the moment of momentum is conserved. This is analogous to the conservation of linear momentum.

Example 7.12. *A smooth straight tube rotates with constant angular velocity Ω in a horizontal plane about a point O in the tube. A particle, mass m, is inside the tube, initially at rest at a distance a from O. Show that after time t*

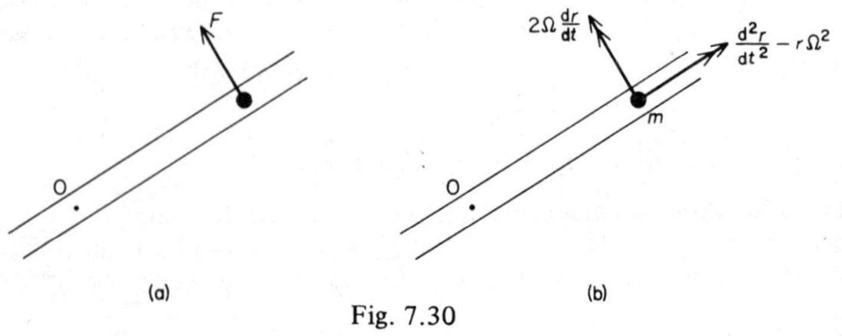

Fig. 7.30

the particle is at a distance a cosh Ωt from O, and find the force exerted on the particle by the tube (Fig. 7.30).

Draw two diagrams, one showing the forces and the other the components of acceleration. Since $d\theta/dt = \Omega$ and $d^2\theta/dt^2 = 0$, the component of acceleration parallel to $\hat{\boldsymbol{\theta}}$ is

$$\frac{1}{r}\frac{d}{dt}(r^2\Omega) = \frac{1}{r}\left(2r\frac{dr}{dt}\Omega\right) = 2\Omega\frac{dr}{dt}$$

Considering forces parallel to $\hat{\mathbf{r}}$,

$$0 = m\left(\frac{d^2r}{dt^2} - r\Omega^2\right)$$

i.e.
$$\frac{d^2r}{dt^2} - \Omega^2 r = 0$$

The solution of this differential equation is $r = A \exp \Omega t + B \exp -\Omega t$ for suitable A, B.

Initially, $\quad r = a \quad$ and $\quad dr/dt = 0,$

$$A + B = a$$

and
$$\Omega A - \Omega B = 0$$

$\therefore$
$$A = B = \tfrac{1}{2}a$$

i.e.
$$r = \frac{a}{2}\exp \Omega t + \frac{a}{2}\exp -\Omega t$$

which can be written $\quad r = a \cosh \Omega t.$

To find the force F exerted by the tube on the particle, consider the motion parallel to $\hat{\boldsymbol{\theta}}$.

$$F = m\left(2\Omega\frac{dr}{dt}\right)$$
$$= 2ma\Omega^2 \sinh \Omega t, \quad \text{since } dr/dt = a\Omega \sinh \Omega t.$$

Example 7.13. *A particle, mass m, on a smooth horizontal table is attached to an equal particle by a light inextensible string which passes through a hole in the table, so that the second particle hangs freely (Fig. 7.31). The first particle is projected at right angles to the string with velocity $\sqrt{(2gh)}$ from a point a distance a from the hole. Prove that the hanging particle will be pulled up through the hole if $2h > a$ and the total length of the string is less than $\frac{1}{2}h + \sqrt{(ah + \frac{1}{4}h^2)}$.*

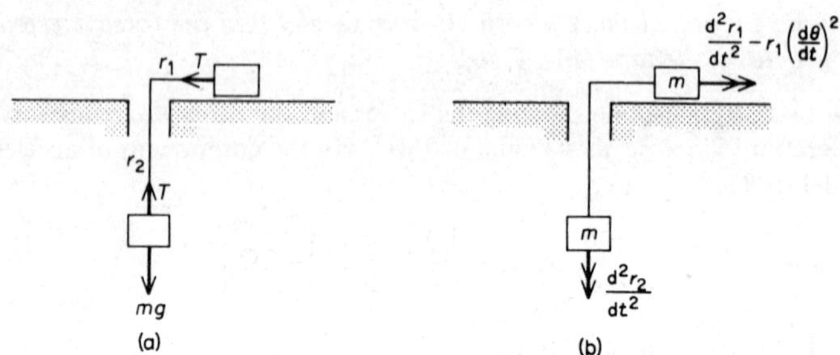

Fig. 7.31

Since the string is inextensible, $r_1 + r_2$ is constant,

i.e. $$\frac{d^2r_1}{dt^2} + \frac{d^2r_2}{dt^2} = 0$$

Considering forces on each particle along the string,

$$mg - T = m\frac{d^2r_2}{dt^2} \tag{7.5}$$

and

$$-T = m\left[\frac{d^2r_1}{dt^2} - r_1\left(\frac{d\theta}{dt}\right)^2\right]$$

$\therefore$ $$mg = -m\left[\frac{d^2r_1}{dt^2} - r_1\left(\frac{d\theta}{dt}\right)^2\right] + m\frac{d^2r_2}{dt^2}$$

But $$\frac{d^2r_2}{dt^2} = -\frac{d^2r_1}{dt^2}$$

so, dropping the suffix after substituting for d^2r_2/dt^2,

$$g = -\left[2\frac{d^2r}{dt^2} - r\left(\frac{d\theta}{dt}\right)^2\right]$$

i.e. $$2\frac{d^2r}{dt^2} - r\left(\frac{d\theta}{dt}\right)^2 + g = 0 \tag{7.6}$$

Since the table is smooth, there is not a force along $\hat{\boldsymbol{\theta}}$,

$\therefore$ $$\frac{1}{r}\frac{d}{dt}\left(r^2\frac{d\theta}{dt}\right) = 0$$

i.e.
$$r^2 \frac{d\theta}{dt} = a\sqrt{(2gh)}$$

from the initial conditions. Substituting in equation 7.6,

$$2\frac{d^2r}{dt^2} - \frac{2a^2gh}{r^3} + g = 0 \qquad (7.7)$$

Multiply by dr/dt and integrate.

$$\left(\frac{dr}{dt}\right)^2 + \frac{a^2gh}{r^2} + gr \quad \text{is constant}$$

Substituting the initial conditions, $r = a$ and $dr/dt = 0$,

$$\left(\frac{dr}{dt}\right)^2 + \frac{a^2gh}{r^2} + gr - g(h + a) = 0 \qquad (7.8)$$

Now this assumes that the second particle is not pulled through the hole, that is, that the string is sufficiently long for the maximum value of r to be less than the length of the string. To find the maximum, put $dr/dt = 0$ in equation 7.8

$$\frac{a^2gh}{r^2} + gr - g(h + a) = 0$$

i.e.
$$r^3 - (h + a)r^2 + a^2h = 0 \qquad (7.9)$$

But initially, $dr/dt = 0$ when $r = a$, so that $(r - a)$ is one factor of equation 7.9,

i.e.
$$(r - a)(r^2 - hr - ah) = 0$$

The largest root of this equation will be

$$r = \tfrac{1}{2}h + \tfrac{1}{2}\sqrt{(h^2 + 4ah)}$$

for this is larger than a since $2h > a$. This condition also ensures that the smallest value of r, $\frac{1}{2}h - \frac{1}{2}\sqrt{(h^2 + 4ah)}$, is greater than O, so that the first particle remains on the table and is not pulled down through the hole.

Central force: tension in the string

In the above example, the tension in the string can now be found from equation 7.5,

For $$T = mg - m\frac{d^2r_2}{dt^2}$$

$$= mg + m\frac{d^2r_1}{dt^2}$$

$$= mg + m\left(-\tfrac{1}{2}g + \frac{a^2gh}{r^3}\right) \quad \text{from equation 7.7}$$

$$= \tfrac{1}{2}mg + \frac{ma^2gh}{r^3}$$

Motion referred to perpendicular axes

We have seen in the early pages of this chapter how to investigate the motion of a particle moving under gravity only. Even when other forces are introduced it may still be convenient to consider components along two perpendicular axes, expressing the position vectors and other vector quantities in terms of **i** and **k**.

Example 7.14. *A particle mass m is projected with velocity U at an angle of elevation α. The forces acting on the particle are the weight of the particle and a resistance mλ***v***. Investigate the subsequent motion of the particle.*

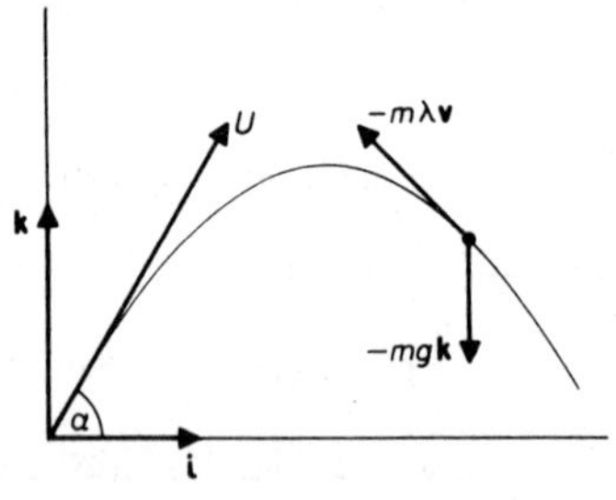

Fig. 7.32

Taking **i** and **k** as our usual unit vectors, since the velocity is $(d/dt)(x\mathbf{i} + y\mathbf{k})$, the resisting force (Fig. 7.32) is

$$-m\lambda\left(\frac{dx}{dt}\mathbf{i} + \frac{dy}{dt}\mathbf{k}\right)$$

The equation of motion therefore is

$$-mg\mathbf{k} - m\lambda\left(\frac{dx}{dt}\,\mathbf{i} + \frac{dy}{dt}\,\mathbf{k}\right) = m\left(\frac{d^2x}{dt^2}\,\mathbf{i} + \frac{d^2y}{dt^2}\,\mathbf{k}\right)$$

Equating the **i** vectors,

$$\frac{d^2x}{dt^2} + \lambda\frac{dx}{dt} = 0$$

$$\Rightarrow x = A + B\,e^{-\lambda t}$$

and from the initial conditions, $A + B = 0$ and $-\lambda B = U\cos\alpha$

$$x = \frac{U\cos\alpha}{\lambda}(1 - e^{-\lambda t}) \tag{7.10}$$

Equating the **k** vectors,

$$\frac{d^2y}{dt^2} + \lambda\frac{dy}{dt} = -g$$

The solution of this equation is

$$y = A + B\,e^{-\lambda t} - \frac{g}{\lambda}t$$

and from the initial conditions

$$A + B = 0 \quad \text{and} \quad U\sin\alpha = -\frac{g}{\lambda} - B\lambda$$

i.e.

$$B = -\frac{1}{\lambda}\left(\frac{g}{\lambda} + U\sin\alpha\right)$$

so that

$$y = \frac{1}{\lambda}\left(\frac{g}{\lambda} + U\sin\alpha\right)(1 - e^{-\lambda t}) - \frac{g}{\lambda}t \tag{7.11}$$

It is tedious to eliminate t between equations 7.10 and 7.11 to obtain the equation of the trajectory and it is best left with t as a parameter. However, we notice that, if λ is small,

$$x = \frac{U\cos\alpha}{\lambda}[1 - (1 - \lambda t\ldots)]$$

$$\simeq U\cos\alpha t$$

and $$y = \frac{1}{\lambda}\left(\frac{g}{\lambda} + U\sin\alpha\right)[1 - (1 - \lambda t + \tfrac{1}{2}\lambda^2 t^2 \ldots)] - \frac{g}{\lambda}t$$

$$= \frac{g}{\lambda}t + U\sin\alpha\, t - \tfrac{1}{2}gt^2 \ldots - \frac{g}{\lambda}t$$

$$= U\sin\alpha\, t - \tfrac{1}{2}gt^2$$

This is the parametric form of the trajectory when air resistance is ignored. Notice that if we include the term in λ

$$x = U\cos\alpha\, t - \tfrac{1}{2}\lambda U\cos\alpha\, t^2, \quad \text{less than when } \lambda = 0.$$

EXERCISE 7(d)

1. A smooth straight wire is made to rotate in a horizontal plane with constant angular velocity Ω. Find the initial conditions if a small ring free to slip along the wire is to describe an equiangular spiral.

2. The velocity of a particle moving in a plane is $\lambda r^2\hat{\mathbf{r}} + \mu\theta^2\hat{\boldsymbol{\theta}}$. Find the polar equation of the path.

3. A small ring which can move on a rough circular wire fixed in a horizontal plane is projected along the wire with initial velocity U. Show that it will come to rest after travelling a distance

$$(a/2\mu)\sinh^{-1}(U^2/ga),$$

where a is the radius of the wire and μ is the coefficient of friction between the bead and the wire.

4. A particle is permanently fixed to the end B of a straight rod AB of negligible mass and length a. The rod is pivoted smoothly at A and rests on a horizontal table. The particle is projected horizontally at time $t = 0$ with a velocity $a\Omega$. There is a resistance to motion equal to kv per unit mass, where k is a constant and v is the velocity at any instant. Prove that the angle through which the rod turns in time t is $\Omega(1 - e^{-kt})/k$. What is the least value of Ω for which the rod will complete a revolution? (O. & C.)

5. A smooth straight wire is made to rotate in a horizontal plane about a fixed point O on the wire with uniform angular velocity ω. A ring of mass m slides on the wire and is repelled from O by a constant force ωkm. The ring is projected from O along the wire with initial velocity k. Obtain (a) the distance of the ring from O after time t, and (b) the horizontal component of the reaction between the wire and the ring after time t. (O. & C.)

6. A particle of mass m slides without friction on the spoke of a horizontal wheel, but is attached to the centre of the wheel by a spring of natural length a and modulus of elasticity λ. When the wheel is fixed the period of small oscillations is $2\pi/n$.
Prove that $\lambda = man^2$. The wheel is made to rotate with a constant angular velocity ω ($<n$). Prove that the particle can remain at rest relative to the wheel at a distance $an^2/(n^2 - \omega^2)$ from the centre, providing the wheel is sufficiently large.
If the particle is slightly disturbed from this position, prove that it executes a simple harmonic motion relative to the spoke of the wheel, period $2\pi/\sqrt{(n^2 - \omega^2)}$. (O. & C.)

7. Two particles each of mass m are connected by a light inextensible string and are lying on a smooth horizontal table with the string taut. The string passes through a small ring O fixed to the table at a point distant a from the first particle. The first particle is given a horizontal velocity V perpendicular to the string. Prove that its subsequent path until the second particle reaches O has the polar equation $r = a \sec(\theta/\sqrt{2})$ relative to O. Prove also that if the point (r, θ) is reached after time t, then $r^2 = a^2 + \frac{1}{2}V^2t^2$. (O. & C.)

8. A body mass m is initially at a point P, and is under the action of a force mk^2/r^3 towards a fixed point O, where OP $= a$. The body is projected with velocity k/a at an angle of $\pi/4$ with OP produced. Show that it describes an equiangular spiral.

9. A particle mass m is projected from a point O with speed U at an angle α above the horizontal. Air resistance at any instant is $-\lambda m\mathbf{v}$, where λ is a constant. Find the time taken to reach the highest point in its path, and the horizontal distance then covered.

10. A particle mass m and electric charge e moves in the plane of two unit vectors $\mathbf{i}, \mathbf{j}$ under the action of constant electric and magnetic fields. These exert a constant force $eE\mathbf{i}$ and also a force eHv along the inward normal, v being the speed of the particle at any instant. Write down the vector equation of motion and show that it is satisfied by

$$\mathbf{r} = (A + B\cos\omega t)\mathbf{i} + (Et/H + B\sin\omega t)\mathbf{j},$$

where $$\omega = eH/m.$$

Find the values of A and B if the particle is initially at rest at O, and show that the particle comes instantaneously to rest at intervals of $2\pi/\omega$ seconds.

8. Moments of Inertia: Dynamics of Rigid Bodies

Rigid body

A rigid body is defined as any body for which the distance between every pair of particles is unalterable. For example, a metal rod, a plank of wood, an empty tea-cup, are rigid bodies; a bicycle chain, a pair of nut crackers, are not rigid bodies.

Kinetic energy of a rigid body

Consider a rigid body rotating about an axis through a fixed point O, not necessarily in the body (Fig. 8.1). When the body is rotating with angular speed ω, an element mass m 'at' a point P distance r

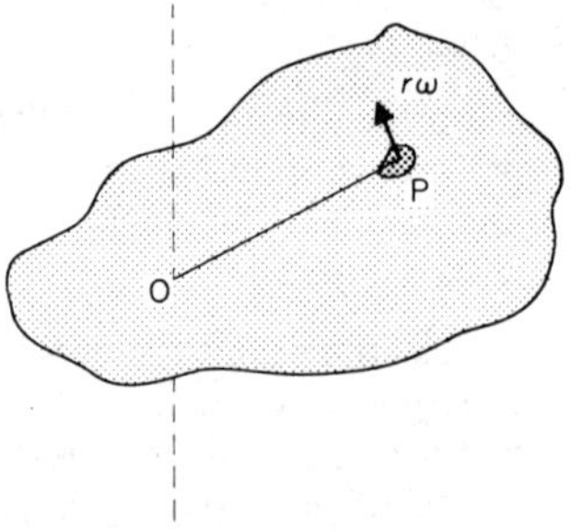

Fig. 8.1

from O has velocity $r\omega$ perpendicular to OP and no velocity along OP, since the distance between O and P cannot be altered. Therefore the kinetic energy of the element is $\frac{1}{2}m(r\omega)^2$, and the kinetic energy of the whole body is $\Sigma\frac{1}{2}m(r\omega)^2$. Since ω is the same for all elements of the body, the kinetic energy is $\frac{1}{2}\omega^2\Sigma(mr^2)$. The quantity

$$\Sigma\, mr^2$$

is called the *moment of inertia* of the body about that axis of rotation*, and depends only on the distribution of the mass relative to the axis. It is generally denoted by I, so that the kinetic energy of the body is written $\frac{1}{2}I\omega^2$.

Radius of gyration

If M is the total mass of a body and I the moment of inertia of the body about a certain axis, it is often convenient to define a quantity k such that $Mk^2 = I$. This quantity is called the radius of gyration of the body about that axis.

Moment of inertia of a uniform rod about an axis parallel to the rod

Consider a rod, mass M, length $2a$, placed a distance b from the straight line HK and parallel to HK (Fig. 8.2). Every element of

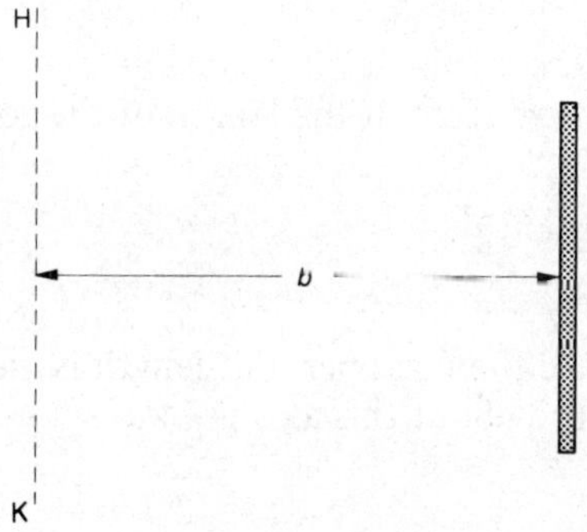

Fig. 8.2

the rod is a distance b from HK, so that $r = b$ for all elements, and

$$\Sigma mr^2 = b^2 \Sigma m$$
$$= Mb^2$$

* The moment of inertia about an axis l will in general be different from the moment of inertia of the same body about another axis l' (see page 215). The expression 'moment of inertia' is sometimes used loosely where there is no ambiguity about the axis to which it refers.

since the total mass Σm of the rod is M. This result is true even if the rod is not uniform. But if the rod is placed perpendicular to HK with one end on HK (Fig. 8.3), all elements of the rod are not the same distance from HK. We must divide the rod, mass m per

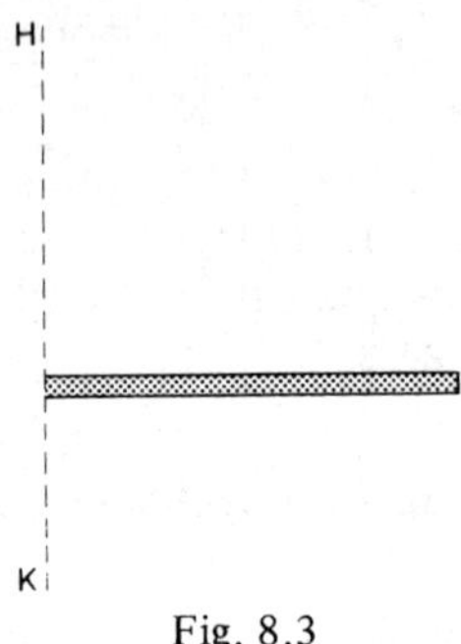

Fig. 8.3

unit length, into elements length δx, and the moment of inertia is $\Sigma(m\delta x)x^2$. Using calculus,

$$I = \int_0^{2a} mx^2\,dx, \quad \text{if the length of the rod is } 2a$$

$$= [\tfrac{1}{3}mx^3]_0^{2a}$$

$$= \tfrac{8}{3}ma^3$$

But $2ma = M$, since the mass per unit length is m, so the moment of inertia of the rod about this axis is $\frac{4}{3}Ma^2$.

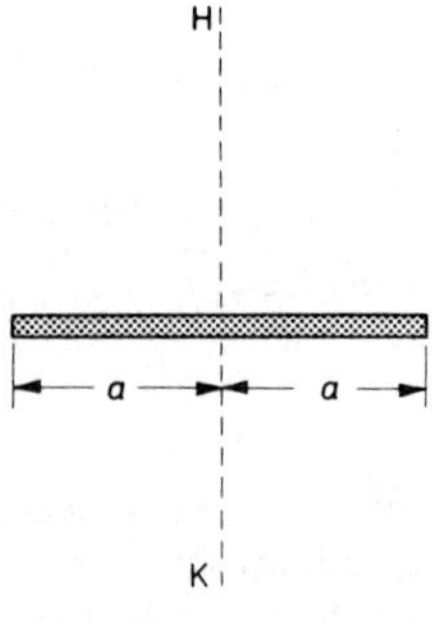

Fig. 8.4

If instead the rod is placed (Fig. 8.4) with its midpoint on HK, the limits of integration are $-a$ to a and

$$I = \int_{-a}^{a} mx^2 \, dx$$

$$= [\tfrac{1}{3}mx^3]_{-a}^{a}$$

$$= \tfrac{1}{3}Ma^2$$

Thus the moment of inertia of any one body is dependent on the axis of rotation. The radii of gyration in each of the three cases considered above are

$$\sqrt{b^2}, \sqrt{(\tfrac{4}{3}a^2)}, \sqrt{(\tfrac{1}{3}a^2)}, \quad \text{i.e., } b, \tfrac{2}{3}\sqrt{3}a \quad \text{and} \quad \tfrac{1}{3}\sqrt{3}a$$

respectively, since $I = Mk^2$.

Moment of inertia about an axis inclined at an angle α to the rod

If the rod is inclined at an angle α to HK (Fig. 8.5), an element distance x from the midpoint of the rod is $x \sin \alpha$ from the axis, so the moment of inertia is

$$\int_{-a}^{a} m(x \sin \alpha)^2 \, dx = \tfrac{1}{3}Ma^2 \sin^2 \alpha$$

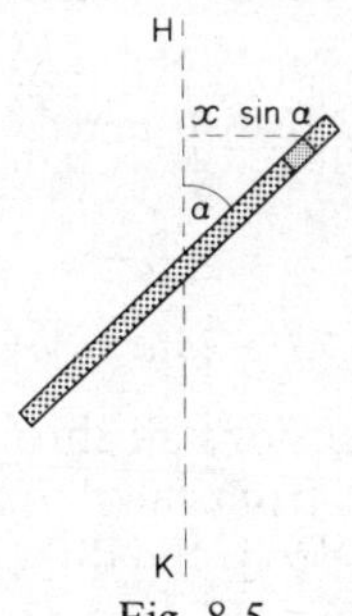

Fig. 8.5

Moment of inertia of a non-uniform rod

If the mass of the rod is distributed so that the density of an element is proportional to its distance from one end (Fig. 8.6), the

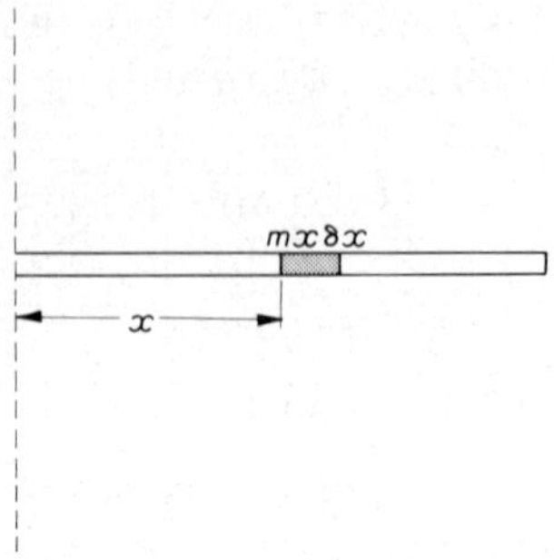

Fig. 8.6

moment of inertia I about an axis through that end perpendicular to the rod is given by

$$I = \int_0^{2a} x^2(mx \, dx)$$

where m is the constant of proportion,

$$= [\tfrac{1}{4}mx^4]_0^{2a}$$

$$= 4ma^4$$

But the mass M of the rod is given by

$$M = \int_0^{2a} mx \, dx$$

$$= 2ma^2$$

$$\therefore \qquad I = 2Ma^2$$

Notice the check of dimensions all through the last example. The dimensions of I are M L^2, from the definition. Since $mx\delta x$ is the mass of an element of the rod, the dimensions of m are M L^{-2} and the dimensions of $4ma^4$ are M L^2, as expected.

Moment of inertia of discrete particles

If two bodies, masses m and $2m$, small enough to be regarded as particles, are placed one at each end of a light rod (Fig. 8.7), the

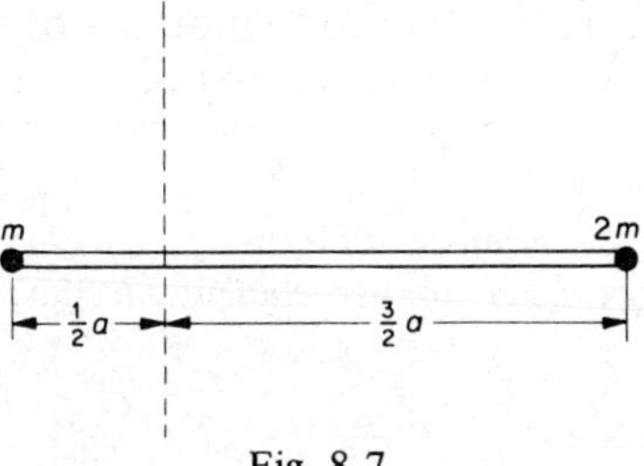

Fig. 8.7

moment of inertia of the lighter body about an axis through a point of quarter section of the rod and perpendicular to the rod is $m(\frac{1}{2}a)^2$ and of the heavier body about the same axis is $2m(\frac{3}{2}a)^2$ i.e. $(19/4)ma^2$. The radius of gyration is found from

$$(3m)k^2 = \tfrac{19}{4}\, ma^2$$

i.e.

$$k = \sqrt{(\tfrac{19}{12})}a$$

N.B. Note the *total* mass is $3m$. This must be used when finding the radius of gyration.

Addition of moments of inertia

Since moments of inertia are, by definition, the sum of a number of scalar quantities, they can be added or subtracted as scalars, though they must, of course, be about the same axis if the result is to be meaningful. The moment of inertia of two equal uniform rods, each mass m, rigidly joined at right angles at B as in Fig. 8.8,

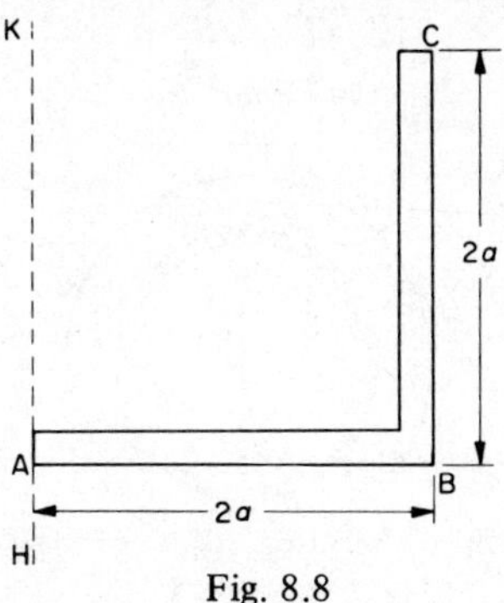

Fig. 8.8

about the axis HK is $(4/3)ma^2$, the moment of inertia of AB about HK, plus $4ma^2$, the moment of inertia of BC about the same axis, i.e., $(16/3)ma^2$.

Example 8.1. *Find the moment of inertia of a circular ring, mass M radius a, about an axis through the centre perpendicular to the plane of the ring.*

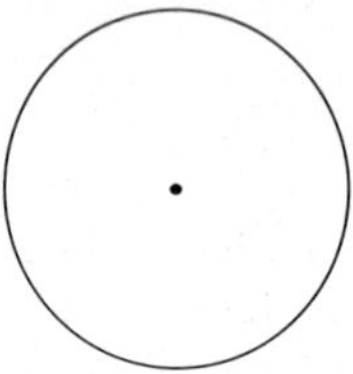

Fig. 8.9

Since each element mass m of a ring of negligible thickness is at the same distance from the axis, (Fig. 8.9), the moment of inertia about this axis is Σma^2,

i.e. $$a^2 \Sigma m$$

i.e. $$Ma^2$$

Example 8.2. *Find the moment of inertia of a uniform circular disc, mass M radius a, about an axis through the centre, perpendicular to the plane of the disc.*

Divide the disc (Fig. 8.10) into concentric rings, radius x, width δx. If m is the mass per unit area, the mass of each ring is approximately $m(2\pi x)\delta x$.

Thus the moment of inertia of the disc is

$$\int_0^a x^2(2\pi mx)\,dx = \int_0^a 2\pi mx^3\,dx$$

$$= \tfrac{1}{2}\pi ma^4$$

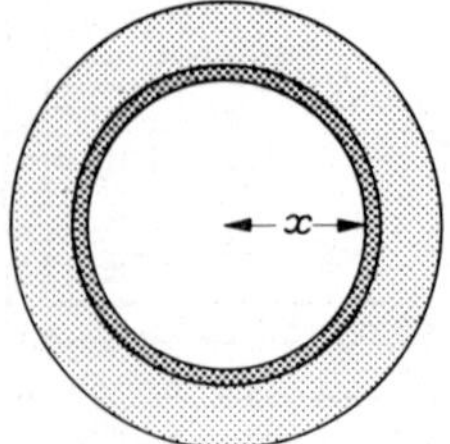

Fig. 8.10

But $$m(\pi a^2) = M, \quad \text{the mass of the disc,}$$

so $$I = \tfrac{1}{2}Ma^2$$

Example 8.3. *A thin uniform washer mass M is in the shape of a circular disc radius 2a from which a concentric circular disc radius a has been removed. Find the moment of inertia of the washer about an axis through the centre perpendicular to the plane of the washer.*

Consider the washer (Fig. 8.11) as the difference of two circular discs. Since the mass is proportional to the surface area, the mass of the larger disc is $\frac{4}{3}M$, and of the smaller disc is $\frac{1}{3}M$, the mass of the washer being given as M.

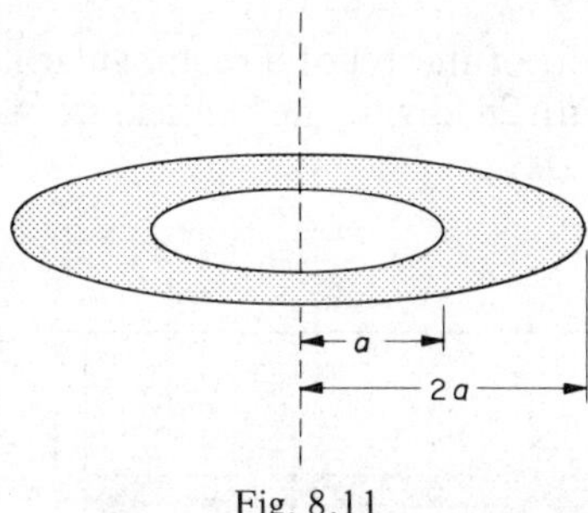

Fig. 8.11

The moment of inertia about the given axis is

$$\tfrac{1}{2}(\tfrac{4}{3}M)(2a)^2 - \tfrac{1}{2}(\tfrac{1}{3}M)(a^2)$$

i.e. $$\tfrac{5}{2}Ma^2$$

Example 8.4. *Find the moment of inertia of a uniform circular ring, mass M, radius a, about a diameter.*

Consider an element of arc (Fig. 8.12), mass $ma\delta\theta$. The moment of inertia of this about the diameter is

$$(ma\delta\theta)(a \sin \theta)^2$$

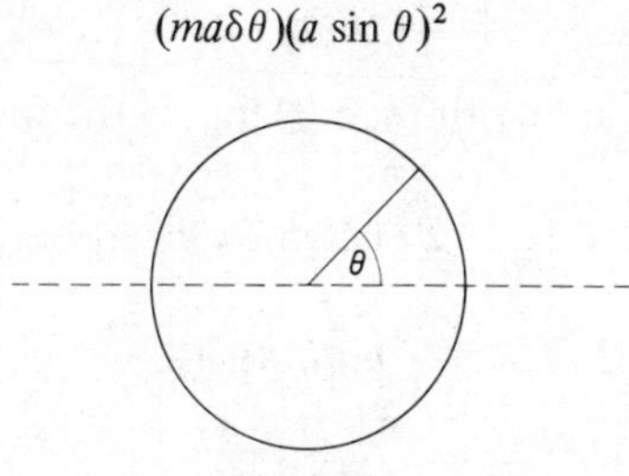

Fig. 8.12

Therefore the moment of inertia of the whole ring is

$$= \int_0^{2\pi} ma^3 \sin^2 \theta \, d\theta$$

$$= \pi ma^3$$

But the mass M of the ring is $2\pi ma$, as m is the mass per unit length,

$$\therefore \qquad I = \tfrac{1}{2}Ma^2$$

The 'stretching' rule

To find the moment of inertia of a rectangular lamina sides $2a$, $2b$, about a side of length $2a$, divide the lamina into strips mass $2bm\ \delta x$,

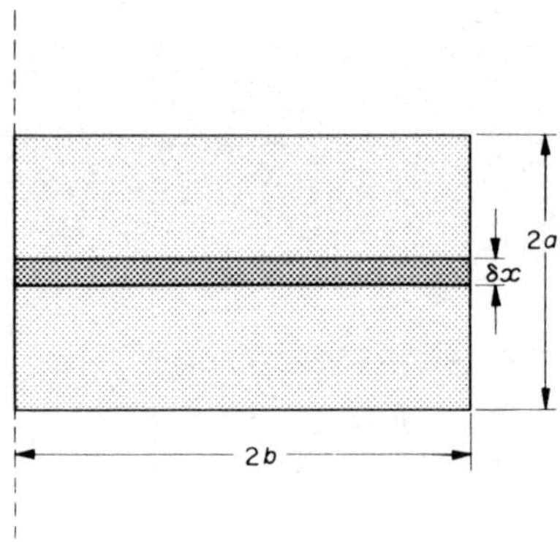

Fig. 8.13

thickness δx perpendicular to the axis of rotation (Fig. 8.13). The moment of inertia of any one strip is

$$\tfrac{4}{3}(2bm\delta x)b^2$$

Since these strips are of the same length, the moment of inertia of the lamina is

$$\Sigma\tfrac{4}{3}(2bm\ \delta x)b^2$$

i.e.
$$\int_0^{2a} \tfrac{8}{3}mb^3\ dx$$

i.e.
$$\tfrac{16}{3}mb^3a$$

i.e. $\frac{4}{3}Mb^2$, since $M = 4mab$

This is the same expression as the moment of inertia of a uniform rod, and the rectangular lamina can be obtained by 'stretching' the rod parallel to the axis of rotation.

This illustrates the 'stretching' rule, that *if a body can be obtained by stretching another body parallel to an axis, the mass being unaltered, then the moments of inertia of the bodies are equal. Thus a hollow cylinder can be obtained from a ring, so the moment of inertia about its axis is* Ma^2, *and a solid cylinder has moment of inertia* $\frac{1}{2}Ma^2$, *about its axis, as it can be obtained by stretching a circular disc.*

EXERCISE 8(a)

Use the definition of the moment of inertia (Σmr^2) or its calculus form to calculate the following:

1. The moment of inertia (M.I.) about the coordinate axis Ox of masses m, m, and $3m$ at points (1, 1), (2, 2), and (−1, 3) respectively. Deduce the radius of gyration about Ox of a light plate to which these masses are fixed.

2. The M.I. about Oy of masses m, $2m$, and $3m$ at (1, 1), (−2, −3), and (−1, 4) respectively.

3. The M.I. about $\mathbf{r} = \lambda\mathbf{i}$ of masses m, $2m$, and $3m$ at points position vectors $\mathbf{i} + 2\mathbf{j}$, $3\mathbf{i} + 4\mathbf{j}$, $\mathbf{i} - \mathbf{j}$, respectively.

4. The M.I. about the line $y = 1$ of masses m, m, and $2m$ at points (1, 1), (2, 1), and (3, −1) respectively.

5. Find the M.I. about Ox of masses m, $2m$, and $2m$ at points position vectors $\mathbf{i} + \mathbf{j}$, $2\mathbf{i} + \mathbf{j}$ and $\mathbf{i} + 2\mathbf{j}$ respectively. Deduce the M.I. about Oy.

6. Find the M.I. of a uniform rod, mass M, length $2a$, about an axis perpendicular to the rod through a point in the rod distance d from the midpoint.

7. Find the M.I. of the rod in Question 6 about an axis perpendicular to the rod through a point in the rod at a distance d from one end of the rod.

8. Find the M.I. of a rod AB, mass M, length $2a$, about an axis through A perpendicular to the rod, if the density of the rod at any point is proportional to its distance from B.

9. The density of a rod AB, length $2a$, increases linearly from a value k at A to $2k$ at B. Find the radius of gyration of the rod about an axis perpendicular to the rod (a) through A, (b) through B.

10. Find the M.I. of a square wire framework ABCD, mass M, of uniform rods, length $2a$, (a) about AB, (b) about AC, (c) about the perpendicular bisector of AB and CD.

11. Write down the M.I. about an axis through the centre perpendicular to its plane of a circular arc, mass M, radius a, which subtends an angle $\pi/2$ at the centre.

12. Find the M.I. of a uniform semi-circular ring, mass M, radius a, about an axis in the plane of the ring, inclined at an angle α to the axis of symmetry passing through the centre of the ring.

13. Find the M.I. of a uniform circular hoop, mass M, radius a, about an axis perpendicular to the plane, distant c from the centre (hint: use $r^2 = a^2 + c^2 - 2ac \cos \theta$).

14. Find the M.I. of a uniform isosceles triangular lamina, mass M, sides a, a, and $2b$, about an axis through the vertex parallel to the base.

15. Find the M.I. of the same lamina about an axis through the vertex perpendicular to the base, in the plane of the lamina.

16. Find the M.I. of a uniform square lamina, mass M, side $2a$, about an axis through the midpoints of two parallel sides of the square.

17. A uniform lamina, mass M, is in the shape of a parallelogram, sides $2a$, $2b$, with each of the smaller angles 60°. Find the M.I. about a side length $2a$.

18. Given that the M.I. of a uniform rectangular lamina, mass M, sides $2a$, $2b$, about an axis through the intersection of the diagonals perpendicular to the lamina is $\frac{1}{3}M(a^2 + b^2)$, find the M.I. of a cube edge $2a$ about an axis through the midpoints of two opposite faces.

Perpendicular axes rule

So far we have considered almost exclusively *laminae*, bodies whose mass may be regarded as in one plane. This rule applies only to such bodies. *If the moments of inertia of a lamina about two perpendicular axes Ox, Oy in the plane of the lamina are I_x and I_y, the moment of inertia about an axis through O perpendicular to the plane of the lamina is $I_x + I_y$.*

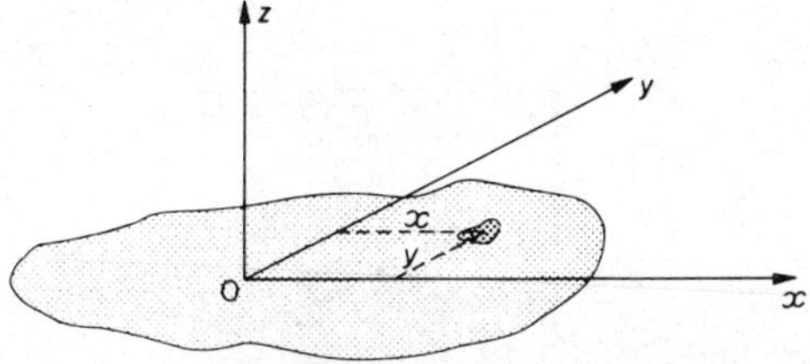

Fig. 8.14

The moment of inertia (Fig. 8.14) about Ox of an element mass m at the point (x, y) is my^2, and about Oy is mx^2. The distance of the element from Oz is $\sqrt{(x^2 + y^2)}$, so the moment of inertia of the lamina about Oz is

$$\begin{aligned} \Sigma m(x^2 + y^2) &= \Sigma mx^2 + \Sigma my^2 \\ &= I_y + I_x \end{aligned}$$

We have seen that the moment of inertia of a uniform ring, mass M, radius a, about a diameter is $\frac{1}{2}Ma^2$. So $I_x = I_y = \frac{1}{2}Ma^2 \Rightarrow I_z = Ma^2$, a result with which we are already familiar. Conversely, if we know only I_z, but realize that $I_x = I_y$ by symmetry, then $I_z = 2I_x$, as in Fig. 8.15.

If Ox is the axis parallel to a side through the midpoint of a square lamina, mass M, side $2a$, it can be seen by the stretching rule that the moment of inertia about Ox is $\frac{1}{3}Ma^2$. If Oy is the perpendicular axis in the plane of the lamina, $I_x = I_y$ by symmetry, and $I_y = \frac{1}{3}Ma^2$.

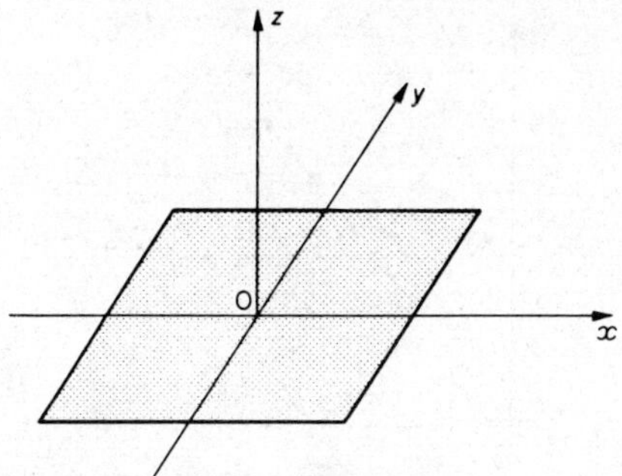

Fig. 8.15

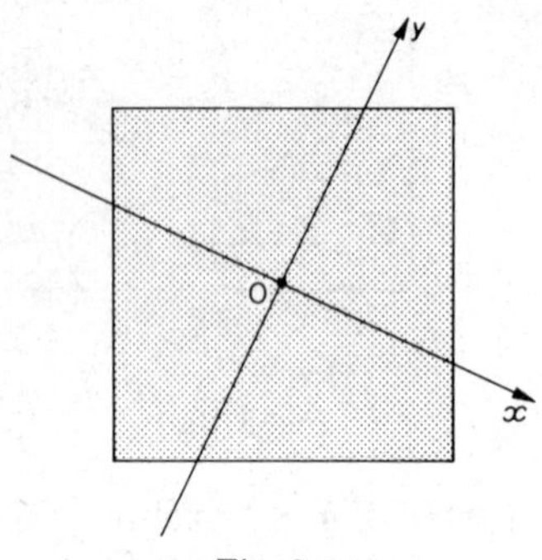

Fig. 8.16

Thus if Oz is perpendicular to both Ox and Oy,

$$I_z = \tfrac{2}{3}Ma^2, \quad \text{by the perpendicular axis theorem}$$

If, instead, Ox and Oy had been any two perpendicular lines in the plane of the lamina meeting at the midpoint (Fig. 8.16), from the rotational symmetry of the square, $I_x = I_y$.

But $$I_z = \tfrac{2}{3}Ma^2 = I_x + I_y$$

$\therefore$ $$I_x = I_y = \tfrac{1}{3}Ma^2$$

whatever the angle made by the axes with the sides of the square.

Example 8.5. *Find the moment of inertia of a uniform rectangular lamina, mass M, sides 2a, 2b, about an axis through a corner perpendicular to the lamina.*

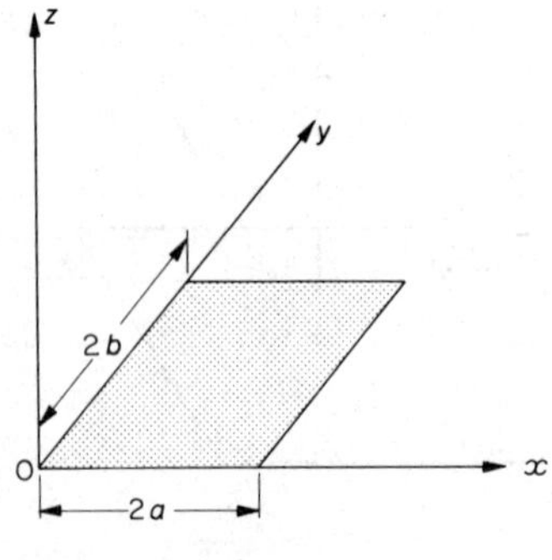

Fig. 8.17

Taking coordinate axes as in Fig. 8.17,

$$I_x = \tfrac{4}{3}Ma^2$$

and $$I_y = \tfrac{4}{3}Mb^2$$

applying the stretching rule to two rods, one parallel to each axis.

$\therefore$ $$I_z = \tfrac{4}{3}M(a^2 + b^2)$$

Example 8.6. *Find the moment of inertia of a uniform elliptic lamina mass M, semi-axes a, b, about an axis through the centre perpendicular to the lamina.*

If each chord parallel to the x axis of a circle radius b is stretched by a factor a/b, this does not alter the distance from the x axis of the mass of that chord (Fig. 8.18).

$\therefore$ $$I_x = \tfrac{1}{4}Mb^2$$

the same as the moment of inertia of the circle radius b. Similarly,

$$I_y = \tfrac{1}{4}Ma^2$$

compressing chords parallel to Oy by a factor b/a.

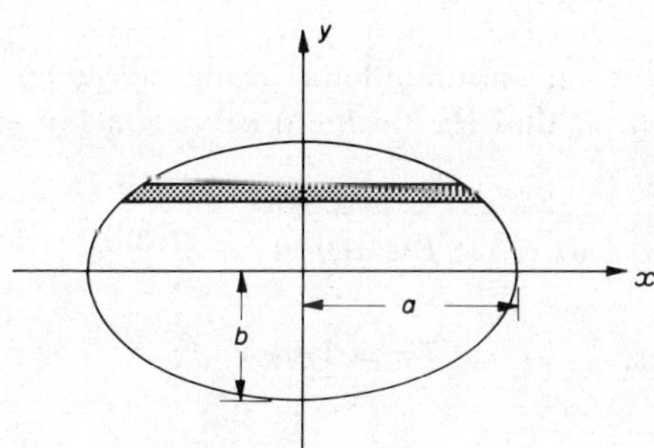

Fig. 8.18

Thus since

$$I_z = I_x + I_y$$
$$I_z = \tfrac{1}{4}M(a^2 + b^2)$$

It must be emphasized that this rule is true only for laminae. If applied to a sphere, centre O, $I_z = I_x + I_y$.

But $$I_x = I_y = I_z, \quad \text{by symmetry}$$

$\therefore$ $$I_x = I_y = I_z = 0, \quad \text{an absurd conclusion}$$

Moment of inertia of a solid

Many solids can be formed by stretching laminae, as the cube in Question 18 of Exercise 8(a). Others can be formed by rotating the area bounded by a plane curve. These latter are called solids of revolution, and can be divided into sections by planes perpendicular to the axis of rotation (Fig. 8.19).

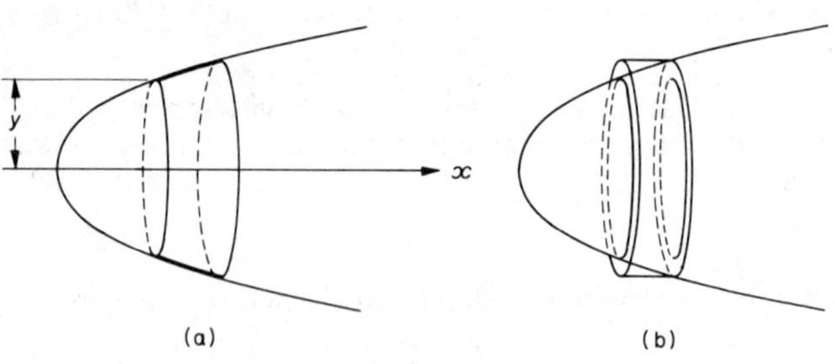

Fig. 8.19

These sections are bounded above and below by cylinders, radii y and $(y + \delta y)$, so that the moment of inertia I of each section is such that

$$\tfrac{1}{2}(m\pi y^2\ \delta x)y^2 < I < \tfrac{1}{2}[m\pi(y+\delta y)^2\ \delta x](y+\delta y)^2$$

Using calculus, $$I = \int \tfrac{1}{2}m\pi y^4\ \mathrm{d}x$$

A similar expression can be obtained for a solid of revolution about Oy.

Example 8.7. *Find the moment of inertia of a uniform solid sphere, mass M, radius a, about an axis through the centre of the sphere.*

Since the sphere can be formed (Fig. 8.20) by rotating about Ox the circle $x^2 + y^2 = a^2$,

$$I = \int_{-a}^{a} \tfrac{1}{2}m\pi y^4\ \mathrm{d}x$$

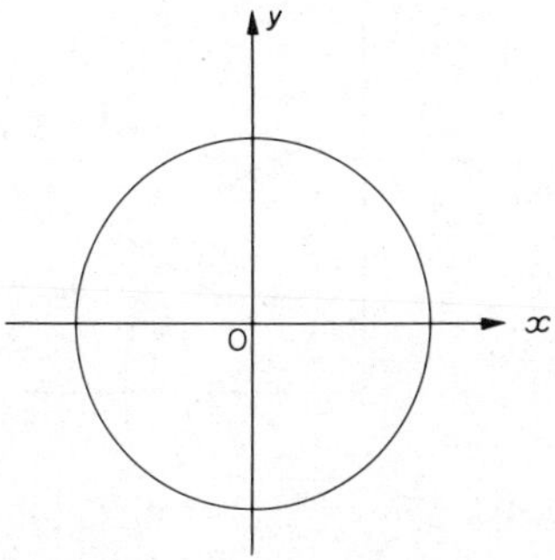

Fig. 8.20

where m is the mass per unit volume,

$$= \tfrac{1}{2} m\pi \int_{-a}^{a} (a^2 - x^2)^2 \, dx, \quad \text{as } y^2 = a^2 - x^2$$

But

$$I = m\pi \int_{0}^{a} (a^4 - 2a^2x^2 + x^4) \, dx$$

since the circle is symmetrical about Oy,

$$= m\pi\left[a^4x - \tfrac{2}{3}a^2x^3 + \tfrac{1}{5}x^5\right]_0^a$$

$$= \tfrac{8}{15} m\pi a^5$$

$$= \tfrac{2}{5} Ma^2, \quad \text{since } M = (\tfrac{4}{3}\pi a^3)m$$

Use of symmetry

When finding moments of inertia, it is most important to use any symmetry the body possesses. This was seen in Example 8.7 to help with the evaluating of the integral; the next example gives a further illustration of this point.

Example 8.8. *Find the moment of inertia of a uniform hollow spherical shell, mass M, radius a, about a diameter.*

The distance of an element of the shell (Fig. 8.21), mass m, coordinates (x, y, z), from the x axis is $\sqrt{(y^2 + z^2)}$.

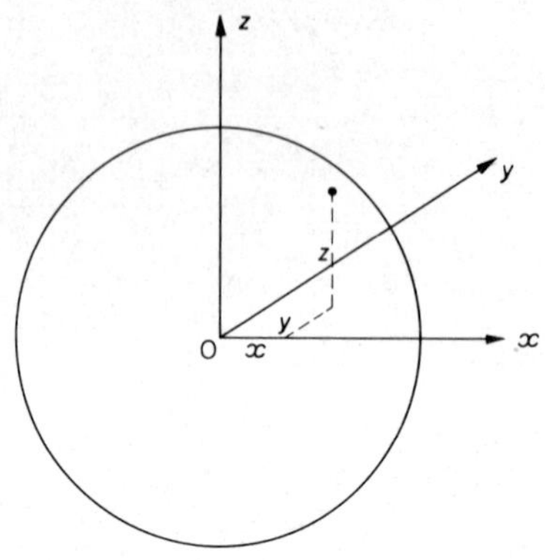

Fig. 8.21

By definition, $I_x = \Sigma m(y^2 + z^2)$

Similarly, $I_y = \Sigma m(z^2 + x^2)$

and $I_z = \Sigma m(x^2 + y^2)$

$$\therefore \quad I_x + I_y + I_z = \Sigma m(2x^2 + 2y^2 + 2z^2)$$
$$= 2\Sigma m(x^2 + y^2 + z^2)$$
$$= 2a^2 \Sigma m, \quad \text{since } x^2 + y^2 + z^2 = a^2$$

for all points on the sphere,

$$= 2Ma^2$$

But $I_x = I_y = I_z$, by symmetry,

$$I_x = \tfrac{2}{3}Ma^2$$

There are two alternative methods, either to divide the spherical shell into rings, or to consider the shell as the limit as $b \to a$ of a hollow sphere, external radius a, internal radius b. Both are very much longer than the above method.

Parallel axis rule

If the moment of inertia of a body mass M about an axis l through the centre of gravity of the body is I_G, then the moment of inertia about any axis parallel to l is $I_G + Mh^2$, where h is the distance between the axes.

We have already seen that the moment of inertia of a uniform rod about an axis through its midpoint perpendicular to the rod is $\frac{1}{3}Ma^2$, with the usual notation. The moment of inertia about a parallel axis through one end is $\frac{4}{3}Ma^2$, which can be written $M(\frac{1}{3}a^2 + a^2)$, and about a parallel axis a distance d from the centre of gravity is $M(\frac{1}{3}a^2 + d^2)$. These are both special cases of the parallel axis theorem.

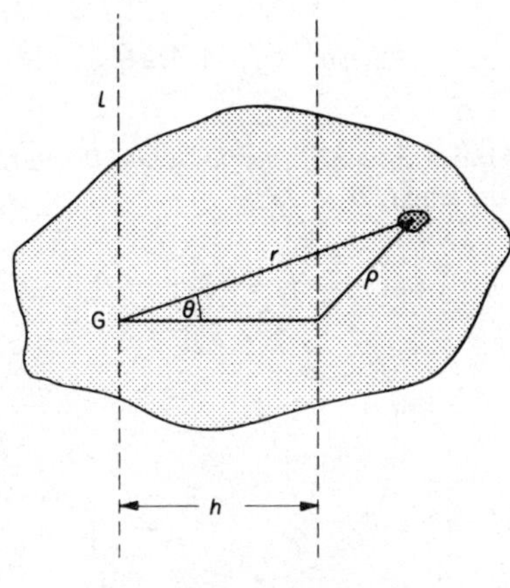

Fig. 8.22

Let the distance of an element mass m from the axis parallel to l be ρ (Fig. 8.22). Then by the cosine formula,

$$\rho^2 = r^2 + h^2 - 2rh\cos\theta$$

so that

$$\begin{aligned}\Sigma m\rho^2 &= \Sigma m(r^2 + h^2 - 2rh\cos\theta)\\ &= \Sigma mr^2 + h^2\Sigma m - 2h\Sigma mr\cos\theta\end{aligned}$$

But $\quad \Sigma mr^2 = I_G$

and $\Sigma mr\cos\theta = 0$, since this is the sum of the moments of the elements of the body about an axis through the centre of gravity.

$\therefore$

$$\begin{aligned}\Sigma m\rho^2 &= I_G + h^2\Sigma m\\ &= I_G + Mh^2\end{aligned}$$

This proof may be written more concisely using vectors, for

$$\boldsymbol{\rho} = \mathbf{r} - \mathbf{h}$$

$$\therefore \quad \Sigma m\rho^2 = \Sigma m(\mathbf{r} - \mathbf{h}) \cdot (\mathbf{r} - \mathbf{h})$$

$$= \Sigma mr^2 - 2\Sigma m\mathbf{r} \cdot \mathbf{h} + \Sigma mh^2$$

$$= \Sigma mr^2 - 2\mathbf{h} \cdot (\Sigma m\mathbf{r}) + h^2 \Sigma m$$

But $\Sigma m\mathbf{r} = 0$ from the definition of the centre of mas

$$\therefore \quad \Sigma m\rho^2 = I_G + Mh^2$$

Example 8.9. *Find the moment of inertia of a uniform ring mass M radius a about a tangent to the ring (Fig. 8.23)*

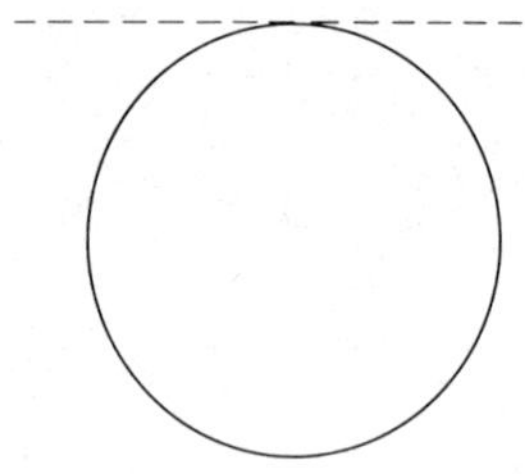

Fig. 8.23

The moment of inertia about a diameter is $\frac{1}{2}Ma^2$. The tangent is parallel to the diameter, and distant a. Therefore the moment of inertia about the tangent is

$$M(\tfrac{1}{2}a^2 + a^2) = \tfrac{3}{2}Ma^2$$

Summary of moments of inertia

The moments of inertia of the bodies which occur most frequently in this book are given in the table below. It will be found convenient to remember these.

Uniform rod, length 2a, axis through midpoint perpendicular to the rod	$\frac{1}{3}Ma^2$
Uniform rod, length 2a, axis through one end perpendicular to the rod	$\frac{4}{3}Ma^2$

Uniform rectangular lamina, 2a by 2b, axis through the midpoint perpendicular to the lamina	$\frac{1}{3}M(a^2 + b^2)$
Uniform hoop, radius a, axis through centre perpendicular to the hoop	Ma^2
Uniform circular disc, radius a, axis through centre perpendicular to the disc	$\frac{1}{2}Ma^2$
Uniform circular disc, radius a, diameter as axis,	$\frac{1}{4}Ma^2$
Uniform solid sphere, radius a, about any diameter	$\frac{2}{5}Ma^2$

The moments of inertia of many other bodies, e.g. cylinders, can be found by stretching one of the above.

Routh's rule

Observing that the denominators of the moments of inertia above are 3, 4, or 5, Routh* proposed that the moment of inertia of a body about a principal axis through its centre of gravity is

$$\text{M} \times \frac{\text{sum of the squares on the two other principal semi-axes}}{3, 4, \text{ or } 5}$$

The denominator is 3 if the body is a rod, a rectangular lamina or a cuboid; it is 4 if the body is circular or elliptic; it is 5 if the body is spherical or ellipsoidal. This is an empirical rule which is found to fit the theoretical results.

As an example, the moment of inertia of a rectangular lamina sides $2a$, $2b$, about an axis through the midpoint perpendicular to the plane of the lamina is

$$M\frac{a^2 + b^2}{3}$$

by Routh's rule. About an axis through the midpoints of the two sides length $2a$ the moment of inertia is

$$M\frac{a^2 + 0^2}{3}, \quad \text{i.e. } \tfrac{1}{3}Ma^2,$$

* E. J. Routh (1831–1907) was Senior Wrangler at Cambridge in 1850 when James Clerk Maxwell was Second Wrangler. Routh became a distinguished dynamicist.

as the other perpendicular semi-axis has zero length. In the case of the uniform circular disc, the axis being perpendicular to the plane of the disc, the moment of inertia is

$$M\frac{a^2+a^2}{4}, \quad \text{i.e. } \tfrac{1}{2}Ma^2$$

EXERCISE 8(b)

1. Find the M.I. of a uniform square lamina, mass M, side $2a$, about an axis through a vertex perpendicular to the plane of the lamina.

2. A uniform lamina, mass M, is in the shape of a rhombus, side $2a$, angle α. Find its moment of inertia about (a) an axis through the intersection of the diagonals, (b) an axis through a vertex, both axes being perpendicular to the plane of the lamina.

3. Find the M.I. of a rectangular lamina, sides $2a$, $2b$, about one of the sides length $2b$.

4. Find the M.I. of a circular cylinder, mass M, radius a, length l, about a diameter of one end.

5. Find the M.I. of the cylinder in Question 4 about a diameter through its centre of gravity.

6. Find the M.I. of a lamina in the shape of an isosceles triangle sides a, a, b about an axis through the vertex perpendicular to the plane of the lamina.

7. Find the M.I. of the lamina in Question 6 about an axis through its centre of gravity perpendicular to the lamina.

8. Find the M.I. of a uniform solid cone mass M, base radius a, and height h about

   (a) its axis,
   (b) a line through the vertex perpendicular to the axis,
   (c) a line through the centre of gravity perpendicular to the axis.

9. Find the radius of gyration of a uniform solid sphere, radius a, about a tangent.

10. Find the radius of gyration of a uniform solid hemisphere, radius a, (a) about a diameter d of the circular face, (b) about an axis through the centre of gravity parallel to d.

11. Find the radius of gyration of a uniform hollow hemispherical shell (a) about a diameter d of its circular section, (b) about an axis through the centre of gravity parallel to d.

12. The density at a point P of a sphere, radius a, is kx, where x is the distance of P from the centre of the sphere. Find the radius of gyration of the sphere about a diameter.

13. A ring, mass M, radius a, is fixed to a thin circular disc, mass $2M$, radius a, so that they are concentric. Find the radius of gyration of the body about an axis through the common centre perpendicular to the plane of the body.

14. Find the volume of the solid of uniform density formed by rotating the portion of the curve $y = a \sin x$ between $x = 0$ and $x = \pi$ through four right angles about the axis of x. Find also the radius of gyration of this solid about the x axis. (O. & C.)

15. A sledge hammer consists of an iron rectangular block 15 cm × 5 cm × 5 cm. A central circular hole of 2.5 cm diameter is bored through it at right angles to one of its longer faces, and a light wooden shaft, 0.9 m long, is fitted into it. Find the M.I. of the hammer about a line drawn through the midpoint of the far end of the shaft normal to the axis of the shaft and parallel to the small face of the block. (Take the density of iron as 7200 kg m^{-3}.) (C.S.)

Applications of moments of inertia

The term 'moment of inertia' was introduced because the quantity Σmr^2 occurred in the kinetic energy of a rigid body rotating about a fixed axis. The principle of the conservation of energy enables us to investigate such motion.

Example 8.10. *A uniform rod AB, mass M, length 2a, (Fig. 8.24) is freely hinged at A so that it can rotate in a vertical plane. Initially the rod is held horizontally, and is then released from rest. Find the angular velocity when the rod is vertical.*

The kinetic energy of the rod is

$$\tfrac{1}{2}I\omega^2, \quad \text{i.e. } \tfrac{1}{2}(\tfrac{4}{3}Ma^2)\omega^2$$

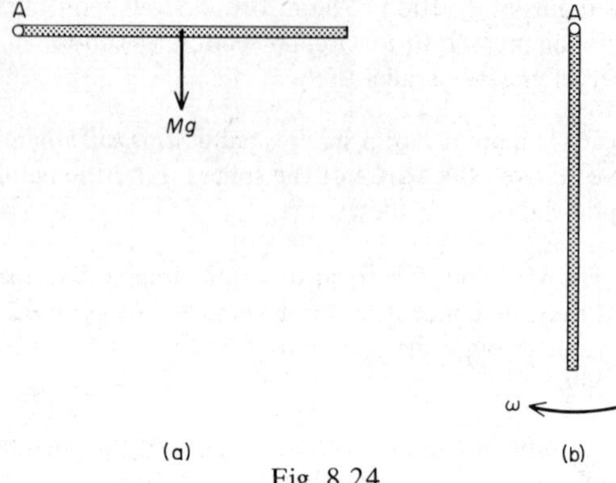

Fig. 8.24

the moment of inertia about an axis through A being required as the rod is rotating about A. When the rod is vertical, the potential energy, measured from the fixed horizontal level through A, is $-Mga$.

$$\therefore \qquad \tfrac{2}{3}Ma^2\omega^2 - Mga = 0$$

by the conservation of energy, i.e.

$$\omega = \sqrt{\frac{3g}{2a}}$$

when the rod is vertical.

Example 8.11. *A bucket, mass m, is raised or lowered by a light rope wrapped round a solid cylindrical axle, mass M, radius a (Fig. 8.25). If the bucket is released from rest, find the velocity when it has fallen a distance h.*

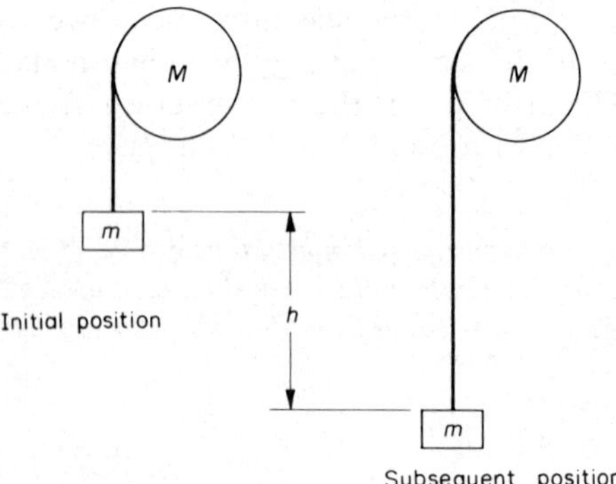

Fig. 8.25

The kinetic energy of the axle is $\frac{1}{2}(\frac{1}{2}Ma^2)\omega^2$, and that of the bucket is $\frac{1}{2}mv^2$. But,

$$v = a\omega$$

$$\therefore \qquad \text{total kinetic energy} = \tfrac{1}{4}(M + 2m)v^2$$

From the conservation of energy,

$$\tfrac{1}{4}(M + 2m)v^2 - mgh = 0$$

$$v = \sqrt{\left(\frac{4mgh}{M + 2m}\right)}$$

Notice that the velocity is less than $\sqrt{(2gh)}$, the value the velocity would attain if the bucket was not connected to the axle. Some of the potential energy lost by the bucket has given kinetic energy to the axle.

Example 8.12. *A non-uniform rod, mass M, is free to rotate in a vertical plane about a horizontal axis through a point C in the rod (Fig. 8.26). The distance of C from the centre of gravity G is h, and the moment of inertia*

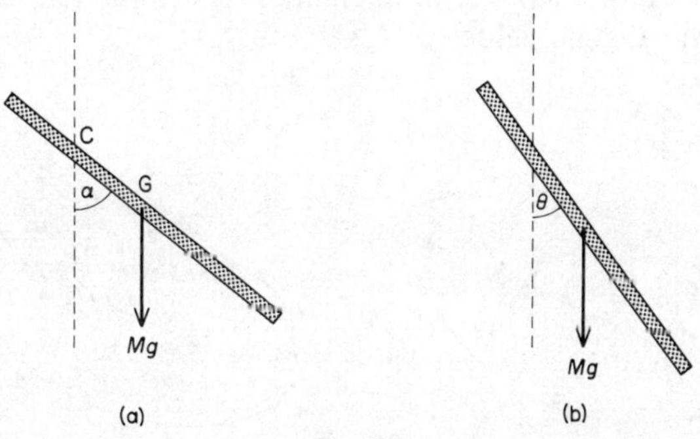

Fig. 8.26

about this axis is I. The rod hangs at rest in a vertical position with G below C. If it is pulled aside a small angular distance α, and then released from rest, investigate the subsequent motion.

From the conservation of energy,

$$-Mgh\cos\alpha = \tfrac{1}{2}I\left(\frac{d\theta}{dt}\right)^2 - Mgh\cos\theta$$

Differentiating,

$$I\frac{d\theta}{dt}\cdot\frac{d^2\theta}{dt^2} + Mgh\sin\theta\,\frac{d\theta}{dt} = 0$$

i.e.

$$\frac{d^2\theta}{dt^2} + \frac{Mgh}{I}\sin\theta = 0$$

If α is small, θ is also small, since $\theta < \alpha$, so that the equation of motion is approximately

$$\frac{d^2\theta}{dt^2} + \frac{Mgh}{I}\theta = 0$$

i.e. simple harmonic motion, period $2\pi\sqrt{\left(\frac{I}{Mgh}\right)}$.

Equation of motion: angular acceleration

If a rigid body is free to rotate about an axis through a fixed point O, and an element of the body is acted on by a force F, as in Fig. 8.27(a), the components of acceleration produced are $r\omega^2$ towards the axis and $r\,d\omega/dt$ at right angles to the radius vector, ω being the angular velocity.

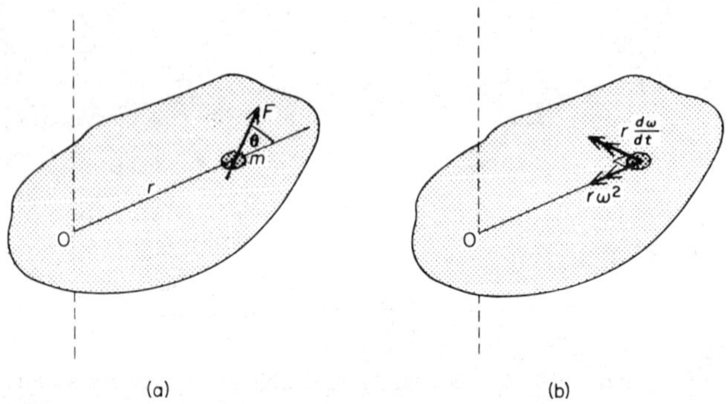

Fig. 8.27

Considering the motion perpendicular to OP,

$$F\sin\theta = mr\frac{d\omega}{dt}$$

i.e.

$$rF\sin\theta = mr^2\frac{d\omega}{dt}$$

so that
$$\Sigma rF \sin \theta = \Sigma mr^2 \frac{d\omega}{dt}$$
$$= I \frac{d\omega}{dt}$$

But $\Sigma rF \sin \theta$ is equal to the sum of the moments of all the external forces acting on the body, so that the equation of motion may be written
$$G = I \frac{d\omega}{dt}$$

where $G = \Sigma rF \sin \theta$, and is a couple acting in the sense of θ increasing.

Alternatively, expressed in vector notation, the equation of motion is
$$F \sin \theta \hat{\boldsymbol{\theta}} = mr \frac{d\omega}{dt} \hat{\boldsymbol{\theta}}$$

whence
$$\mathbf{r} \times (F \sin \theta \hat{\boldsymbol{\theta}}) = \mathbf{r} \times \left(mr \frac{d\omega}{dt} \hat{\boldsymbol{\theta}} \right),$$

i.e.
$$\mathbf{r} \times \mathbf{F} = \mathbf{r} \times \left(mr \frac{d\omega}{dt} \hat{\boldsymbol{\theta}} \right)$$

i.e.
$$\mathbf{r} \times \mathbf{F} = mr^2 \frac{d\omega}{dt} \hat{\mathbf{n}}$$

where $\hat{\mathbf{n}}$ is a unit vector perpendicular to both $\mathbf{r}$ and $\hat{\boldsymbol{\theta}}$.

Again
$$\mathbf{r} \times \mathbf{F} = G\hat{\mathbf{n}}$$

so
$$G = I \frac{d^2\theta}{dt^2}$$

Deducing the energy equation

The equation
$$G = I \frac{d^2\theta}{dt^2}$$

can be written
$$G \frac{d\theta}{dt} = I \frac{d\theta}{dt} \cdot \frac{d^2\theta}{dt^2}$$

and integrated to give

$$\tfrac{1}{2}I\left(\frac{d\theta}{dt}\right)^2 = \int G \, d\theta$$

a generalized form of the energy equation we have already used. Many problems can be solved with equal ease by either method, but usually if we wish to show that a certain motion is simple harmonic, $G = I\,d^2\theta/dt^2$ is slightly shorter, as there is no need to differentiate.

Example 8.13. *Show that the rod in Example 8.12 executes simple harmonic motion when slightly disturbed from the equilibrium position.*

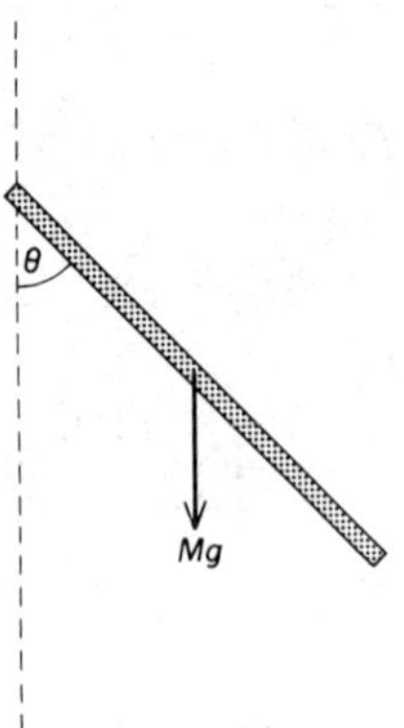

Fig. 8.28

The moment about the horizontal axis through A of the forces acting on the rod in Fig. 8.28 is

$$Mg(h \sin \theta)$$

in the sense of θ decreasing,

$$\therefore \qquad -Mgh \sin \theta = I\frac{d^2\theta}{dt^2}$$

$$\therefore \qquad \frac{d^2\theta}{dt^2} + \frac{Mgh}{I}\sin \theta = 0, \quad \text{as before, (page 236)}$$

Example 8.14. *A uniform circular disc, mass M, radius 2a, has a concentric disc radius a cut away. The remaining body is freely pivoted at a point P on the inside circumference so that it can rotate in a vertical plane. Show that it executes simple harmonic motion if slightly disturbed from an equilibrium position and find the period of small oscillations.*

There are, of course, two positions of equilibrium, but the only one which will produce small oscillations is that in which the circular hole is below P (Fig. 8.29).

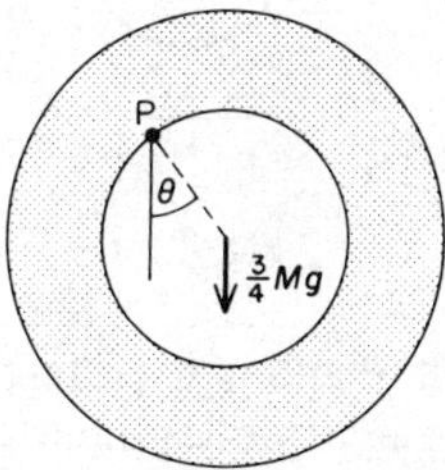

Fig. 8.29

The mass of the piece remaining is $\frac{3}{4}M$ and its moment of inertia about an axis through the common centre is

$$\tfrac{1}{2}M(2a)^2 - \tfrac{1}{2}(\tfrac{1}{4}M)a^2 = \tfrac{15}{8}Ma^2$$

Thus the moment of inertia about the axis through P is

$$\tfrac{3}{4}M(\tfrac{5}{2}a^2 + a^2), \quad \text{i.e. } \tfrac{21}{8}Ma^2$$

by the parallel axis theorem.

Considering the rotation about P,

$$-\tfrac{3}{4}Mga \sin\theta = \tfrac{21}{8}Ma^2 \frac{d^2\theta}{dt^2}$$

i.e.
$$\frac{d^2\theta}{dt^2} + \frac{2g}{7a}\sin\theta = 0$$

approximately simple harmonic motion, period $2\pi\sqrt{(7a/2g)}$ when θ is small.

Connected bodies: pulleys

Fig. 8.30 shows a smooth light string, one end of which is wrapped around a uniform solid circular axle A, mass m, radius a. The string

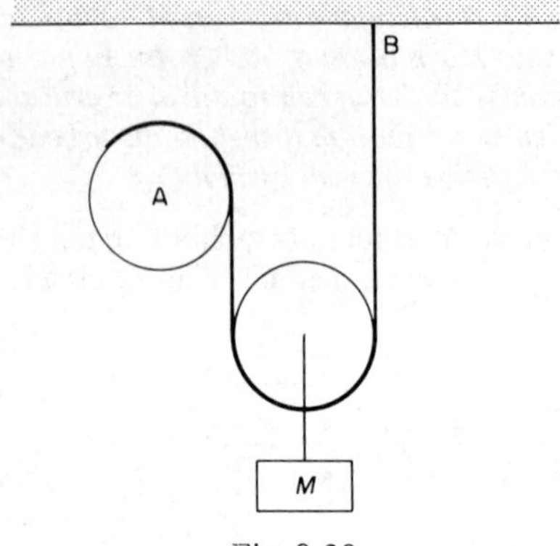

Fig. 8.30

passes under a light pulley and is then fastened at a fixed point B in the ceiling. From the light pulley hangs a load mass M.

In investigating the motion of the system, suppose first that the axle can rotate freely. As M descends a distance x, a length $2x$ of string is required. Since the end B is fixed, this string must come from that wound on the axle, so the axle must rotate through an angle $2x/a$ radians. Thus if v is the velocity of M and ω the angular velocity of the axle,

$$v = \frac{a\omega}{2}$$

From the conservation of energy,

$$\tfrac{1}{2}(\tfrac{1}{2}ma^2)\omega^2 + \tfrac{1}{2}Mv^2 - Mgx = 0$$

when the mass M has fallen a distance x.

$$\therefore \qquad (m + \tfrac{1}{2}M)v^2 = Mgx, \quad \text{using } v = a\omega/2$$

Thus the velocity v after falling a distance x is obtained.

To find the acceleration,

$$(m + \tfrac{1}{2}M)2v\frac{\mathrm{d}v}{\mathrm{d}t} = Mgv, \quad \text{since } v = \frac{\mathrm{d}x}{\mathrm{d}t}$$

$$\therefore \qquad \frac{\mathrm{d}v}{\mathrm{d}t} = \frac{Mg}{2m + M}$$

Couple acting at an axle

In the above example, if there is a couple G acting at the axle A, the work done in turning the axle through an angle θ is $G\theta$

$\therefore$ the energy equation becomes

$$\tfrac{1}{2}(\tfrac{1}{2}ma^2)\omega^2 + \tfrac{1}{2}Mv^2 - Mgx + G\theta = 0$$

i.e.
$$(m + \tfrac{1}{2}M)v^2 - Mgx + 2G\frac{x}{a} = 0$$

Thus
$$v^2 = \frac{2Mgax - 4Gx}{a(2m + M)}$$

and
$$\frac{dv}{dt} = \frac{Mga - 2G}{a(2m + M)}$$

As we expect, both the velocity and the acceleration are less than when the axle can rotate freely.

EXERCISE 8(c)

1. A uniform rod AB, mass M, length $2a$, can rotate freely in a vertical plane about a horizontal axis through A. To the end B is fixed a small body mass $2M$. Initially the rod is at rest in a horizontal position. If it is then released, find the angular velocity when the rod is vertical.

2. A circular disc, mass M, radius a, can rotate freely in a vertical plane about a horizontal axis through the centre O. A small body, mass M, is fixed at a point P on the circumference of the disc, and is held so that OP makes an angle of 60° with the downward vertical. Find the velocity of P when OP is vertical.

3. A square lamina, side $2a$, mass M, has four equal small bodies mass M attached, one to each vertex. If the lamina can rotate in a vertical plane about an axis through a vertex, find the period of small oscillations when slightly disturbed from equilibrium.

4. A uniform solid sphere, radius a, can rotate freely about a fixed horizontal axis which is a tangent to the sphere at a point A. The sphere is initially at rest with its centre vertically above the axis. If it is then given a small displacement, find the greatest angular velocity in the subsequent motion.

5. If the sphere in Question 4 is initially at rest below the axis, and is then given an angular velocity $\sqrt{(5g/7a)}$, find the angle through which the sphere oscillates in the subsequent motion.

6. A uniform hollow spherical shell, mass m, radius a, has a small body, mass m, fixed at a point X on the shell. The system can rotate freely either about a horizontal axis through the centre of the shell, or about a parallel axis touching the shell at the point diametrically opposite X. Find the period of small oscillations in each case, when slightly disturbed from equilibrium.

7. Two particles, each mass m, are attached one to each end of a diameter PQ of a uniform circular disc, mass $4m$, radius a, centre O. The system is free to rotate about a horizontal axis through A, a point on PQ such that OA = b. The system is released from rest when PQ is horizontal. Show that the M.I. about the axis is $2m(2a^2 + 3b^2)$, and that the angular velocity ω when PQ is vertical is given by

$$\omega^2 = \frac{6gb}{2a^2 + 3b^2}$$

(O. & C.)

8. A uniform rod, mass M, length $4l$, can rotate freely in a vertical plane about a horizontal axis through a point in it distant l from one end. Find the period of small oscillations if released from rest at a small angle α to the vertical.

9. P and Q are midpoints of adjacent sides of a rectangular lamina mass M, sides $2a$, $2b$. P is the midpoint of a side $2a$. If T_1, T_2 are the periods of small oscillations in a vertical plane about axes through P, Q perpendicular to the plane of the lamina, respectively, find $T_1^2 : T_2^2$.

10. Three equal uniform rods, each of length $2l$ and mass m, are rigidly joined together at their ends to form a triangular frame. The frame can rotate freely about a fixed horizontal axis through one vertex, perpendicular to the plane containing the rods. If the frame is released from rest in a position with the rod opposite the axis vertical, prove that the greatest angular velocity in the ensuing motion is $\sqrt{(2g/l\sqrt{3})}$.

(O. & C.)

11. A uniform rod AB is free to rotate about a horizontal axis through the end A. A small body M, equal in mass to the rod, is fixed at a point in the rod. When M is at B, the period of small oscillations is T_1: when M is at the midpoint of AB, the period of small oscillations is T_2. Find the ratio $T_1^2 : T_2^2$.

12. An engine is driving a flywheel, M.I. about the axis of rotation 1000 kg m^2 at 120 revolutions per minute. When the engine is suddenly switched off the flywheel comes to rest after 100 revolutions. Find the magnitude of the retarding couple.

13. A top, M.I. about the axis of rotation 0.01 kg m^2, is set in motion by pulling a string 1 metre long with a constant force of 50 N. Find the angular velocity with which the top begins to spin.

14. Two solid cylindrical drums, each mass m, radius a, are free to rotate about their horizontal axes. A smooth light rope is wound around the drums and passes under a light pulley which supports a load mass M (Fig. 8.31). Find the velocity of the load when it has fallen a distance h, assuming that the rope is so long that the free lengths may be regarded as vertical.

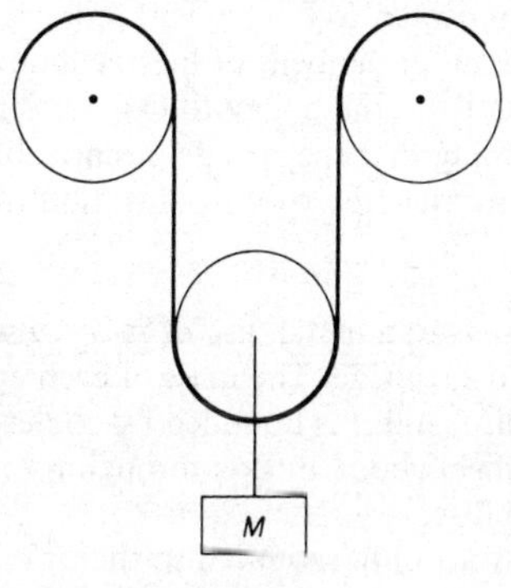

Fig. 8.31

A braking couple G is then applied to each axis. Find the further distance the load descends before it comes to rest.

15. A heavy pulley which may be regarded as a uniform circular disc of mass $6m$, centre O, and radius a, can turn freely in a vertical plane about a horizontal axis through O. A light inextensible string passes over the pulley, and particles of mass $2m$ and $3m$ are attached at its free ends. The system is released from rest and the string does not slip on the pulley. Show that the acceleration of the heavier particle is $g/8$. After time t a constant frictional couple is applied to the pulley and in consequence the system comes to rest again in a further time t. Assuming that the heavier particle does not reach the ground throughout the motion, calculate (a) the total distance covered by the heavier particle, (b) the magnitude of the frictional couple. (A.E.B.)

16. A flywheel has a horizontal axle radius r. The system has mass M and radius of gyration k about its axis, and rotates without friction. A string is wound around the axle and carries a mass m hanging freely. If the system is released from rest, prove that the acceleration of the mass is

$$\left(\frac{mr^2}{Mk^2 + mr^2}\right)g$$

If the string slips off the axle after the mass m has descended a distance $8r$, find the magnitude of the constant retarding couple which is necessary to bring the flywheel to rest after n more revolutions.

(A.E.B.)

17. A particle P of mass m rests on a rough horizontal table. The coefficient of friction between the particle and the table is $\mu, <1$. Another particle Q, mass m, is connected to P by a light string which passes over a rough pulley, radius a, moment of inertia about the axis of rotation I, so that the string from the pulley to Q is vertical. The system is released from rest. Assuming that the string does not slip on the pulley and that the pulley rotates freely on its axis, find the acceleration of the system.

18. A flywheel consists of a metal disc of radius a with an annulus welded concentrically to each side. The mass of each annulus is the same as the mass M of the disc, and it is bounded by circles radii a, $\frac{3}{4}a$. Find the M.I. of the flywheel about an axis through its centre perpendicular to the plane of the disc.
The flywheel is smoothly mounted so that it can rotate about this axis, which is horizontal, and a small particle mass m is attached at a point on the outside edge of the flywheel. Find the maximum angular speed of the flywheel if the system is slightly disturbed from rest with the particle at its highest point.
Prove that the period of small oscillations of the system about its position of stable equilibrium is

$$\frac{\pi}{2}\sqrt{\left[\frac{a(33M + 16m)}{mg}\right]}$$

(S.U.J.B.)

19. The couple produced by the motor driving a shaft is $G(1 - \cos 2\theta)$, where θ is the angle through which the shaft has turned. There is a constant load on the shaft exerting a couple G. A flywheel is attached to the shaft, which is designed to run within x per cent of an average speed of ω rad s^{-1}. Show that the M.I. of the flywheel about the axis of rotation is $50G/\omega^2 x$.

20. When a magnet, magnetic moment M, is at angle θ to a field of strength H, a restoring couple $MH \sin\theta$ acts on the magnet. If such a magnet is freely suspended in the field about a pivot at its centre of gravity, and is then slightly disturbed, prove that it will execute s.h.m., period $2\pi\sqrt{(I/MH)}$, where I is the M.I. of the magnet about the axis.

21. A certain type of torpedo is propelled by using the energy stored in a flywheel. The flywheel may be regarded as a uniform circular disc, mass 100 kg, radius 0.6 m, and is initially rotating at 12 000 r.p.m. If the average resistance experienced by the torpedo is 3000 N, find the rate at which the flywheel is rotating after the torpedo has travelled 500 m.

22. A drum of radius a is mounted with its axis horizontal and a light inextensible string is attached at a point on the circumference of the drum. Part of the string is wound around the drum and the remainder hangs vertically with a mass M attached at the lower end. A constant couple G is applied to the drum, causing the mass to rise a distance x. Prove that the speed of the mass is given by

$$v^2 = \frac{2xa(G - Mag)}{I + Ma^2}$$

where I is the moment of inertia of the drum about its axis, and deduce that the upward acceleration of the mass is

$$\frac{a(G - Mag)}{I + Ma^2}$$

(M.E.I.)

23. A light rod AB, of length l, has a particle mass m fixed at A and a particle mass $4m$ fixed at B. A point P of the rod, where AP $= x$, is freely pivoted to a fixed point. Prove that, if $x < \frac{4}{5}l$, the rod can swing like a pendulum in a vertical plane through P with B below P. Prove that the period of oscillation is

$$2\pi\left[\frac{4(l-x)^2 + x^2}{4g(l-x) - gx}\right]^{1/2}.$$

Prove that there is a minimum value of this period and find the value of x for which it occurs. (O. & C.)

24. A rough string passes over a pulley and supports masses M and $2m$ at its ends when the pulley is held fixed. The moment of inertia of the pulley is na^2, where a is the radius and $m < M < 2m$. The system is now released. Find, from considerations of energy or otherwise, the velocity

V of the mass M when it has risen a height h. At this moment half of the $2m$ mass falls off. Find the velocity U of the mass M as it reaches the position it had at the beginning of the whole motion and show that

$$\frac{U^2}{V^2} = \frac{m(n + 2M)}{(2m - M)(n + M + m)}$$

There is no slipping between the string and the pulley. (O. & C.)

9. Conservation of Energy and Momentum: Further Applications of Newton's Law

Newton's law $\mathbf{F} = m\mathbf{a}$, we have seen, is fundamental to our study of mechanics. The alternative time-integral form

$$\int F \, dt = \text{change in momentum}$$

and the distance-integral form

$$\int \mathbf{F} \, . \, d\mathbf{s} = \text{change in kinetic energy}$$

do give us other methods of solving problems which are sometimes easier than a direct application of $\mathbf{F} = m\mathbf{a}$.

Systems of pulleys

Consider a body mass m on a smooth horizontal table. A string, one end of which is attached to m, passes over a smooth pulley fixed at the edge of the table and under a smooth heavy pulley mass M, then is fastened at a fixed point in the ceiling (Fig. 9.1).

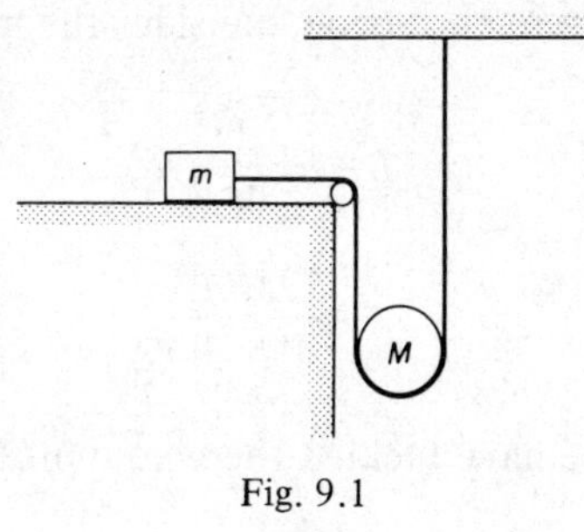

Fig. 9.1

When the pulley M descends a distance x, a length of string $2x$ is required so that the mass m moves a distance $2x$ towards the edge of the table. The velocity of M is $\mathrm{d}x/\mathrm{d}t$ and the velocity of m is $(\mathrm{d}/\mathrm{d}t)(2x)$, i.e. $2\ \mathrm{d}x/\mathrm{d}t$. Denoting $\mathrm{d}x/\mathrm{d}t$ by v, the kinetic energy of the system is

$$\tfrac{1}{2}Mv^2 + \tfrac{1}{2}m(2v)^2, \quad \text{i.e. } \tfrac{1}{2}Mv^2 + 2mv^2$$

The external forces acting on the system are the weight of the heavy pulley Mg, and the equal and opposite forces, the weight of m and the reaction of the table. Thus taking $-\mathbf{k}$ as a unit vector vertically downwards, if the pulley M has descended a distance x since the system was released from rest,

$$\int \mathbf{F} \,.\, \mathrm{d}\mathbf{s} = \text{change in kinetic energy}$$

$$\Rightarrow (-Mg\mathbf{k}) \,.\, (-x\mathbf{k}) = \tfrac{1}{2}Mv^2 + 2mv^2$$

i.e.
$$Mgx = \tfrac{1}{2}Mv^2 + 2mv^2$$

Thus the velocity of M is equal to

$$\sqrt{\left(\frac{2Mgx}{M+4m}\right)}$$

To find the acceleration of the pulley, differentiating,

$$Mg\frac{\mathrm{d}x}{\mathrm{d}t} = (\tfrac{1}{2}M + 2m)2v\frac{\mathrm{d}v}{\mathrm{d}t}$$

i.e.
$$\frac{\mathrm{d}v}{\mathrm{d}t} = \frac{Mg}{M+4m}, \quad \text{since } v = \frac{\mathrm{d}x}{\mathrm{d}t}$$

To find the tension in the string, consider the mass m. Newton's law gives

$$T = m\frac{\mathrm{d}}{\mathrm{d}t}(2v)$$

i.e.
$$T = \frac{2Mmg}{M+4m}$$

We could of course have tackled the whole problem using Newton's law (Fig. 9.2):

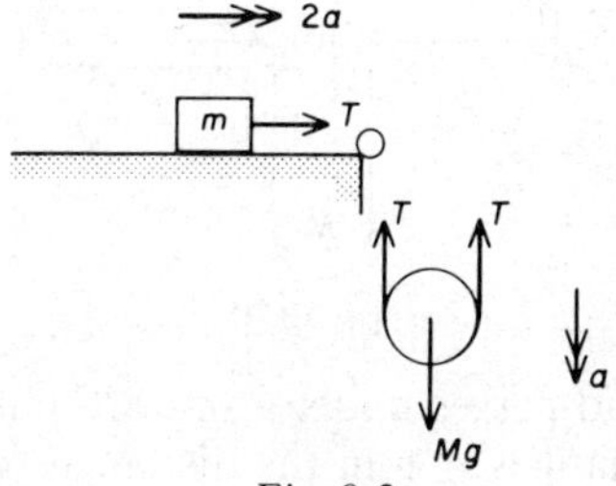

Fig. 9.2

For the mass m, $T = m(2a)$

and for the pulley $Mg - 2T = Ma$

$$\Rightarrow a = \frac{Mg}{M + 4m} \quad \text{and} \quad T = \frac{2Mmg}{M + 4m}$$

The velocity v can be found writing $a = v\,\mathrm{d}v/\mathrm{d}s$ and integrating, or since the acceleration is constant, from $v^2 = u^2 + 2as$. The two methods of solution show that if the velocities of such a system are required, it is easier to consider energy; if forces or accelerations are required, Newton's law is usually better.

Rough table, rough pulleys

If the table is rough, with coefficient of friction μ between the table and the mass m, the energy equation becomes

$$Mgx - \mu mg(2x) = \tfrac{1}{2}Mv^2 + 2mv^2$$

$$\Rightarrow v = \sqrt{\left[\frac{(2M - 4\mu m)g}{M + 4m}\right]}$$

assuming $M > 2\mu m$, the condition that the system moves from rest.

If either pulley is rough it will rotate and so acquire kinetic energy due to that rotation and we need to know the moment of inertia of that pulley and proceed as in Chapter 8.

Moving pulleys

As problems become more complicated it is important to study the geometry carefully to ensure that correct velocities and accelerations are used. If a string connects two bodies m, m' on smooth

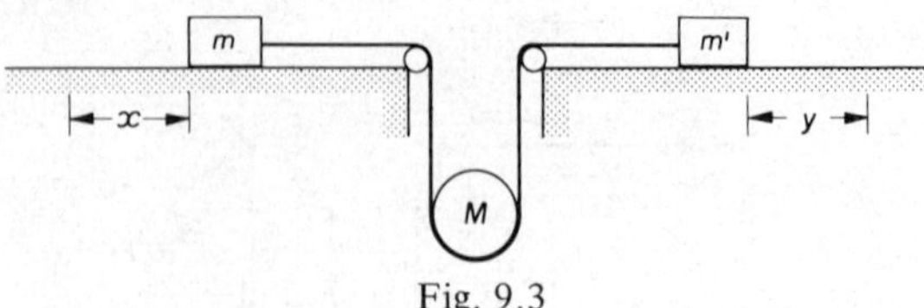

Fig. 9.3

horizontal tables and passes under a smooth pulley mass M hanging freely (Fig. 9.3), changes x, y in the distances of m, m' from the edge of the table allow a change $\frac{1}{2}(x + y)$ in the height of M, assuming that the string is vertical from the edge of the tables to M. Further, when a string passes over a moving pulley, care must be taken to ensure that the total acceleration is used and not the acceleration relative to a pulley which is itself moving.

Example 9.1. *Two bodies, masses m, 2m, are connected by a light inextensible string which passes over a smooth pulley, mass m. The axle of the pulley is fastened to one end of a second string which passes over a smooth fixed pulley and has a mass 4m attached at the other end. The system is free to move in a vertical plane. Find the acceleration of the body mass 4m.*

Fig. 9.4 shows the accelerations and forces on each part of the system, T and T' being the tensions in the strings. If the acceleration of the mass $2m$ is a'

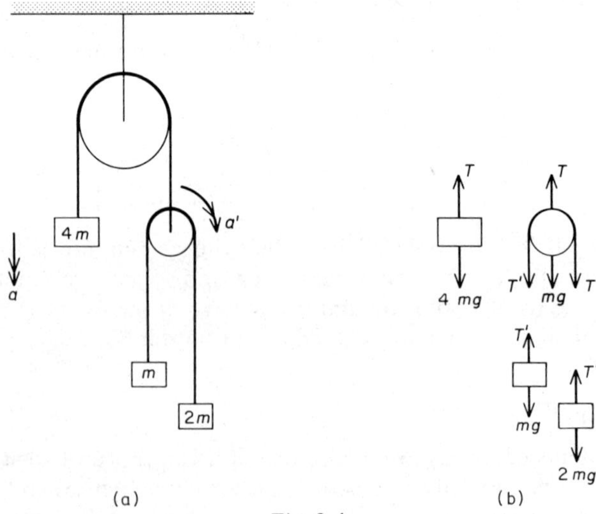

Fig. 9.4

relative to the pulley mass m, since the pulley itself has acceleration a upwards, the mass $2m$ has acceleration $(a' - a)$ downwards, and the mass at the other end of the string has acceleration $(a' + a)$ upwards.

Applying Newton's law to the pulley and each of the three masses,

$$T - mg - 2T' = ma \tag{9.1}$$

$$T' - mg = m(a' + a) \tag{9.2}$$

$$2mg - T' = 2m(a' - a) \tag{9.3}$$

and

$$4mg - T = 4ma \tag{9.4}$$

We have four equations in four unknowns and we wish to find a. T occurs only in equations 9.1 and 9.4, a' only in equations 9.2 and 9.3,

so

$$3mg - 2T' = 5ma$$

and

$$4mg - 3T' = -4ma$$

giving

$$a = \tfrac{1}{23}g$$

Notice that if the masses m, $2m$ had been replaced by equal masses $(3/2)m$, the system could have stayed at rest: as it is, there is a small acceleration $(1/23)g$ downwards for the mass $4m$.

Motion on the surface of a wedge

When considering the motion of bodies on the surface of a wedge it is most important to be clear what unknowns we are using for the accelerations (or velocities). Suppose that a wedge, mass M, angle α, is at rest on a smooth horizontal table, and a particle mass m is placed on the inclined face of the wedge (Fig. 9.5). If the acceleration of the wedge is $\mathbf{a}$ and the acceleration of the particle relative to the face of the wedge is $\mathbf{a}'$, the acceleration of the particle will be the vector sum of $\mathbf{a}$ and $\mathbf{a}'$. Since these are not in the same directions we must emphasize that they are vectors; in the earlier examples in this chapter that has not been necessary.

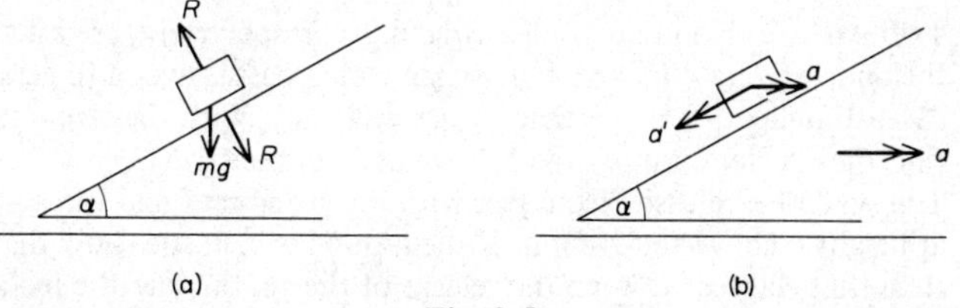

Fig. 9.5

The acceleration of the wedge is caused by the force between the particle and the wedge. The weight of the wedge and the reaction of the table on the wedge are equal and opposite and do not affect the motion of the wedge, so they are not marked in the figure. Thus for the wedge,

$$R \sin \alpha = Ma \tag{9.5}$$

To find the acceleration of the wedge, consider the motion of the particle perpendicular to the face of the wedge,

$$mg \cos \alpha - R = m(a \sin \alpha)$$

i.e. $$m(g \cos \alpha - a \sin \alpha) \sin \alpha = Ma$$

$\Rightarrow$ $$a = \frac{mg \sin \alpha \cos \alpha}{M + m \sin^2 \alpha}$$

Notice that the dimensions are L T^{-2}, those of acceleration, also that when M is large relative to m, the acceleration is very small, as expected.

To find the acceleration of the particle down the face of the wedge, the components of force and acceleration in that direction give

$$mg \sin \alpha = m(a' - a \cos \alpha)$$

whence $$a' = \frac{(M + m)g \sin \alpha}{M + m \sin^2 \alpha}$$

From equation 9.5, the reaction R is $Ma/\sin \alpha$,

i.e. $$R = \frac{Mmg \cos \alpha}{M + m \sin^2 \alpha}$$

EXERCISE 9(a)

1. Two particles P and Q, of mass m and $2m$, respectively, are attached to the ends of a light inextensible string which passes over a fixed small smooth pulley. If the particles move vertically, with the string taut, find the acceleration of P and the tension in the string.
   The system is released from rest with the string taut and the particle Q at height h above the ground. If the ground is inelastic show that the time that elapses between the release of the system and the instant that Q is next at instantaneous rest above the ground is $2\sqrt{(6h/g)}$. (C.)

2. A heavy uniform chain of length $2l$ and mass M hangs over a smooth peg. A body mass M is attached at one end of the chain and the system is released from rest when the body is at a distance l below the peg, both parts of the chain being vertical. By considering the conservation of energy prove that the velocity of the body just before the other end of the chain has left the peg is $\sqrt{(3lg/2)}$.

3. A light inextensible string passes over a fixed smooth pulley. To one end is fixed a body of mass $6m$, to the other end a pulley of mass $3m$, over which passes a similar string carrying masses $2m$ and m at its ends. Find the acceleration of the mass $6m$.

4. Two particles A and B, of masses m and M respectively are attached to the ends of a light inextensible string of length l which passes over a small smooth pulley P at the edge of a rough horizontal table. A is placed on the table a distance a from the edge and B hangs vertically. When the system is released from rest, B moves vertically downwards. Prove that the acceleration f of each particle and the tension T in the string before A reaches P are given by

$$f = \frac{(M - \mu m)g}{M + m} \quad \text{and} \quad T = \frac{Mmg(1 + \mu)}{M + m}$$

where μ ($\mu < M/m$) is the coefficient of friction between A and the table. (O. & C.)

5. A light inextensible string has one end fixed. The string passes under a smooth movable pulley mass M, over a smooth fixed pulley, and has a mass m attached at the other end. All parts of the string not in contact with a pulley are vertical. Find the velocity of the mass m when it has descended a distance x, given $2m > M$.

6. A wedge of mass M and angle α is at rest on a smooth horizontal table. A particle mass m is placed on the smooth inclined face on the wedge, and a horizontal force F is applied towards the edge of the wedge. Show that the acceleration of the wedge is $(F - mg \sin \alpha \cos \alpha)/(M + m \sin^2 \alpha)$ and the reaction between the wedge and the particle is

$$\frac{m(F \sin \alpha + Mg \cos \alpha)}{M + m \sin^2 \alpha}$$

7. A wedge of mass M and angle α is at rest on a rough horizontal plane. A particle mass m slides down the smooth inclined face of the wedge. Find the least value of the coefficient of friction between the wedge and the table if the wedge stays at rest during this motion.

8. A wedge, mass M, angle α, is at rest on a rough horizontal plane. The coefficient of friction between the wedge and the plane is μ. A particle of mass m is placed gently on the smooth inclined face of the wedge. If friction is not sufficiently great to prevent motion, show that the wedge moves with acceleration

$$\frac{m\cos\alpha(\sin\alpha - \mu\cos\alpha) - \mu M}{m\sin\alpha(\sin\alpha - \mu\cos\alpha) + M}g$$

9. A symmetrical double wedge of mass M and isosceles cross-section rests on a smooth horizontal table. The lines of greatest slope in the two inclined faces (both smooth) each make an angle α with the horizontal. Particles of mass m_1 and m_2 are initially at rest on the faces and are connected by a light inextensible string which lies entirely in a line of greatest slope and which passes over a smooth pulley at the apex of the wedge. Prove that the wedge begins to move with acceleration

$$\frac{g(m_1 - m_2)\sin\alpha\cos\alpha}{M + (m_1 + m_2)\sin^2\alpha}$$

Find the tension in the string during the initial part of the motion. (C.)

10. A smooth wedge of mass M whose inclined face makes an angle α with the horizontal, rests on a smooth horizontal table on which it is free to move. A particle of mass m falls vertically on to the inclined face of the wedge, the velocity at impact being V. If the coefficient of restitution between the particle and the wedge is e, show that the wedge moves with velocity

$$\frac{mV(1 + e)\sin\alpha\cos\alpha}{M + m\sin^2\alpha}$$

after impact. (A.E.B.)

Harder examples, including variable mass

Example 9.2. *Two equal bodies A, B, mass m, are connected by a light string and are initially at rest on a smooth horizontal table with the string just taut. The body A is projected with a horizontal velocity at right angles to AB. Find the velocities of A and B when the string has turned through a right angle.*

Since the table is smooth and there are not any horizontal forces on the system, both linear momentum and kinetic energy are conserved. Since momentum is conserved parallel to the initial direction of AB, and the masses

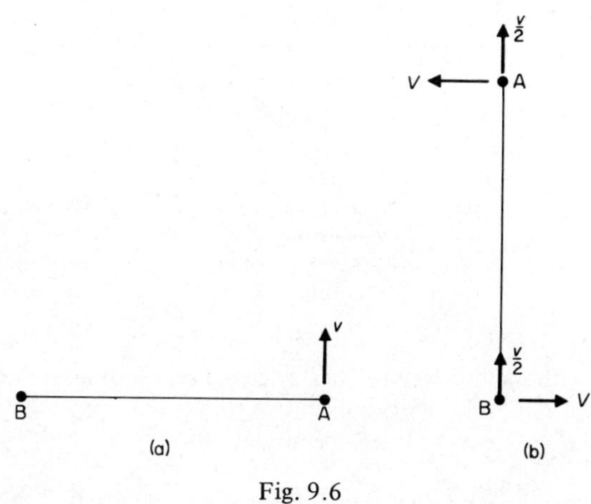

Fig. 9.6

of A and B are equal, the components V of velocity in this direction must be equal and opposite [Fig. 9.6(b)]. Since momentum is also conserved perpendicular to the initial direction of AB, and the string remains taut, the component of each body in that direction is $\frac{1}{2}v$. But kinetic energy is also conserved,

i.e. $$\tfrac{1}{2}mv^2 = 2[\tfrac{1}{2}m(\tfrac{1}{4}v^2 + V^2)]$$

whence $$V = \tfrac{1}{2}v$$

the velocities of each body are $\frac{1}{2}v\sqrt{2}$, inclined at 45° to the line of the string on opposite sides of the string.

Example 9.3. *To one end of a light rod length 2l is attached a small body, mass m; to the other end is attached a ring, mass m, which can slide freely on a smooth horizontal wire so that the system moves in a vertical plane. The rod is held just underneath the wire and is then released from rest. Find the angular speed of the rod when it makes an angle θ with the horizontal (Fig. 9.7).*

Our experience probably suggests that the rod is going to oscillate about the ring, which itself oscillates on the wire. Since there is not a horizontal force acting on the system, the centre of mass moves in a vertical line, confirming our idea of the likely motion. None of our familiar systems of coordinates, e.g. Cartesian (x, y), polar (r, θ), is adequate to describe this motion, and we need to devise our own. The motion can be described completely in terms of the distance x of the ring from a fixed point on the wire and the angle θ made

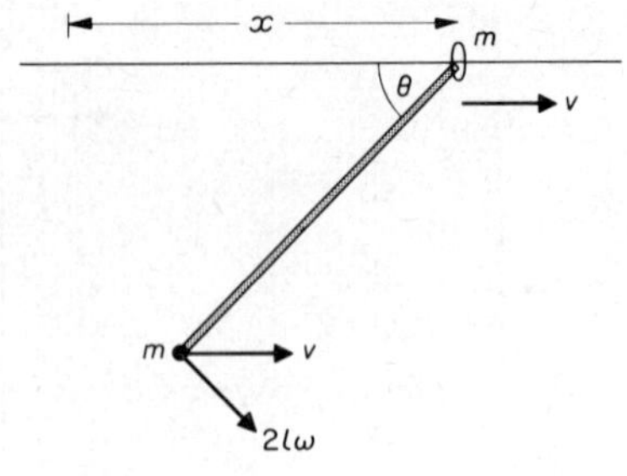

Fig. 9.7

by the rod with the horizontal. Then since the centre of mass moves in a vertical line,

$$x - l\cos\theta \text{ is constant}$$

i.e. $$\frac{\mathrm{d}x}{\mathrm{d}t} + l\sin\theta\,\frac{\mathrm{d}\theta}{\mathrm{d}t} = 0, \quad \text{say } v + l\omega\sin\theta = 0$$

The velocity V of the mass m is the vector sum of the components v, the velocity of the ring, and $2l\omega$, the velocity relative to the ring. Thus

$$\begin{aligned} V^2 &= v^2 + 4l^2\omega^2 + 4v^2l^2\omega\sin\theta \\ &= l^2\omega^2(\sin^2\theta + 4 - 4\sin^2\theta), \quad \text{since } v = -l\omega\sin\theta \\ &= l^2\omega^2(\sin^2\theta + 4\cos^2\theta) \end{aligned}$$

Thus the work done on the system by the external force, the weight of the mass m, gives

$$\begin{aligned} mg(2l\sin\theta) &= \tfrac{1}{2}mv^2 + \tfrac{1}{2}mV^2 \\ &= \tfrac{1}{2}ml^2\omega^2\sin^2\theta + \tfrac{1}{2}ml^2\omega^2(\sin^2\theta + 4\cos^2\theta) \\ &= ml^2\omega^2(1 + \cos^2\theta) \end{aligned}$$

∴ the angular speed of the rod at an angular distance θ from the horizontal is

$$\sqrt{\left[\frac{2g\sin\theta}{l(1 + \cos^2\theta)}\right]}$$

Variable mass

The form in which Sir Isaac Newton stated his second law was 'the rate of change of momentum of a body is proportional to the force applied',

i.e. $$\frac{\mathrm{d}}{\mathrm{d}t}(m\mathbf{v}) = \mathbf{F}$$

is clearly equivalent to the form in which we have used it, $\mathbf{F} = m\mathbf{a}$, if and only if the mass of the body is constant. There are, however, many situations in which the mass of the body is not constant, e.g. a raindrop falling through a cloud, a rocket propelling itself by ejecting some of its own mass. We shall first investigate the motion of a raindrop to find the acceleration while it is falling through a cloud and its mass is increasing through condensation.

Motion of a raindrop

Suppose a raindrop, mass per unit volume m, is falling through a cloud that is at rest, and that the rate at which the mass is increasing is proportional to the surface area of the raindrop. Then

$$\frac{\mathrm{d}}{\mathrm{d}t}\left(\tfrac{4}{3}\pi m r^3\right) = 4\pi k m r^2$$

assuming the raindrop to be spherical and taking the constant of proportion to be km,

i.e. $$\frac{\mathrm{d}r}{\mathrm{d}t} = k$$

$\Rightarrow$ $$r = a + kt$$

if the radius of the raindrop was initially a.

Ignoring resistances, the only force on the raindrop is its weight,

$\therefore$ $$\tfrac{4}{3}\pi m r^3 g = \frac{\mathrm{d}}{\mathrm{d}t}\left(\tfrac{4}{3}\pi m r^3 v\right)$$

i.e. $$r^3 g = \frac{\mathrm{d}}{\mathrm{d}t}(r^3 v)$$

i.e. $$r^3 v = \int r^3 g \,\mathrm{d}t$$

But $$r = a + kt,$$

i.e. $$(a + kt)^3 v = \int (a + kt)^3 g \,\mathrm{d}t$$

$$= \frac{g}{4k}(a + kt)^4 - \frac{g}{4k}a^4$$

if the raindrop started from rest.

$$\therefore \qquad v = \frac{g}{4k}(a + kt) - \frac{ga^4}{4k(a + kt)^3}$$

Differentiating, the acceleration is

$$\frac{g}{4} + \frac{3ga^4}{4(a + kt)^4}$$

which approaches the value $\frac{1}{4}g$ as t becomes large, and had the initial value g.

Motion of a rocket

The acceleration of a rocket is produced by ejecting burnt fuel with a velocity, often assumed constant, relative to the rocket. To investigate this, we consider the change in the momentum over a small interval of time δt.

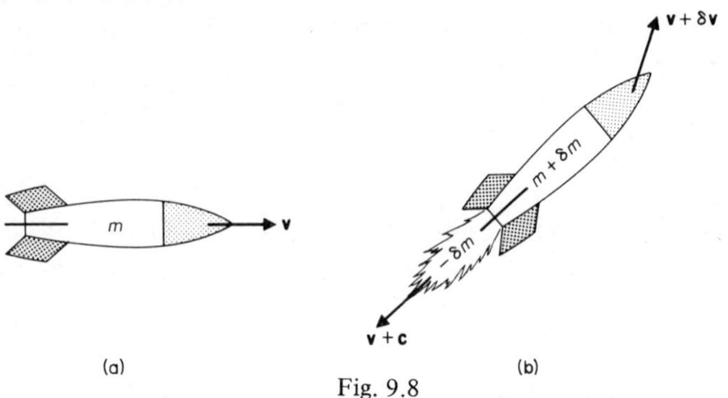

Fig. 9.8

Suppose that a force **F** is acting on the rocket, mass m, velocity **v**, and that fuel is ejected with velocity **c** relative to the rocket (Fig. 9.8).

Denote the mass of fuel ejected in time t by $-\delta m$; since m is decreasing, $-\delta m$ is positive. Considering the change in momentum over the time δt,

$$\mathbf{F}\delta t = (m + \delta m)(\mathbf{v} + \delta\mathbf{v}) + (-\delta m)(\mathbf{v} + \mathbf{c}) - m\mathbf{v}$$

$$= m\delta\mathbf{v} + (-\delta m)\mathbf{c}$$

$$\mathbf{F} = m\frac{\mathrm{d}\mathbf{v}}{\mathrm{d}t} - \mathbf{c}\frac{\mathrm{d}m}{\mathrm{d}t}$$

Example 9.4. *A rocket in space, mass (including fuel) M, ejects directly behind the rocket a quantity kM of its fuel with velocity c relative to the rocket. Find the increase in the velocity of the rocket caused by the ejection of this fuel.*

As the rocket is in space, **F** = 0. Since the fuel is ejected behind the rocket the relative velocity is $-c$ in the direction of motion of the rocket, so the equation of motion becomes

$$m\frac{dv}{dt} + c\frac{dm}{dt} = 0$$

i.e.

$$v = -c\int\frac{dm}{m}$$

$$v = -c\log_e\left(\frac{m}{M}\right) + U, \quad \text{if } m = M \text{ when } v = U$$

∴ when

$$m = (1 - k)M$$

$$v - U = -c\log_e(1 - k)$$

Since $(1 - k)$ is less than 1, $\log(1 - k)$ is negative, v is greater than U, and the velocity has increased by an amount

$$|c\log_e(1 - k)|$$

Thus the increase in velocity of the rocket depends only on the velocity of ejection of the fuel and the fraction of the load of the rocket which is fuel. It is not dependent on the rate at which fuel is consumed.

Rocket under gravity

When the rocket in Example 9.4 is launched vertically, the force **F** is the weight of the rocket, so that the equation of motion is

$$mg = m\frac{dv}{dt} - c\frac{dm}{dt}$$

If the rate at which the fuel is burnt is constant, say α per unit interval of time, and the mass of the rocket initially is M, and if all the motion takes place in a straight line

$$-(M - \alpha t)g = (M - \alpha t)\frac{dv}{dt} - \alpha c$$

i.e.
$$\frac{dv}{dt} + g = \frac{\alpha c}{M - \alpha t}$$

$$\Rightarrow \qquad v + gt = -c \log_e \left(\frac{M - \alpha t}{M} \right)$$

since $v = 0$ and $m = M$ when $t = 0$,

i.e.
$$v = -gt + c \log_e \left(\frac{M}{M - \alpha t} \right) \tag{9.6}$$

This form for the velocity shows the term $-gt$ we should expect from the gravitational attraction of the Earth and the term due to the propulsion of the rocket, assuming that it lifts off when $t = 0$. However, dv/dt must be positive, so the rocket will only launch when $t = 0$ if

$$\frac{\alpha c}{M} - g > 0, \quad \text{i.e., } \alpha c > Mg$$

If this is not so, the rocket stays at rest on the ground until the mass has been reduced to the value $\alpha c/g$, unless the fuel is first exhausted. If the fuel is exhausted before this mass is attained, the rocket does not launch.

Height attained by rocket

To find the distance travelled by a rocket while burning fuel, integrate equation 9.6,

$$s = -\tfrac{1}{2}gt^2 + c \int \log \left(\frac{M}{M - \alpha t} \right) dt$$

$$= -\tfrac{1}{2}gt^2 + (c \log M)t - c \int \log (M - \alpha t)\, dt$$

$$= -\tfrac{1}{2}gt^2 + ct\left[1 + \log \left(\frac{M}{M - \alpha t} \right)\right] + \frac{cM}{\alpha} \log \left(\frac{M - \alpha t}{M} \right)$$

If the velocity attained by the rocket when all the fuel has been exhausted is V, it will then travel under gravity, if still applicable, and the total height attained will be $s + V^2/2g$.

EXERCISE 9(b)

1. A raindrop of variable mass m is falling through a cloud which is at rest. The mass of the raindrop increases by an amount km per unit distance of its fall. The raindrop starts from rest with mass m_0. Prove that its mass after it has fallen through a distance x is $m_0\,e^{kx}$. Obtain the equation of motion of the raindrop, and prove that its velocity v after falling through a distance x is given by

$$v^2 = g(1 - e^{-2kx})/k$$

(O. & C.)

2. A rocket has an initial total mass M, including a mass m of fuel. The fuel burns at a rate of α units of mass per unit time so as to produce a uniform thrust F. The rocket is fired vertically upwards from rest. Show that, if air resistance is neglected, the greatest velocity attained is

$$\frac{m\,[mg + 2(F - Mg)]}{2(M - m)\alpha}$$

Deduce that the height attained at time T ($T \leqslant m/\alpha$) is

$$\int_0^T \frac{2(F - Mg) + \alpha gt}{2(M - \alpha t)}\, t\, dt$$

(O. & C.)

3. A uniform chain of length l lies in a loose heap near the edge of a horizontal table, with one end of the chain hanging over the edge. Show that the velocity of the vertical part of the chain when a length x has slipped off the table is $\sqrt{(2gx/3)}$ and that the whole chain has slipped off in time $\sqrt{(6l/g)}$. (O.S.)

4. A space probe is moving free from gravitational fields, and it expels a mass m of gas per unit time from its rocket engine, with a speed a relative to the probe, where m and a are constant. The probe experiences a resistive force equal to a constant multiple k times the square of its velocity. Show that the equation of motion is

$$(M - mt)\frac{dv}{dt} = ma - kv^2$$

where M is the initial mass of the probe.
Hence show that if the probe is initially at rest then the velocity is related to time t by the relation

$$\frac{M - mt}{M} = \left[\frac{(ma)^{1/2} - k^{1/2}v}{(ma)^{1/2} + k^{1/2}v}\right]^{\left(\frac{m}{4ak}\right)^{\frac{1}{2}}}$$

(C.S.)

5. A rocket whose initial mass is M, of which half is accounted for by the fuel it initially contains, is fired vertically upwards. The velocity of the exhaust gases relative to the rocket is constant and equal to u, and the mass of fuel burnt per unit time is constant and equal to A. Assuming g constant and neglecting air resistance, show that the altitude of the rocket at the instant when the fuel becomes exhausted is

$$\frac{Mu}{2A}(1 - \log_e 2) - \frac{M^2 g}{8A^2}$$

and find the velocity at this instant. (O.S.)

6. A machine gun of mass M stands on a horizontal plane and contains shot of mass M'. The shot is fired horizontally at the rate of mass m per unit time with velocity u relative to the gun. If the coefficient of friction between the gun and the plane is μ and sliding begins at once, show that the velocity of the gun after all the shot is fired is

$$u \log(1 + M'/M) - \mu M' g/m$$ (C.S.)

7. A rocket is propelled vertically upwards by the backwards ejection of matter at a uniform rate and with constant speed V relative to the rocket. The total mass of propelling matter available is m and it is completely ejected at a time τ after launching, when the mass remaining to the rocket is km. Show that, when the time t is less than τ, the velocity of the rocket varies according to the equation

$$\frac{dv}{dt} = -g + \frac{V}{(k+1)\tau - t}$$

If $g\tau(k+1) < V$ and the initial velocity is zero, show that the rocket will rise to the height

$$\frac{V^2}{2g}\left(\log\frac{k+1}{k}\right)^2 - V\tau\left[(k+1)\log\frac{k+1}{k} - 1\right]$$ (C.S.)

8. A rocket burns fuel at a rate equal to k times its instantaneous mass, the fuel being ejected with a fixed velocity P relative to the rocket. It is initially at rest on the surface of the Earth and is fired vertically upwards. The gravitational attraction caused by the Earth may be taken to be ga^2/r^2, where a is the radius of the Earth and r the distance of the rocket from the centre of the Earth. Show that if $kP > g$, the rela-

tion between the mass m and the position r of the rocket is given by

$$\log m = \log m_0 - \int_a^r \left[\frac{k^2 x}{2(x-a)(kPx - ag)} \right]^{1/2} dx$$

where m_0 is the initial mass of the rocket. (C.S.)

9. A shell is at rest in space, when it bursts into two fragments, the energy released being E. Show that the relative speed of the fragments after separation cannot be less than $2\sqrt{(2E/M)}$. (C.S.)

10. A ring of mass m slides on a smooth vertical rod; attached to the ring is a light string passing over a smooth peg distant a from the rod, and at the other end of the string is a mass $M(>m)$. The ring is held on a level with the peg and released: show that it first comes to rest after falling a distance

$$\frac{2mMa}{M^2 - m^2}$$

(C.S.)

10. Statics

Equilibrium of large bodies

In *Additional Applied Mathematics* we investigated some easy problems on large bodies in equilibrium. We saw that:

(a) since there is no acceleration of the body the sum of all the forces acting on the body is zero,

i.e. $$\Sigma \mathbf{F} = 0$$

More especially, the sum of the resolved parts of the forces in any direction is zero;

(b) since there is no rotation of the body, the sum of the moments about any axis of all the forces acting on the body is zero. This may be extended to say that the sum of the moments about any point is zero,

i.e. $$\Sigma \mathbf{r} \times \mathbf{F} = 0$$

but we shall not use the vector product in this chapter.

The use of these principles is illustrated in the examples that follow.

Example 10.1. *A uniform rod AB of length 2l, weight W, rests against a smooth vertical wall with one end B on smooth horizontal ground, as in Fig. 10.1. The rod is prevented from slipping by a light inelastic string OC which is perpendicular to the rod. Find the tension T in the string.*

Resolving horizontally and vertically,

$$T \sin \theta - R = 0 \tag{10.1}$$

and $$T \cos \theta - S + W = 0 \tag{10.2}$$

Taking moments about the horizontal axis through O,

$$S(2l \cos \theta) - W(l \cos \theta) - R(2l \sin \theta) = 0$$

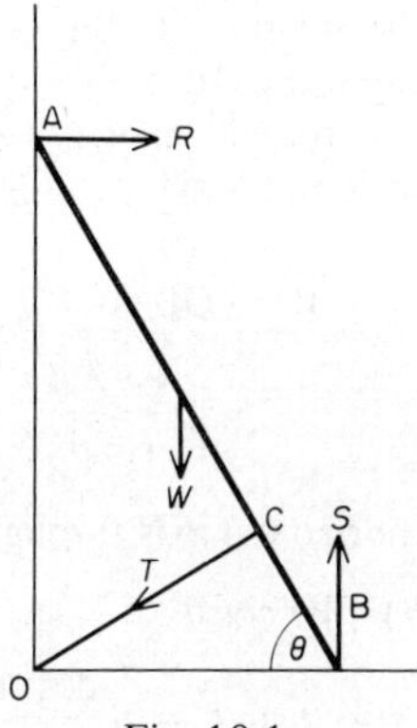

Fig. 10.1

Substituting from equations 10.1 and 10.2,

$$T(2l\cos^2\theta) + W(l\cos\theta) - T(2l\sin^2\theta) = 0$$

$$\therefore \quad T(2l\sin^2\theta - 2l\cos^2\theta) = W(l\cos\theta)$$

i.e.
$$T = \frac{W\cos\theta}{2(\sin^2\theta - \cos^2\theta)}$$

The selection of horizontal and vertical directions for the resolution of forces was obvious; we chose the horizontal axis through O because the perpendicular distances onto the lines of action of the forces could be found easily. If we had used an axis through B, the perpendicular distance onto the line of action of

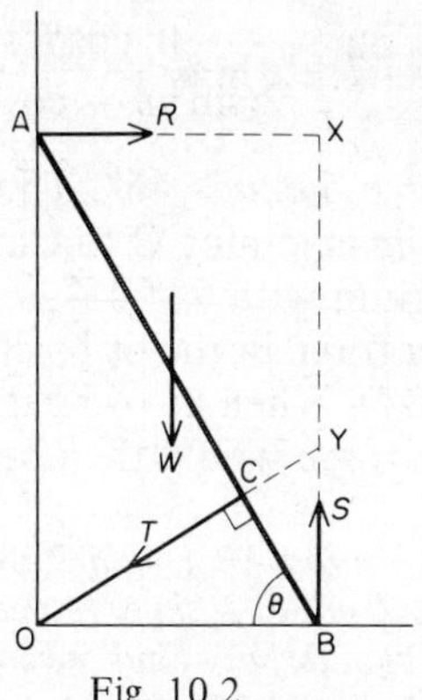

Fig. 10.2

the tension T would have been OB $\cos\theta$. But OB $= 2l\cos\theta$, so BC $= 2l\cos^2\theta$. This is slightly less easy than using OB.

Notice that we could have found T merely from an equation of moments. For if the lines of action of R and S meet at X, and OC produced meets BX at Y, (Fig. 10.2),

$$\text{BY} = \text{OB}\cot\theta$$

$$= 2l\frac{\cos^2\theta}{\sin\theta}$$

Taking moments about a horizontal axis through X,

$$T(\text{XY}\sin\theta) = Wl\cos\theta$$

But $$\text{XY} = 2l\sin\theta - 2l\frac{\cos^2\theta}{\sin\theta}$$

$\therefore$ $$\text{XY}\sin\theta = 2l(\sin^2\theta - \cos^2\theta)$$

$\therefore$ $$T = \frac{W\cos\theta}{2(\sin^2\theta - \cos^2\theta)}, \quad \text{as before}$$

It is easier in this example to find three equations and to eliminate the unknowns R and S, but we shall see in other examples that some problems can be solved easily by taking moments about an axis through a suitable point.

Least value of θ

Since T is a tension in a string, T must be positive. But

$$T = \frac{W\cos\theta}{2(\sin^2\theta - \cos^2\theta)}$$

so that $\sin^2\theta > \cos^2\theta$, i.e. $\theta > 45°$. Thus equilibrium is only possible when a *string* is joining O to C if $\theta > 45°$. If it is required to maintain equilibrium with $\theta < 45°$, a light rod must be used so that it can provide a force in the opposite direction, (often called a thrust; see page 287). When $\theta = 45°$, it is not possible to have equilibrium, for the force would then be infinite.

Example 10.2. *A uniform rod AB, length 2l, weight W, is connected by two strings AC, BC, lengths 2l cos α, 2l sin α, respectively, to a fixed point C. The system hangs freely in equilibrium. Find the angle made by AB with the vertical, and the tension in each string.*

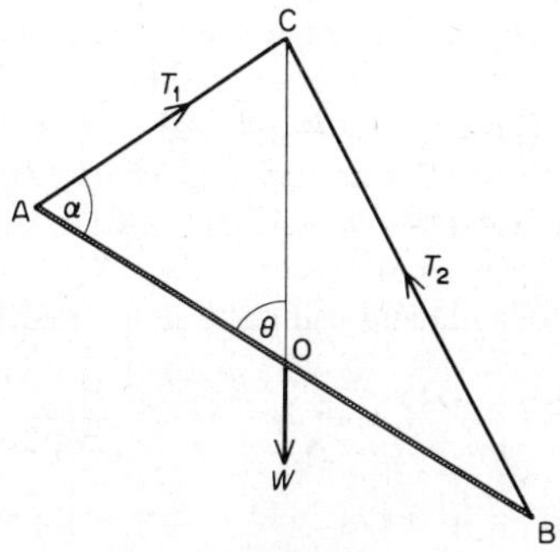

Fig. 10.3

Since the lengths of the strings are $2l \cos \alpha$ and $2l \sin \alpha$ and AB = $2l$, angle ACB = 90° and angle CAB = α. Now the rod AB is uniform, so that the weight acts through its midpoint O (Fig. 10.3), and O is the centre of a circle radius l, through A, C, and B (since ACB is a right angle). Thus

$$\text{angle OCA} = \text{angle OAC} = \alpha$$

and
$$\text{angle COB} = 2\alpha$$

so the rod AB is inclined at an angle 2α to the vertical.

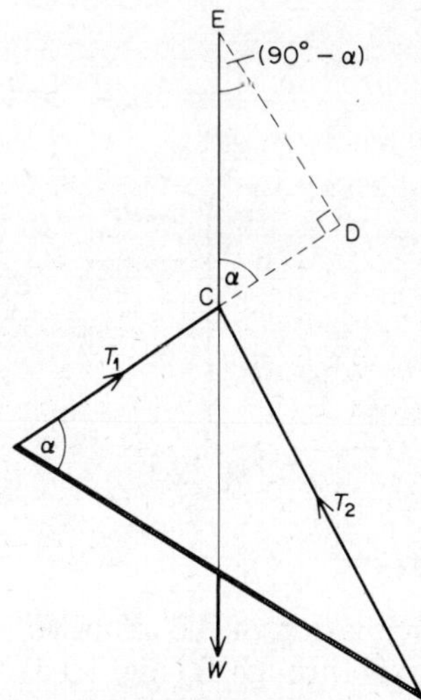

Fig. 10.4

To find the tensions in the strings, we see that the lines of action of the three forces acting on the rod pass through C (so that the sum of the moments about an axis through C is zero). *It is, of course, always true that when a body is in equilibrium under the action of three non-parallel forces, the lines of action of those forces must concur.* Triangle CDE in Fig. 10.4 is the triangle of forces for this system.

Applying the sine formula and using the angles marked in Fig. 10.4,

$$\frac{T_1}{\sin (90° - \alpha)} = \frac{T_2}{\sin \alpha} = \frac{W}{\sin 90°}$$

i.e. $$T_1 = W \cos \alpha \quad \text{and} \quad T_2 = W \sin \alpha$$

Use of Lami's theorem

This result could have been obtained using Lami's theorem (*Additional Applied Mathematics*, page 83). The forces at C are shown in Fig. 10.5,

$$\frac{T_1}{\sin (90° + \alpha)} = \frac{T_2}{\sin (180° - \alpha)} = \frac{W}{\sin 90°}$$

i.e. $$T_1 = W \cos \alpha \quad \text{and} \quad T_2 = W \sin \alpha$$

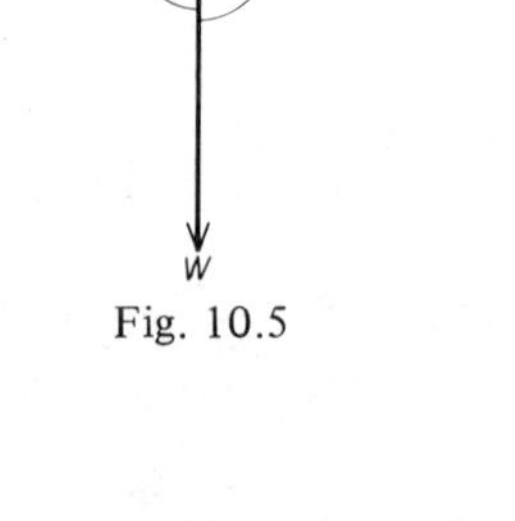

Fig. 10.5

Alternative solution

Having found the inclination of AB as above, we can take moments about a horizontal axis through B (Fig. 10.3). Then,

$$Wl \sin (180° - 2\alpha) = T_1 2l \sin \alpha$$

i.e. $$W(2 \sin \alpha \cos \alpha) = T_1(2 \sin \alpha)$$

$$\Rightarrow \qquad T_1 = W \cos \alpha$$

as before. T_2 is found similarly. There will often be several methods for solving these problems, and by experience the reader will come to discover which method is most suitable for which problem.

In Example 10.2, the strings AC, BC were separate, with different tensions. The next example shows a continuous string in which the tension must be constant, as it passes over a smooth peg.

Example 10.3. *A uniform rod AB of weight W and length 6l is suspended in equilibrium by a light inextensible string which passes over a smooth peg. One end of the string is fixed at A; the other is fixed at C, the point of trisection of the rod nearer to B. If P is the point of contact of the string with the peg, show that AP : PC = 3 : 1, providing the length of the string is between 4l and 8l.*

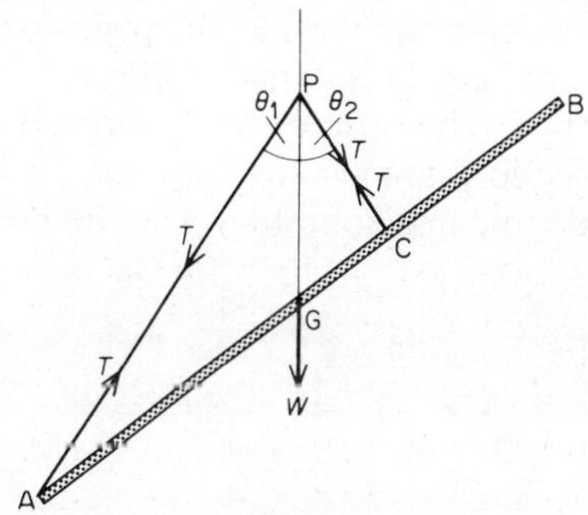

Fig. 10.6

Since the peg is smooth (Fig. 10.6), the magnitude of the tension in the string is not altered as the string passes round the peg. Resolving horizontally,

$$T \sin \theta_1 = T \sin \theta_2$$

$$\therefore \qquad \theta_1 = \theta_2$$

i.e. the portions AP, PC of the string are equally inclined to the vertical. Further, since the rod is uniform, the line of action of the weight passes through G, the midpoint of AB. Thus,

$$AG : GC = 3l : l = 3 : 1.$$

Since PG is the internal bisector of angle APC, by the converse of the internal bisector theorem,

$$\text{AP} : \text{PC} = 3 : 1, \quad \text{as required}$$

Alternatively, using the sine formula,

$$\frac{\text{AP}}{\sin \text{AGP}} = \frac{\text{AG}}{\sin \theta_1} \quad \text{and} \quad \frac{\text{PC}}{\sin \text{PGC}} = \frac{\text{GC}}{\sin \theta_2}$$

But $\sin \text{AGP} = \sin \text{PGC}$ and $\theta_1 = \theta_2$

$\therefore$ $\text{AP} : \text{PC} = \text{AG} : \text{GC}$

$= 3 : 1$

Inclination of rod

Notice that in this example we cannot find the inclination of the rod to the vertical unless we know the length of the string, but we can show that whatever the length of the string the end B of the rod is at the same horizontal level as the peg. For since AP : PC = 3 : 1 and AP, PC are equally inclined to the vertical, their vertical projections must be in the ratio of 3 : 1. But AB : BC = 3 : 1, and their vertical projections are also in the ratio 3 : 1 [see Fig. 10.7(b)], so that B is at the same horizontal level as the peg.

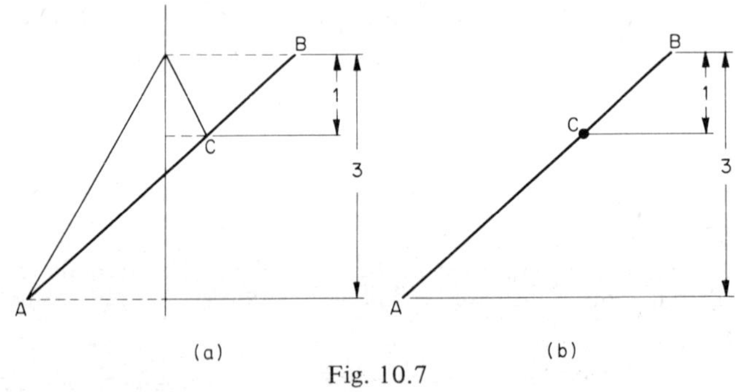

Fig. 10.7

Three-dimensional problems

These problems have been confined to two dimensions. Three-dimensional problems are usually solved by considering two-dimensional sections.

Example 10.4. *A uniform solid sphere of radius r and weight W rests in equilibrium symmetrically placed on three fixed smooth rods, lengths a, which form an equilateral triangle in a horizontal plane (Fig. 10.8). Find the force exerted by each rod on the sphere.*

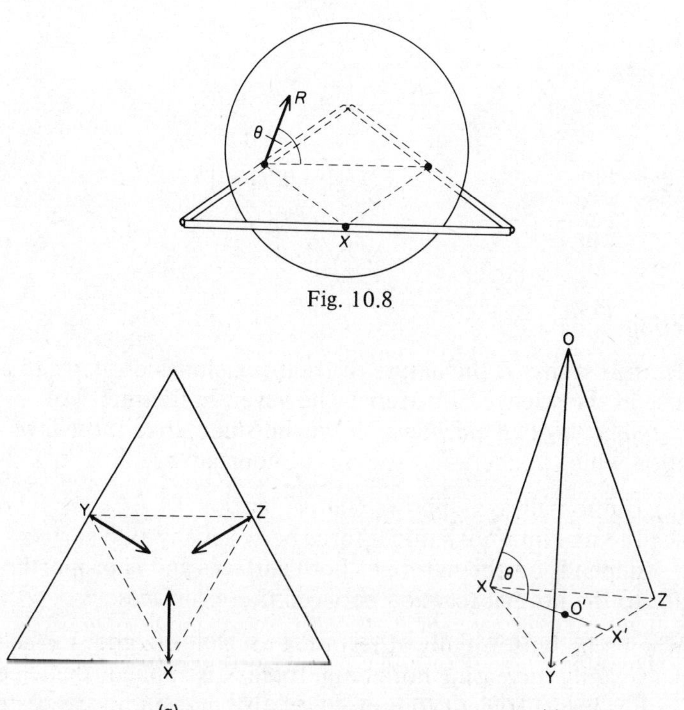

Fig. 10.8

Fig. 10.9

By symmetry, the vertical component of each of the three required forces must equal one third of the weight of the sphere, and the lines of action of the three forces must pass through the centre of the sphere.

The points of contact X, Y, Z of the sphere on the rods are the vertices of an equilateral triangle [Fig. 10.9(a)], and the centre O of the sphere is the fourth vertex of a tetrahedron [Fig. 10.9(b)] in which OX = OY = OZ = r. If O′ is the point in the plane XYZ vertically below O, and X′ is the midpoint of YZ,

$$\begin{aligned} XO' &= \tfrac{2}{3}XX' \\ &= \frac{2}{3}\left(\frac{a\sqrt{3}}{4}\right) = \frac{a}{2\sqrt{3}} \end{aligned}$$

Thus
$$\cos\theta = \frac{a}{(2\sqrt{3})r}$$

As the force R at X acts along XO,

$$R\sin\theta = W/3$$

$$\therefore \qquad R = \frac{W}{3\sin\theta}$$

$$= \frac{W}{3\sqrt{[1-(a^2/12r^2]}}$$

$$= \frac{2Wr}{\sqrt{3}\sqrt{(12r^2-a^2)}}$$

Friction

A detailed study of the nature of friction belongs properly to a course in the science of materials; however, in Chapter 9 of *Additional Applied Mathematics* we did summarize those laws of friction which concern us. The most important are:

(a) friction always opposes *relative* motion;
(b) the maximum frictional force between any two surfaces depends on the nature of both surfaces and is proportional to the normal reaction between those surfaces.

When a body is initially at rest on a rough horizontal surface and a steadily increasing horizontal force **X** is applied, the frictional force **F** is just sufficient to prevent relative motion until a certain

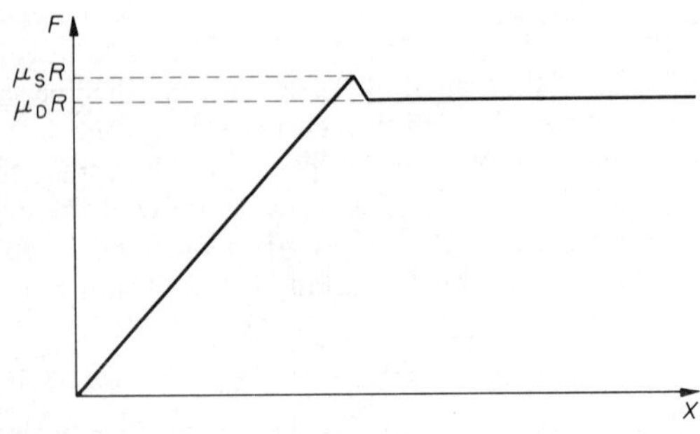

Fig. 10.10

maximum value is attained (limiting friction). When **X** increases beyond this value, there is still a frictional force acting, though the coefficient of dynamic or sliding friction μ_D (the ratio of the frictional force to the normal reaction) is usually slightly less than the coefficient of static friction μ_s (Fig. 10.10). Such differences do not often concern us at this stage.

To illustrate friction opposing relative motion, consider this example.

Example 10.5. *A box of mass m is at rest on a long plank of wood, mass M, which is itself at rest on a horizontal table. The surfaces of the box and the upper face of the plank are rough; the lower face of the plank and the surface of the table are smooth. The plank is suddenly given an initial horizontal velocity U***i**. *Investigate the subsequent motion.*

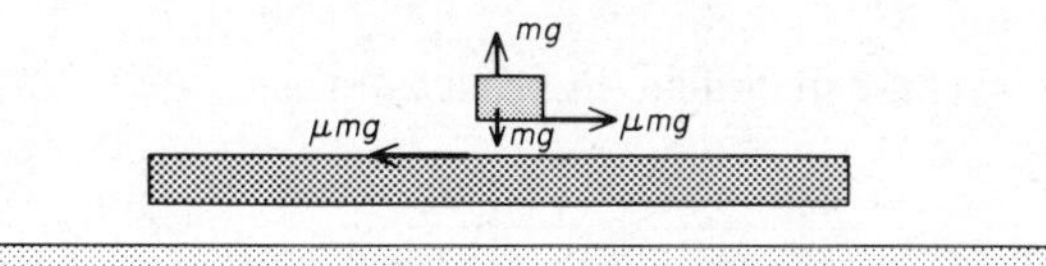

Fig. 10.11

The normal reaction of the plank on the box in Fig. 10.11 is mg, so that the maximum frictional force is μmg. When the plank suddenly moves with velocity $U\mathbf{i}$ the frictional force cannot suddenly induce a velocity $U\mathbf{i}$ in the box, so the box slips on the plank. Thus while slipping takes place the acceleration of the box is $\mu g\mathbf{i}$; the acceleration of the plank is $\mu(m/M)g\mathbf{i}$. So if $\mathbf{v}$ and $\mathbf{V}$ are the velocities of the box and plank respectively,

$$\mathbf{v} = \mu gt\mathbf{i} \quad \text{and} \quad \mathbf{V} = \left(U - \mu\frac{m}{M}gt\right)\mathbf{i}$$

Slipping started because the frictional force was not large enough to produce sufficient acceleration to keep the box in place on the plank. Slipping ceases when the velocities of the box and the plank are equal,

i.e. when
$$\mu gt = U - \mu\frac{m}{M}gt$$

i.e.
$$t = \frac{MU}{\mu g(M+m)}$$

Then both the box and the plank have velocity $MU/(M+m)$. Notice that momentum is conserved, since the frictional forces are equal and opposite and act for the same period of time, and we could have found the final velocity V' from the conservation of momentum,

$$(M+m)V' = MU$$

While acquiring this velocity the box will have travelled a distance

$$\tfrac{1}{2}(\mu g)\left[\frac{MU}{\mu g(M+m)}\right]^2 \quad \text{i.e.} \quad \frac{M^2U^2}{2\mu g(M+m)^2}$$

and the plank a distance

$$\tfrac{1}{2}\left(U+\frac{MU}{M+m}\right)\left(\frac{MU}{\mu g(M+m)}\right), \quad \text{from } S=\tfrac{1}{2}(u+v)t$$

i.e. $$\frac{1}{2}\frac{M(2M+m)U^2}{\mu g(M+m)^2}$$

so the box will have slipped on the plank a distance

$$\frac{1}{2}\frac{M(2M+m)U^2}{\mu g(M+m)^2} - \frac{M^2U^2}{2\mu g(M+m)^2}$$

i.e. $$\frac{MU^2}{2\mu g(M+m)}$$

Notice that if the surfaces between the plank and the table had been rough (Fig. 10.12), say with the same coefficient of friction as between the plank and the box, the normal reaction between the plank and the table is

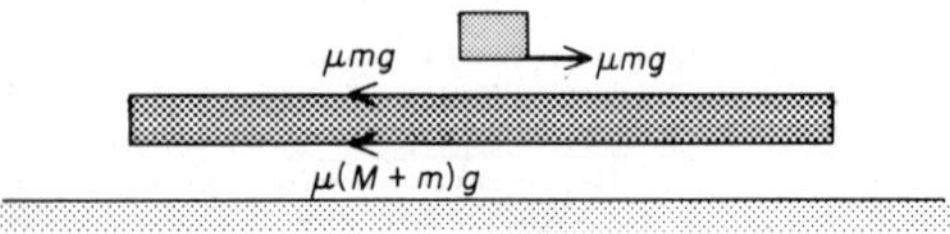

Fig. 10.12

$(M+m)g$, so the frictional force between these two is $\mu(M+m)g$, and the acceleration **a** of the plank is given by

$$-\mu(M+m)g\mathbf{i} - \mu mg\mathbf{i} = M\mathbf{a}$$

i.e. $$\mathbf{a} = \frac{-\mu(M+2m)g}{M}\mathbf{i}$$

$$\mathbf{v} = \mu gt\mathbf{i} \quad \text{and} \quad \mathbf{V} = \left(U - \frac{\mu(M+2m)}{M}gt\right)\mathbf{i}$$

Thus slipping ceases after a time $MU/2(M+m)\mu g$ when the box and the plank have a common velocity $MU/2(M+m)$ and their total momentum is $\frac{1}{2}MU$. Momentum $\frac{1}{2}MU$ has been lost by the plank and the box because an external force $\mu(M+m)g$ has been acting for a time $\frac{1}{2}\,[MU/(M+m)\mu g]$.

Sliding or toppling

When a rectangular block is at rest on a rough horizontal table, by symmetry the weight of the block acts through the midpoint M of the base and the normal reaction R also acts through M. But when a horizontal force F is applied to the block, the data are no longer symmetrical and R may not act through M (Fig. 10.13).

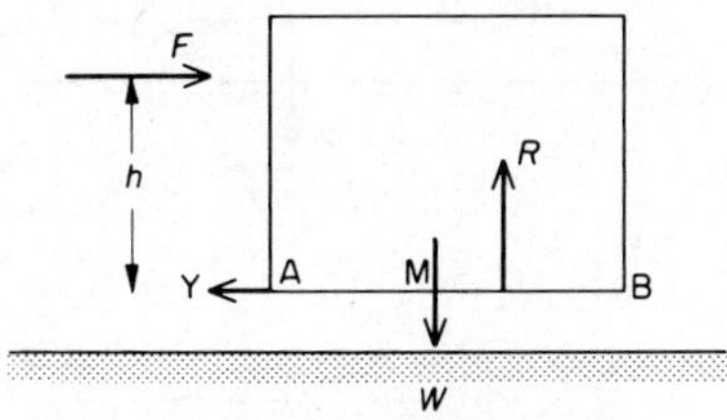

Fig. 10.13

Suppose the block is a cube of edge $2a$, and the force F is applied at a height h above the horizontal table. Then since there is no vertical acceleration of the cube,

$$R - W = 0$$

i.e.

$$R = W$$

Since the cube is in equilibrium, considering the moments of the forces about an axis along the edge through A,

$$Fh + Wa - Rx = 0$$

where x is the distance from A of the line of action of R,

i.e.

$$x = \frac{Fh + Wa}{R}$$

$$= a + \frac{Fh}{W}, \quad \text{since } R = W$$

Thus R always acts to the right of M, assuming F to be positive. As F increases, equilibrium can be broken by the cube slipping or tilting about the edge through B. The cube slips when $F = \mu W$; the cube tilts when the reaction acts through the edge through B, i.e. when $x = 2a$, i.e. $F = Wa/h$. Thus the cube slips or tilts according as a/h is greater or less than μ. When the cube is on the point of slipping, $F = \mu W$, and R acts as shown in Fig. 10.14.

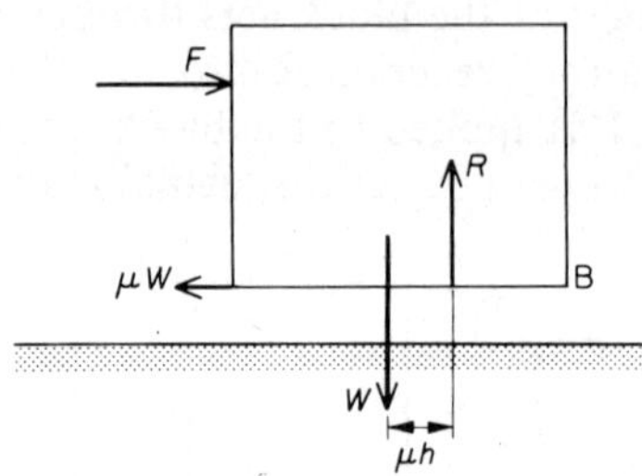

Fig. 10.14

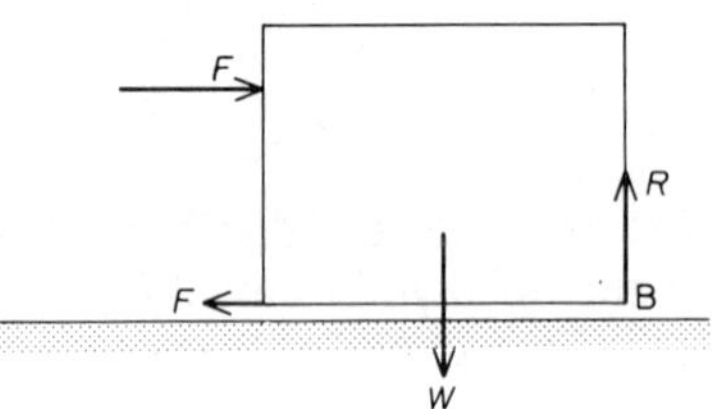

Fig. 10.15

When the cube is on the point of tilting, $F = Wa/h$, and R acts as shown in Fig. 10.15. Similar considerations enable us to see whether a body can rest in equilibrium on an inclined plane.

Example 10.6. *Show that a uniform cube cannot rest in equilibrium on a plane inclined at more than 45° to the horizontal, however rough the plane.*

The centre of gravity of a uniform cube, edge $2a$, by symmetry is a height a above the base (Fig. 10.16). Thus when the cube is placed on a plane inclined at 45° to the horizontal the weight acts through a point X in the lowest edge of the cube. When the inclination of the plane is increased, the weight acts to the left of X with a counter-clockwise moment about the edge through X.

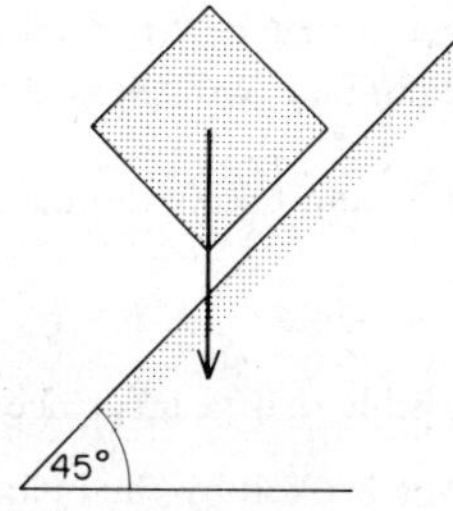

Fig. 10.16

But there is not a force with a clockwise moment about this edge so the cube cannot rest in equilibrium.

Example 10.7. *A uniform circular cylinder of radius a and weight W rests between the two fixed planes AB, AC, which are equally inclined to the horizontal at an angle α. The plane AB is smooth but the coefficient of friction between the plane AC and the cylinder is μ. A horizontal force W is applied to the top of the cylinder perpendicular to the highest generator. Show that equilibrium is impossible whatever the value of μ unless $\alpha \geqslant 45°$, and find the least value of μ if the cylinder can rest in equilibrium when $\sin \alpha = 4/5$.*

Fig. 10.17 shows a plane section of the cylinder with the forces acting on the cylinder. This distinguishes them from the equal and opposite forces

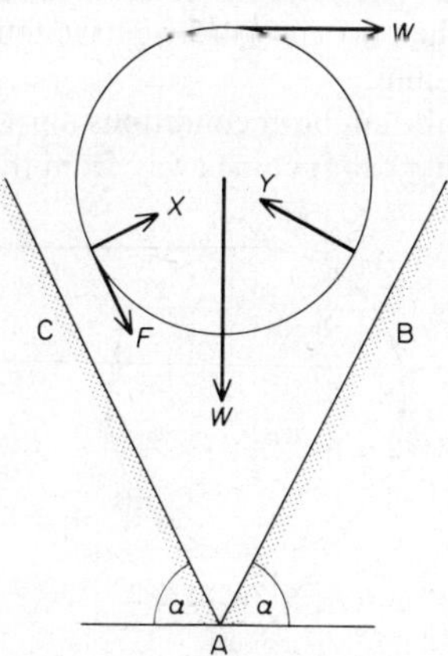

Fig. 10.17

exerted by the cylinder. Since the plane AB is smooth, there is not a frictional force along the generator in contact with the plane (shown here as the point B).

If the cylinder is in equilibrium, taking moments about the axis of the cylinder,

$$Fa = Wa, \quad \text{i.e. } F = W$$

Thus equilibrium is only possible if $W \leqslant \mu X$, since $F \leqslant \mu X$.

But equilibrium can also be broken by the cylinder coming away from the plane at C, when $X = 0$. To find X, we can resolve vertically and horizontally, and write $F = W$.

$$W(1 + \sin\alpha) - (X + Y)\cos\alpha = 0 \qquad (10.3)$$

$$W(1 + \cos\alpha) + (X - Y)\sin\alpha = 0 \qquad (10.4)$$

Multiply equation 10.3 by $\sin\alpha$ and equation 10.4 by $\cos\alpha$, and subtract.

$$W(\sin\alpha + \sin^2\alpha - \cos\alpha - \cos^2\alpha) - 2X\sin\alpha\cos\alpha = 0$$

i.e.
$$X\sin 2\alpha = W(\sin\alpha - \cos\alpha)(1 + \sin\alpha + \cos\alpha) \qquad (10.5)$$

Thus $X \geqslant 0$ if and only if $(\sin\alpha - \cos\alpha) \geqslant 0$, i.e. $\alpha \geqslant 45°$. So whatever the value of μ, if the cylinder is in equilibrium, $\alpha \geqslant 45°$. If $\sin\alpha = 4/5$

equation 10.5 gives
$$\tfrac{24}{25}X = \tfrac{12}{25}W$$

i.e. $X = \frac{1}{2}W$. But the cylinder will rotate unless $W \leqslant \mu X$, so that equilibrium will only be possible if $\alpha \geqslant 45°$ *and* the surfaces are sufficiently rough to prevent slipping at C; when $\alpha = \sin^{-1} 4/5$ we have found that $\mu \geqslant 2$ if equilibrium is to be possible.

Notice that for equilibrium both conditions must be satisfied; the cylinder must not slip at C, neither can it come away from the plane at C.

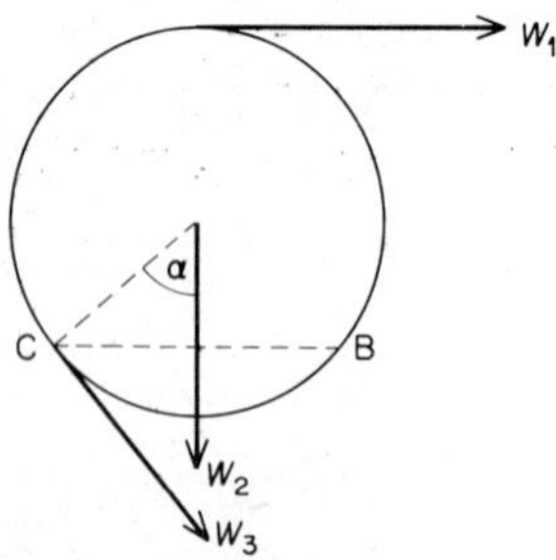

Fig. 10.18

Equation 10.5 could have been obtained by taking moments about a horizontal axis through B (Fig. 10.18). We distinguish the three forces equal to W by suffices so that the perpendicular distances onto their lines of action can be identified easily.

Since the radius of the cylinder is a,

$$X(a \sin 2\alpha) + W_1(a + a \cos \alpha) - W_2(a \sin \alpha) - W_3[a + a \cos (180° - 2\alpha)] = 0$$

i.e. $X \sin 2\alpha = W(-\cos \alpha + \sin \alpha - \cos 2\alpha)$

$= W(\sin \alpha - \cos \alpha)(1 + \sin \alpha + \cos \alpha)$ as in equation 10.5.

EXERCISE 10(a)

1. A uniform rod AB, weight W, rests with one end A on smooth horizontal ground and the other end B against a smooth vertical wall. The rod is kept in equilibrium by a horizontal force F applied at A. If the rod makes an angle of 45° with the horizontal, show that $F = \frac{1}{2}W$.

2. If the rod in Question 1 is inclined at α to the horizontal, instead of 45°, show that $F = \frac{1}{2}W \cot \alpha$.

3. A uniform ladder AB of weight W and length $2a$ rests with one end A against a smooth vertical wall and the other end B on smooth horizontal ground. The ladder is prevented from slipping by a horizontal rope which joins a point C in the ladder to a point on the wall. If BC = x, and the ladder is inclined at an angle α to the horizontal, find the tension in the rope.

4. A light inextensible string, length $3a$, joins two points A, D which are on the same horizontal level, a distance $2a$ apart. Two small bodies, each weight W, are tied to the string at points B and C, where AB = BC = CD = a. If the system hangs in equilibrium, find the inclination to the horizontal of the portion AB of the string, and the tensions in AB and BC.

5. Three particles each of weight W are attached to the points B, C, and D of a light inextensible string ABCDE which hangs with A and E attached to fixed pegs. If the portions AB and DE each make an angle α with the horizontal, show that the angles made by the portions BC and CD of the string with the horizontal are also equal.
   If $\alpha = 60°$, find in terms of W the tensions in the four portions of the string, and the angle made by BC with the horizontal. (C.)

6. The ends of a string of length l are attached to two points A and B on a fixed horizontal beam at a distance a apart ($a < l$). A smooth ring of weight W slides on the string and is in equilibrium under a horizontal force F when W is vertically below B. Prove that $F = aW/l$, and find the tension in the string.
If now the horizontal force on the ring is Q, acting in the same direction as F, and the part of the string attached to B makes an angle of 45° with AB produced when the ring is again in equilibrium, prove that $Q = W(l + a\sqrt{2})/l$. (O. & C.)

7. A uniform lamina of weight W is in the form of a triangle ABC in which AB = a, AC = $3a$ and the angle A is a right angle. One end of a light string is attached to the lamina at B and the other end is attached at C. The string passes over a smooth peg, and when the lamina hangs at rest the edge AC is horizontal and B is vertically above A. Show that the two parts of the string make the same angle with the vertical and find this angle.
Find what weight must be suspended from C for the lamina to hang at rest with BC horizontal and with A below BC. (A.E.B.)

8. Two smooth pegs C and D are at the same horizontal level and CD = $4a$; A is the middle point of CD. A uniform rod AB, of length $2a$ and weight W, is smoothly hinged at A and, with B below the level of A, is free to move in the vertical plane containing CD. A string attached to the rod at B passes over C and carries a weight $\frac{1}{2}\sqrt{3}W$; a second string also attached at B passes over D and carries a weight w. Prove that, if the system is in equilibrium when angle CAB = 60°, then (a) $w = W$, and (b) the reaction of the rod on the hinge is $\frac{1}{2}W$ and acts parallel to BD. (O. & C.)

9. A uniform rod AB rests in equilibrium inclined at an angle α to the horizontal with one end A on a rough horizontal floor and the other end B against a smooth vertical wall. The plane of the rod is vertical and perpendicular to the wall. Show that the coefficient of friction between the rod and the ground is not less than $\frac{1}{2}\cot\alpha$.

10. A uniform ladder rests in a vertical plane with the lower end on a rough horizontal plane and the upper end against a rough vertical wall, perpendicular to the plane of the ladder. If the coefficient of friction between the ladder and the ground is μ, and that between the ladder and the wall is $\frac{1}{2}\mu$, find the least angle the ladder can make with the horizontal if it is to remain in equilibrium.

11. A uniform cone, base radius r and height h, is placed on a rough horizontal plane. The inclination of the plane to the horizontal is increased

slowly. Prove that the cone will slide down the plane (and not topple) if the coefficient of friction between the cone and the plane is less than $4r/h$.

12. A uniform cube is placed on a rough plane inclined at an angle $\tan^{-1}(\frac{3}{4})$ to the horizontal so that four of the edges of the cube are horizontal. Show that the cube can only rest in equilibrium if the coefficient of friction between the cube and the plane is greater than $\frac{3}{4}$.
When the cube is in equilibrium on the plane, a steadily increasing force parallel to and up the plane is applied at the midpoint of the lowest edge of the upper face of the cube. Show that equilibrium is broken by the cube toppling about a horizontal edge.

13. A uniform cube is placed on a rough inclined plane so that four of its edges are horizontal. If α is the inclination of the plane to the horizontal and μ is the coefficient of friction, show that the cube can only rest in equilibrium if $\mu > \tan\alpha$ and $\alpha < \frac{1}{4}\pi$.
A steadily increasing horizontal force is applied at the midpoint of the lower horizontal edge of the face opposite to that in contact with the plane. The force is in the vertical plane containing the centre of the cube, and tends to push the cube up the plane. If $\tan\alpha = \frac{1}{3}$, prove that equilibrium is broken by sliding or tilting according as μ is less than or greater than $\frac{1}{2}$. (O. & C.)

14. Two fixed and equally rough pegs P and Q are a distance a apart, $\overrightarrow{PQ}$ making an angle $\alpha(<90^\circ)$ with the upward vertical; AB is a uniform rod, length $2l$ and weight W, which is placed over P and under Q, the end B being uppermost. The rod is about to slip when $QB = x$. If R and S are the reactions on the rod at P and Q respectively, prove that

$$R\cos(\lambda+\alpha) = S\cos(\lambda-\alpha)$$

and

$$x = l - \tfrac{1}{2}a - \tfrac{1}{2}a\cot\lambda\cot\alpha$$

where λ is the angle of limiting friction between each peg and the rod. (O. & C.)

15. A uniform rod length $2a$ rests against a fixed rough cylinder whose axis is horizontal. The rod is perpendicular to the axis of the cylinder and inclined at an angle θ to the horizontal, and is kept in this position by a horizontal string attached at the highest point of the rod, also perpendicular to the axis of the cylinder. Show that the length x of the rod above the point of contact with the cylinder must be such that

$$a\cos\theta(\cos\theta - \mu\sin\theta) \leqslant x \leqslant a\cos\theta(\cos\theta + \mu\sin\theta)$$

where μ is the coefficient of friction between the rod and the cylinder and $\mu < \tan\theta$.

16. A modern substitute for an office paper-clip is shown in section in Fig. 10.19. The frame, fastened to a wall as shown, has three inner plane surfaces of which one is vertical and another inclined at 30° to the vertical: lodged between these is a cylinder of negligible weight with its axis horizontal. Papers inserted between the cylinder and the vertical face become jammed and cannot be released by a downward pull. Determine the least angle of friction between the cylinder and the surfaces in contact with it for the apparatus to work, explaining your argument carefully. (M.E.I.)

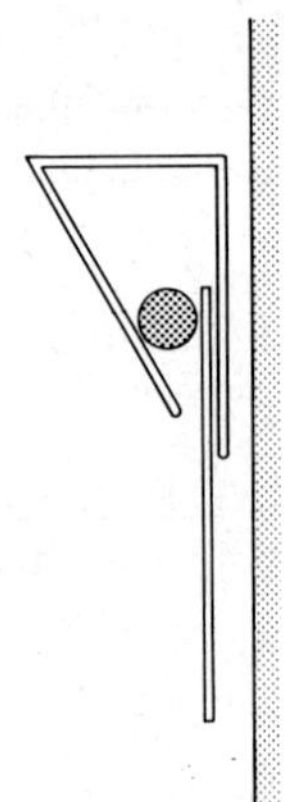

Fig. 10.19

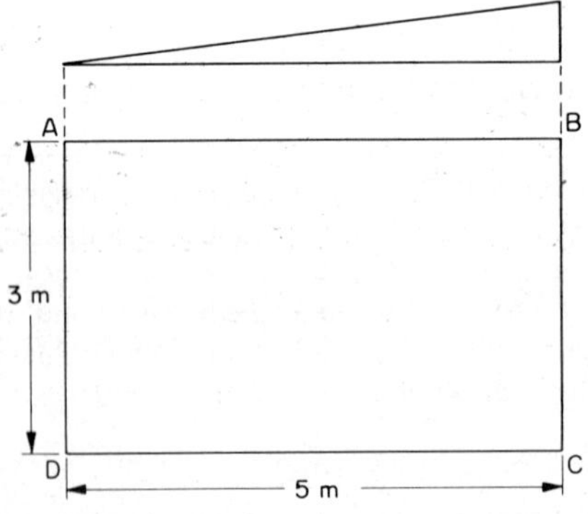

Fig. 10.20

17. Fig. 10.20 shows the plan and elevation of a rigid rectangular plate of uniform material which varies in thickness from 0.01 m at the end AD to 0.015 m at the end BC. (The figure exaggerates the thickness.) Show that the centre of gravity of the plate is $2\frac{2}{3}$ m from the edge AD. The plate, weight 4800 N, rests horizontally at A, B, C, D on point supports which may be regarded as slightly adjustable vertically. It has a load of 4000 N placed on it at the middle point. The reactions of the supports A, B, C, D are R_A, R_B, R_C, and R_D N respectively. To obtain the values of these reactions the plate with its load may be regarded as equivalent to loads R_A, R_B, R_C, and R_D at its corners. Show that $R_B + R_C = 4560$.
Obtain further equations for R_A, R_B, R_C, and R_D and show that a full solution cannot be obtained without more data. Solve for the case in which the supports are adjusted to make R_A zero. (M.E.I.)

18. An insect has six legs and it may be assumed that when it is 'standing' on the ceiling its weight is distributed equally on the feet which are attached at the vertices of a regular hexagon. Any foot will become detached when required to exert a pull greater than or equal to twice that required for 'standing'.
Examine whether the insect can detach just two legs at the same time, making clear for which pair of legs this is possible. Assume that the centre of mass of the insect does not move as legs are detached from the ceiling. (M.E.I.)

19. A wheelbarrow of weight W has a rusty wheel so that a friction couple opposes its turning. It rests with the wheel on rough ground (coefficient of friction μ) and its handles against a smooth vertical wall. The centre of gravity G of the barrow is on the line joining the centre C of the wheel to the middle point A of the line joining the points of contact of the handles with the wall. The radius of the wheel is a, CG = b, CA = c. If there is equilibrium with AC making an angle θ with the vertical, show that

$$\mu > \frac{b \tan \theta}{c + a \sec \theta}$$

and find the magnitude of the frictional couple. (M.E.I.)

20. A drawer jams when I attempt to open it by pulling only one of the handles. If the depth of the drawer is d and the distance of the handle from the centre of the front is a, prove that the coefficient of friction at the side of the drawer is not less than $d/2a$.

21. When a car is on level ground, the centre of gravity is a height h above the ground. The front and rear axles are then at horizontal distances a and b respectively from the centre of gravity. If the car can be parked

facing up a hill inclined at an angle α above the horizontal with the rear wheels locked, prove that the coefficient of friction must not be less than $(a+b)/(h+a\cot\alpha)$. Deduce the least value of the coefficient of friction if the car is to be parked facing downhill on the same slope.

22. Two rough circular cylinders of equal radius and length (and uniform density) lie side by side on a rough plane inclined at an angle α to the horizontal and they touch each other along a common generator. The weight of the upper cylinder is W_1, and the coefficient of friction between it and the plane is μ_1. The corresponding quantities for the lower cylinder are W_2 and μ_2 respectively, and the coefficient of friction between the two cylinders is μ_3. Show that equilibrium is impossible for any value of α unless $(\mu_3-1)W_1 \geqslant (\mu_3+1)W_2$.
Suppose that this condition holds and that the angle α is slowly increased from zero. Show that if

$$(W_1+W_2)\mu_1\mu_2 - W_1\mu_1 + W_2\mu_2 = 0$$

then friction becomes limiting between the plane and both cylinders simultaneously. (C.S.)

23. A uniform rod AB of length $2l$ rests with its end A on a rough horizontal plane and with a point C of the rod, distant $2a$, $(a<l<2a)$ from A, in contact with a fixed smooth sphere of radius a, which is standing on the rough horizontal plane. The rod and the centre of the sphere are in the same vertical plane. If μ is the coefficient of friction between the rod and the ground, show that $\mu \geqslant 12l/(50a-9l)$.
By considering the fact that the centre of the rod must lie between A and C, show that for equilibrium to be maintained for all admissible values of the ratio $l:a$, μ must be greater than $\frac{3}{4}$. (C.)

24. A ladder of length $2a$ and weight W is leaning against a smooth vertical wall at an angle α to the horizontal. A man weight w climbs up the ladder. Show that he will reach the top of the ladder safely providing the coefficient of friction between the foot of the ladder and the ground satisfies the inequality

$$\mu > \frac{2w+W}{2(w+W)\tan\alpha}$$

If the wall is rough and the coefficient of friction between the ladder and the wall is also μ, find the condition that the ladder will not slip as the man climbs it. If $w \ll W$, show that this condition reduces to

$$\mu > \frac{1-\sin\alpha}{\cos\alpha}\left(1+\frac{w}{W}\right)$$

when terms in w^2/W^2 are neglected. (O.S.)

Jointed rods: heavy and light rods

Many problems occur involving bodies freely joined together, and the simplest of such bodies are light rods. By a 'heavy' rod we mean a rod whose weight is considerable compared with the forces acting on it; a 'light' rod by contrast is a rod whose weight is so small in comparison to the other forces acting on the rod that it can be neglected. The 'free' joints ensure that the friction at the joints is also negligible.

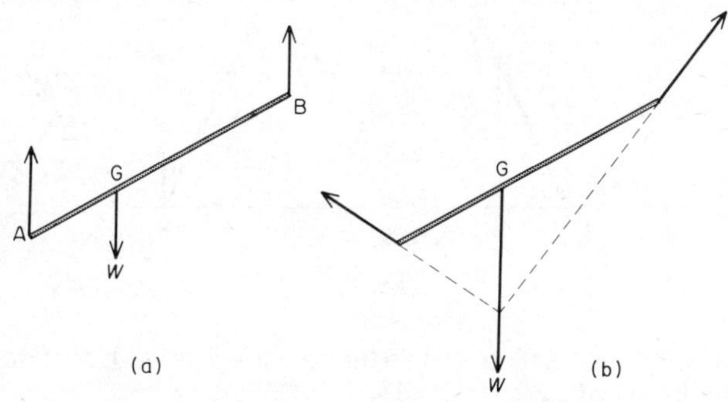

Fig. 10.21

Consider first a heavy rod freely jointed at its ends A, B (Fig. 10.21). Then the weight of the rod acts through the centre of gravity G (not necessarily the midpoint of AB, of course), and in order to keep the rod in equilibrium the lines of action of the forces at A and B must either be vertical or must meet on the vertical through G. They cannot both act along the rod, for then the only force with a component at right angles to the rod would be the weight of the rod; nor can one act along the rod and the other not, for then the lines of action of the forces would not meet in a point. Thus the forces at the hinges A and B act along the rod AB if and only if the weight of the rod is taken as zero. The following examples illustrate this difference between light and heavy rods.

Example 10.8. *Two equal heavy uniform rods AB, BC, weight W and length 2a, are freely jointed at B and rest with the ends A and C on a rough horizontal table. If the rods make an angle α with the horizontal, find the force exerted by each rod on the other.*

As the hinge at B is in equilibrium the forces exerted by each rod on the hinge must be equal and opposite, and are usually called the *reactions* at the hinge. However, as the configuration is symmetrical about a vertical axis through B, there cannot be a vertical component of the reaction at the hinge B. Fig. 10.22 shows the rods separated at the joint so that the nature of the equal and opposite forces can be marked.

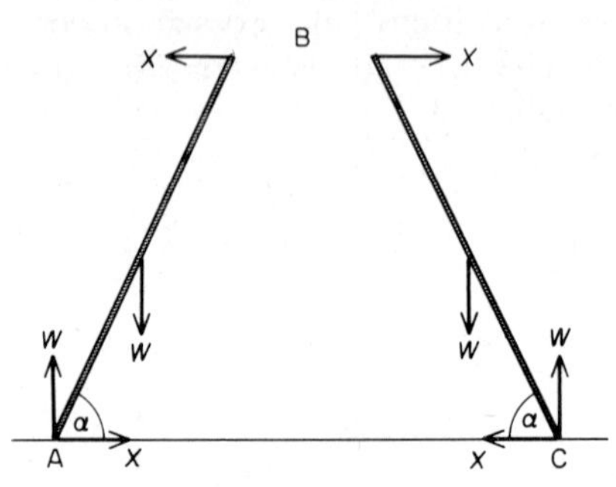

Fig. 10.22

Considering the moments about a horizontal axis through A of the forces acting on the rod AB,

$$Wa\cos\alpha - X(2a\sin\alpha) = 0$$

i.e. $$X = \tfrac{1}{2}W\cot\alpha$$

the force exerted by each rod on the other is a horizontal force $\frac{1}{2}W\cot\alpha$ acting as shown in Fig. 10.22.

Considering the horizontal and vertical forces acting on AB, we see that the force exerted by the table on AB at A has a horizontal component $X(=\frac{1}{2}W\cot\alpha)$ and a vertical component W. Thus the rods can only rest in equilibrium in this manner if the coefficient of friction μ between the rods and the table is such that

$$X \leqslant \mu W, \quad \text{i.e. } \mu \geqslant \tfrac{1}{2}\cot\alpha$$

Notice that in the case of heavy rods we do not at this stage attempt to find the forces (tension, etc.) in the rods.

Example 10.9. *Light rods AB, BC, lengths a and 2a respectively, are freely hinged at B, and the ends A and C are fixed to a vertical wall. A small body weight W is fixed at B. Find the forces exerted on the wall by the frame at A and C.*

Since the only forces at A are the force T_1 in the rod AB and the force exerted by the wall on the rod, the force exerted by the rod on the wall will be equal to T_1 in magnitude and direction (Fig. 10.23). Similarly the force exerted at C will be equal to the force T_2 in BC.

Since the small body is in equilibrium at B, resolving the forces horizontally and vertically,

$$T_2 \sin 60^\circ - W = 0, \quad \text{since angle ABC} = 60^\circ$$

and

$$T_1 - T_2 \cos 60^\circ = 0$$

$$\therefore \qquad T_2 = \frac{2W}{\sqrt{3}} \quad \text{and} \quad T_1 = \frac{W}{\sqrt{3}}$$

the force at A is $W/\sqrt{3}$ and the force at C is $2W/\sqrt{3}$, acting as in Fig. 10.23.

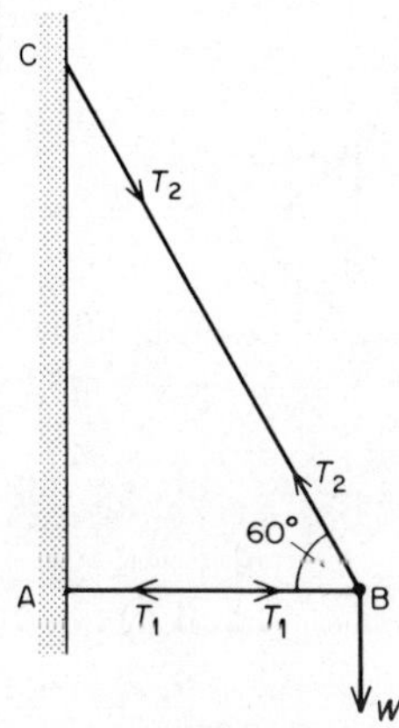

Fig. 10.23

Tension and thrust

Notice that the force T_2 acts at B in the direction from B to C, so the weight of the body is exerting an equal and opposite force on the rod and is tending to stretch the rod. This force is called a *tension*. By contrast, the force in the rod AB on the body is from A to B, so that the equal and opposite force exerted by the body on the rod is from B to A, and is tending to compress the rod. This force is called a *thrust*. It is advisable to mark the diagram to indicate the nature of these forces (Fig. 10.23).

More examples on problems involving light rods are given on page 290. The next example illustrates a jointed framework containing both light and heavy rods.

Example 10.10. *Four equal heavy uniform rods of length 2a and weight W are freely jointed together to form a square ABCD. The system is suspended from the joint A and kept in equilibrium at 45° to the vertical by a light rod AC. Find the tension in this light rod and the reactions at the hinges B and D.*

The forces (Fig. 10.24) are symmetrical about the vertical through A and C, so we shall mark only those to the right of AC. If the tension in the light rod AC is T, then by symmetry there is an upward force $\frac{1}{2}T$ acting at C on the rod BC and at C on the rod CD.

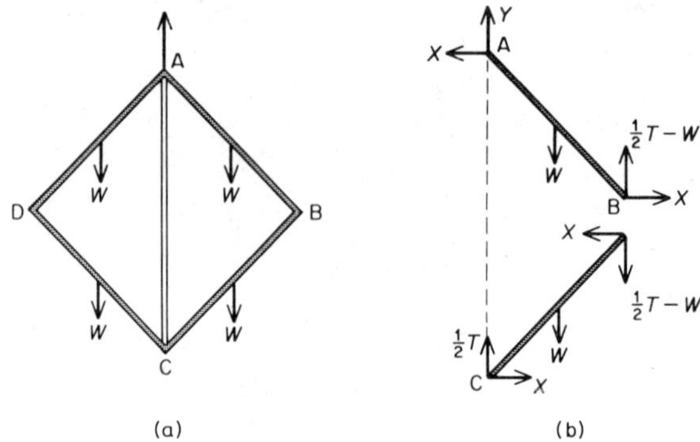

Fig. 10.24

If the horizontal component of the reaction at C is X, then considering the horizontal forces on BC, the horizontal component of the reaction at B is also X. Similarly, so is the horizontal component of the reaction at A.

Considering the vertical forces on BC, the vertical component of the reaction at B is $\frac{1}{2}T - W$. From the moments about a horizontal axis through A of the forces acting on the rod AB,

$$Wa\cos 45° - X(2a\sin 45°) - (\tfrac{1}{2}T - W)(2a\cos 45°) = 0 \qquad (10.6)$$

and about a horizontal axis through C of the forces on the rod BC,

$$Wa\cos 45° - X(2a\sin 45°) + (\tfrac{1}{2}T - W)(2a\cos 45°) = 0$$

Subtracting, $\frac{1}{2}T - W = 0$, i.e. the vertical component of the reaction at B is zero and $T = 2W$, so the tension in the light rod is $2W$.

To find the magnitude of the reaction at B, we have shown that $\frac{1}{2}T - W = 0$, so from equation 10.6,

$$Wa \cos 45^\circ - X(2a \sin 45^\circ) = 0$$

i.e. $X = \frac{1}{2}W$, the reaction at B (and at D) is horizontal and equal to $\frac{1}{2}W$.

Hinged rods at rest on a rough horizontal plane

In Example 10.8 we considered a pair of rods AB, BC freely jointed at B. As the rods were equal, by symmetry the forces at A and C were equal, so that if one rod slips at A the other will slip at C. But if the rods are not equal, it may be that one end will slip and not the other; similarly, a horizontal force applied anywhere would destroy the symmetry of the data.

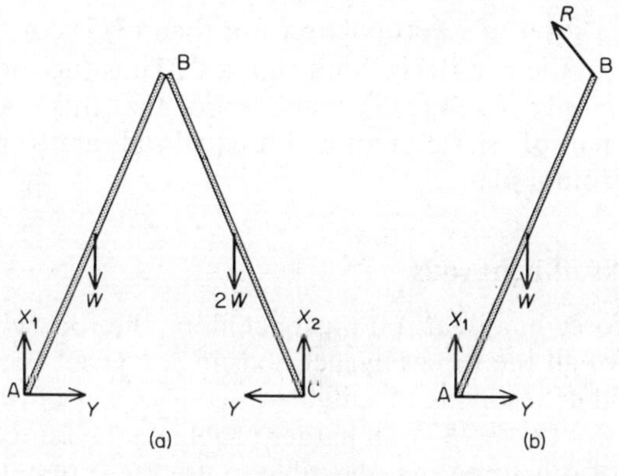

Fig. 10.25

If we have two rods AB, BC equal in length, say $2a$, but with weights W and $2W$ respectively (Fig. 10.25), from the moments about a horizontal axis through A of all the forces acting on the rods,

$$W(a \cos \alpha) + 2W(3a \cos \alpha) - X_2(4a \cos \alpha) = 0$$

where α is the angle between the rods and the horizontal,

i.e. $$X_2 = \tfrac{7}{4}W$$

whence $$X_1 = \tfrac{5}{4}W$$

Now the horizontal components of the reactions at A and C are equal in magnitude, and considering the moments about a horizontal axis through B of the forces on AB,

$$W(a\cos\alpha) + Y(2a\sin\alpha) - X_1(2a\cos\alpha) = 0$$

i.e.
$$Y = \tfrac{1}{2}(2X_1 - W)\cot\alpha$$
$$= \tfrac{3}{4}W\cot\alpha, \quad \text{since } X_1 = \tfrac{5}{4}W$$

Thus the rod will not slip at A if the coefficient of friction μ between the rod and the table is such that

$$Y \leqslant \mu X_1$$

i.e.
$$\tfrac{3}{4}W\cot\alpha \leqslant \mu(\tfrac{5}{4}W)$$

i.e.
$$\mu \geqslant \tfrac{3}{5}\cot\alpha$$

If $\mu > (3/5)\cot\alpha$, μ is certainly greater than $(3/7)\cot\alpha$, so that $Y < \mu X_2$ and the rod BC will not slip at C. Thus the rods will be in equilibrium only if $\mu \geqslant (3/5)\cot\alpha$. Notice that this is greater than the coefficient of friction required if equal rods are to rest on a rough horizontal plane.

Frameworks of light rods

Since the force in a light rod must act along the rod, we know the directions of all the forces in such rods in any given framework. The method of resolving in suitable directions was illustrated in Example 10.9 (page 287). In harder problems the same method is required but it is sometimes possible to use the symmetry of the data to reduce the number of unknown forces.

Example 10.11. *A framework ABCDE is made of seven light rods of equal length, as in Fig. 10.26. The framework is supported at A and C and loads of 20 N are placed at D and at E. Find the force in each rod, indicating whether this force is a tension or a thrust.*

The external forces on the framework are the two loads of 20 N, and the upward reactions at A and C. By symmetry, these reactions are equal and since they total 40 N, each must be 20 N.

Let $T_1, T_2, T_3, \ldots$ be the magnitudes in newtons of the forces in the rods, as in Fig. 10.26. Since there is an upward force exerted by the support at A, the rod AE is the only means whereby a downward force can be applied at A, so that the force at A must act as in Fig. 10.26. This force is a thrust, or we can say that the rod is in *compression*. Similarly T_2 must act at A as shown, and therefore is a tension.

Equating to zero the sum of the vertical components of the forces at A,

$$T_1 \sin 60^\circ - 20 = 0$$

i.e.

$$T_1 = 40/\sqrt{3}$$

and from the horizontal components,

$$T_1 \cos 60 - T_2 = 0$$

$$T_2 = 20/\sqrt{3}$$

By symmetry, the forces in BD and BE must be equal. But these are the only forces acting at B that have vertical components, so their sum must be zero, and so each force separately is zero.

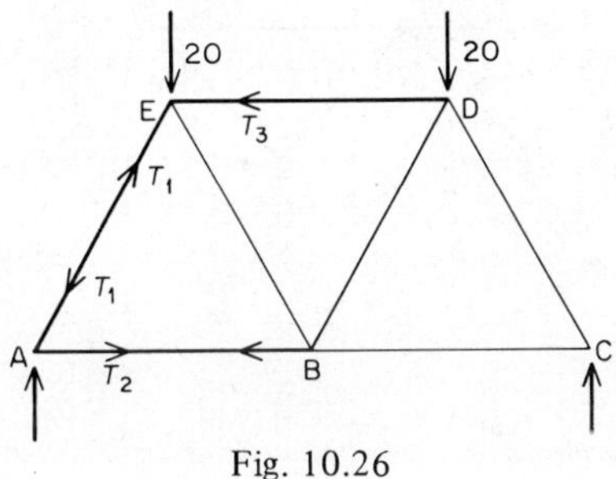

Fig. 10.26

Considering the horizontal forces at E,

$$T_3 - T_1 \cos 60 = 0$$

i.e.

$$T_3 = 20/\sqrt{3}$$

The remaining forces can now be written down by symmetry. Thus we have

thrusts of $40/\sqrt{3}$ N in AE and CD,
thrusts of $20/\sqrt{3}$ N in DE,
tensions of $20/\sqrt{3}$ N in AB and BC,

and no force in either BE or BD. These two rods could be removed without upsetting the equilibrium of the framework when the loading is symmetrical.

Example 10.12. *The light framework ABCDEF in Fig. 10.27 is formed of rods so that AB, BC, DE, and EF are horizontal and AE, EB, BD, and DC are* *inclined at 45° to the horizontal. The framework is smoothly jointed to a rigid wall at A and F, and a load of 100 N applied at C. Find the force in each rod and the reactions at A and F.*

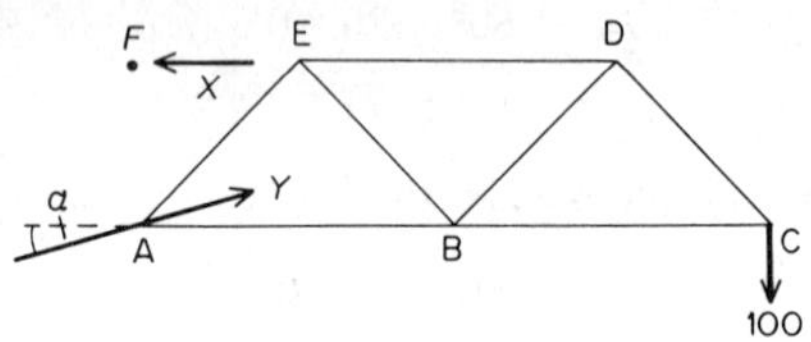

Fig. 10.27

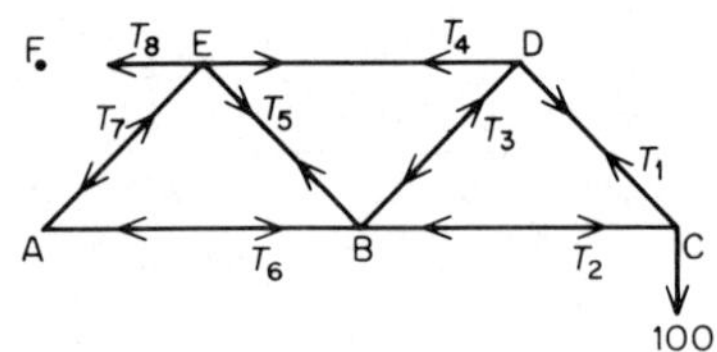

Fig. 10.28

The external force X at F must act along EF, and the third external force Y on the framework must act through the point of intersection of the lines of action of X and the load 100 N. So from the horizontal and vertical components of the forces,

$$Y \cos \alpha - X = 0 \quad \text{and} \quad Y \sin \alpha - 100 = 0$$

But if the length of AB is $2a$, the height of the framework is a and $\tan \alpha = \frac{1}{4}$, so

$$Y = 100\sqrt{17} \quad \text{and} \quad X = 400$$

Denoting the size of the forces in newtons by T_1, T_2, etc., as in Fig. 10.28, we must start at a joint such as C where there are only two unknown forces. At each joint we shall consider the vertical and horizontal components of the forces.

At C, $T_1 \sin 45^\circ = 100$ and $T_2 = T_1 \cos 45^\circ$

$$\Rightarrow T_1 = 100\sqrt{2} \quad \text{and} \quad T_2 = 100$$

At D, $T_3 \sin 45^\circ = T_1 \sin 45^\circ$ and $T_4 = T_3 \cos 45^\circ + T_1 \cos 45^\circ$

$$\Rightarrow T_3 = 100\sqrt{2} \quad \text{and} \quad T_4 = 200$$

At B, $T_5 \sin 45^\circ = T_3 \sin 45^\circ$ and $T_6 - T_2 - T_3 \cos 45^\circ - T_5 \cos 45^\circ = 0$

$$\Rightarrow T_5 = 100\sqrt{2} \quad \text{and} \quad T_6 = 300$$

At E, $T_7 \sin 45^\circ = T_5 \sin 45^\circ$ and $T_8 - T_4 - T_5 \cos 45^\circ - T_7 \cos 45^\circ = 0$

$$\Rightarrow T_7 = 100\sqrt{2} \quad \text{and} \quad T_8 = 400$$

As a check, at F, $T_8 = X$, and we have already found T_8 to be 400, equal to the value we previously obtained for X.

The directions of the forces at each joint can often be found by inspection. If the direction taken as positive is clearly marked on the figure, a negative value can be easily interpreted. Thus if we had thought that the force from BC at C was to the left, we should have obtained $T_2 = -100$, and realized our error.

We see that the rods CD, BC, ED, and EF are in tension, the rest are in compression (with thrusts). These results can be summarized

rod	AB	thrust	300 N
rod	BC	thrust	100 N
rod	CD	tension	$100\sqrt{2}$ N
rod	DE	tension	200 N
rod	BD	thrust	$100\sqrt{2}$ N
rod	BE	tension	$100\sqrt{2}$ N
rod	AE	thrust	$100\sqrt{2}$ N
rod	EF	tension	400 N

and the reactions at A and F are $100\sqrt{17}$ N and 400 N respectively. Alternatively a sign convention of positive for tension and negative for thrust (or vice versa) can be adopted.

Bow's notation

A graphical method of solving framework problems was devised by R. H. Bow and published in 1873. This is really only an extension of the triangle of forces (*Additional Applied Mathematics*, page 82), but since the force polygons become very complicated a clear notation is vital.

Consider first the forces at C in the framework in Example 10.12. Knowing the directions of the forces in BC and CD, if we draw a line 100 units long to represent the load 100 N, the forces in BC and CD can be found from this triangle (Fig. 10.29). Their directions can also be obtained since, as the forces are in equilibrium, they must act in order, as shown in the smaller triangle. This order is determined by the direction of the load of 100 N.

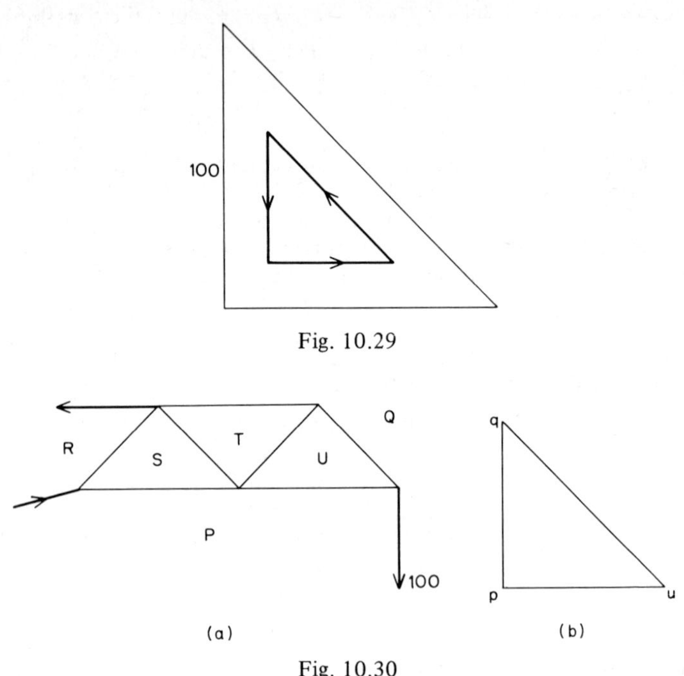

Fig. 10.29

Fig. 10.30

Bow's notation consists of lettering the regions bounded by the lines of action of the forces with capital letters [Fig. 10.30(a)] and lettering the vertices of the corresponding polygons of forces with small letters. Regions P and Q are separated by the line of action of the load so the load is represented by a vertical line *pq* length 100 units. The lines *qu, pu* represent the forces whose lines of action separate the regions Q, U and P, U respectively. Thus we can letter the triangle of forces acting at C.

As when calculating the forces, we can still only find the forces at points where there are not more than two unknown forces. Consider the point D, which is surrounded by the regions Q, U, and T. We have drawn *qu* and we know the directions of the forces separating Q, T and T, U, so we know the directions of the lines *qt* and *tu*. Add these to Fig. 10.30(b).

Consider next the forces at B, where there are only unknown forces in BA and BE. The lines of action of the forces separate the regions P, S, T, and U. We know the positions of all the corresponding points except *s*, and we know that *ps* is horizontal, *ts* parallel to *qu*. We can extend Fig. 10.30(b) to show the point *s*. Likewise *sr* is parallel to *tu* and *rq* is horizontal, so that Fig. 10.31 gives the

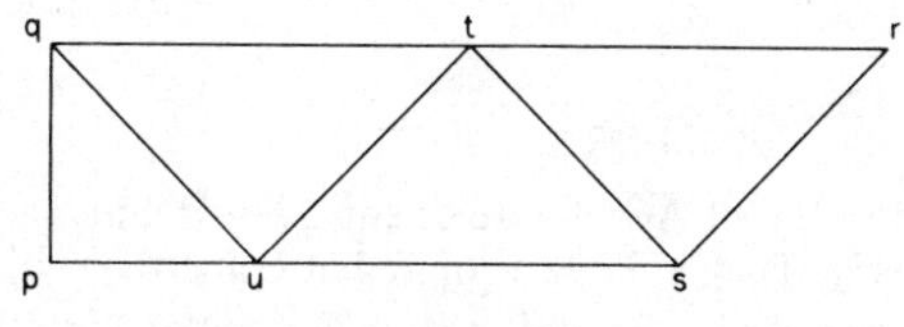

Fig. 10.31

complete force diagram for the framework. The magnitude of each force can be read and tabulated.

Force in rod AB, represented by *ps*, 300 N
Force in rod BC, represented by *pu*, 100 N
Force in rod CD, represented by *qu*, 140 N
Force in rod DE, represented by *qt*, 200 N
Force in rod BD, represented by *tu*, 140 N
Force in rod BE, represented by *st*, 140 N
Force in rod AE, represented by *rs*, 140 N
Reaction at A, represented by *pr*, 410 N
Reaction at F, represented by *rq*, 400 N

Since the lines of action of the reactions at A and F separate the regions P, R and R, Q respectively, the reactions are represented by the lines *pr* and *rq*. Since the load was represented by *qp*, the order *qp, pr, rq* must be preserved for equilibrium.

The directions of the forces can be found in the same way as with the triangle of forces *pqu*. Since regions P, S, T, U surround the point B, the forces at B are given by the quadrilateral *pust*. The force exerted by BC on B is equal to and opposite to the force by BC on C, whose direction is marked in Fig. 10.30(b), so the forces in

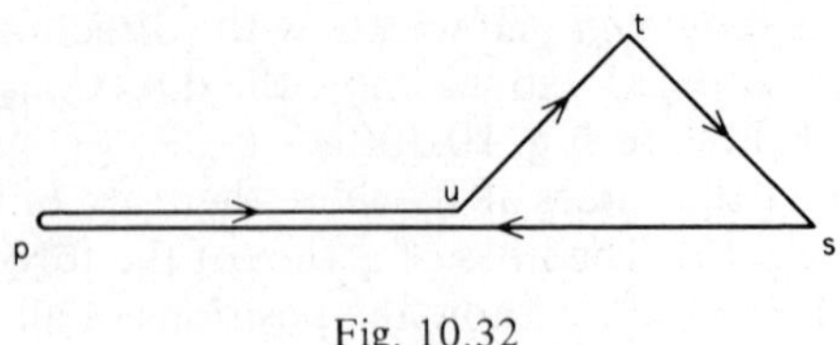

Fig. 10.32

pust act as in Fig. 10.32, enabling us to mark the appropriate forces in the framework.

EXERCISE 10(b)

1. Two uniform rods AC, BC are of equal length but weights W_1, W_2 respectively. They are freely jointed at C and the ends A and B are fixed to smooth hinges on the same horizontal level. In equilibrium the rods rest in a vertical plane with C below the level of AB, and with both rods inclined at an angle 45° to the horizontal. Find the horizontal and vertical components of the reaction of the rod AC on the other rod.

2. Two equal uniform rods AB, BC, weight W, are freely jointed at B. They rest in a vertical plane inclined at an angle α to the horizontal with the ends A and C on a rough horizontal plane. If the plane is sufficiently rough to prevent slipping, find the components along and perpendicular to the plane of the forces at the hinge B.

3. Two uniform rods AB and AC, each of weight W and length $4a$, are smoothly hinged together at A. At B and C are small light rings which run on a rough horizontal wire. The rods hang down below the wire, each making an acute angle θ with the vertical. A particle of weight $5W$ is fastened to the rod AB at a point D, where BD $= a$. If the system is in equilibrium, find the friction force and the normal reaction of the wire on each ring in terms of W and θ.
If the coefficients of friction at B and C are $\frac{1}{3}$ and 1 respectively, find the largest value of θ for which the system will stay in position without slipping. (C.)

4. Fig. 10.33 represents a uniform rod AB, length $2a$ and weight W hinged at A and supported at C by a fixed smooth vertical circular disc with AD horizontal; the angle DAB $= \theta$ and AD $= c(a < c < 2a)$. A weight W is suspended from B. Prove that if P and Q are the vertical and

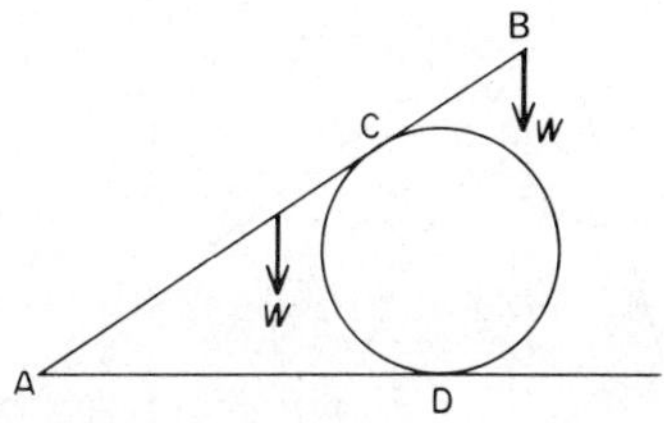

Fig. 10.33

horizontal components respectively of the reaction of the hinge on the rod, then

$$Q = \frac{3Wa \sin 2\theta}{2c}$$

and that, if the resultant of P and Q makes the same angle θ with the upward vertical, then $\cos^2 \theta = c/3a$. (O. & C.)

5. Fig. 10.34 (in which every angle is either 45° or 90°) represents a framework of light rigid rods freely jointed at A, B, C, D, and E and supported at A and D, AD being horizontal. Weights U and V are

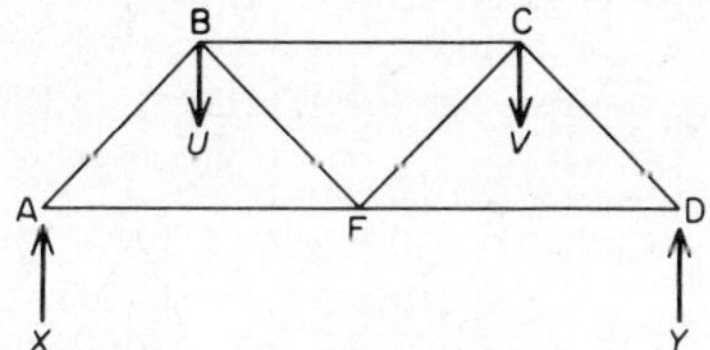

Fig. 10.34

suspended from B and C. Prove that the vertical thrusts X and Y at A and D respectively are given by the equations

$$4X = 3U + V, \quad 4Y = U + 3V$$

Find also the thrust or tension in each rod; draw a diagram from which these can be read, distinguishing clearly thrusts from tensions. (O. & C.)

6. ABCDE (Fig. 10.35) is a smoothly pinjointed framework of light rods. AB = BC, CD = DE, and the perpendicular from E to AC meets AC at a point one fifth of its length from A; the angle ACE = 36°.

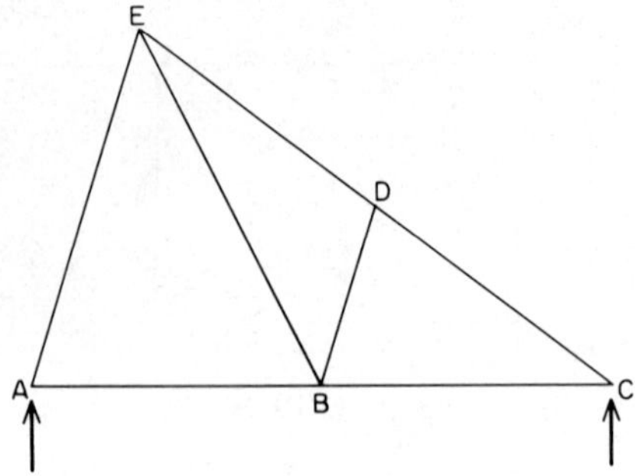

Fig. 10.35

The framework is supported at A and C with AC horizontal, and equal loads W are applied at E and D. Calculate (or find graphically) the supporting forces at A and C, and find graphically the stress in each rod, indicating which rods are in tension and which are in compression. (S.U.)

7. The framework ABCDEF shown in Fig. 10.36 consists of eight smoothly jointed light rods. The framework is smoothly hinged to a vertical wall at A and B and is in a vertical plane with BCD and AFE

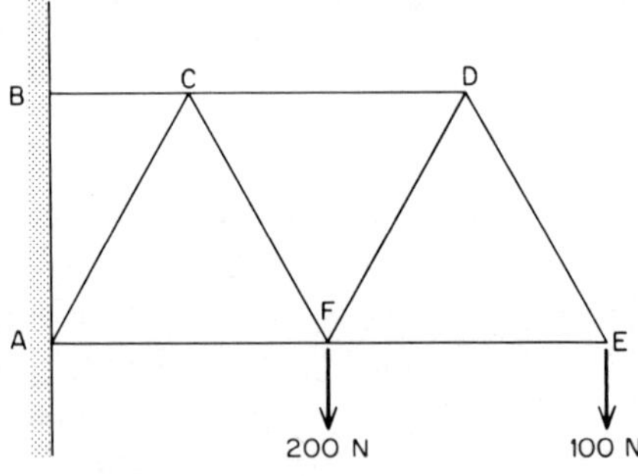

Fig. 10.36

horizontal. The triangles ACF, CDF, and DEF are equilateral. The framework is in equilibrium with weights 100 N and 200 N acting at E and F respectively. Find the reactions at A and B and the forces in the rods, stating which rods are in compression. (A.E.B.*)

8. A light framework ABCD (Fig. 10.37) consists of five smoothly jointed rods of equal length. The framework carries a load W at D and is smoothly hinged and fixed at A. The framework is kept in equilibrium in a vertical plane with AC horizontal by a force P applied at B

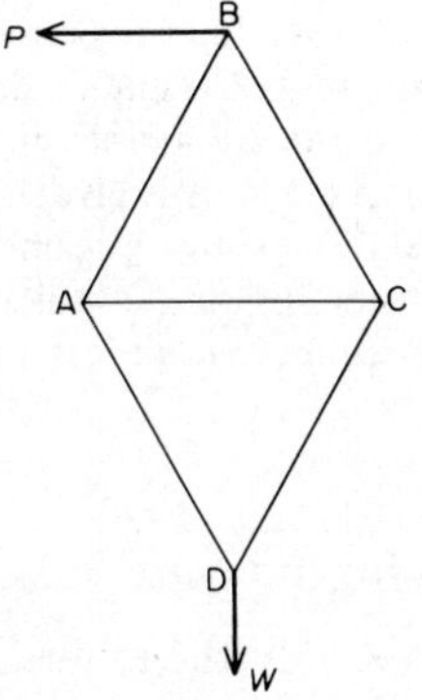

Fig. 10.37

in a direction parallel to CA. Find the magnitude of P and the magnitude and direction of the reaction at A. Find, graphically or otherwise, the forces in the five rods and state which rods are in compression. (A.E.B.)

9. Fig. 10.38 represents a smoothly jointed framework formed by nine light rods. AB = BC; ADB, BFC are equilateral triangles, and the angles BDE, BFE are right angles; ABC is horizontal and BE is vertical. Loads

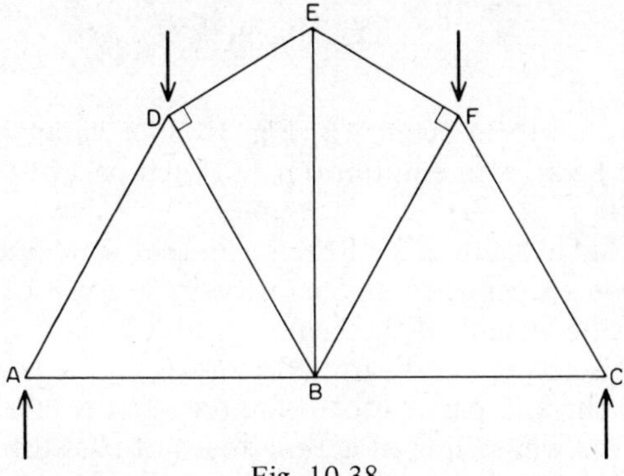

Fig. 10.38

W, $3W$ are hung from D, F and the framework is supported at A, C by vertical forces. Find these forces, show that there is no stress in the rod BD, and find the stress in the other rods, giving both the magnitude and the sense in each case. (O. & C.)

10. A framework is made of seven light rods freely jointed at their ends. Five of them form a square ABCD and its diagonal BD; CE is equal and parallel to DB; BE is equal to AB and lies in the same line as AB. The framework is in a vertical plane, A is pivoted to a fixed point of a smooth vertical wall, D rests below A against the wall and at E is hung a weight W. Find the reactions on the wall at D and at A. Find also the stress in each rod, indicating whether it is a thrust or a tension. (O. & C.)

Shearing force and bending moment

So far we have considered only the external forces on a rod and the forces at the joints of a framework. The latter show whether a rod is in tension or compression, and the tension or thrust is an internal force in the rod. There may of course be other internal forces in a rod, not necessarily along the rod.

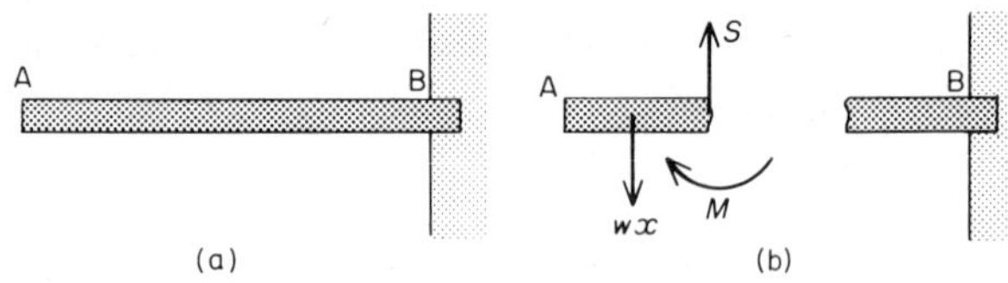

Fig. 10.39

Consider a uniform beam AB (Fig. 10.39), clamped at one end B. Then the beam is in equilibrium and each part of the beam is in equilibrium.

If we consider a length x of the beam that is in equilibrium, there must be a vertical force S exerted by the rest of the beam on this part. If the weight of the beam per unit length is w, $S = wx$. The force S is called the shearing force.

But since the end part of the beam does not rotate and there is only one force whose line of action does not pass through the point at which S acts, there must also be a couple M on the beam, where

$$M - wx\left(\frac{x}{2}\right) = 0, \quad \text{i.e. } M = \tfrac{1}{2}wx^2$$

The couple M is called the bending moment. The shearing force has been taken with the upward direction positive, and M with the clockwise sense positive. Sometimes other sign conventions are used so it is always wise to make clear the direction of S and the sense of M.

Shearing force and bending moment graphs

The variation of S and M with x can easily be illustrated graphically and this often gives a clearer indication of the manner in which S and M vary with x. If the length of the beam is a, $0 \leqslant x \leqslant a$ and we have only *part* of a straight line graph and *part* of a quadratic graph (Fig. 10.40).

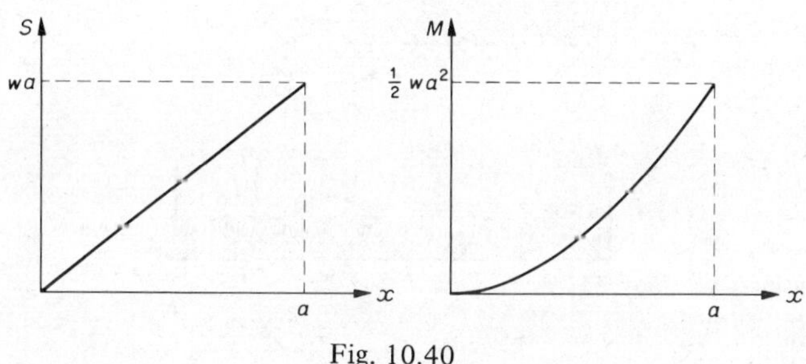

Fig. 10.40

Shearing force and bending moment for a light beam

When a light beam AB is supported at each end and loads $3W$ and $6W$ applied at each point of trisection, the forces at the supports are $4W$ and $5W$ (Fig. 10.41).

The beam is divided into three parts, and the shearing force and bending moment of each part must be found separately. Taking the length of the beam as $3a$, we wish to find the shearing force and bending moment at a point P, a distance x from A. We shall

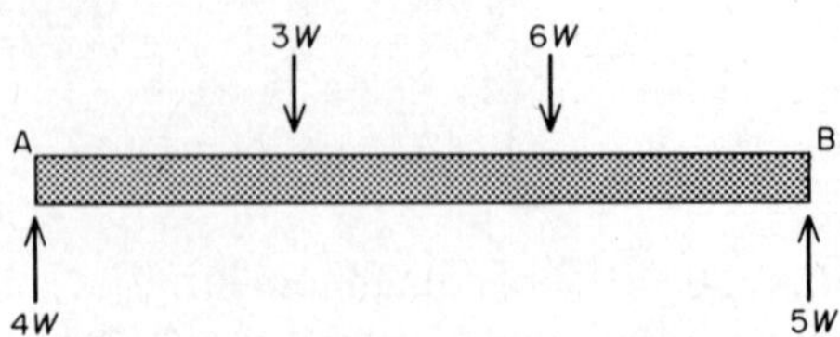

Fig. 10.41

consider for each part the vertical forces to find S and the moments about a horizontal axis through P to find M.

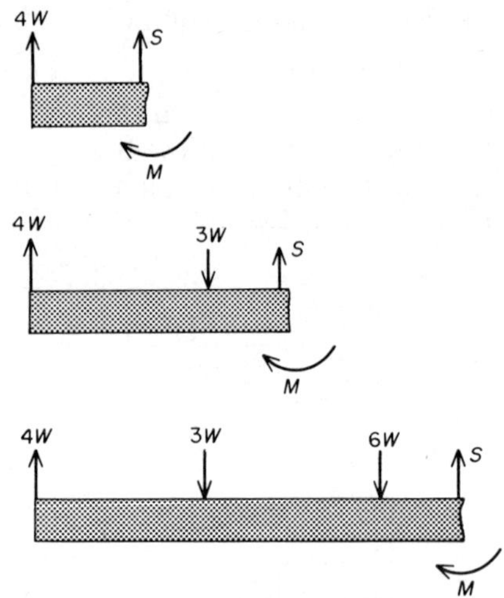

Fig. 10.42

When $0 \leqslant x < a$,

$$S \text{ (upwards)} = -4W$$
$$M \text{ (clockwise)} = -4Wx$$

When $a < x < 2a$,

$$\begin{aligned} S \text{ (upwards)} &= 3W - 4W \\ &= -W \\ M \text{ (clockwise)} &= 3W(x - a) - 4Wx \\ &= -Wx - 3Wa \end{aligned}$$

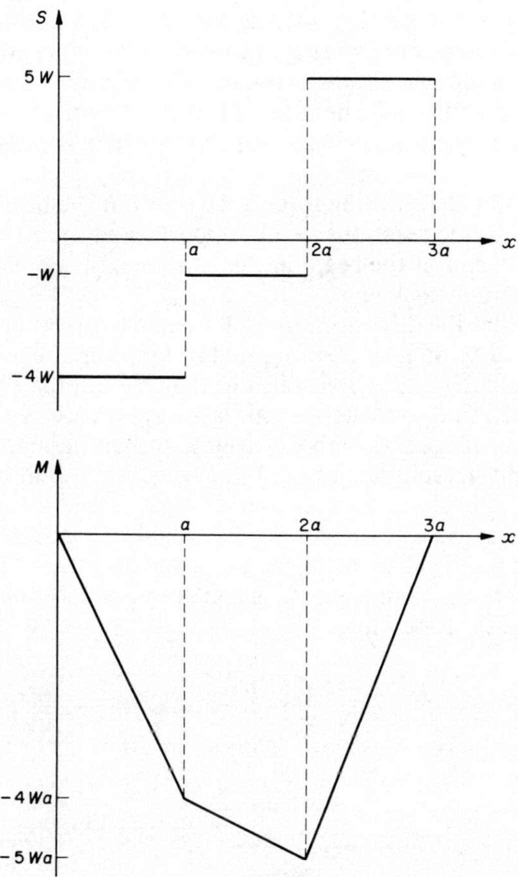

Fig. 10.43

When $2a < x < 3a$,

$$S \text{ (upwards)} = 6W + 3W - 4W$$
$$= 5W$$
$$M \text{ (clockwise)} = 6W(x - 2a) + 3W(x - a) - 4Wx$$
$$= 5Wx - 15Wa$$

The shearing force and bending moment diagrams are given in Fig. 10.43.

The graph of the shearing force against x is discontinuous (Fig. 10.43), the discontinuities being at the points of application of the loads and equal in magnitude to the loads. The graph of the bending moment is continuous but has a discontinuous gradient, the discontinuities again occurring at the points where the loads are applied.

The values of the shearing force at the ends of the beam are of course equal to the reactions at the supports, and since there is not a couple at an end of the beam in this example, the bending moment is zero at each end.

Noticing that the discontinuities of S and $\mathrm{d}M/\mathrm{d}x$ occur at the same values of x, we may be prompted to look for a relation between S and $\mathrm{d}M/\mathrm{d}x$, and we observe that in both the examples $S = \mathrm{d}M/\mathrm{d}x$. To find out whether this is always true, consider a small element of beam, length δx, average weight per unit length w. The weight per unit length need not be constant, but can vary with x.

With our usual sign convention, Fig. 10.44 shows all the forces and couples on the element of the beam and also the equal and opposite force and couple on the beam at one side of the element. Then for the shearing force

$$S + w\delta x - (S + \delta S) = 0$$

i.e.
$$\delta S = w\ \delta x$$

$$\frac{\mathrm{d}S}{\mathrm{d}x} = w \text{ in the limit}$$

and for the bending moment

$$(M + \delta M) - w\ \delta x\left(\frac{\delta x}{2}\right) - S\ \delta x - M = 0$$

i.e.
$$\delta M - w\ \delta x\left(\frac{\delta x}{2}\right) - S\ \delta x = 0$$

$\mathrm{d}M/\mathrm{d}x = S$ in the limit. Thus not only have we found that for a beam without loading at a particular point $\mathrm{d}M/\mathrm{d}x = S$, but also that $\mathrm{d}S/\mathrm{d}x = w$, the weight per unit length at that point.

If a vertical load is applied at a point on the beam, similar analysis shows that there is a discontinuity in S and dM/dx at that

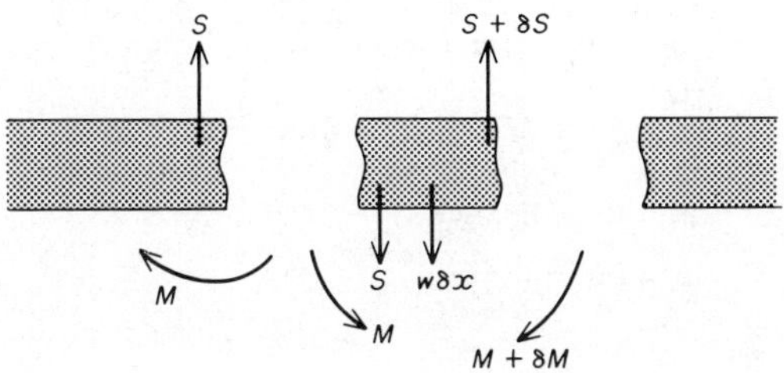

Fig. 10.44

point equal to the size of the load, but that at all other points S and dM/dx are continuous and such that

$$\frac{dM}{dx} = S, \quad \frac{dS}{dx} = w$$

This result can often be used in solving problems, as in the next example.

Example 10.13. *A uniform beam AB, length 2a, weight per unit length w, has a load wa applied at its midpoint. The beam is held in a horizontal position by two supports, one at each end. Draw the shearing force and bending moment diagrams for the beam.*

Considering the whole of the beam (Fig. 10.45), the reaction at each support is $(3/2)wa$. Now consider a length x of the beam.

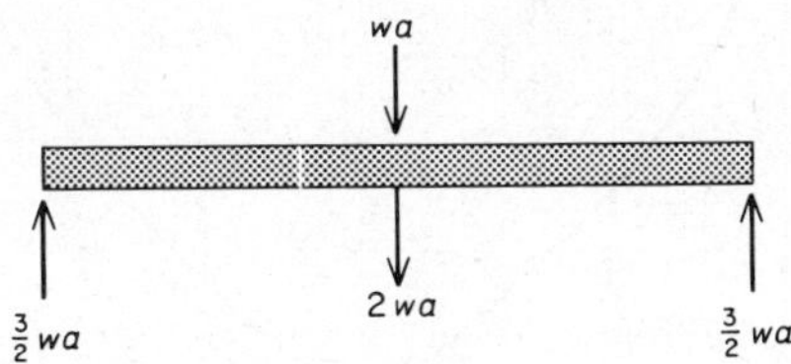

Fig. 10.45

When $\quad 0 \leqslant x < a, \quad \dfrac{dS}{dx} = w \quad \Rightarrow S = wx + C$

But $\quad S = -\frac{3}{2}wa \quad$ when $x = 0, \quad \therefore C = -\frac{3}{2}wa$

$$S = wx - \tfrac{3}{2}wa$$

Also $\quad \dfrac{dM}{dx} = S \quad \Rightarrow M = \frac{1}{2}wx^2 - \frac{3}{2}wax + C$

But $\quad M = 0 \quad$ when $x = 0, \quad \therefore C = 0$

and $\quad M = \frac{1}{2}wx^2 - \frac{3}{2}wax$

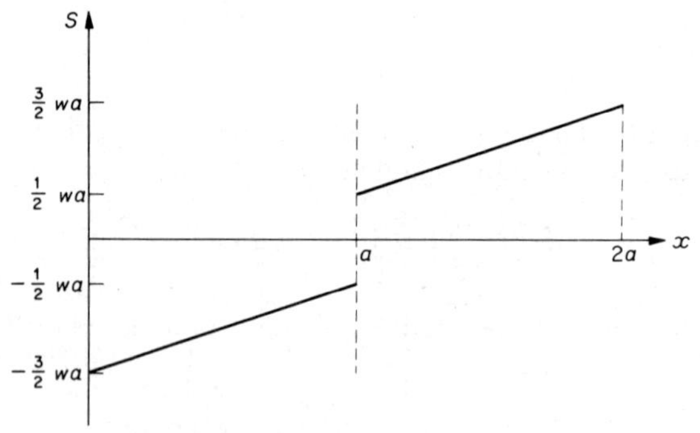

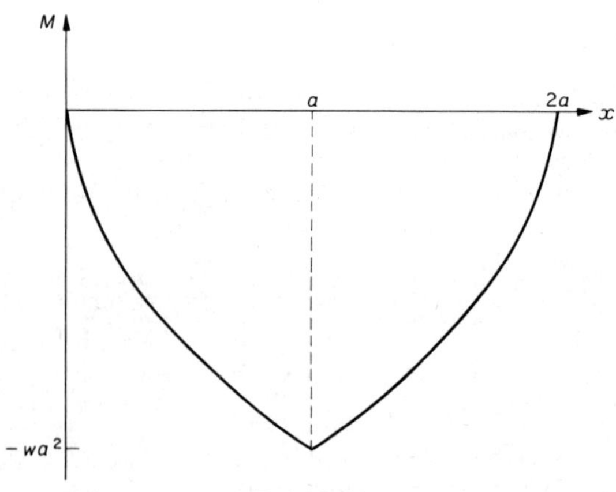

Fig. 10.46

When $\qquad a < x \leqslant 2a, \quad \dfrac{dS}{dx} = w \Rightarrow S = wx + C$

But when x is less than a,

$$S = wx - \tfrac{3}{2}wa$$

and the discontinuity at $x = a$ must be wa, the applied load, so $C = -\tfrac{1}{2}wa$ and $S = wx - \tfrac{1}{2}wa$. Also

$$\frac{dM}{dx} = S \Rightarrow M = \tfrac{1}{2}wx^2 - \tfrac{1}{2}wxa + C$$

Now M is continuous when $x = a$,

$\therefore \qquad \tfrac{1}{2}wa^2 - \tfrac{3}{2}wa(a) = \tfrac{1}{2}wa^2 - \tfrac{1}{2}wa(a) + C$

i.e. $\qquad C = -wa^2$

$$\Rightarrow M = \tfrac{1}{2}wx^2 - \tfrac{1}{2}wax - wa^2$$

As a check, when $x = 2a$, $S = (3/2)wa$, the reaction at B, and $M = 0$ as expected. The shearing force and bending moment diagrams are shown in Fig. 10.46.

Forces along the beams

In all these problems we consider only the vertical forces acting on the beams or parts of the beams. It would not have affected the results if the beams had been in tension or compression, but it is not usual at this stage to consider the shearing force and bending moments inside a beam which is in tension or compression.

EXERCISE 10(c)

1. A straight uniform plank AB, length $4a$ and total weight $4wa$, is held in a horizontal position by supports at A and B. A load $2wa$ is placed on the plank at a point distant a from A. Find the shearing force and bending moment at the point distant x from A, and draw the shearing force and bending moment diagrams.

2. A straight plank is such that its density at any point is proportional to the distance of that point from the end A. Neglecting the thickness of the plank, find the shearing force and bending moment at a point x from A, if the weight of the plank is W, the length is l, and the plank is held in a horizontal position by supports at each end.

3. A uniform straight plank of length $2a$ and total weight $2aw$ is held in a horizontal position by a clamp at one end. A man of weight aw stands

on the plank at a distance x from the clamp. Find the force and couple that the clamp must exert.
Find expressions for the bending moment along the plank.
Due to a weakness in the plank it will snap at the midpoint if the bending moment there exceeds $\frac{3}{4}a^2w$. Prove that the man cannot safely walk more than five-eighths of the length of the plank from the clamp. (O. & C.)

4. A uniform beam of weight $2W$ and length $6l$ is supported in a horizontal position by two trestles placed at the same distance l from each end. Two particles, each of weight w, where $2w > W$, can be moved along the beam. Calculate the bending moment and the shearing force at a point distant x from the left hand end, when each particle is y units from its nearest end and $3l > x > y$.
Show that y can be chosen so that the bending moment is zero at the midpoint of the beam and that, with the particles in this position, the bending moment is independent of w at all points of the beam between them. (S.U.)

5. On a light rigid beam ACDB of length $4l$, the points C and D are such that AC = DB = l. A weight $2W$, is attached at C and a uniformly distributed load of $4W$ is spread over the beam from C to B. The beam is held at rest in a horizontal position by means of two vertical strings attached at A and D. Draw the shearing force and bending moment diagrams for this loading of the beam. State the maximum bending moment to which the beam is subjected and where this occurs.
An additional weight is now attached at B. Find its magnitude if it is just sufficient to reduce the tension in one string to zero. Draw the shearing force and bending moment diagrams in this case. (A.E.B.)

6. The light beam ABCDE is simply supported at A, C, and E, and is hinged at B. It is subject to the loads shown in Fig. 10.47. Sketch the shearing force and bending moment diagrams, giving numerical values at A, B, C, D, and E. State the convention used for positive bending moments and shear forces. (C.S.)

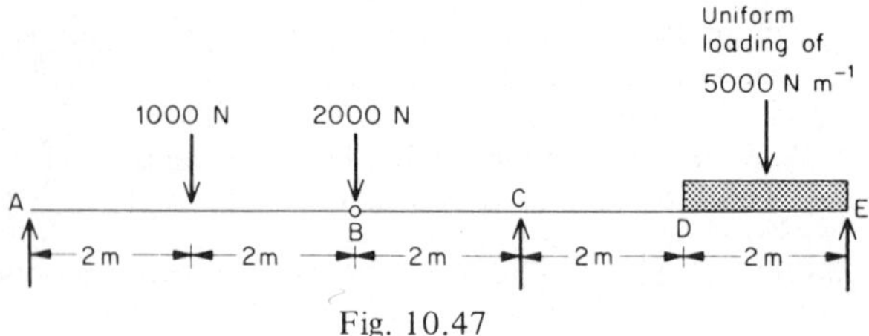

Fig. 10.47

11. Further Investigation of the Motion of Rigid Bodies

Motion of the centre of mass of a rigid body

Using the standard notation, suppose a force **F** acts on an element mass m position vector **r**, of a rigid body. Then

$$\mathbf{F} = m\,\frac{\mathrm{d}^2\mathbf{r}}{\mathrm{d}t^2}$$

Summing over the body,

$$\Sigma\mathbf{F} = \Sigma m\,\frac{\mathrm{d}^2\mathbf{r}}{\mathrm{d}t^2}$$

But the centre of mass of the system, position vector $\bar{\mathbf{r}}$, is given by

$$\bar{\mathbf{r}}\Sigma m = \Sigma m\mathbf{r}$$

$$\therefore \qquad \left(\frac{\mathrm{d}^2\bar{\mathbf{r}}}{\mathrm{d}t^2}\right)\Sigma m = \Sigma m\,\frac{\mathrm{d}^2\mathbf{r}}{\mathrm{d}t^2}$$

i.e.

$$\Sigma\mathbf{F} = M\left(\frac{\mathrm{d}^2\bar{\mathbf{r}}}{\mathrm{d}t^2}\right), \text{ where } M = \Sigma m$$

Some of the forces in $\Sigma\mathbf{F}$ will be internal forces, which are equal and opposite, so that the final summation is only over the external forces.

Thus the centre of mass of a rigid body moves as though all the external forces on the body acted at the centre of mass of the body. We have already used this result, unproved, when investigating the motion of large bodies, and this justifies our treating them as particles.

Force on the axis during the rotation of a rigid body

We have considered already the rotation of rigid bodies about an axis. We can now use the result above to find the force on the axis due to the rotation of a rigid body.

Example 11.1. *A uniform rod AB, mass m, length 2a, is freely pivoted at A. It is held horizontal and then released from rest. Find the horizontal and vertical components of the force at the hinge when the rod is vertical.*

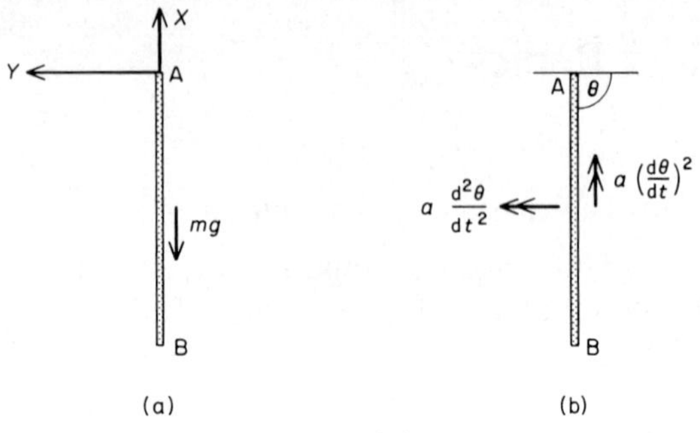

Fig. 11.1

The forces on the rod [Fig. 11.1(a)] must be sufficient to produce the acceleration of the centre of mass of the rod [Fig. 11.1(b)].

∴ When $\theta = \dfrac{\pi}{2}$,
$$X - mg = ma\left(\frac{d\theta}{dt}\right)^2 \tag{11.1}$$

and
$$Y = ma\frac{d^2\theta}{dt^2} \tag{11.2}$$

But from the conservation of energy throughout the motion

$$\tfrac{1}{2}(\tfrac{4}{3}ma^2)\left(\frac{d\theta}{dt}\right)^2 - mga\sin\theta = 0$$

∴
$$ma\left(\frac{d\theta}{dt}\right)^2 = \tfrac{3}{2}mg\sin\theta$$

and
$$ma\frac{d^2\theta}{dt^2} = \tfrac{3}{4}mg\cos\theta$$

Substituting in equations 11.1 and 11.2,

$$X = mg + \tfrac{3}{2}mg\sin\theta$$

and
$$Y = \tfrac{3}{4}mga\cos\theta$$

Thus when the rod is vertical, i.e. $\theta = \pi/2$, the force on the hinge is also vertical, and equal to $(5/2)mg$.

Example 11.2. *A uniform rod AB, length 2a, mass m, is held at an angle π/6 to the vertical with the lower end resting on a rough horizontal table. The rod is then released. Find an inequality satisfied by μ, the coefficient of friction between the rod and the table if the rod does not immediately slip on the table.*

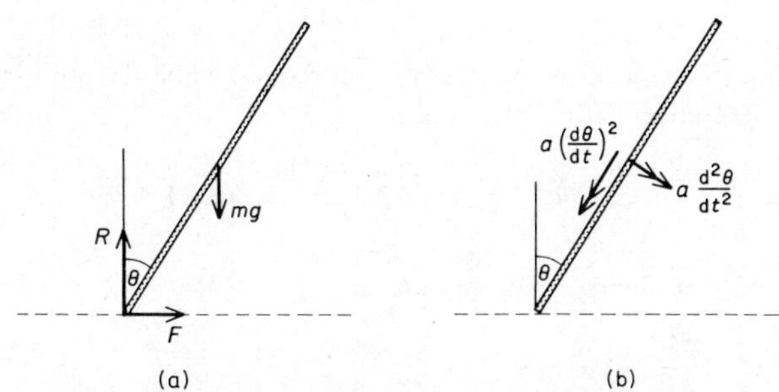

Fig. 11.2

Considering the vertical and horizontal components of the acceleration of the centre of mass of the rod (Fig. 11.2),

$$mg - R = m\left[a\frac{d^2\theta}{dt^2}\sin\theta + a\left(\frac{d\theta}{dt}\right)^2\cos\theta\right]$$

and

$$F = m\left[a\frac{d^2\theta}{dt^2}\cos\theta - a\left(\frac{d\theta}{dt}\right)^2\sin\theta\right]$$

But while the rod is rotating about a fixed point,

$$\tfrac{4}{3}ma^2\frac{d^2\theta}{dt^2} = mga\sin\theta \qquad (11.3)$$

Now initially

$$a\frac{d^2\theta}{dt^2} = \tfrac{3}{4}g\sin\pi/6 \quad \text{and} \quad \frac{d\theta}{dt} = 0$$

$\therefore$

$$R = mg - \tfrac{3}{4}mg(\tfrac{1}{2})^2, \quad \text{using } \sin\pi/6 = \tfrac{1}{2}$$
$$= \tfrac{13}{16}mg$$

and

$$F = \tfrac{3}{4}(\tfrac{1}{2})\left(\frac{\sqrt{3}}{2}\right)mg$$
$$= \frac{3\sqrt{3}}{16}mg$$

Since the rod does not slip, $F \leqslant \mu R$

$$\therefore \qquad \frac{3\sqrt{3}}{16} mg \leqslant \mu \tfrac{13}{16} mg$$

$$\therefore \qquad \mu \geqslant \frac{3\sqrt{3}}{13}$$

To find the forces exerted by the table on the rod while the rod is rotating, we can integrate equation 11.3 to give

$$\tfrac{2}{3} ma^2 \left(\frac{d\theta}{dt}\right)^2 = mga\left(\frac{\sqrt{3}}{2} - \cos\theta\right)$$

since $d\theta/dt = 0$ when $\theta = \pi/6$, so that as

$$a\frac{d^2\theta}{dt^2} = \tfrac{3}{4} g \sin\theta$$

$$R = mg - m\left[\tfrac{3}{4} g \sin^2\theta + \tfrac{3}{2} g\left(\frac{\sqrt{3}}{2} - \cos\theta\right)\cos\theta\right]$$

$$= \tfrac{1}{4} mg(\sin^2\theta + 3\sqrt{3}\cos\theta - 2\cos^2\theta)$$

and

$$F = mg\left[\tfrac{3}{4} g \sin\theta\cos\theta - \tfrac{3}{2} g\left(\frac{\sqrt{3}}{2} - \cos\theta\right)\sin\theta\right]$$

$$= \frac{3\sqrt{3}}{4} mg \sin\theta(\sqrt{3}\cos - 1)$$

Notice that this time we use the rotational form of Newton's law

$$G = I\frac{d^2\theta}{dt^2}$$

whereas in Example 11.1, we used the energy equation. Since the energy equation is merely the distance-integral of Newton's law, we shall in general be able to use either. It is often slightly easier to use the energy equation and then differentiate to find $d^2\theta/dt^2$, rather than to use $G = I\, d^2\theta/dt^2$ and integrate to obtain $d\theta/dt$.

EXERCISE 11(a)

1. A thin circular hoop mass m can rotate freely in a vertical plane about an axis through a point P in the hoop. The hoop is held with its centre O vertically above P, and is then given a small displacement. Show that the force on the axis when the centre O is below P is $3mg$.

2. A uniform circular disc mass m can rotate freely in the vertical plane of the disc about an axis through a point P in the circumference of the disc. Initially the disc is held so that the centre O of the disc is at the same height as P. The disc is then released from rest. Show that when OP is vertical the force on the axis is $(7/3)mg$.

3. The disc in Question 2 is initially at rest with O vertically below P. The disc is then projected with angular velocity Ω so that it just completes circles in a vertical plane. Find the greatest and least force on the hinge in the subsequent motion.

4. A uniform cubical block, mass m, rotates freely about a horizontal axis along one edge of the cube. It is held initially so that the centroid of the cube is at the same height as the axis. The cube is then released from rest. Show that the force on the axis in the subsequent motion has components $(5/2)mg \sin \theta$ and $\frac{1}{4}mg \cos \theta$ in certain directions, and that the greatest force on the axis is $(5/2)mg$, where θ is the angle through which the block has rotated.

5. A rough uniform rod AB, mass m and length $2a$, is pivoted at its mid-point and is free to rotate without friction in a vertical plane. A small ring, also of mass m, is placed on the rod at a distance $\frac{1}{2}a$ from B. The coefficient of friction between the rod and the ring is μ. The system is released from rest with the rod horizontal. Prove that when the rod has rotated through an angle θ, slipping not having occurred,

$$7a\left(\frac{d\theta}{dt}\right)^2 = 12g \sin \theta$$

Show that the ring will slip on the rod when $\tan \theta$ exceeds $4\mu/13$.
(J.M.B.)

6. A uniform rough rod of length a and mass m rests in equilibrium with half its length on a horizontal table and the other half sticking out beyond the table at right angles to the edge. A ring of mass M is slipped on this part of the rod and held at a distance r from the centre of the rod. The system is then released. Prove that, if the coefficient of friction is the same for the rod and the table and for the rod and the ring, slipping occurs first at the point of contact of the rod and the ring.
(O. & C.)

7. A uniform rod is released from rest in a horizontal position with one end supported by a small rough peg. The coefficient of friction between the rod and the peg is μ. Find the inclination of the rod to the horizontal when it slides off the peg. (O. & C.)

8. A uniform solid half-cylinder has radius a and mass m. The centre of mass G is at a distance b from the flat face. The moment of inertia

about the axis through G parallel to the generators is mk^2. The solid is held on a smooth horizontal table with generators horizontal, the flat face being vertical. From this position it is released. Prove that when the flat face makes an angle θ with the vertical,

$$(k^2 + b^2 \cos^2 \theta)\left(\frac{d\theta}{dt}\right)^2 = 2gb \sin \theta$$

Find the reaction of the table on the solid just after it has been released. (O. & C.)

Kinetic energy of a rigid body

If $\mathbf{r}$ is the position vector (Fig. 11.3) of an element mass m of a rigid body, and $\bar{\mathbf{r}}$ is the position vector of the centre of mass G of

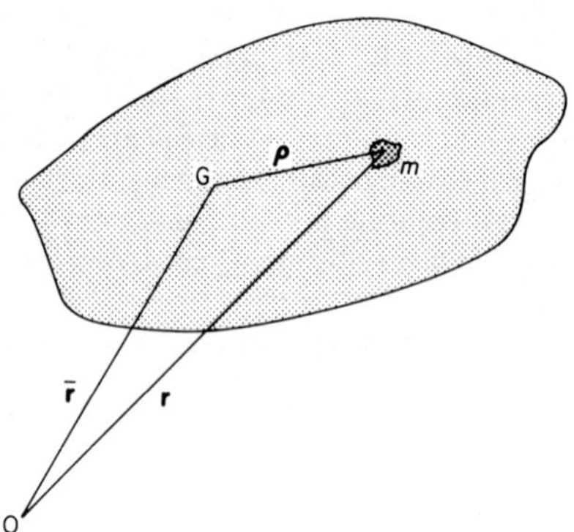

Fig. 11.3

the body, the position vector of the element relative to G is $\boldsymbol{\rho}$, where $\mathbf{r} = \bar{\mathbf{r}} + \boldsymbol{\rho}$. Now from the definition of the centre of mass,

$$\Sigma m\boldsymbol{\rho} = 0$$

whence
$$\Sigma m \frac{d}{dt}(\boldsymbol{\rho}) = 0 \tag{11.4}$$

To determine the kinetic energy of the body in terms of the velocity of the centre of mass, let $\bar{\mathbf{v}}$ denote the velocity of G,

i.e.
$$\bar{\mathbf{v}} = \mathrm{d}\bar{\mathbf{r}}/\mathrm{d}t$$

Then the kinetic energy of the body is

$$\Sigma \tfrac{1}{2} m \left(\frac{\mathrm{d}\mathbf{r}}{\mathrm{d}t}\right)^2 = \tfrac{1}{2}\Sigma m \left[\frac{\mathrm{d}}{\mathrm{d}t}(\bar{\mathbf{r}} + \boldsymbol{\rho})\right]^2$$

$$= \tfrac{1}{2}\Sigma m \left[\bar{\mathbf{v}} + \frac{\mathrm{d}}{\mathrm{d}t}(\boldsymbol{\rho})\right]^2$$

$$= \tfrac{1}{2}(\Sigma m)\bar{\mathbf{v}}^2 + \bar{\mathbf{v}}\Sigma m \frac{\mathrm{d}}{\mathrm{d}t}(\boldsymbol{\rho}) + \tfrac{1}{2}\Sigma m \left[\frac{\mathrm{d}}{\mathrm{d}t}(\boldsymbol{\rho})\right]^2$$

But $\Sigma m\, \mathrm{d}\boldsymbol{\rho}/\mathrm{d}t = 0$ from equation 11.4, and $\mathrm{d}\boldsymbol{\rho}/\mathrm{d}t$ is the velocity relative to the centre of mass. For a rigid body, $|\mathrm{d}\boldsymbol{\rho}/\mathrm{d}t| = \rho\omega$, where $\boldsymbol{\omega}$ is the angular velocity vector of the body.

Thus the kinetic energy of the body is

$$\tfrac{1}{2}M\bar{\mathbf{v}}^2 + \tfrac{1}{2}I\omega^2$$

where M is the mass of the body,
$\bar{\mathbf{v}}$ is the velocity of the centre of mass G,
I is the moment of inertia of the body about an axis through G perpendicular to the plane of rotation, and
and $\boldsymbol{\omega}$ is the angular velocity vector of the body.

Although we shall only use this result for a rigid body, the expression

$$\tfrac{1}{2}M\bar{v}^2 + \tfrac{1}{2}\Sigma m \left(\frac{\mathrm{d}\boldsymbol{\rho}}{\mathrm{d}t}\right)^2$$

is the kinetic energy of a system of particles not necessarily forming a rigid body.

Motion of a body rolling without slipping down an inclined plane

The result obtained above can be used to find the acceleration of a rolling body in many problems. Consider a tennis ball (Fig. 11.4), which may be taken as a hollow sphere of mass m and radius a. When it is rolling without slipping, the velocity $\bar{v}$ of the centre of mass is related to the angular velocity ω by $\bar{v} = a\omega$. When it has rolled a distance x down a plane inclined at an angle α to the horizontal, from the conservation of energy

$$\tfrac{1}{2}M\bar{v}^2 + \tfrac{1}{2}I\omega^2 - Mgx \sin\alpha = 0$$

i.e. $$\tfrac{1}{2}M\bar{v}^2 + \tfrac{1}{2}(\tfrac{2}{3}Ma^2)\frac{\bar{v}^2}{a^2} - Mgx \sin \alpha = 0$$

i.e. $$\tfrac{5}{6}\bar{v}^2 = gx \sin \alpha \qquad (11.5)$$

$$\bar{v} = \sqrt{(\tfrac{6}{5}gx \sin \alpha)}$$

The acceleration of the centre can be found by differentiating, for

$$\mathrm{d}x/\mathrm{d}t = \bar{v}$$

From equation 11.5, $$\tfrac{5}{6}\left(2\bar{v}\frac{\mathrm{d}\bar{v}}{\mathrm{d}t}\right) = g \sin \alpha \frac{\mathrm{d}x}{\mathrm{d}t}$$

i.e. $$\frac{\mathrm{d}\bar{v}}{\mathrm{d}t} = \tfrac{3}{5}g \sin \alpha$$

(An alternative method of obtaining this result is shown in Example 11.4.)

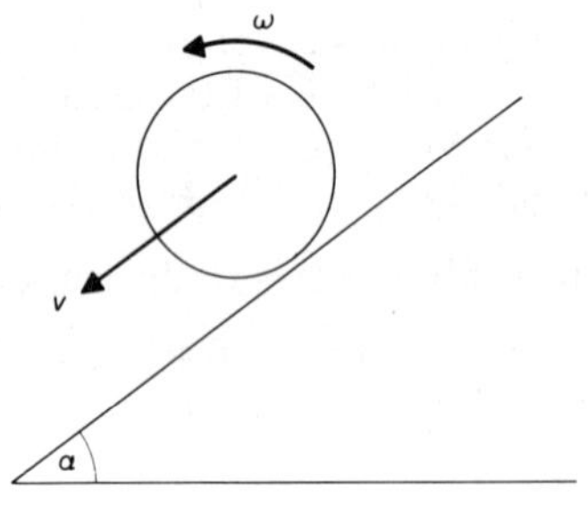

Fig. 11.4

Since the acceleration is constant, the velocity attained t seconds after starting from rest is $(\tfrac{3}{5}g \sin \alpha)t$ and the distance travelled is $(\tfrac{3}{10}g \sin \alpha)t^2$.

Example 11.3. *A uniform solid cylinder, mass m, radius r, rolls without slipping inside a fixed hollow cylinder radius 4r, the axes of both cylinders being horizontal and parallel. Find the period of small oscillations about the position of stable equilibrium.*

Consider a cross-section of the cylinders, as in Fig. 11.5. Then if θ is the angle made by the line of centres with the vertical, and ω is the angular velocity of the rolling cylinder, the point of contact P of the circles of cross-section has velocity $r\omega$ relative to the centre of the rolling cylinder, which itself has velocity $3rd\theta/dt$ relative to the fixed centre O of the larger cylinder. Since the velocity of P is zero,

$$r\omega = 3r\frac{d\theta}{dt}$$

N.B. Note the term 3r. This is often erroneously thought to be 4r, the radius of the larger cylinder.

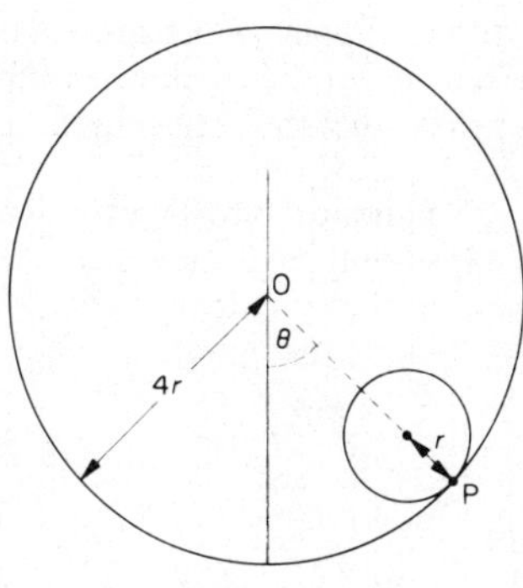

Fig. 11.5

Since the velocity of the centre of mass is $3r\ d\theta/dt$, the conservation of energy gives

$$\tfrac{1}{2}m\left(3r\frac{d\theta}{dt}\right)^2 + \tfrac{1}{2}(\tfrac{1}{2}mr^2\omega^2) - mg(3r\cos\theta) = C$$

i.e.
$$\tfrac{27}{4}mr^2\left(\frac{d\theta}{dt}\right)^2 - 3mgr\cos\theta = C$$

Differentiating and simplifying,

$$\frac{d^2\theta}{dt^2} + \frac{2g}{9r}\sin\theta = 0$$

For small oscillations, this is approximately s.h.m., period $2\pi\sqrt{(9r/2g)}$.

EXERCISE 11(b)

1. A solid sphere rolls without slipping down a rough plane inclined at an angle of 30° to the horizontal. Show that the acceleration of the centre of the sphere is $(5/14)g$.

2. A uniform solid cylinder starts with its axis horizontal and rolls without slipping parallel to a line of greatest slope of a rough plane inclined at an angle α to the horizontal. A uniform solid sphere rolls from rest without slipping down a similar rough plane inclined at β to the horizontal. If the accelerations of the centres of mass of the two bodies are equal, show that $14 \sin \alpha = 15 \sin \beta$.

3. A truck mass M has four circular wheels, each mass m and radius r. The truck is pushed without slipping along a rough horizontal surface by a force F. Find the velocity of the truck when it has travelled a distance s from rest. Hence show that the acceleration of the truck is $F/(M + 2m)$.

4. Fig. 11.6 shows a fixed hollow circular cylinder, internal radius a. One half of the surface is smooth, and the other half rough. The lowest horizontal generator of the cylinder divides the rough surface from the

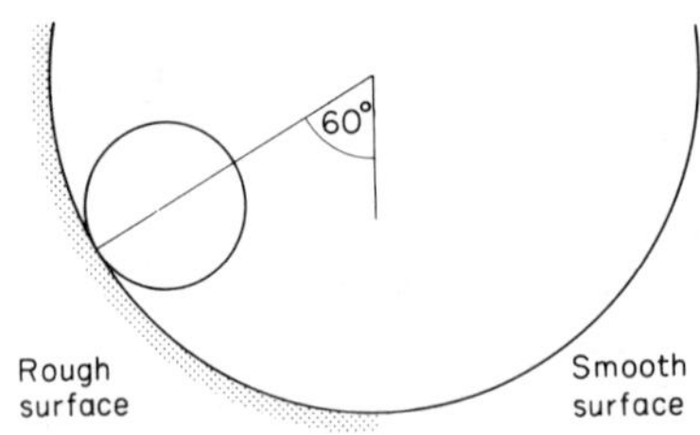

Fig. 11.6

smooth. A uniform solid disc, radius $\frac{1}{4}a$, is held initially in contact with the rough part of the cylinder, so that the disc is in a vertical plane and the common normal at the point of contact is inclined at 60° to the vertical. The disc is then released from rest. If the disc does not slip on the rough surface of the cylinder, so that energy is conserved, show that it comes instantaneously to rest at a height $\frac{1}{4}a$ above its lowest position.

5. In the system shown in Fig. 11.7, two drums radii a, are free to rotate without friction about their axes. A light rope is wound around each drum, and passes under a light pulley C, from which hangs a body mass M. If the M.I. of each drum about its axis is kMa^2, find the velocity of C when it has descended a distance x.

6. Fig. 11.8 shows two pulleys which can rotate without friction about axles through their centres. The pulley centre A, which is fixed, has

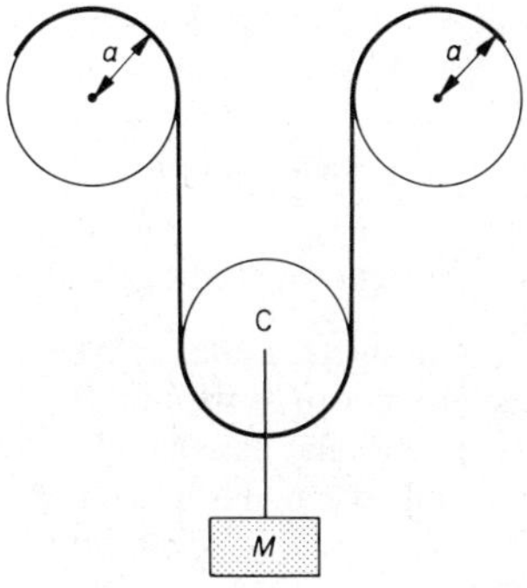

Fig. 11.7

radius a and M.I. about A of $\frac{1}{2}ma^2$. The pulley centre C is light and carries a load mass $3m$.
A light inelastic string has one end fixed, passes under the movable pulley, over the heavy pulley and then is attached to a load of mass $2m$. The string does not slip on either pulley.
Find the kinetic energy of the system at a time t after it is released from rest, and the angular velocity of the heavy pulley at this time.
(S.U.J.B.)

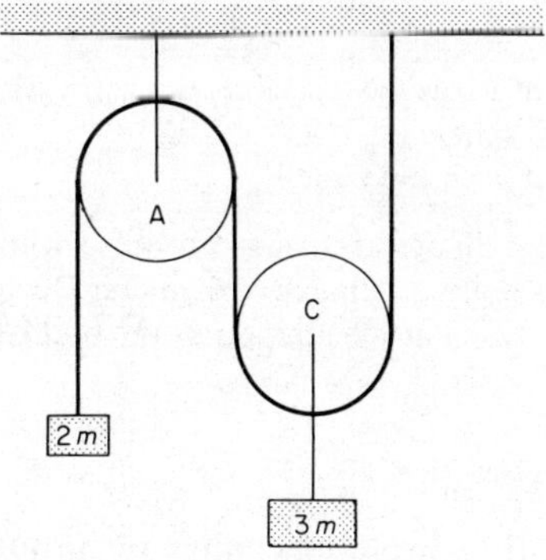

Fig. 11.8

A particle of mass m is placed on the top of a uniform solid circular cylinder, mass $6m$, radius a, which is free to turn about its axis. While the particle has not slipped on the cylinder, show that the angular velocity ω of the cylinder is given by

$$\omega^2 = \frac{g}{a} \sin^2 \tfrac{1}{2}\theta$$

where θ is the angle through which the cylinder has turned.

8. A uniform smooth hemisphere, radius a, is held with a point of its circular rim touching a smooth horizontal floor, its apex touching a smooth vertical wall and its flat base parallel to the wall. It is then released. Prove that while it remains in contact with the floor and the wall,

$$a\left(\frac{\mathrm{d}\theta}{\mathrm{d}t}\right)^2 = \tfrac{15}{8} g \sin\theta$$

where θ is the angle through which it has turned.
Find the reaction of the wall and floor on the hemisphere when (a) $\theta = 45°$, (b) $\theta = 90°$. (O. & C.)

9. A uniform sphere of radius a and mass m has a particle mass M stuck to its surface at the point A. The sphere rests in equilibrium on a horizontal table with A at its highest point. When slightly disturbed, it rolls without slipping on the table. Prove that the energy equation can be written

$$[\tfrac{7}{10} ma^2 + Ma^2(1 + \cos\theta)]\left(\frac{\mathrm{d}\theta}{\mathrm{d}t}\right)^2 = Mga(1 - \cos\theta)$$

Prove that when A reaches the table, the vertical reaction of the table on the weighted sphere is $[M + m + 20M^2/(7m)]g$, assuming the sphere is still in contact with the table. (O. & C.)

10. A uniform solid cylinder of diameter d rolls without slipping inside at the bottom of a hollow cylinder of diameter D which is fixed with its axis horizontal. Calculate the period of the oscillations assumed small. (O.S.)

Moment of momentum: rate of change of moment of momentum

When a particle mass m velocity $\mathbf{v}$ is acted on by a force $\mathbf{F}$, Newton second law gives

$$\mathbf{F} = \frac{\mathrm{d}}{\mathrm{d}t}(m\mathbf{v})$$

The moment of a force **F** about a point position vector **a** has been defined as $(\mathbf{r} - \mathbf{a}) \times \mathbf{F}$, where **r** is the position vector of any point on the line of action of **F**. Thus the moment of the force **F** about the origin is $\mathbf{r} \times \mathbf{F}$, and

$$\mathbf{r} \times \mathbf{F} = \mathbf{r} \times \frac{\mathrm{d}}{\mathrm{d}t}(m\mathbf{v})$$

Summing over a rigid body,

$$\Sigma(\mathbf{r} \times \mathbf{F}) = \Sigma\left[\mathbf{r} \times \frac{\mathrm{d}}{\mathrm{d}t}(m\mathbf{v})\right]$$

Now $\mathbf{v} = \frac{\mathrm{d}}{\mathrm{d}t}(\mathbf{r})$, by definition,

$$\therefore \qquad \left[\frac{\mathrm{d}}{\mathrm{d}t}(\mathbf{r})\right] \times \mathbf{v} = \mathbf{v} \times \mathbf{v} = 0$$

$$\therefore \qquad \Sigma\mathbf{r} \times \frac{\mathrm{d}}{\mathrm{d}t}(m\mathbf{v}) = \Sigma\frac{\mathrm{d}}{\mathrm{d}t}(\mathbf{r} \times m\mathbf{v})$$

$$= \frac{\mathrm{d}}{\mathrm{d}t}\Sigma(\mathbf{r} \times m\mathbf{v})$$

Moreover, since the internal forces on the elements of the body are equal and opposite (Newton's third law),

$$\Sigma\mathbf{r} \times \mathbf{F}$$

is equal to the sum of the moments of the external forces acting on the body. The quantity $\Sigma(\mathbf{r} \times m\mathbf{v})$ is defined as the moment of momentum of the rigid body (sometimes called the angular momentum) so that the sum of the moments about a fixed point O of the external forces acting on a rigid body is equal to the rate of change of the moment of momentum about O of that body.

This is the analogue for rotational motion of Newton's second law; the sum of the external forces acting on a body is equal to the rate of change of momentum of that body.

Moment of momentum of a body rotating about an axis through the centre of mass.

When a rigid body (Fig. 11.9) is rotating about a fixed centre of mass G, the moment of momentum $\Sigma(\mathbf{r} \times m\mathbf{v})$ is equal to

$$\Sigma\mathbf{r} \times (mr\omega\hat{\boldsymbol{\theta}}) = (\Sigma mr^2)\omega\hat{\mathbf{n}}$$

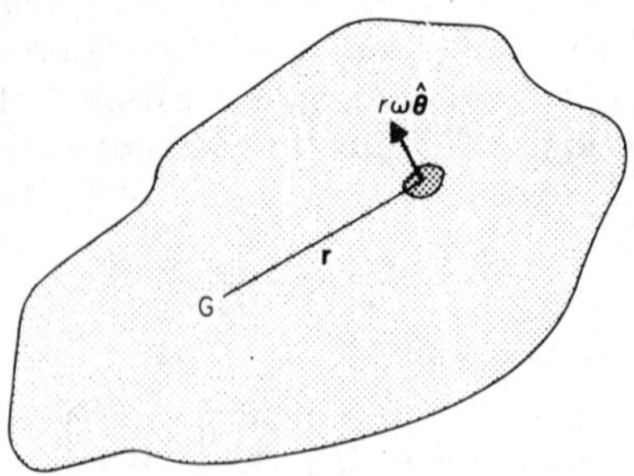

Fig. 11.9

where $\hat{\mathbf{n}}$ is a unit vector perpendicular to $\mathbf{r}$ and θ,

$$= I\omega\hat{\mathbf{n}}$$

Taking the scalar product with a unit vector along the axis of rotation through the centre of mass, the moment of momentum about the axis through the centre of mass is $I\omega$.

Moment of momentum referred to the motion of the centre of mass

With the usual notation, to find the moment of momentum of a rigid body (Fig. 11.10) referred to the motion of the centre of

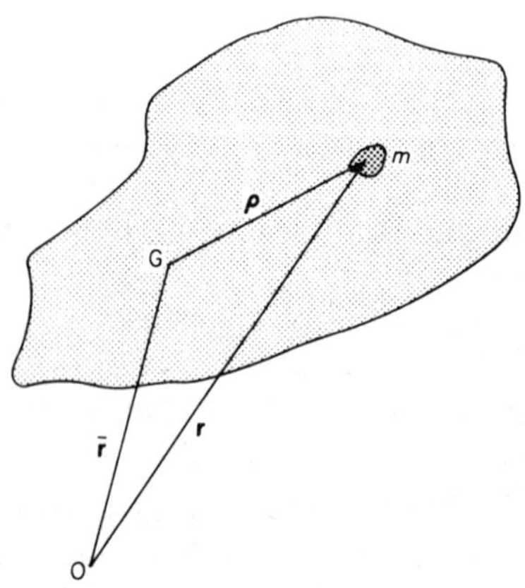

Fig. 11.10

mass of the body,

$$\Sigma(\mathbf{r} \times m\mathbf{v}) = \Sigma\left[(\bar{\mathbf{r}} + \boldsymbol{\rho}) \times m\left(\bar{\mathbf{v}} + \frac{\mathrm{d}\boldsymbol{\rho}}{\mathrm{d}t}\right)\right]$$

$$= (\Sigma m)\bar{\mathbf{r}} \times \bar{\mathbf{v}} + \bar{\mathbf{r}}\Sigma m\frac{\mathrm{d}\boldsymbol{\rho}}{\mathrm{d}t} + (\Sigma m\boldsymbol{\rho}) \times \bar{\mathbf{v}}$$

$$+ \Sigma\boldsymbol{\rho} \times m\frac{\mathrm{d}\boldsymbol{\rho}}{\mathrm{d}t}$$

Now $$\Sigma m\boldsymbol{\rho} = 0 \quad \text{and} \quad \Sigma m\frac{\mathrm{d}\boldsymbol{\rho}}{\mathrm{d}t} = 0$$

$\therefore$ $$(\Sigma m\boldsymbol{\rho}) \times \bar{\mathbf{v}} = 0 \quad \text{and} \quad \bar{\mathbf{r}} \times \Sigma m\frac{\mathrm{d}\boldsymbol{\rho}}{\mathrm{d}t} = 0$$

$\therefore$ $$\Sigma(\mathbf{r} \times m\mathbf{v}) = \bar{\mathbf{r}} \times M\bar{\mathbf{v}} + \Sigma\left(\boldsymbol{\rho} \times m\frac{\mathrm{d}\boldsymbol{\rho}}{\mathrm{d}t}\right) \tag{11.6}$$

Thus the moment of momentum of a rigid body mass M about a fixed point, here taken as the origin of the position vectors, is equal to the moment of the linear momentum of a particle mass

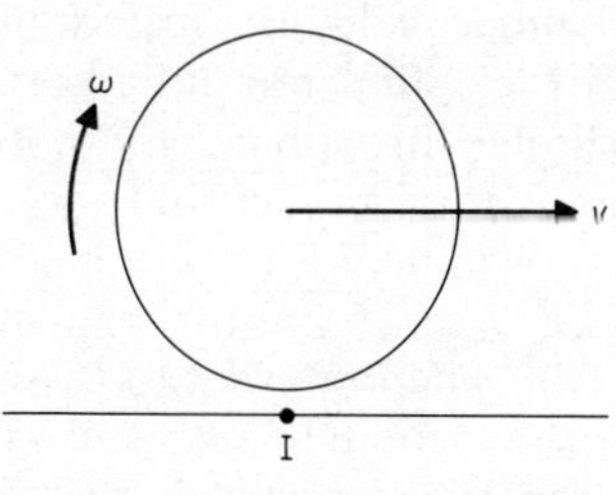

Fig. 11.11

M at the centre of mass G of the rigid body, plus the moment of momentum of the body relative to G. For example, a solid circular cylinder radius a (Fig. 11.11) rolling without slipping on a rough horizontal surface with velocity v has moment of momentum about the point of contact I

$$(mv)a + (\tfrac{1}{2}ma^2)\frac{v}{a}, \quad \text{i.e. } \tfrac{3}{2}mva$$

Angular acceleration

From equation 11.6, putting $\bar{\mathbf{r}} = 0$, we see that the moment of momentum of a body about its centre of mass is $I\omega\hat{\mathbf{n}}$, whether the centre of mass is fixed or not. Thus

$$\Sigma\mathbf{r} \times \mathbf{P} = \frac{\mathrm{d}}{\mathrm{d}t}\,(I\omega\hat{\mathbf{n}})$$

$$= I\frac{\mathrm{d}^2\theta}{\mathrm{d}t^2}\,\hat{\mathbf{n}}$$

Taking the scalar product with a unit vector along an axis through the centre of mass,

$$G = I\frac{\mathrm{d}^2\theta}{\mathrm{d}t^2}$$

This we have used when a body was rotating about a fixed axis. We now see this is always true for the angular acceleration about an axis through the centre of mass.

Instantaneous centre

The point of contact I of the section of the cylinder (page 317) is momentarily at rest, and is called the instantaneous centre. The moment of inertia of the cylinder about a horizontal axis parallel to the axis of the cylinder through I is $\frac{3}{2}ma^2$, by the parallel axis theorem, and the moment of momentum about this axis is $\frac{3}{2}mav$. Many of the results proved here for a fixed axis, e.g. the kinetic energy is $\frac{1}{2}I\omega^2$, $G = I\,\mathrm{d}^2\theta/\mathrm{d}t^2$,* and the angular momentum is $I\omega$, can be shown to be true when referred to the instantaneous centre. The extensive use of the instantaneous centre is beyond the range of this book, but it is instructive to note that Example 11.12 and many similar problems can be solved easily using the instantaneous centre. There are, of course, pitfalls awaiting unwary users—see comment at the end of Example 11.5.

* $G = I\,\mathrm{d}^2\theta/\mathrm{d}t^2$ is only true if the instantaneous centre is at a constant distance from the c. of m.; it gives the initial value of $\mathrm{d}^2\theta/\mathrm{d}t^2$ when the body starts from rest, and it is a good approximation for small oscillations.

Example 11.4. *Find the acceleration of the centre of a hollow sphere rolling without slipping down a rough plane inclined to the horizontal at an angle α (Fig. 11.12).*

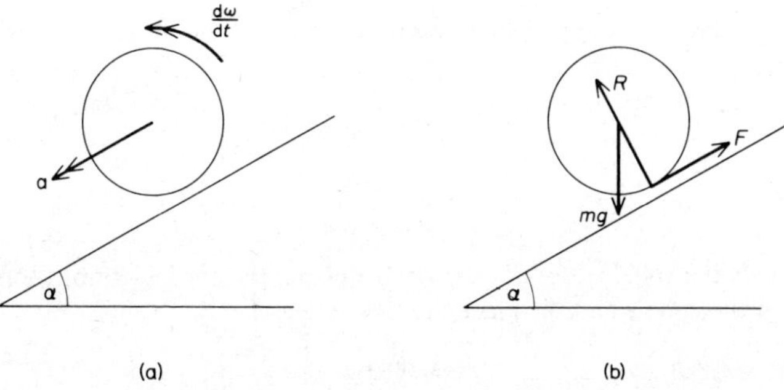

Fig. 11.12

This is the same problem that we solved using the conservation of energy on page 316.

If the sphere has mass m and radius r,

$$mg \sin \alpha - F = m \frac{dv}{dt}$$

from the motion of the centre of mass, and

$$rF = \tfrac{2}{5}mr^2 \frac{d^2\theta}{dt^2}, \quad \text{from } G = I \frac{d^2\theta}{dt^2}$$

about an axis through the centre of mass.

But $$r \frac{d^2\theta}{dt^2} = \frac{dv}{dt}$$

∴ $$mg \sin \alpha - \tfrac{2}{5}m \frac{dv}{dt} = m \frac{dv}{dt}$$

i.e. $$\frac{dv}{dt} = \tfrac{5}{7}g \sin \alpha, \quad \text{as before}$$

Alternatively, considering the motion about the instantaneous centre, in this case the point of contact of the sphere and the plane,

$$mg \sin \alpha = \tfrac{7}{5}mr^2 \frac{d^2\theta}{dt^2}$$

giving $$\frac{dv}{dt} = \tfrac{5}{7}g \sin \alpha$$

Since there is no slipping between the sphere and the plane,

$$F \leqslant \mu R$$

But
$$F = \tfrac{2}{5}mg \sin \alpha$$

$\therefore$
$$\tfrac{2}{5}mg \sin \alpha \leqslant \mu mg \cos \alpha,$$

$\therefore$
$$\mu \geqslant \tfrac{2}{5} \tan \alpha$$

Thus since the sphere does not slip on the plane, the coefficient of friction between the sphere and the plane must be at least

$$\tfrac{2}{5} \tan \alpha$$

Example 11.5. *A wedge of mass M and angle α is free to move on a smooth horizontal table. A solid sphere, mass m, radius r, can roll without slipping down the rough inclined face of the wedge. Find the acceleration of the wedge as the sphere rolls down (compare the particle on a wedge, on page 251).*

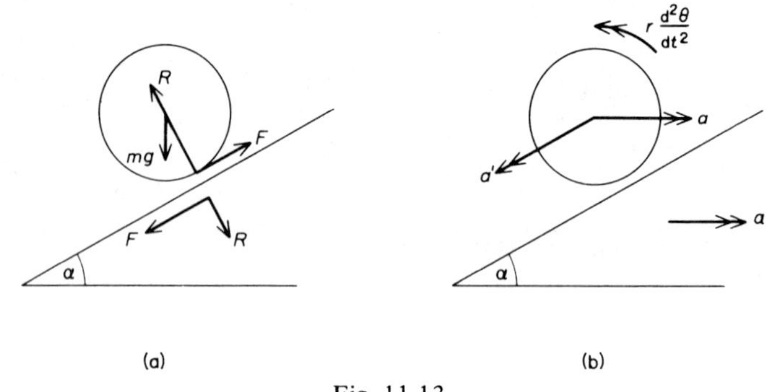

Fig. 11.13

Considering the forces on the sphere parallel to the face of the wedge (Fig. 11.13),

$$mg \sin \alpha - F = m(a' - a \cos \alpha) \tag{11.7}$$

where a is the acceleration of the wedge and a' is the acceleration of the sphere relative to the wedge.

Considering the forces on the sphere perpendicular to the face of the wedge,

$$mg \cos \alpha - R = ma \sin \alpha \tag{11.8}$$

Considering the horizontal forces on the wedge,

$$R \sin \alpha - F \cos \alpha = Ma \tag{11.9}$$

and finally $G = I\, \mathrm{d}^2\theta/\mathrm{d}t^2$ about a horizontal axis through the centre of the sphere,

$$rF = \tfrac{2}{5}mr^2 \frac{\mathrm{d}^2\theta}{\mathrm{d}t^2}$$

i.e.

$$F = \tfrac{2}{5}ma' \tag{11.10}$$

a' only occurs in equations 11.7 and 11.10, so

$$mg \sin\alpha - \tfrac{7}{2}F = -ma\cos\alpha \tag{11.11}$$

Eliminating F between equations 11.9 and 11.11, then R using equation 11.10, we have

$$a = \frac{5mg \sin\alpha \cos\alpha}{7M + m(2 + 5\sin^2\alpha)}$$

Notice that in this example the point of contact of the sphere on the wedge is not the instantaneous centre, as the wedge is moving. It is not easy to find the instantaneous centre, yet it is of course still correct to use $G = I\, \mathrm{d}^2\theta/\mathrm{d}t^2$ about an axis through the centre of mass.

Bodies rolling and sliding

Friction resists relative motion, or tendency to relative motion. Thus in the previous examples the component of the weight down the plane causes acceleration of the centres of the bodies, and if the bodies are not to slip there must be angular acceleration. The friction force acts to produce that acceleration, if it is sufficiently great to do so.

When the centre of a body (Fig. 11.14) of circular cross-section radius r, say a sphere or cylinder, has velocity v, if the body is rolling without slipping the angular velocity is v/r. If the body is moving on a horizontal surface and there is not a force causing acceleration, then the velocity of the body and the angular velocity

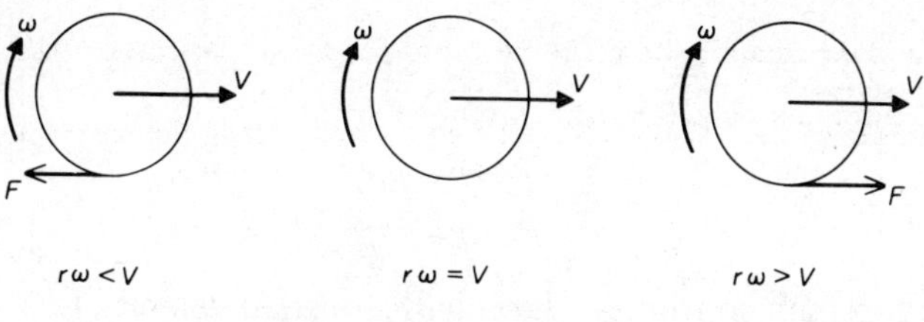

Fig. 11.14

are constant, there is no tendency for relative motion, and there will not be a frictional force.

If the angular velocity ω is such that $r\omega < v$, friction acts to reduce v and increase ω, if possible until $v = r\omega$: if $r\omega > v$, friction increases v and reduces ω, again if possible until $v = r\omega$ (Fig. 11.15).

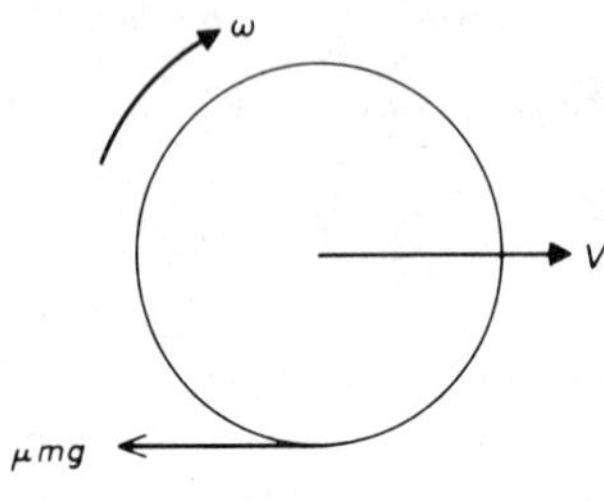

Fig. 11.15

If a circular hoop, mass m, radius r, is projected along a rough horizontal surface, with velocity U and angular velocity initially zero, then in the subsequent motion

$$-\mu mg = m\frac{\mathrm{d}v}{\mathrm{d}t}, \quad \text{by Newton's law,}$$

and

$$\mu mgr = (mr^2)\frac{\mathrm{d}\omega}{\mathrm{d}t}$$

from the motion about a horizontal axis through the centre of mass.

$$\therefore \qquad v = U - \mu gt$$

and $\quad r\omega = \mu gt, \quad$ since $v = U \quad$ and $\quad \omega = 0 \quad$ when $t = 0$.

Slipping ceases after time T where

$$U - \mu gT = \mu gT$$

i.e.

$$T = U/2\mu g$$

The hoop then continues to roll with constant velocity $\frac{1}{2}U$, constant angular velocity $U/2r$.

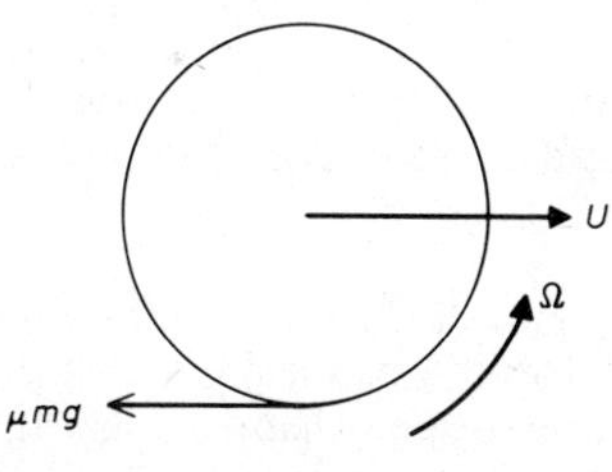

Fig. 11.16

If instead the hoop initially has a 'back-spin', angular velocity Ω (Fig. 11.16), as before

$$v = U - \mu gt$$

and
$$r\omega = -r\Omega + gt$$

Slipping ceases when $t = (U + r\Omega)/2\mu g$. The velocity then is $\frac{1}{2}(U - r\Omega)$. If $U > r\Omega$, the hoop rolls forward; if $U = r\Omega$, the hoop is at rest; and if $U < r\Omega$, the hoop returns rolling without slipping towards the point from which it was projected.

EXERCISE 11(c)

1. A uniform solid sphere is placed in contact with a fixed rough plane inclined at 30° to the horizontal. The sphere is released from rest and rolls without slipping down a line of greatest slope of the plane. Show that the centre of the sphere acquires a speed of 7 m s^{-1} after rolling 7 m down the plane. What is the least value of the coefficient of friction, if the sphere does not slip on the plane?

2. A uniform circular hoop rolls down a line of greatest slope of a rough plane inclined at an angle α to the horizontal. If the hoop does not slip on the plane, show that the acceleration of the centre of the hoop is $\frac{1}{2}g \sin \alpha$, and that the coefficient of friction between the hoop and the plane is not less than $\frac{1}{2} \tan \alpha$.

3. A uniform circular hoop, radius a, mass m, rolls and slips down a line of greatest slope of a plane inclined at an angle α to the horizontal. If the coefficient of friction between the hoop and the plane is $\frac{1}{4} \tan \alpha$, find the acceleration of the centre of the hoop and the angular acceleration of the hoop. Find also the kinetic energy of the hoop when it has travelled a distance k down the plane, and the energy lost in sliding down the plane.

4. A truck mass M has four circular wheels, each mass m and radius r. The truck is pushed without slipping along a rough horizontal surface by a force F. Show that the acceleration of the centre of mass of the truck and wheels is $F/(M + 2m)$.

5. A uniform solid cylinder and a thin uniform cylindrical ring roll from rest down parallel lines of greatest slope of a plane inclined to the horizontal at an angle α. Show that the solid cylinder covers a distance $\frac{1}{12}gt^2 \sin \alpha$ more than the ring in time t. Find the minimum value of the coefficient of friction for this to be possible. (A.E.B.)

6. A hollow right circular cylinder is projected up a rough inclined plane, of inclination α, with its generators perpendicular to the lines of greatest slope. If the cylinder is projected with velocity U and no angular velocity, show that it stops slipping after time $U/g(2\mu \cos \alpha + \sin \alpha)$, where μ is the coefficient of friction. If $\mu \geqslant \frac{1}{2} \tan \alpha$, show that the cylinder then begins to roll without slipping. (O. & C.)

7. A solid circular cylinder radius a is spinning with angular velocity Ω about its horizontal axis. It is then placed gently onto a rough plane, inclined to the horizontal at an angle α. The coefficient of friction between the cylinder and the plane is $\tan \alpha$. If the sense of rotation is such that it causes slipping down the line of greatest slope, show that the axis of the cylinder will remain at rest for a time $a\Omega/2g \sin \alpha$.

8. A uniform solid sphere is at rest on a rough horizontal plane; the coefficient of friction between the sphere and the plane is μ. A constant horizontal force F is applied through the centre of the sphere. Show that the sphere rolls without slipping if $F \leqslant (7/2)mg$.

9. A uniform circular disc of mass m and radius r rolls without slipping down a line of greatest slope of a rough plane inclined at an angle α to the horizontal. Find the acceleration of the centre of the disc and the total reaction of the plane on the disc.

10. A uniform solid sphere, mass m, radius a, is projected horizontally along the surface of a rough horizontal plane. The initial velocity of the centre is V and the initial angular velocity is zero. Prove that, whatever the coefficient of friction the sphere ends up rolling along the plane with angular velocity $(5/7)V/a$.
A similar sphere is projected in a similar way up a line of greatest slope of a rough plane inclined to the horizontal at an angle α. Prove that, if $\tan \alpha > (7/2)\mu$, the sphere will never maintain a motion of rolling on the plane. (O. & C.)

Impulses on a rigid body

When an impulse **J** acts on a body mass m, the change in the velocity of the body is $\mathbf{J}/m$, since momentum is conserved. Thus if the initial velocity is **u** and the final velocity is **v**,

$$\mathbf{J} = m\mathbf{v} - m\mathbf{u}$$

$$\therefore \qquad \mathbf{r} \times \mathbf{J} = (\mathbf{r} \times m\mathbf{v}) - (\mathbf{r} \times m\mathbf{u}),$$

where **r** is the position vector of the point of the body at which the impulse is applied. Since an impulse is supposed to act instantaneously, **r** is also the position vector of the body both before and after the application of the impulse. Therefore *the moment of the impulse about a point P is equal to the change in the moment of momentum of the body about the same point P.*

Example 11.6. *A uniform rod AB, mass m, length 2a, is at rest on a smooth horizontal table. A horizontal impulse* **J** *is applied at A, at right angles to AB (Fig. 11.17). Investigate the subsequent motion.*

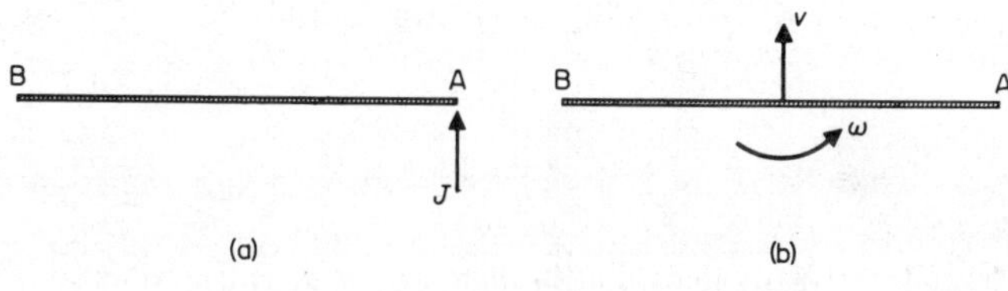

Fig. 11.17

If **v**, ω are the velocity and angular velocity respectively immediately after the impulse, from the conservation of linear momentum

$$\mathbf{J} = m\mathbf{v}$$

The moment of momentum of the rod about an axis perpendicular to AB through the centre of mass G is $\frac{1}{3}ma^2\omega$. Therefore from the conservation of the moment of momentum about the axis through G

$$Ja = \tfrac{1}{3}ma^2\omega$$

Thus the centre of mass moves with velocity J/m perpendicular to the rod, and the rod rotates with angular velocity $3J/ma$. Since the table is smooth, the velocity and angular velocity will remain constant in the subsequent motion.

Notice that we could have considered the conservation of moment of momentum about any axis. Thus about a vertical axis through B, the moment of momentum is

$$a(mv) + \tfrac{1}{3}ma^2\omega$$

$$\therefore \qquad a(mv) + \tfrac{1}{3}ma^2\omega = (2a)J$$

But $mv = J$, $\therefore \omega = 3J/ma$, as before.

It is almost invariably easiest to consider the conservation of moment of momentum about an axis through the centre of mass, as the term $\bar{\mathbf{r}}$ is then zero.

Example 11.7. *Two equal uniform rods AB, BC, each mass m and length 2a, are freely jointed at B (Fig. 11.18). Initially A, B, and C are in a straight line and are at rest on a smooth horizontal table. A horizontal impulse J is applied at A perpendicular to AB. Find the velocity with which C begins to move.*

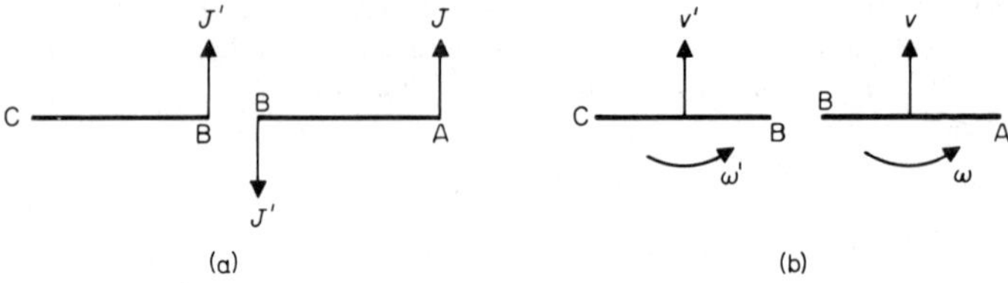

Fig. 11.18

Since the rods are freely jointed at B, there will be equal and opposite impulses at the hinge at B; these will be at right angles to AB. The velocities of the end B of the two rods will also be equal,

i.e. $$v' + a\omega' = v - a\omega \qquad (11.12)$$

using the notation of Fig. 11.18.

From the conservation of linear momentum of each rod,

$$J - J' = mv$$

and $$J' = mv'$$

From the conservation of moment of momentum about a vertical axis through the centre of mass of each rod,

$$(J + J')a = \tfrac{1}{3}ma^2\omega$$

and $$J'a = \tfrac{1}{3}ma^2\omega'.$$

To solve these equations in the easiest manner, notice that v, v', ω, and ω' are given explicitly in each of the last four equations in terms of J and J'.

Multiplying equation 11.12 by m and substituting,

$$J' + 3J' = (J - J') - 3(J + J')$$

$$\therefore \qquad J' = -\tfrac{1}{4}J$$

Thus $v = 5J/4m$, $v' = -J/4m$, $\omega = 9J/4ma$ and $\omega' = -3J/4ma$. The velocity of C is $v' - a\omega'$, which is $J/2m$.

Example 11.8. *A uniform rod AB, mass m, length 2a, is freely hinged at A so that it can rotate in a vertical plane. Initially the rod hangs at rest vertically below A. A horizontal impulse J is applied to the end B. If the rod makes complete revolutions in the subsequent motion, show that* $J^2 \geqslant (4m^2ga)/3$.

When the impulse is applied at B (Fig. 11.19), there may be an impulse at the hinge at A.

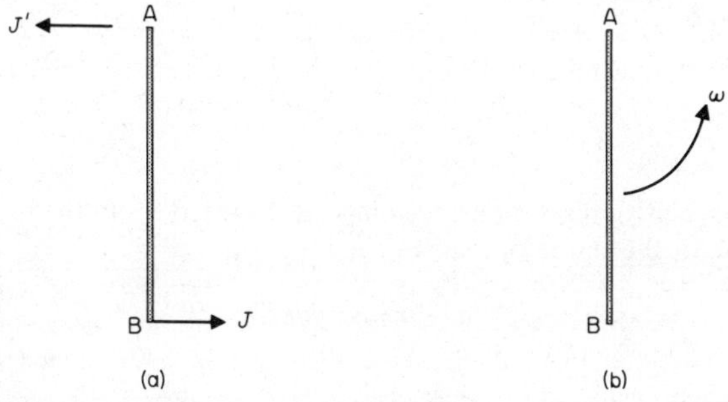

Fig. 11.19

Considering the conservation of the moment of momentum about an axis through A perpendicular to the plane in which the rod rotates,

$$(2a)J = (mv)a + \tfrac{1}{3}ma^2\omega$$

$$\therefore \qquad J = \tfrac{2}{3}ma\omega, \quad \text{since } v = a\omega$$

$$\text{i.e.} \qquad \omega = \frac{3J}{2ma}$$

Notice the moment of momentum is equal to $(4/3)ma^2\omega$, the same figure we should have obtained by considering $I\omega$ about an axis through the fixed point A.

The rod will make complete revolutions only if the kinetic energy at the lowest position is greater than or equal to the increase in potential energy necessary to attain the highest position,

i.e. $$\tfrac{1}{2}mv^2 + \tfrac{1}{2}(\tfrac{1}{3}ma^2)\omega^2 \geqslant mg(2a)$$

i.e. $$\tfrac{2}{3}ma^2\omega^2 \geqslant 2mga$$

i.e. $$\frac{3J^2}{2m^2} \geqslant 2ga\,,$$

$$J^2 \geqslant \frac{4m^2ga}{3}$$

The dimensions of the result serve as a useful check. J, being a change in linear momentum, has dimensions M L T^{-1}, so the dimensions of J^2 are M^2 L^2 T^{-2}. The dimensions of m^2ga are M^2(L T^{-2}) L, i.e. M^2 L^2 T^{-2}, the same as those of J^2.

Example 11.9. *A uniform rod AB, mass m, length 2a, is freely hinged at A so that it can rotate in a vertical plane (Fig. 11.20). When the rod is vertical it strikes a peg P, so placed that there is not an impulse on the hinge at A. Find the distance of P from A.*

Since the impulsive reaction on the hinge at A is zero, from the linear momentum of the centre of mass of the rod,

$$J - ma\omega = ma\Omega$$

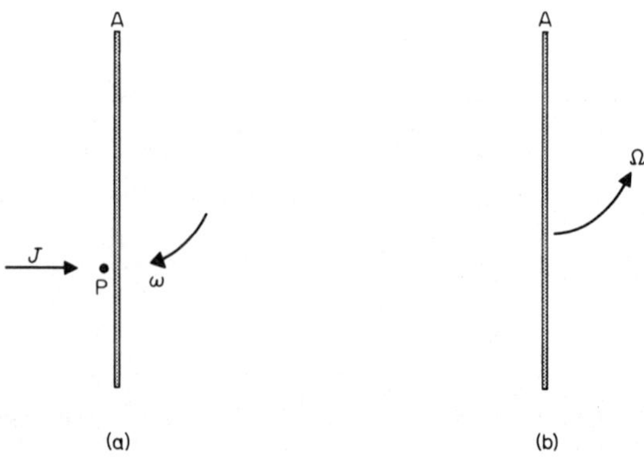

Fig. 11.20

where ω and Ω are the angular velocities before and after impact. From the moment of momentum about A,

$$Jx - \tfrac{4}{3}ma^2\omega = \tfrac{4}{3}ma^2\Omega$$

$$\therefore \quad ma(\Omega + \omega)x = \tfrac{4}{3}ma^2(\Omega + \omega)$$

$$\therefore \quad x = \tfrac{4}{3}a$$

Notice that x, the distance of P from A, is independent of the angular velocity ω of the rod before impact.

The point at which the impulse is applied to the rod is called the *centre of percussion.* Impulses applied at this point do not produce impulses at the hinge. Thus a doorstop will ideally be placed at this point, to minimize the impulsive forces at the hinge when the door strikes the stop; likewise a cricketer will try to strike the ball with this point of his bat, to reduce the impulse at his wrist when he hits the ball.

Example 11.10. *A hoop, mass m, radius a, is rolling without slipping along a rough horizontal floor with speed U (Fig. 11.21). It strikes a rough inelastic step, height (2/5)a, at a point P. Investigate the subsequent motion.*

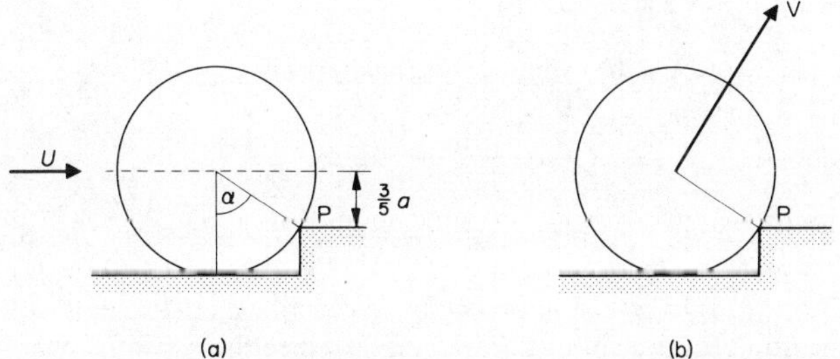

Fig. 11.21

Since the step is rough and inelastic, we can suppose that the hoop does not slip on the step and does not rebound from the step. From the moment of momentum about P,

$$mU(\tfrac{3}{5}a) + (ma^2)U/a = mVa + (ma^2)V/a$$

$$\therefore \quad V = \tfrac{4}{5}U$$

The hoop then begins to describe a circle radius a, centre P, with velocity $(4/5)U$. But if the hoop is to continue to describe a circle centre P, it must remain in contact with the step, so the normal reaction X must not become zero (Fig. 11.22).

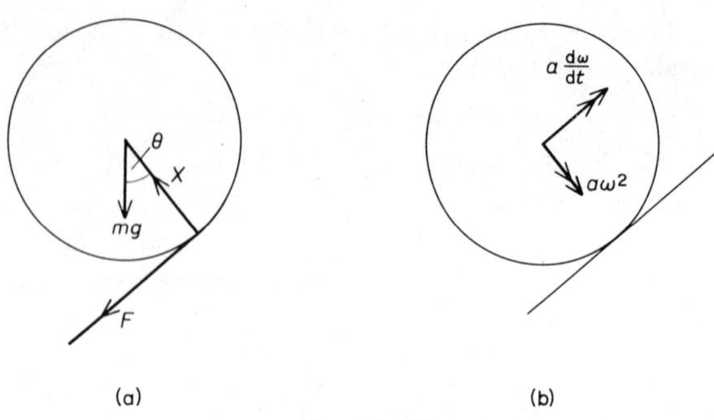

Fig. 11.22

Considering the linear motion of the centre of mass, parallel to the tangent at P,

$$mg \cos \theta - X = ma\omega^2$$

i.e. $$X = mg \cos \theta - ma\omega^2$$

Initially $\cos \theta = 3/5$ and $a\omega = (4/5)U$,

$\therefore$ $$X \geqslant 0 \quad \text{when } \theta = \alpha, \quad \text{where } \cos \alpha = 3/5,$$

if $$\tfrac{3}{5}mg - \tfrac{16}{25}m\frac{U^2}{a} \geqslant 0$$

i.e. $$U^2 \leqslant \tfrac{15}{16}ga$$

Thus if $U^2 \leqslant (15/16)ga$ the hoop begins to describe a circle, centre P.

As the hoop rotates about P, ω decreases, since the potential energy increases, and $\cos \theta$ increases, since θ is decreasing. Thus if X is non-zero when $\theta = \alpha$, X will remain non-zero. So if the hoop does not leave P immediately, it will not do so in the subsequent motion.

If the hoop is to mount the step, the kinetic energy at the bottom after impact must not be less than the potential energy the hoop will gain in mounting the step,

i.e. $$\tfrac{1}{2}mV^2 + \tfrac{1}{2}(ma^2)\frac{V^2}{a^2} \geqslant mg(\tfrac{2}{5}a)$$

i.e. $$V^2 \geqslant \tfrac{2}{5}ga$$

i.e. $$\tfrac{16}{25}U^2 \geqslant \tfrac{2}{5}ga,$$

$$U^2 \geqslant \tfrac{5}{8}ga$$

If V' is the velocity of the centre of the hoop when rolling on the top of the step,

$$\tfrac{1}{2}mV^2 + \tfrac{1}{2}(ma^2)\frac{V^2}{a^2} = \tfrac{1}{2}mV'^2 + \tfrac{1}{2}(ma^2)\frac{V'^2}{a^2} + mg(\tfrac{2}{5}a)$$

$$V^2 = V'^2 + \tfrac{2}{5}ga$$

$$V'^2 = \tfrac{16}{25}U^2 - \tfrac{2}{5}ga$$

$$V' = \tfrac{4}{5}\sqrt{(U^2 - \tfrac{5}{8}ga)}$$

Thus if $U^2 < \frac{5}{8}ga$, the hoop rotates about P until the angular velocity is zero, then rotates back to the ground, along which it will roll with velocity

$$\tfrac{4}{5}(\tfrac{4}{5}U), \quad \text{i.e. } \tfrac{16}{25}U$$

from the symmetry of the impulse applied on striking the ground to that applied when the hoop strikes the step at P; the weight of the hoop, being a force, does not affect the symmetry of the momenta.

If

$$\tfrac{5}{8}ga \leqslant U^2 \leqslant \tfrac{15}{16}ga$$

the hoop rotates about P and then rolls along the step with velocity

$$\tfrac{4}{5}\sqrt{(U^2 - \tfrac{5}{8}ga)}$$

If

$$U^2 > \tfrac{15}{16}ga,$$

the hoop leaves the step on impact, and the centre of mass of the hoop describes a parabola, like all projectiles.

EXERCISE 11(d)

1. A uniform rod AB mass m, is at rest on a smooth horizontal table. A horizontal impulse J is applied at the midpoint of AB, at right angles to AB. Show that the rod does not rotate in the subsequent motion, and find the velocity of the centre of mass.

2. A uniform rod AB, mass m, length $2a$, is at rest on a smooth horizontal table. A horizontal impulse J is applied at a point of trisection of AB, at right angles to AB. Find the velocity of the centre of mass and the angular velocity immediately after the impulse.

3. A uniform rod AB, mass m, has a particle mass m fixed at A. The rod is free to move on a smooth horizontal table. A horizontal impulse J is

applied at the midpoint of AB, at right angles to AB. Find the velocity of the centre of mass and the angular velocity immediately after the impulse.

4. A uniform circular disc, mass m, radius a, is at rest with one of its plane faces in contact with a smooth horizontal table. A horizontal impulse J is applied to the disc along a tangent to the disc. Find the angular velocity of the disc.

5. A uniform circular disc, centre O, mass m, radius a, can rotate freely about a horizontal axis which is a tangent to the disc at a point P; this axis is in the plane of the disc. The disc receives an impulse J at O, so that it describes complete revolutions about the axis. Show that $J^2 \geqslant 5m^2ga$.

6. The circular disc in Question 5 is initially at rest vertically below the axis. A particle, mass m, travelling horizontally with velocity U strikes the disc at O and adheres to the disc. If the disc oscillates through an angle 2θ in the subsequent motion, show that $\cos\theta = 1 - U^2/9ga$.

7. A uniform rod, mass m, length $2a$, is freely hinged at a fixed point at one of its ends and hangs freely in a position of stable equilibrium. The rod is suddenly made to rotate with initial angular velocity $\sqrt{(3g/a)}$ as a result of a horizontal impulse applied at its free end.
   (a) Find the magnitude of the impulse.
   (b) Show that the rod just reaches its position of unstable equilibrium.
   (c) Find the reaction at the hinge when the rod is horizontal. (A.E.B.)

8. Uniform rods AB, BC, CD, each of length $2l$ and mass m are freely jointed at B and C. They are at rest on a smooth horizontal table so that A, B, C, D lie in order along a straight line. An impulse J is applied at A in a direction at right angles to the rod and in the plane of the table. Find the initial velocities of A and D. (O. & C.)

9. A uniform cylindrical log AB, mass M, is at rest on a sheet of perfectly smooth ice. A small stone serves to make it pivot freely about a vertical axis through its midpoint. A cat, mass m, sits on the log at A. If $6m = \pi M$, show that it is possible for the cat to jump from A to the other end B without passing over the midpoint of the log.

10. A uniform rod AB of length $2a$ moves on a smooth horizontal table. When the rod is rotating about A as instantaneous centre with angular velocity ω, the point P of the rod at a distance x from A strikes an inelastic peg. Find the angular velocity after impact and the position of P which makes it a maximum. If half the energy is lost by the impact show that P is at a distance $2a/\sqrt{3}$ from B. (O. & C.)

11. A rod of length $2l$ and mass M can rotate freely on a smooth horizontal table about one end which is hinged to a fixed point on the table. Initially the rod is rotating with angular velocity Ω when its midpoint strikes a small ball of mass m which was initially at rest on the table. The coefficient of restitution between the ball and the rod is e, and the impulsive reaction on impact is horizontal and perpendicular to the rod. Find the velocity of the ball and the angular velocity of the rod immediately after impact, and show that the sense of rotation of the rod is unchanged if $4M > 3em$.
Prove that, if $4M > 3em$, the rod will not strike the ball again provided that

$$e > \frac{4M(3\sqrt{3} - \pi)}{4\pi M + 9m\sqrt{3}}$$

(O. & C.)

12. Fig. 11.23 shows a uniform solid spherical ball, mass m and radius a, moving in a vertical plane, just before it bounces on a rough horizontal floor. At this instant just before impact the centre of the ball has

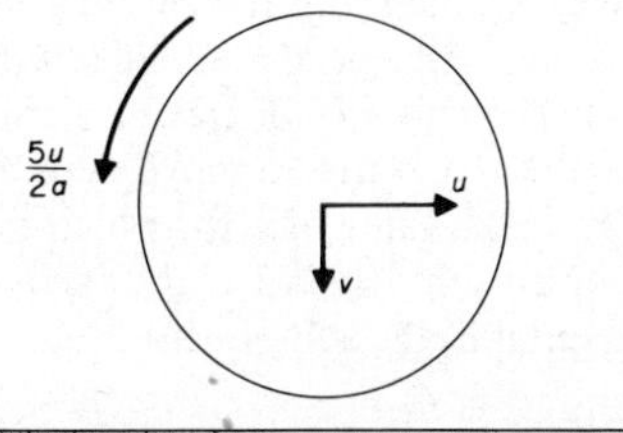

Fig. 11.23

horizontal and vertical components u and v respectively, and it is spinning in the direction shown, about the diameter normal to its plane of motion with angular velocity $5u/2a$. If the coefficient of restitution between the ball and the floor is e and the floor is sufficiently rough to prevent slipping, find the horizontal and vertical components of the impulsive force created by the impact. Show that the ball rises vertically without spin after impact and calculate the loss in kinetic energy that occurred. (A.E.B.)

13. A uniform rod, mass m and length $2a$, lies freely on a smooth horizontal table; it is struck at one end by a particle of mass M moving with velocity V perpendicular to the length of the rod. The coefficient of restitution between the rod and the particle is e. Prove that the impulse of the blow is

$$\frac{(1 + e)MmV}{m + 4M}$$

Find the relation that must hold between m, M, and e, if the rod after one complete revolution hits the particle, and deduce that m must be greater than $2M$. (O. & C.)

14. A thin uniform rod ABC, mass m, length l, is free to rotate in a vertical plane about a frictionless pivot at B, where AB = $\frac{1}{3}l$ and BC = $\frac{2}{3}l$. The end C is held vertically above B and then released. When the rod has swung through $180°$ it strikes a fixed peg P without rebounding. Determine how far P is below B if the impulse at the pivot is $m\sqrt{6gl}/18$. (C.S.)

15. A uniform thin rod AB, mass M, is smoothly pivoted at A and is held with B vertically above A. It is then allowed to fall, and when B is vertically below A it strikes a small stationary particle mass m, which sticks to B. If the end B swings up only to the level of A, prove that $M = 6m$.

16. A uniform rod AB of mass m and length $2a$ is suspended from a smooth fixed pivot at its end A. The rod is hanging at rest when a particle mass m, moving horizontally with speed u, collides with the rod at a point a distance x below A. The particle adheres to the rod. Prove that immediately after impact the rod starts to move with angular velocity $3ux/(3x^2 + 4a^2)$. Find the value of x for which the angular velocity is a maximum and find, for this value of x, the value of u for which the rod just becomes horizontal in the subsequent motion. (J.M.B.)

17. A uniform spherical asteroid mass M and radius a is spinning with angular speed ω about a diameter, but may otherwise be considered to be at rest. A meteor mass m and negligible dimensions is moving with speed V along a line through its centre and perpendicular to the axis of rotation. After the collision the meteor adheres to the surface of the asteroid. Find the mass centre of the resulting composite body and the speed of the mass centre. Show also that the angular speed of the body about an axis through the mass centre is

$$\frac{2(M + m)}{2M + 7m}$$

(M.E.I.)

18. A uniform circular hoop radius a is rolling without slipping along a rough horizontal plane. The velocity of the centre of the hoop is U. The hoop strikes a step of height $\frac{1}{5}a$ and rotates around the edge of the step and then rolls along the step. Show that

$$20ga < 81U^2 < 80ga$$

19. A solid spherical ball, radius a, rolls without slipping along a rough horizontal plane. The velocity of the centre of the ball is U. The ball strikes a rough inelastic step, height h. If the ball fails to mount the step, show that

$$\left(1 - \frac{5h}{7a}\right)^2 U^2 < \tfrac{10}{7} gh$$

The ball rolls back and strikes the floor, then rolls away with angular velocity V/a. Show that

$$V = U\left(1 - \frac{5h}{7a}\right)^2$$

20. A hoop which is symmetrical about its axis has mass M and radius a. It rolls in a vertical plane down a line of greatest slope of a rough plane inclined at an angle 30° to the horizontal. After rolling through a distance d from rest, the hoop strikes a step which projects $\frac{1}{2}a$ perpendicular to the plane. Find the minimum value of d for which the hoop will surmount the step, on which it does not slip. (C.S.)

21. A cubical brick, edge $2a$, slides down a smooth inclined plane that makes an acute angle α with the horizontal, where $\tan\alpha = 5/12$. The brick strikes a fixed bar, perpendicular to the direction of motion of the brick, and a perpendicular distance $\frac{1}{4}a$ from the plane. If the brick has sufficient velocity to surmount the bar, show that it must have slipped a distance at least equal to $(107/60)a$ down the plane.

22. A gramophone turntable with radius a and moment of inertia I is rotating freely with angular velocity ω_1 about a vertical frictionless spindle. An insect of mass m (to be regarded as a particle) flies with velocity u along a horizontal line tangential to the rim of the turntable, and alights on it, coming to rest relative to the turntable. Find the new angular velocity ω_2.
The insect then walks with constant velocity v to the centre of the turntable. Prove that the turntable makes

$$\frac{a\omega_2}{2\pi v}(\gamma + \gamma^{-1}) \tan^{-1}\gamma$$

revolutions during the walk, γ being defined by $\gamma^2 = ma^2/I$. (C.S.)

23. A rope hangs over a pulley of radius a and M.I. I, which is perfectly rough to the rope but perfectly smooth on its bearings. Two monkeys of equal mass m, hanging at the same level, are one at each end of the rope. Starting at the same instant, the monkeys climb with constant speeds u_1 and u_2 relative to the rope ($u_1 > u_2$). Show that when the monkey speed u_1 is at a height h above his initial position, he is at a height

$$\frac{hI(u_1 - u_2)}{(I + ma^2)u_1 + ma^2u_2}$$

above the other monkey. (C.S.)

24. A man mass m stands at a point A on a horizontal platform which can rotate freely about a fixed vertical axis through a point O of the platform. Initially both man and platform are at rest. The man starts to walk and describes (relative to the platform) a circle having OA as diameter, and returns to his starting point on the platform. Show that when he reaches A, the angular displacement of the platform relative to the ground is given by

$$\pi\left[1 - \sqrt{\left(\frac{I}{I + ma^2}\right)}\right]$$

where I is the M.I. of the lamina about the axis through O, and a is the distance of A from O. (O.S.)

25. A wedge of mass m has a rough sloping face inclined at $\pi/4$ to its base which is placed on a smooth horizontal plane. A uniform solid cylinder of mass m and radius a is placed on the sloping face of the wedge with its axis perpendicular to a line of greatest slope. The system is released from rest, and the cylinder rolls down the wedge without slipping.
(a) Show that the acceleration of the wedge is $g/5$.
(b) Find the condition satisfied by the coefficient of friction between the cylinder and the wedge.
(c) Find the time taken for the cylinder to descend a vertical distance d. (S.U.J.B.)

26. A solid spherical ball rests in equilibrium at the bottom of a fixed spherical globe whose inner surface is very rough. The ball is struck a horizontal blow such that the initial speed of the centre is v. Prove that, if v lies between $\sqrt{(10gd/7)}$ and $\sqrt{(27gd/7)}$, the ball will leave the surface of the globe, where d is the difference between the radii of the ball and the globe. (C.S.)

27. A uniform disc of radius a rolls along the ground with angular velocity Ω towards a flight of steps. The height of each tread of the steps is $\frac{1}{2}a$.

Assuming that there is no rebounding, and no slipping where the disc is in contact with a step, prove that just after hitting the first step the disc has angular velocity $\frac{2}{3}\Omega$. Prove also that if

$$\Omega^2 = \frac{6g}{5a}\,[(\tfrac{3}{2})^{2n} - 1]$$

the disc will come to rest balanced on the edge of the nth step.

(O. & C.)

12. Equilibrium and Stability

The energy test for positions of equilibrium

Let T denote the kinetic energy of a system with one degree of freedom*, and V the potential energy of that system. Then by the principle of the conservation of energy,

$$T + V \text{ is constant}$$

Differentiating, we see that the stationary values of T occur with the stationary values of V. But the stationary values of T occur when the velocity is stationary, that is, the acceleration is zero, i.e. the sum of the forces causing the acceleration is zero, so the system is in equilibrium. Therefore the positions of equilibrium occur with the stationary values of V. The use of the term 'velocity' above is not precise, because the body may of course have angular as well as linear velocity. But a rigorous treatment of this method is more suitable for university courses.

The statements above are most easily understood when $T = \frac{1}{2}mv^2$.

Then $$\frac{\mathrm{d}T}{\mathrm{d}t} = mv\frac{\mathrm{d}v}{\mathrm{d}t}, \quad \text{i.e.} \quad \frac{\mathrm{d}T}{\mathrm{d}t} = 0 \Leftrightarrow \frac{\mathrm{d}v}{\mathrm{d}t} = 0$$

since v is not always zero, otherwise the body does not move from the point to which it was displaced.

Example 12.1. *A particle of mass m is suspended by an elastic string, natural length l, modulus mg. Find the extension of the string when hanging vertically in equilibrium.*

In Fig. 12.1, let x be the extension in the string. Then the potential energy of the system is

$\frac{1}{2}\frac{mg}{l}x^2$ since the elastic string is stretched,

and $-mgx$ since the particle is at distance x below

* A system with 'one degree of freedom' is one whose configuration can be described completely in terms of one variable. This can be linear (e.g. Ex. 12.1) or angular (e.g. Ex 12.2).

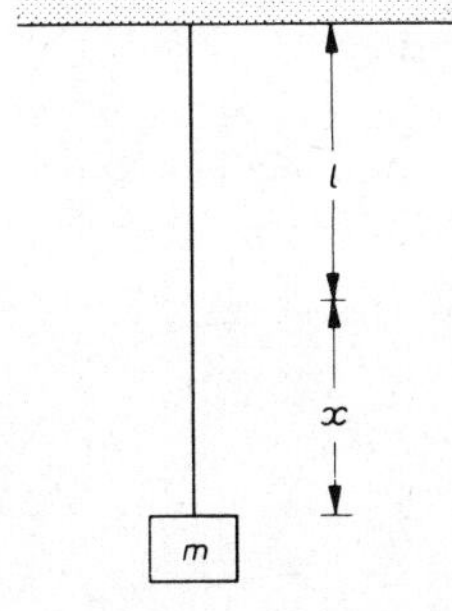

Fig. 12.1

a fixed point. The kinetic energy is $\frac{1}{2}m\dot{x}^2$, supposing the particle to be displaced in a straight line (one degree of freedom).

$$\therefore \qquad \frac{1}{2}\frac{mg}{l}x^2 - mgx + \tfrac{1}{2}m\dot{x}^2 = C$$

i.e.

$$\frac{mg}{l}x\dot{x} - mg\dot{x} + m\dot{x}\ddot{x} = 0$$

In equilibrium, $\ddot{x} = 0$

$$\therefore \qquad \frac{mgx}{l} - mg = 0, \quad \text{since } \dot{x} \neq 0,$$

$$x = l, \quad \text{as anticipated}$$

It is easy to see that

$$\frac{dT}{dt} = 0 \Leftrightarrow \frac{dV}{dt} = 0$$

so that the position of equilibrium is found from $dV/dt = 0$, and we do not need to write down an expression for T.

Example 12.2. *A non-uniform circular cylinder, mass m, radius a, has its centre of gravity G a distance k from O the centre of the cylinder. Find the positions of equilibrium when the cylinder is placed on a smooth horizontal table.*

Suppose the line OG makes an angle θ with the vertical (Fig. 12.2). Then

$$V = mg(r - k\cos\theta)$$

$$\frac{dV}{d\theta} = mgk\sin\theta$$

Thus $$\frac{dV}{d\theta} = 0 \Rightarrow \sin\theta = 0, \quad \text{i.e. } \theta = 0 \text{ or } 180^\circ$$

As expected, the only positions of equilibrium occur when G is vertically above or below 0.

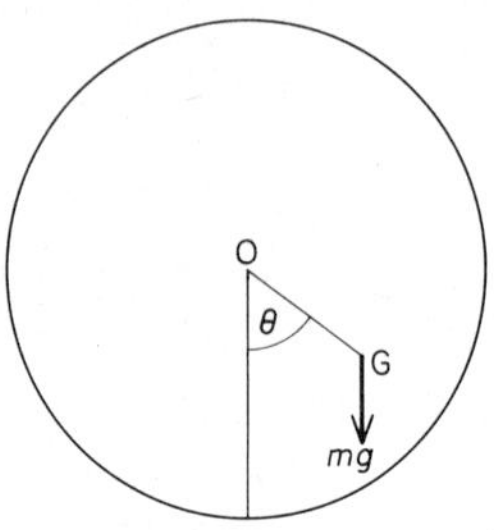

Fig. 12.2

Stable and unstable equilibrium

If a position of equilibrium is such that when the system is displaced slightly it returns to that position, the position is called a position of *stable* equilibrium. If the system when displaced moves further away from the original position, it is called a position of *unstable* equilibrium. Thus the position in Example 12.1, by experience, is stable. In Example 12.2, when G is vertically below O the equilibrium is stable; when G is vertically above O the equilibrium is unstable.

Consider a sphere moving on the surface of a sheet of corrugated iron (Fig. 12.3). Positions A and B are positions of equilibrium. When displaced from A, the sphere moves away from A, so that the K.E. increases. Since the sum of the K.E. and the P.E. is constant, the P.E. must decrease. This is true for displacements to

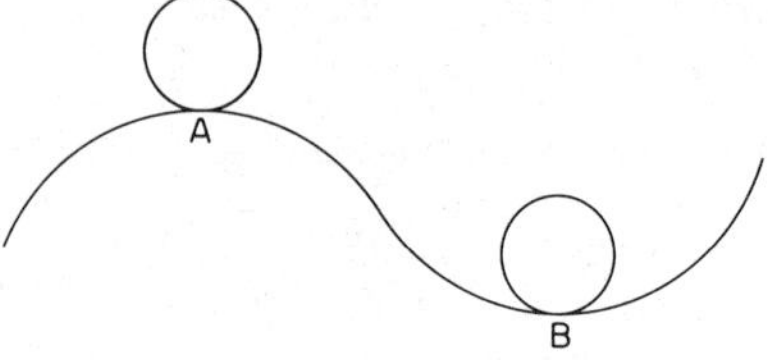

Fig. 12.3

any point in the neighbourhood of A, so that the P.E. must have a maximum value at A. Similarly, if the sphere is released from rest after a small displacement from B, the sphere returns to B with increased K.E., i.e. the P.E. at B must be a minimum.

More general problems may be considered with the help of a graph of V against any parameter θ (Fig. 12.4). At points A and B

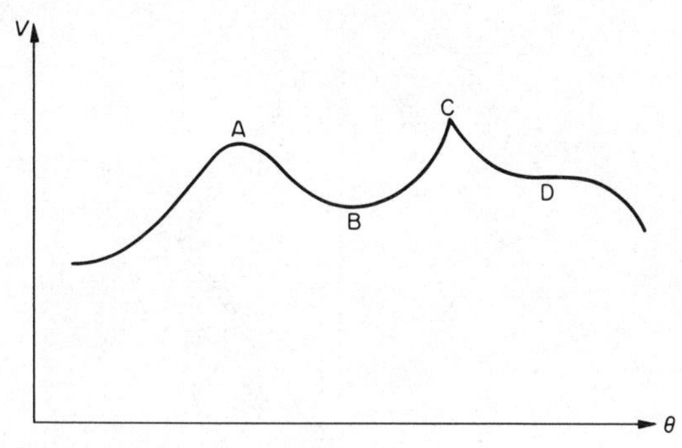

Fig. 12.4

V has a maximum and a minimum respectively, and they correspond to positions of unstable and stable equilibrium. Points C and D are reminders that not all stationary values are maxima or minima, nor are all maxima and minima stationary values.

Example 12.3. *Four equal uniform rods, each mass m and length a, are smoothly jointed to form a rhombus ABCD. This is suspended at A, and an elastic spring, length a, modulus λ joins A and C (Fig. 12.5). Find the positions of equilibrium and investigate the stability of each.*

The extension in the spring is $2a \cos\theta - a$, so the energy in the elastic spring is $\frac{1}{2}(\lambda/a)(2a\cos\theta - a)^2$. The P.E. of the rods is $-4mga\cos\theta$, so that

$$V = \tfrac{1}{2}\lambda a(2\cos\theta - 1)^2 - 4mga\cos\theta$$

and

$$\frac{dV}{d\theta} = \lambda a(2\cos\theta - 1)(-2\sin\theta) + 4mga\sin\theta$$

$$= \sin\theta\,\{2a[2mg - \lambda(2\cos\theta - 1)]\}$$

$$= 0 \quad \text{when } \sin\theta = 0 \quad \text{or} \quad \cos\theta = \frac{2mg + \lambda}{2\lambda}$$

Thus there are always positions of equilibrium with $\theta = 0$ (the geometry of the figure restricts θ so that $0 < \theta < 90°$), but if

$$\frac{2mg + \lambda}{2\lambda} < 1, \quad \text{i.e. } 2mg < \lambda$$

there is another solution.

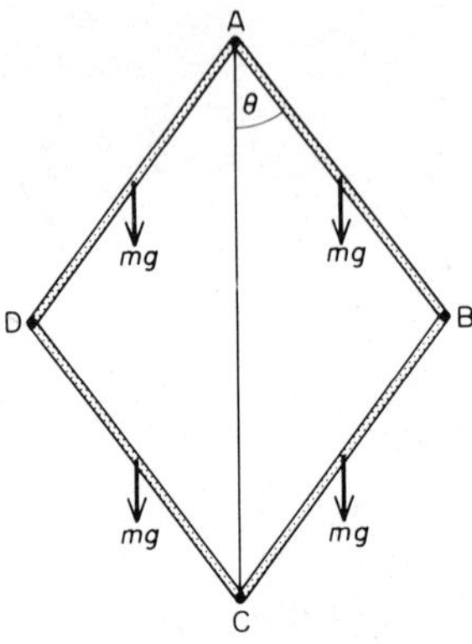

Fig. 12.5

To examine the stability of the solution where $\theta = 0$, it is useful to notice that when

$$\frac{\mathrm{d}V}{\mathrm{d}\theta} = \sin\theta\,\mathrm{F}(\theta), \quad \text{where } \mathrm{F}(\theta) \text{ is any function of } \theta,$$

$$\frac{\mathrm{d}^2 V}{\mathrm{d}\theta^2} = \sin\theta\,\frac{\mathrm{dF}}{\mathrm{d}\theta} + \cos\theta\,\mathrm{F}(\theta)$$

When $\theta = 0$, $\mathrm{d}^2V/\mathrm{d}\theta^2 = F(0)$, so the value of $\mathrm{d}^2V/\mathrm{d}\theta^2$ when $\theta = 0$ can be found without differentiating, by merely substituting $\theta = 0$ in $\mathrm{F}(\theta)$. This can be generalized in other problems when

$$\frac{\mathrm{d}V}{\mathrm{d}\theta} = \sin\theta\,\mathrm{F}(\theta) + \theta\,\mathrm{G}(\theta)$$

and also for non-zero positions of equilibrium, using Taylor's theorem.

In this example,

$$\frac{\mathrm{d}^2 V}{\mathrm{d}\theta^2} = 2a(2mg - \lambda) \quad \text{when } \theta = 0$$

which is negative when $\theta = 0$ if $\lambda > 2mg$, positive if $\lambda < 2mg$. Thus if $\lambda > 2mg$, $\theta = 0$ is a position of unstable equilibrium; if $\lambda < 2mg$, $\theta = 0$ is a position of stable equilibrium. It can also be shown that the other position, when it exists, is a position of stable equilibrium.

This conclusion could have been reached by examining the sign of $\mathrm{d}V/\mathrm{d}\theta$ either side of $\theta = 0$. When $\lambda > 2mg$, $4mg - 2\lambda(2\cos\theta - 1)$ is negative when θ is nearly equal to zero. When θ is negative, $\mathrm{d}V/\mathrm{d}\theta$ is positive, and when θ is positive, $\mathrm{d}V/\mathrm{d}\theta$ is negative, so that $\theta = 0$ gives a maximum, a position of unstable equilibrium. Likewise, when $\lambda < 2mg$, the root $\theta = 0$ is the only solution, and $\theta = 0$ is a position of stable equilibrium.

We have not yet examined the case when $\lambda = 2mg$. Then

$$\frac{\mathrm{d}V}{\mathrm{d}\theta} = 8mga\sin\theta(1 - \cos\theta)$$

and

$$\frac{\mathrm{d}^2V}{\mathrm{d}\theta^2} = 0 \quad \text{when } \sin\theta = 0$$

But near $\theta = 0$, $1 - \cos\theta$ is positive, so that as θ increases through 0, $\mathrm{d}V/\mathrm{d}\theta$ is negative, zero then positive, and $\theta = 0$ is a position of stable equilibrium. It is, of course, the only position of equilibrium, as

$$\cos^{-1}\frac{2mg + \lambda}{2\lambda} = 0$$

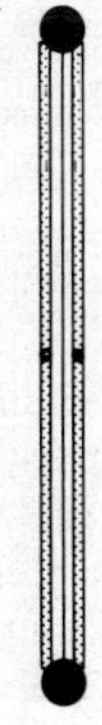

$\lambda \leqslant 2\,mg$

Only one position of equilibrium, $\theta = 0$, stable

(a)

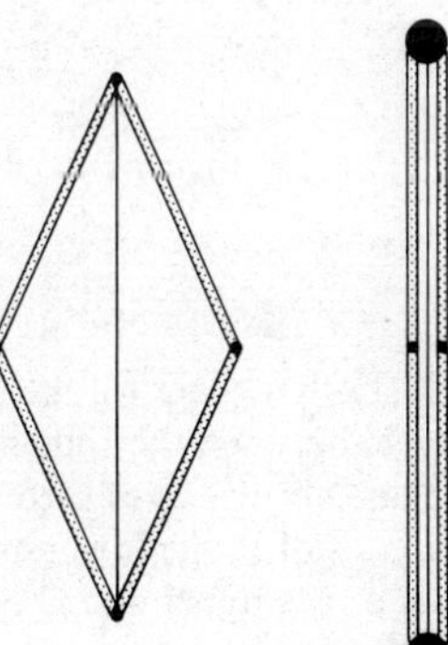

$\lambda > 2\,mg$

Two positions of equilibrium, $\theta = \cos^{-1}\left(\frac{2mg + \lambda}{2\lambda}\right)$, stable; $\theta = 0$, unstable

(b)

Fig. 12.6

The inequality $\lambda < 2mg$ describes the modulus of elasticity as small compared with the weights of the rods. Then the spring cannot support the rods in a position inclined to the vertical, so the only equilibrium position is when the rods hang vertically [Fig. 12.6(a)]. After a small displacement from that position, the rods return to it, and the position is one of stable equilibrium. By contrast, if $\lambda > 2mg$, the spring is strong enough to support the rods inclined to the vertical, and this position is one of stable equilibrium. When $\theta = 0$, the rods, assumed thin, can be in equilibrium in a vertical position, but when displaced they do not return to that position. These results are in accord with our experience.

Example 12.4. *A uniform rod, length 2l, mass m, rests in a trough whose cross-section is a parabola latus rectum 4a (Fig. 12.7). Investigate the possible positions of equilibrium.*

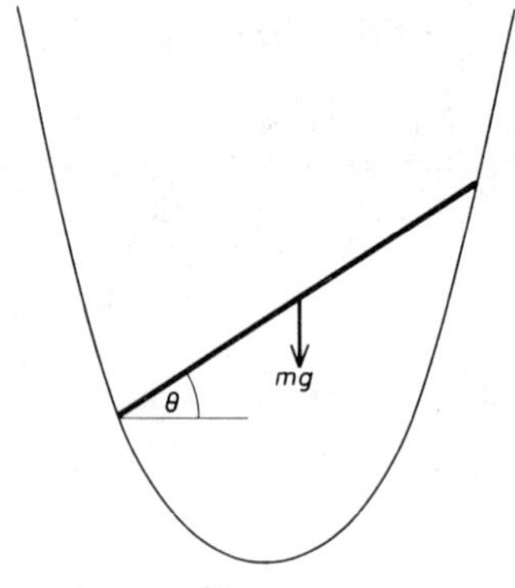

Fig. 12.7

It seems likely that there will be a horizontal position of equilibrium, so take θ as the angle between the rod and the horizontal. If the x and y axes are horizontal and vertical axes through the vertex of the parabola, respectively, the coordinates of P, the lower end of the rod can be $(2at, at^2)$, and the coordinates of the upper end Q are $(2at + 2l \cos\theta, at^2 + 2l \sin\theta)$. Since Q lies on the parabola,

$$(2at + 2l\cos\theta)^2 = 4a(at^2 + 2l\sin\theta)$$

i.e.
$$2at\cos\theta + l\cos^2\theta = 2a\sin\theta$$

i.e.
$$2at + l\cos\theta = 2a\tan\theta \tag{12.1}$$

The potential energy V is

$$mg(at^2 + l\sin\theta)$$

so
$$\frac{dV}{d\theta} = mg\left(2at\frac{dt}{d\theta} + l\cos\theta\right)$$

From equation 12.1 $\quad 2a\dfrac{dt}{d\theta} = l\sin\theta + 2a\sec^2\theta$

$$\therefore \qquad \frac{dV}{d\theta} = mg\left[(2a\tan\theta - l\cos\theta)\frac{l\sin\theta + 2a\sec^2\theta}{2a} + l\cos\theta\right]$$

$$= 2mga\sin\theta\left(\sec^3\theta - \frac{l^2}{4a^2}\cos\theta\right)$$

after some simplification.

Thus $dV/d\theta = 0$ when $\sin\theta = 0$ or $\cos^4\theta = 4a^2/l^2$. If $2a \geqslant l$, the only position of equilibrium is $\theta = 0$, when the rod is horizontal, but if $2a < l$, $\cos\theta = \pm\sqrt{(2a/l)}$, so there are two other positions of equilibrium, equally inclined to the horizontal, as we expect, by symmetry.

When $2a > l$ and $\theta = 0$, $\sec^3\theta - (l^2/4a^2)\cos\theta$ is positive, so the only position is one of stable equilibrium. But when $2a < l$, i.e. the rod is long relative to the latus rectum of the parabola, the position $\theta = 0$ is unstable, since $1 - l^2/4a^2$ is negative.

To show that the other positions of equilibrium are stable, let $\theta = \alpha$ describe one of them, where α is acute. Then the other is given by $\theta = \pi - \alpha$, and by symmetry the equilibrium must be the same at both.

Write $dV/d\theta$ as

$$2mga\sin\theta\sec^3\theta\left(1 - \frac{l^2}{4a^2}\cos^4\theta\right)$$

Sin θ and sec θ are positive near $\theta = \alpha$ and do not change sign as θ increases through α, so we only need to consider

$$\left(1 - \frac{l^2}{4a^2}\cos^4\theta\right)$$

Cos$^4\,\theta = 4a^2/l^2$, therefore when θ is a little less than α, $\cos\theta > \cos\alpha$ and

$$\left(1 - \frac{l^2}{4a^2}\cos^4\theta\right)$$

is negative. But when θ is a little greater than α, $\cos\theta < \cos\alpha$ and

$$\left(1 - \frac{l^2}{4a^2}\cos^4\theta\right)$$

is positive. Thus near $\theta = \alpha$, the sign of $dV/d\theta$ is negative, zero then positive, so the position $\theta = \alpha$ is a minimum and the equilibrium is stable.

Example 12.5. *A uniform rough plank, weight W and thickness 2b, rests horizontally in equilibrium across a fixed rough circular cylinder of radius a. A small body, weight w, is fixed to the midpoint of the plank (Fig. 12.8). Investigate the possible positions of equilibrium.*

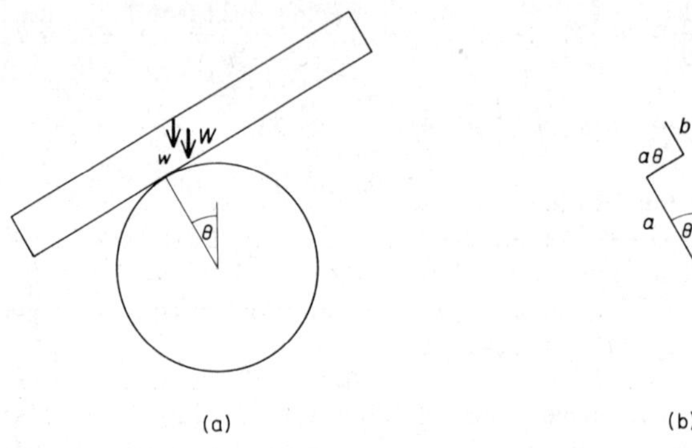

Fig. 12.8

Assuming that the surfaces are sufficiently rough to prevent slipping, the centre of gravity of the plank is

$$a \cos \theta + a\theta \sin \theta + b \cos \theta$$

above the centre of the cylinder, [Fig. 12.8(b)], the term in $a\theta$ being due to the rotation of the plank on the cylinder.

Thus for the system of the plank and the body,

$$V = W(a \cos \theta + a\theta \sin \theta + b \cos \theta) + w(a \cos \theta + a\theta \sin \theta + 2b \cos \theta)$$

$$\therefore \quad \frac{dV}{d\theta} = W(a\theta \cos \theta - b \sin \theta) + w(a\theta \cos \theta - 2b \sin \theta)$$

$$= (W + w)a\theta \cos \theta - (W + 2w)b \sin \theta$$

$$\therefore \quad \frac{dV}{d\theta} = 0 \quad \text{when } \theta = 0 \quad \text{or when}$$

$$\tan \theta = \frac{(W + w)a}{(W + 2w)b}\theta$$

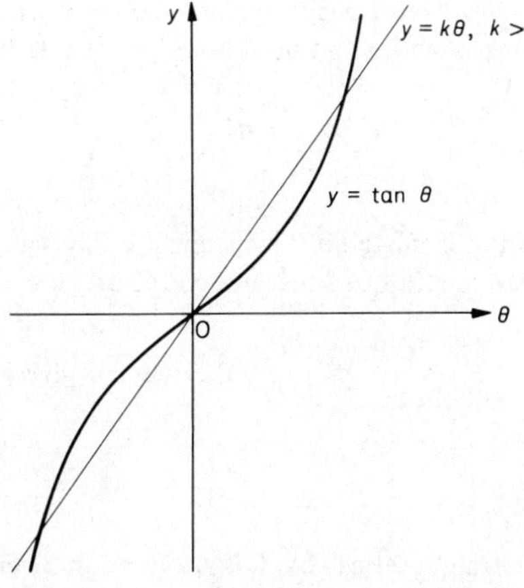

Fig. 12.9

Considering the graphs of $y = \tan\theta$ and $y = k\theta$ (Fig. 12.9), there are non-zero solutions if and only if

$$\frac{(W+w)a}{(W+2w)b} > 1$$

To investigate the nature of the position $\theta = 0$, $\mathrm{d}V/\mathrm{d}\theta$ is of the form

$$\sin\theta\,\mathrm{F}(\theta) + \theta\,\mathrm{G}(\theta)$$

so that when $\theta = 0$,

$$\frac{\mathrm{d}^2 V}{\mathrm{d}\theta^2} = (W+w)a - (W+2w)b$$

When

$$\frac{(W+w)a}{(W+2w)b} < 1$$

$\mathrm{d}^2V/\mathrm{d}\theta^2$ is negative, making $\theta = 0$ a position of unstable equilibrium. Thus if

$$\frac{(W+w)a}{(W+2w)b} < 1$$

$\theta = 0$ is the only position of equilibrium and is unstable. If

$$\frac{(W+w)a}{(W+2w)b} > 1$$

there are two other positions equally inclined to the horizontal. The horizontal position is stable, and it can be shown that the inclined positions are unstable. When

$$\frac{(W+w)a}{(W+2w)b} = 1,$$

the horizontal position is unstable. This is most easily seen by considering the expansion in power series of $\sin\theta$ and $\cos\theta$, as

$$\frac{dV}{d\theta} = \frac{d^2V}{d\theta^2} = \frac{d^3V}{d\theta^3} = 0 \quad \text{when } \theta = 0$$

EXERCISE 12(a)

1. Two smooth straight wires OA, OB are fixed in a vertical plane. Angle AOB is a right angle, and AO makes an angle of α with the horizontal. A uniform rod is free to slide with its ends constrained to move, one on each of OA and OB. Show that there is one position of equilibrium and that this is a position of unstable equilibrium.

2. Four equal uniform rods, AB, BC, CD, DA, of mass m and length $2a$, are freely jointed to form a rhombus ABCD. This is suspended from A, and two elastic springs, modulus $2mg$ and natural length a, join A to C and B to D. Find the angle made by AB with the vertical in equilibrium and show that this is a position of stable equilibrium.

3. Three equal uniform rods AB, BC, CD, each of length $2a$ and mass m, are freely jointed at B and C. The rods hang freely in a vertical plane, hinged with A and D at the same horizontal level, a distance $2a$ apart. B and D are joined by an elastic string, natural length a and modulus $2mg$, so that ABCD is a rhombus. If angle BAD = 2θ, show that the potential energy of the system is $mga[(4\sin\theta - 1)^2 - 4\sin 2\theta]$. With the aid of a sketch graph, show that there is only one position of equilibrium, and that this is a position of stable equilibrium.

4. A particle P of weight W is attached to fixed points A and B by an inextensible string AP of length $4a$ and an elastic string BP of unstretched length $2a$ and modulus $(8/5)W$. The points A and B are a distance $5a$ apart at the same level. Prove that when the system is in equilibrium the string AP makes an angle θ with the horizontal given by

$$(4 - \cot\theta)(41 - 40\cos\theta)^{1/2} = 8$$

Confirm that this equation is satisfied if the strings supporting the particle are mutually perpendicular. (C.)

5. A uniform rod AB, of mass m and length a, is free to turn in a vertical plane about a hinge at A. The rod is supported at B by an elastic string modulus $3mg$ and unstretched length a joining B to a point C which is at a height a vertically above A. Prove that the potential energy of the system is given by

$$V = \tfrac{1}{2}mga(-5\cos\theta - 12\sin\tfrac{1}{2}\theta) + \text{constant}$$

where θ is the angle CAB. Deduce the equilibrium positions of the rod and discuss their stability. (O. & C.)

6. A uniform square plate ABCD of weight W and side $2a$ is placed in a vertical plane with the sides BC and CD resting on smooth parallel rails $2a$ apart at the same level. Prove that, if θ is the inclination of AC to the vertical, the depth of C below the level of the rails is $a\cos 2\theta$. Write down an expression for the potential energy of the system and show that the positions of equilibrium are given by $\theta = 0$ and $4\cos\theta = \sqrt{2}$. Show that the equilibrium is stable when $\theta = 0$. (O. & C.)

7. A uniform sphere of radius b and weight W is placed on a fixed rough sphere of radius a and a weight w is attached to the upper sphere at the point of contact. Show that the potential energy when the upper sphere has rolled into a position where the common radius is inclined at an angle θ to the vertical is

$$V = (W + w)(a + b)\cos\theta - wb\cos\frac{a+b}{b}\theta + \text{constant}$$

Hence show that the sphere can rest in stable equilibrium with $\theta = 0$ if $wa > Wb$. (O. & C.)

8. A light bar AB of length $2a$ is rigidly attached at its centre C to a second light bar CD of length $4a$, the two bars being at right angles. Particles of masses m, $2m$, and $4m$ are attached to the bars at A, B, D respectively and the system can turn in a vertical plane about a pivot through the midpoint E of CD. Show that there are two positions of equilibrium and discuss their stability. (O. & C.)

9. A uniform prism of mass m is placed on two smooth horizontal rails which are at the same level and a distance c apart. The cross-section of the prism is perpendicular to the rails and is an equilateral triangle of side a. The lines of contact of the rails and the prism appear in the cross-section as points P, Q on AB, AC and AP $= x$, AQ $= y$. Prove that

the potential energy of the system is

$$\tfrac{1}{3}mg\left(\frac{a-x}{x}+\frac{a-y}{y}-1\right)z + \text{constant}$$

where z is the depth of A below PQ.
Show that this can be written

$$\frac{mg\sqrt{3}}{6c}\,[c^2 + a(x+y) - (x+y)^2] + \text{constant}$$

Show that there are two oblique positions of equilibrium if $\tfrac{1}{4}a < c < \tfrac{1}{2}a$. (O. & C.)

10. A thin rectangular sheet of metal of mass M, width a, and length $2\pi b$ is bent into a hollow circular cylinder so that two of the edges of length a are soldered together without overlap. The solder forms a thin line of mass m. The cylinder is placed on an inclined plane of angle α which is sufficiently rough to prevent slipping so that the line of the solder is in contact with the plane and at right angles to the lines of greatest slope. Prove that, when the cylinder has rolled through an angle θ down the plane, its potential energy V is given by

$$V = K - mgb\cos(\theta+\alpha) - (m+M)gb\theta\sin\alpha$$

where K is a constant.
Prove that the cylinder can rest in equilibrium on the plane with the solder not touching the plane and perpendicular to the lines of greatest slope if $m(1-\sin\alpha) \geqslant M\sin\alpha$ and that, if this condition holds, there are two positions of equilibrium, one of which is stable. (S.U.J.B.)

Period of small oscillations

The work in this chapter has depended on the sum of the kinetic energy and the potential energy being constant, and we have seen that the positions of equilibrium can be found from $\mathrm{d}V/\mathrm{d}\theta = 0$, for a parameter θ. But in Example 12.1 we found that when we differentiated the energy equation, we had

$$\frac{mg}{l}x\dot{x} - mg\dot{x} + m\dot{x}\ddot{x} = 0$$

Since $\dot{x} \neq 0$,

$$\ddot{x} + \frac{g}{l}(x-l) = 0$$

which we recognize as s.h.m., period $2\pi\sqrt{(l/g)}$, about the position $x = l$.

This method can clearly be used for finding the period of small oscillations about positions of stable equilibrium, and also for investigating the subsequent motion when a body has been disturbed from a position of unstable equilibrium.

Example 12.6. *Two small identical rings mass m are free to slide on a smooth circular wire, radius a, in a vertical plane. The rings are joined by a light rod, length a. Find the period of small oscillations about the position of stable equilibrium.*

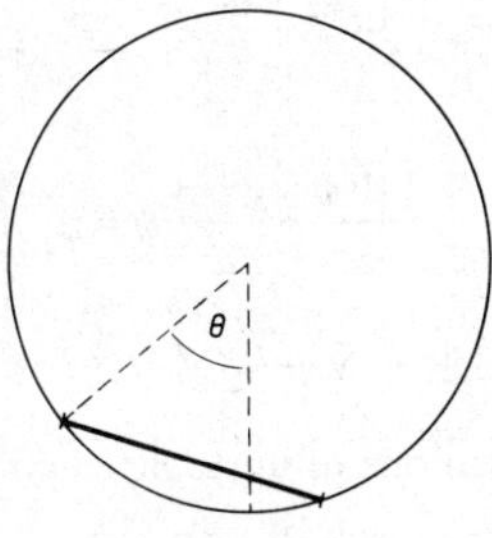

Fig. 12.10

If θ is the angle between the radius through one ring and the vertical (Fig. 12.10),

$$V = -mga\left[\cos\theta + \cos\left(\frac{\pi}{3} - \theta\right)\right]$$

$$= -mga\sqrt{3}\cos\left(\frac{\pi}{6} - \theta\right)$$

But

$$\frac{dV}{d\theta} = mga\sqrt{3}\sin\left(\frac{\pi}{6} - \theta\right)$$

so that $\theta = \pi/6$ is a position of equilibrium, as expected, with the rod horizontal.

Since the rings are moving around the circumference of a circle radius a, the velocity of each ring is $a\ d\theta/dt$, and the kinetic energy of both rings is $ma^2(d\theta/dt)^2$.

Since $T + V$ is constant,

$$ma^2\left(\frac{d\theta}{dt}\right)^2 - mga\sqrt{3}\cos\left(\frac{\pi}{6} - \theta\right) \quad \text{is constant}$$

Differentiating,

$$2ma^2\frac{d\theta}{dt}\cdot\frac{d^2\theta}{dt^2} - mga\sqrt{3}\sin\left(\frac{\pi}{6} - \theta\right)\frac{d\theta}{dt} = 0$$

Substituting $\phi = \pi/6 - \theta$,

$$2ma^2\frac{d^2\phi}{dt^2} + mga\sqrt{3}\sin\phi = 0$$

For small values of ϕ,

$$\frac{d^2\phi}{dt^2} + \frac{g\sqrt{3}}{2a}\phi = 0$$

Thus we have s.h.m., period $2\pi\sqrt{(2a/g\sqrt{3})}$, about the position $\phi = 0$, i.e. about the position $\theta = \pi/6$.

If the position had been one of unstable equilibrium, the equation would have been of the form

$$\frac{d^2\phi}{dt^2} - k^2\phi = 0$$

for which solutions can be found,

$$\phi = A\,e^{kt} + B\,e^{-kt}$$

Example 12.7. *A uniform beam of length 2a, mass m, is hinged at one end so that it can rotate in a vertical plane. One end of a spring of modulus λ, natural length a, is fixed to a point (3/2)a vertically above the hinge. The other end of the spring is fixed at a point on the beam (3/2)a from the hinge (Fig. 12.11). Find the possible positions of equilibrium, and discuss their stability when (a)λ = mg or (b) λ = ½mg. Investigate the ensuing motion in each case after the beam has been disturbed from the equilibrium positions.*

If the angle between the rod and the upward vertical is 2θ, the energy in the spring is

$$\frac{1}{2}\frac{\lambda}{a}(3a\sin\theta - a)^2$$

and

$$V = mga\cos 2\theta + \frac{1}{2}\frac{\lambda}{a}(3a\sin\theta - a)^2$$

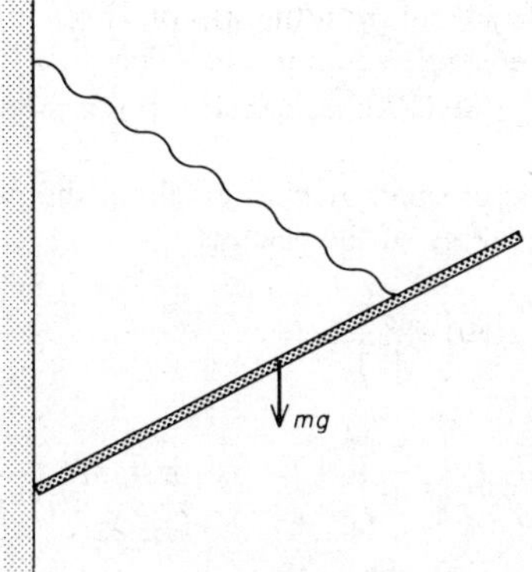

Fig. 12.11

Therefore

$$\frac{dV}{d\theta} = -2mga \sin 2\theta + \frac{\lambda}{a}(3a \sin\theta - a)(3a \cos\theta)$$

$$= \cos\theta\,[(9\lambda a - 4mga) \sin\theta - 3\lambda a] \qquad (12.2)$$

$$\therefore \qquad \frac{dV}{d\theta} = 0 \quad \text{when } \cos\theta = 0, \quad \text{i.e. } \theta = \frac{\pi}{2}$$

or when $\quad \sin\theta = \dfrac{3\lambda}{9\lambda - 4mg}$

But for real θ, $\sin\theta \leqslant 1$, so

$$\frac{3\lambda}{9\lambda - 4mg} \leqslant 1$$

i.e. $\frac{2}{3}mg < \lambda$ for a real value of θ other than $\pi/2$, the value $\lambda = \frac{2}{3}mg$ giving $\theta = \pi/2$.

Thus if $\lambda > \frac{2}{3}mg$, there are two positions of equilibrium, otherwise there is only one position, $\theta = \pi/2$, when the beam hangs vertically downwards. Physically this means that if the spring is sufficiently strong ($\lambda > \frac{2}{3}mg$) it can support the beam inclined at an angle to the vertical; otherwise, the beam falls into the vertical position.

To investigate the nature of the equilibrium, when $\lambda = mg$,

$$\frac{dV}{d\theta} = \cos\theta(5mga \sin\theta - 3mga), \quad \text{from equation 12.2}$$

$$= 5mga \cos\theta(\sin\theta - \tfrac{3}{5})$$

When $\cos\theta = 0$, $\theta = \pi/2$ and from the sign of $\mathrm{d}V/\mathrm{d}\theta$ either side of $\theta = \pi/2$, this is a position of unstable equilibrium. When $\sin\theta = 3/5$, $\cos\theta$ is positive, so again from the sign of $\mathrm{d}V/\mathrm{d}\theta$ either side, this is a position of stable equilibrium.

To find the period of small oscillations about the position inclined to the vertical, the kinetic energy of the beam is

$$\tfrac{1}{2}(\tfrac{4}{3}ma^2)\left(2\frac{\mathrm{d}\theta}{\mathrm{d}t}\right)^2$$

$$\therefore \qquad \tfrac{1}{2}(\tfrac{4}{3}ma^2)\left(2\frac{\mathrm{d}\theta}{\mathrm{d}t}\right)^2 + V \quad \text{is constant}$$

i.e.
$$\tfrac{16}{3}ma^2\,\frac{\mathrm{d}^2\theta}{\mathrm{d}t^2}\cdot\frac{\mathrm{d}\theta}{\mathrm{d}t} + 5mga\cos\theta(\sin\theta - \tfrac{3}{5})\frac{\mathrm{d}\theta}{\mathrm{d}t} = 0$$

i.e.
$$\frac{\mathrm{d}^2\theta}{\mathrm{d}t^2} + \frac{15g}{16a}\cos\theta(\sin\theta - \tfrac{3}{5}) = 0 \qquad (12.3)$$

Substitute $\phi = \theta - \alpha$, where $\sin\alpha : \cos\alpha : 1 = 3:4:5$, so that ϕ is small for small oscillations about this equilibrium position.

Then
$$\frac{\mathrm{d}^2\phi}{\mathrm{d}t^2} + \frac{15g}{16a}\cos(\phi+\alpha)[\sin(\phi+\alpha) - \tfrac{3}{5}] = 0$$

i.e.
$$\frac{\mathrm{d}^2\phi}{\mathrm{d}t^2} + \frac{15g}{16a}(\tfrac{4}{5}\cos\phi - \tfrac{3}{5}\sin\phi)(\tfrac{4}{5}\sin\phi + \tfrac{3}{5}\cos\phi - \tfrac{3}{5}) = 0$$

i.e.
$$\frac{\mathrm{d}^2\phi}{\mathrm{d}t^2} + \frac{15g}{16a}(\tfrac{16}{25}\phi) = 0$$

using $\sin\phi \simeq \phi$, $\cos\phi \simeq 1$, as ϕ is small,

i.e.
$$\frac{\mathrm{d}^2\phi}{\mathrm{d}t^2} + \frac{3g}{5a}\phi = 0$$

This is s.h.m. about $\theta = \alpha$, period $2\pi\sqrt{(5a/3g)}$.

To find the nature of the motion about $\theta = \pi/2$, substituting $\phi = \theta - \pi/2$ in equation 12.3,

$$\frac{\mathrm{d}^2\phi}{\mathrm{d}t^2} - \frac{15g}{16a}\sin\phi(\cos\phi - \tfrac{3}{5}) = 0$$

When ϕ is small,

$$\frac{\mathrm{d}^2\phi}{\mathrm{d}t^2} - \frac{3g}{8a}\phi = 0$$

This is not s.h.m., having a solution of the form

$$\phi = A\,\mathrm{e}^{kt} + B\,\mathrm{e}^{-kt}, \quad \text{where } k^2 = \frac{3g}{8a}$$

For case (b), $\lambda = \frac{1}{2}mg$, the energy equation is

$$\tfrac{1}{2}(\tfrac{4}{3}ma^2)\left(2\frac{\mathrm{d}\theta}{\mathrm{d}t}\right)^2 + V \quad \text{is constant}$$

i.e.
$$\tfrac{16}{3}ma^2\frac{\mathrm{d}^2\theta}{\mathrm{d}t^2}\frac{\mathrm{d}\theta}{\mathrm{d}t} + \tfrac{1}{2}mga\cos\theta(\sin\theta - 3)\frac{\mathrm{d}\theta}{\mathrm{d}t} = 0$$

i.e.
$$\frac{\mathrm{d}^2\theta}{\mathrm{d}t^2} + \frac{3g}{32a}\cos\theta\,(\sin\theta - 3) = 0$$

The only position of equilibrium now is $\theta = \pi/2$; substituting $\phi = \theta - \pi/2$,

$$\frac{\mathrm{d}^2\phi}{\mathrm{d}t^2} - \frac{3g}{32a}\sin\phi(\cos\phi - 3) = 0$$

i.e.
$$\frac{\mathrm{d}^2\phi}{\mathrm{d}t^2} + \frac{3g}{16a}\phi = 0, \quad \text{if } \phi \text{ is small.}$$

This is s.h.m., period $2\pi\sqrt{(16a/3g)}$, about the vertical position.

EXERCISE 12(b)

1. A uniform rod AB, length $2a$, can oscillate in a vertical plane about a horizontal axis through A, perpendicular to the plane of oscillation. Use the methods of this chapter to find the positions of equilibrium and the period of small oscillations about the position of stable equilibrium.

2. Two small identical rings are free to slide on a smooth circular wire, radius a, in a vertical plane. The rings are joined by a light rod length $6a/5$. Find the period of small oscillations about the position of stable equilibrium.

3. Three points A, B, and C are in a straight line on a smooth horizontal table; AC = CB = a. A particle mass m is placed on the table at C and is attached to A and B by two equal elastic strings, modulus of elasticity mg, unstretched lengths $\frac{3}{4}a$. The particle is given a small horizontal displacement at right angles to AB and is then released from rest. Find the period of small displacements about the equilibrium position.

4. A uniform rod AB, of length $6a$ and mass $3M$, has a smooth ring of mass M attached at each of its ends. The rings are threaded on to a smooth fixed vertical circular wire of radius $5a$, whose centre is O. Calculate, in terms of a and g, the period of small oscillations of the system if it is slightly disturbed from its stable equilibrium position. (A.E.B.)

5. A smooth wire is bent into the shape of a circle of radius a and held fixed in a vertical plane. Light elastic threads of natural length a and modulus λ are attached to the wire at the upper and lower extremities A and C of the vertical diameter of the circle. The other ends of the two threads are both attached to a small bead B of mass m, which is free to slide on the wire. The system rests in equilibrium with angle CAB $= \alpha$, where $\sin \alpha = 3/5$. Deduce that $5\lambda = 24mg$.
The bead is now slightly displaced. Show that in the ensuing motion

$$2ma \frac{d^2\theta}{dt^2} = \lambda(\cos\theta - \sin\theta) - mg \sin 2\theta$$

where θ denotes CAB.
Show that the period of small oscillations is

$$10\pi \sqrt{\left(\frac{a}{91g}\right)}$$

(C.S.)

6. A uniform sphere of radius a and mass M has a particle of mass m attached at a point of its surface, and rolls on a perfectly rough horizontal table. With the help of the energy equation, or otherwise, show that, if the sphere is released from rest in a position slightly different from that of stable equilibrium, its period of oscillation is

$$2\pi \sqrt{\left(\frac{7Ma}{5mg}\right)}$$

(C.S.)

7. A particle of mass m is attached at the midpoint of a light elastic string of natural length $2l$ and modulus λ. The ends of the string are fixed at two points distance $2a$ apart on a smooth horizontal table ($a > l$). Show that the particle can perform small oscillations either in the line of the string or perpendicular to it, and that the periods in these two cases are in the ratio of $\sqrt{(a - l)}$ to $\sqrt{a}$. (O.S.)

8. A thin uniform rod AB of length a and mass M is pivoted smoothly at A. The end B is attached to a light elastic string BC, whose natural length is a and whose end C is held at a fixed point. In equilibrium, the rod is horizontal, C is vertically above B, and the distance between B and C is b ($>a$). Calculate the elastic modulus of the string and show

that the system can make small oscillations about the equilibrium configuration, with period

$$2\pi\sqrt{\left[\frac{2(b-a)}{3g}\right]} \qquad \text{(C.S.)}$$

9. A uniform rod AB of length $2a$ and mass m can move freely under gravity about a smooth, fixed horizontal axis through A. A light elastic string of natural length $2a$ and modulus $3mg/2$ has one end fixed to B and the other to a fixed point C, vertically above A, where AC = $2a$. Show that there is a position of equilibrium in which AB makes an angle α with the downward vertical where $\cos\alpha = \frac{1}{8}$.
Find the period of small oscillations about the equilibrium position. (S.U.J.B.)

10. A circle of radius a lies inside a circle of radius $2a$ and touches it. The two circles form the boundary of a uniform lamina which is free to rotate in a vertical plane about a fixed horizontal axis through a point P on the line of centres. Show that as P is varied the minimum period of small oscillations is

$$2\pi\left(\frac{a}{g}\right)^{1/2}\left(\frac{74}{9}\right)^{1/4} \qquad \text{(C.S.)}$$

Answers

EXERCISE 1(a) (page 13)

3. $\frac{5}{3}$. **4.** 3. **5.** $\frac{5}{2}$. **6.** $(2\mathbf{i} + \mathbf{j})$. **7.** $(\frac{2}{3}\mathbf{i} + \frac{1}{3}\mathbf{j})$. **8.** $\frac{4}{13}(3\mathbf{i} + \mathbf{j})$.

10. $2\mathbf{v}_1 + \mathbf{v}_2$. **11.** 15; $\frac{2}{15}, \frac{10}{15}, \frac{11}{15}$. **12.** 9; $\frac{1}{9}, -\frac{4}{9}, -\frac{8}{9}$. **13.** $\frac{4}{\sqrt{21}}$.

14. $\frac{1}{\sqrt{19}}$. **15.** $-\frac{1}{\sqrt{18}}$. **16.** $\overrightarrow{AC}$.

17. Force equal and parallel to $\overrightarrow{DB}$, through A. **18.** $2\overrightarrow{AC}$. **19.** $2\overrightarrow{AB}$.

23. $\mathbf{a} + \mathbf{b}$, $2\mathbf{b}$, $2\mathbf{b} - \mathbf{a}$, $\mathbf{b} - \mathbf{a}$. **24.** $\mathbf{b}$. **25.** $(\mathbf{i} - \mathbf{j} + 2\mathbf{k})$. **26.** $-\frac{1}{2}\mathbf{k}$.

27. $-12, -15$. **29.** $\frac{2}{9}, -\frac{4}{9}, -\frac{1}{9}$. **30.** $\frac{\alpha\delta_2 - \beta\delta_1}{\gamma_1\delta_2 - \gamma_2\delta_1}, \frac{\alpha\gamma_2 - \beta\gamma_1}{\delta_1\gamma_2 - \delta_2\gamma_1}$; $\mathbf{c} = \lambda\mathbf{d}$.

31. (c) $3\overrightarrow{OG}$, (d) 0.

33. (a) Couple, magnitude equal to twice that of the area of the triangle ABC.
(b) Force $2\overrightarrow{AB}$ through the midpoint of BC.

EXERCISE 1(b) (page 24)

2. Yes; $t = 3$. **3.** $t = 1$; $\sqrt{5}$. **4.** $5\sqrt{2}$ km; 1 hr. **5.** 2. **6.** 4.

7. 2. **9.** $\sqrt{8}$. **10.** $\sqrt{(15/2)}$, when $t = \frac{1}{2}$.

11. $(3 - 2T)\mathbf{i} + (4 - 5T)\mathbf{j} + (T - 2)\mathbf{k}$; $\sqrt{(\frac{43}{15})}$; $(\frac{17}{15}\mathbf{i} - \frac{2}{3}\mathbf{j} - \frac{16}{15}\mathbf{k})$

12. $(-\mathbf{i} - 2\mathbf{j})$, $\frac{6}{5}\sqrt{5}$ **13.** $\mathbf{r} = \lambda(3\mathbf{i} + 4\mathbf{j})$. **14.** $\mathbf{r} = \mathbf{i} + 4\mathbf{j} + \lambda(\mathbf{i} + \mathbf{j})$.

17. $\mathbf{r} = \lambda(3\mathbf{i} + 4\mathbf{j} + 5\mathbf{k})$. **18.** $\mathbf{r} = \mathbf{i} + 4\mathbf{j} + \mathbf{k} + \lambda(\mathbf{i} + \mathbf{j} - \mathbf{k})$.

19. No; lines of action are skew. **20.** $\sqrt{3}$. **21.** $\sqrt{14}$ N.

22. $\mathbf{F}_1\sqrt{2}$. **24.** $\pm\frac{4}{5}(3\mathbf{i} + 4\mathbf{j})$

EXERCISE 1(c) (page 37)

1. (a) 6, (b) 0, (c) 0, (d) 0. Vectors are perpendicular. **2.** $\frac{1}{\sqrt{3}}(\mathbf{i} - \mathbf{j} + \mathbf{k})$.

4. $x - 2y + 3z - 11 = 0$. **5.** $x - y + 2z - 4 = 0$. **6.** 0. **7.** $-\frac{1}{10}\sqrt{3}$.

8. $-\frac{1}{3}$. **9.** $-\frac{1}{3}\sqrt{3}$. **10.** 0. **11.** $-\frac{1}{9}\sqrt{6}$. **12.** $\frac{5}{9}\sqrt{3}$. **13.** $\frac{119}{169}$.

14. $\cos^{-1}(\frac{1}{3}\sqrt{3})$. **15.** 3. **16.** 4 units, parallel to OW, through Y.

17. 3(**i** + **j** + **k**); 6(**i** + 2**j** + 2**k**); 54. **18.** $\frac{1}{\sqrt{3}}\mathbf{u} + \sqrt{(\frac{2}{3})}\mathbf{v}$ **19.** $\cos^{-1}\left(\frac{\mathbf{a}\cdot\mathbf{c}}{ac}\right)$

20. $9\mathbf{i} + \frac{11}{3}\mathbf{j}$; $4\mathbf{i} + \frac{4}{3}\mathbf{j}$; $\frac{80}{3}$; $-4\mathbf{i} - \frac{4}{3}\mathbf{j}$. **21.** 40. **22.** $2\sqrt{2}$. **23.** $4\sqrt{(\frac{5}{7})}$.

24. $3\sqrt{14}$; $\mathbf{r} = 2\mathbf{i} + 5\mathbf{j} + 5\mathbf{k} + \lambda(3\mathbf{i} + \mathbf{j} + 2\mathbf{k})$; $\frac{x-2}{3} = \frac{y-5}{1} = \frac{z-5}{2}$; $\frac{5\sqrt{39}}{78}$.

25. True for all λ, μ, **a** when **Q** = 0.

29. (a) 4**i** – 3**j** + **k**; (b) **i** + **j** – **k**; (c) 2**j** – 2**k**; (d) 0. **30.** –2**j** + 2**k**.

31. 10**i** + 6**j** – 4**k**. **32.** $\sqrt{2}$ **33.** $8/\sqrt{3}$

34. $\frac{1}{6}(\mathbf{a} - \mathbf{b})\cdot(\mathbf{a}\times\mathbf{c} + \mathbf{c}\times\mathbf{d} + \mathbf{d}\times\mathbf{a})$. **36.** $10\sqrt{(\frac{2}{3})}$.

37. $\frac{P}{15}(12\mathbf{i} + 29\mathbf{j} + 28\mathbf{k})$; $\frac{2}{13}(12\mathbf{i} + 29\mathbf{j} + 28\mathbf{k})$; $\frac{4P}{3\sqrt{102}}$.

38. 12J, 28J; $\mathbf{F}_3 = -5\mathbf{i} - 5\mathbf{j} + 17\mathbf{k}$. $\sqrt{(5171)}$, parallel to **i** + **j** + **k**.

39. $9860/19\sqrt{(152)}$ Nm.

40. $9\sqrt{11}$; $3\sqrt{6}$; $\mathbf{r} = 5\mathbf{i} + 3\mathbf{j} - 2\mathbf{k} + \lambda(-7\mathbf{i} + \mathbf{j} + 2\mathbf{k})$.

EXERCISE 2(a) (page 50)

1. 1.5 m s^{-1}, 3 m s^{-1}. **2.** **i** m s^{-1}, 1.4**i** m s^{-1}. **3.** **i** m s^{-1}, $\frac{7}{2}$**i** m s^{-1}.

4. 17**i** m s^{-1}, 20**i** m s^{-1}. **5.** –4**i** m s^{-1}, 10**i** m s^{-1}. **7.** $\frac{1}{2}$.

9. $(1 - e) : (1 + e)$. **10.** $\frac{1}{3}(1 - 2e)u$, $\frac{1}{3}(1 + 4e)u$. **12.** 0, 1.6 m s^{-1}.

13. 1.6**i** m s^{-1}, 3.6**i** m s^{-1}. **14.** 0.49 m. **15.** $3\frac{1}{3}$ s.

16. $\frac{1}{2}m(1 + e)(u - v)$. **17.** $\frac{1}{2}(1 + e)u$; $e < 3 - \sqrt{8}$. **19.** $\frac{2}{7}$. **20.** $2t/e$.

22. $1/\sqrt{2}$. **24.** $\frac{1}{2}(1 + e^{2n})u$, $\frac{1}{2}(1 - e^{2n})u$.

EXERCISE 2(b) (page 57)

1. (–**i** + 3**j**) m s^{-1}, **j** m s^{-1}; 2J. **2.** ($1\frac{1}{4}$**i** – 3**j**) m s^{-1}, ($1\frac{1}{2}$**i** + **j**) m s^{-1}.

3. (2**i** – **j**) m s^{-1}, (4**i** + **j**) m s^{-1}; $\sqrt{\frac{81}{85}}$, $-\sqrt{\frac{49}{85}}$. **4.** $\frac{1}{3}\sqrt{5}$.

5. $2\sqrt{3}$ m s^{-1}, $\frac{4}{3}$ m s^{-1}.

6. $\frac{1}{5}\sqrt{1009}$ m s^{-1} at $\tan^{-1}(\frac{15}{28})$ with $\overrightarrow{BA}$, $\frac{1}{5}\sqrt{769}$ m s^{-1} at $\tan^{-1}(\frac{25}{12})$ with $\overrightarrow{AB}$.

8. $\tan^{-1}[b(1 - e)/2h]$. **12.** $\frac{1}{3}$. **14.** $\left(u + \frac{I}{m}\right)\mathbf{i} + \left(v + \frac{J}{m}\right)\mathbf{j}$.

15. 1:2; $\frac{1}{8}u$. **16.** $\tan^{-1}(\frac{3}{5})$. **17.** $\tan^{-1}(\frac{1}{2})$. **18.** $\tan^{-1}\sqrt{\left(\frac{1-e}{2}\right)}$.

19. $\frac{1}{2}V(1 - e)\cos(\alpha - \beta)$, $V\sin(\alpha - \beta)$; $\frac{1}{2}V(1 + e)\cos(\alpha - \beta)$, 0.

EXERCISE 2(c) (page 63)

1. 2 m s^{-1}, 4 N s, 12 J. **2.** $\frac{1}{4}u, \frac{3}{4}u; \frac{2a}{u}; \frac{u}{2}$. **3.** $\frac{1}{4}mu\sqrt{2}$.

4. $\frac{4}{3}\sqrt{5}$ m s^{-1}, $\frac{2}{3}\sqrt{2}$ m s^{-1}. **5.** $\frac{u}{2(M+m)}\sqrt{(4m^2+6mM+3M^2)}; \frac{mu}{2(M+m)}$

8. $\frac{1}{4}u\sqrt{3}; \frac{1}{4}u\sqrt{5}$ at $\tan^{-1}(\frac{1}{2})$ to line of string. **9.** 7 : 2.

10. $\frac{I}{2m}, \frac{I\sqrt{2}}{4m}, \frac{I\sqrt{2}}{4m}$, 0.

EXERCISE 3(a) (page 70)

1. $4x + \frac{1}{y} + C = 0$. **2.** $\log_e(4+y) = x + C$. **3.** $\log_e(4+y^2) = 2x + C$.

4. $\frac{1}{2}\tan^{-1}\left(\frac{y}{2}\right) = \log x + C$. **5.** $4 + y^2 = Cx^2$. **6.** $4 + y^2 = A\,e^{x^2}$.

7. $\log_e y = C - \cos x$. **8.** $\tan y = C - \cos x$. **9.** $y = A(x+1)$.

10. $\log_e(Ay) = \frac{1}{a}\tan^{-1}\left(\frac{x}{a}\right)$. **11.** $2x = y\log_e(Ax)$. **12.** $y = x\log_e(Ax)$.

EXERCISE 3(b) (page 75)

1. 256. **2.** 212; 23 minutes. **3.** £2000; £3500; £1500.
5. 1 cm, 1.08 cm. **6.** $I = 10 - \frac{1}{2}kx^2$; 5.68 **7.** 46 min.
8. 48.5°C; 46 min. **9.** 29°C; 28 min. **11.** 0.8 min; 679. **12.** 2.41 hr.
13. $\frac{1}{k}[m + (kp - m)\,e^{kt}]$; 231. **14.** 12 s. **19.** 21 days.
22. 23 days. **23.** (a) £12 800. Fall from 10 000 to 5120. (b) £45 000.
24. £312 500. **26.** $\frac{1}{384}kl^4$ **31.** 62; 91. **33.** $x = \frac{1}{6}gt^2$.

EXERCISE 3(c) (page 89)

1. $x = 5\cos 3t$. **2.** $x = 2\sin 5t$. **3.** $x = 2\sin 10t$. **4.** $x = 9\cos 4t$.
5. $x = 8\sqrt{2}(\cos 5t + \sin 5t)$. **6.** $x = 10\sin 5t$. **7.** $x = 5\cos 4t$.
8. 5; $x = 10\cos 5t$. **9.** $5\cos\omega t + \frac{10}{\omega}\sin\omega t$; $5\sqrt{5}$ cm.

10. $x = 5 \sin 2t$; π s. **11.** $x = -3 \cos \frac{1}{2}t$; 4π hr.
12. $y = 5 - 4 \cos \frac{1}{2}t$; 3.06 p.m. **13.** 3 m s^{-1}; 3 m s^{-2}.
14. 60π cm s^{-1}; 4π m s^{-1}. **16.** $x = 3\,\mathrm{e}^{-t} - 2\,\mathrm{e}^{-2t}$.

17. $r = \frac{a}{2}(\mathrm{e}^{\Omega t} + \mathrm{e}^{-\Omega t})$; $a\Omega\sqrt{7}$.

19. $\theta = \mathrm{e}^{-kt}\left[\frac{1}{2}\left(1+\frac{k}{p}\right)\theta_0\,\mathrm{e}^{pt} + \frac{1}{2}\left(1-\frac{k}{p}\right)\theta_0\,\mathrm{e}^{-pt}\right]$ where $p = \sqrt{(k^2 - \omega^2)}$;

$\theta = \theta_0\,\mathrm{e}^{-kt}\left[\cos qt + \frac{k}{q}\sin qt\right]$ where $q = \sqrt{(\omega^2 - k^2)}$.

20. $\theta = 2\,\mathrm{e}^{-t} - \mathrm{e}^{-2t}$.

EXERCISE 3(d) (page 96)

1. $x = A\,\mathrm{e}^{-t} + B\,\mathrm{e}^{-4t}$. **2.** $x = A\,\mathrm{e}^{4t} + B\,\mathrm{e}^{-2t}$. **3.** $x = A\,\mathrm{e}^{2t} + B\,t\,\mathrm{e}^{2t}$.
4. $x = A\,\mathrm{e}^{t} + Bt\,\mathrm{e}^{t}$. **5.** $x = \mathrm{e}^{2t}(A\cos t + B\sin t)$.
6. $x = \mathrm{e}^{-3t}(A\cos t + B\sin t)$. **7.** $x = \mathrm{e}^{-4t} + 4\,\mathrm{e}^{t}$. **8.** $x = (1+t)\,\mathrm{e}^{-t}$.
9. $x = \mathrm{e}^{-t}\cos t$. **10.** $6\,\mathrm{e}^{-3t}\sin t$. **12.** $(\mathrm{e}^{t} - \mathrm{e}^{-2t})$ m; $(\mathrm{e} + 2\,\mathrm{e}^{-2})$ m s^{-1}.
13. $\mathrm{e}^{-3t}\sin 2t$ m s^{-1}. **14.** $1 : \mathrm{e}^{-\pi/2}$.

EXERCISE 3(e) (page 104)

1. $x = \frac{k}{p^2}(1 - \cos pt)$; $\frac{k}{p}$. **2.** $A/[(p^2 - q^2)^2 + 4k^2q^2]^{1/2}$; $\tan^{-1}\left(\frac{2kq}{p^2 - q^2}\right)$.

$B\cos(qt - \alpha) + \frac{Bq}{k}\,\mathrm{e}^{-kt}\sin\alpha\cosh t\sqrt{(k^2 - p^2)}$.

3. $x = A\,\mathrm{e}^{-\frac{1}{2}kt}\cos[t\sqrt{(n^2 - \frac{1}{4}k^2)} + \alpha]$. **4.** $3\sqrt{2}$; $-\pi/4$ or $-3\sqrt{2}$, $\frac{3\pi}{4}$;
$-6\,\mathrm{e}^{-\pi/2}$.

5. $\mathrm{e}^{-at}(A\,\mathrm{e}^{bt} + B\,\mathrm{e}^{-bt})$ where $a = \mu/2M$, $b^2 = (\mu^2 - 4\lambda M)/2M$; $\mathrm{e}^{-at}(A + Bt)$.
$\mathrm{e}^{-at}(A\cos pt + B\sin pt)$ where $p^2 = (4\lambda M - \mu^2)/2M$.

EXERCISE 4(a) (page 109)

1. 3 m s^{-1}; $\frac{22}{3}$ m. **2.** 0.90 m s^{-1}. **3.** 0.16 m s^{-1}. **4.** 4s; 0.4 m s^{-1}; $\frac{4}{15}$ m.

5. 4000. **6.** $ut + \frac{\lambda}{km}\left[t + \frac{1}{k}(\mathrm{e}^{-kt} - 1)\right]$. **7.** 8 s; 28.9 s; Yes.

8. $83\frac{1}{3}$ m. **9.** $\frac{F}{M}\left(2t - \frac{t^2}{2T}\right)$. **10.** 7.2 m s^{-1}.

EXERCISE 4(b) (page 114)

1. 0.55 s; 3.2 m. **2.** 0.64 s; 1.37 s. **3.** 5.5 s; 11.5 m.
4. 0.07 s; 0.1 m; 0.2 m. **5.** 8.7 s. **6.** 2.16 s; 27.8 m. **7.** 39 s; 97 s.
8. 105 s. **9.** $\frac{M}{2k}\log_e\left(\frac{5}{2}\right)$. **10.** 4; $u - 2\lambda$, 5.
11. 0.04 s; 5 mm; 0.245 m s^{-1}. **13.** $\frac{1}{2k}\log_e\left(\frac{4}{3}\right)$; $\frac{1}{2kc}\log_e(3)$; $c(1 - e^{-2kd})^{1/2}$.
14. $\frac{1}{2k}\log_e\left(\frac{8}{5}\right)$; $\frac{u}{k}\left[\frac{3}{2}\log_e\left(\frac{5}{3}\right) - 1\right]$. **17.** $\frac{U^2}{2a}$; $\frac{1}{6}aT^2 + UT$.
18. $\frac{m}{2Q}, \frac{Q}{P}$; 512 m. **19.** 16 m s^{-1}. **20.** 1240 m.

EXERCISE 4(c) (page 119)

1. 2 m s^{-1}. **2.** 0.3 m s^{-1}; 1.5 s. **3.** 1.5 m s^{-1}; 0.46 s. **4.** 5.3 m s^{-1}.
5. 12**i** m s^{-1}. **6.** 6.4**i** m s^{-1}; 1.05 s. **7.** 21 m s^{-1}. **8.** 10.3 m s^{-1}, 10.6 m s^{-1}
10. $\sqrt{[2k(a-b)/ab]}$. **11.** 1.12×10^4 m s^{-1}.

EXERCISE 5(a) (page 127)

1. 0.02 m. **2.** 50 N. **3.** 0.098 m. **4.** 0.098 m. **5.** 0.049 m.
6. 0.09 m. **7.** 100 N. **8.** 0.9 m.

EXERCISE 5(b) (page 131)

1. 2 J, 12.5 J, 37.5 J, 62.5 J, 87.5 J. **2.** 7 m s^{-1}, 25 m s^{-1}.
3. 6 m s^{-1}, 0.5 m. **4.** $\frac{1}{2}U\sqrt{3}$. **5.** $\sqrt{[g(2l + a)]}$; $\sqrt{[a(2l + a)]}$.
7. 0.28 m. **8.** 7.67 m s^{-1}, 0.91 m, 7 m s^{-1}. **9.** $\frac{1}{2}a$, $\frac{3}{2}a$. **10.** $3a/k$.
11. $2a/3$, $3a/2$. **12.** 3 m; $\sqrt{5}$ m. **13.** $3mg$. **14.** $\frac{2}{3}h$; $2h$, $(1 + \frac{2}{9}\sqrt{6})h$.

EXERCISE 5(c) (page 141)

1. $2\pi/7$ s; $2\pi/7$ s; 0.01 m; 0.005 m. **2.** $g/16\pi^2$.
3. $5/2\pi$ cm; none, as the string remains taut. **4.** 0.01 m, $2\pi\sqrt{(15)}/70$ s.
5. $4\pi/7$ s; $7\sqrt{3}/20$ m s^{-1}; 49/40 m s^{-2} upwards; 49/40 m s^{-2} downwards.
6. $2\pi\sqrt{(b/g)}$ s; c metres. **8.** 196 N, $\frac{\pi}{7}$ s, 0.989 m.
9. $7/2\ a$; $\frac{1}{2}a$; $\pi\sqrt{(2a/g)}$. **10.** It leaves the table.
11. 3:1. Radius to m turns through $3\pi/4$. **15.** $3l\lambda/(3\lambda - ml\omega^2)$.
16. $\pi\sqrt{(b/g)}$; $a - 4\mu b$.

EXERCISE 6(a) (page 150)

7. $a\mathbf{j}, a\mathbf{i} + a\dfrac{\pi}{2}\mathbf{k}; a\mathbf{i} + a\mathbf{k}, -a\mathbf{j} + a\mathbf{k}; \dfrac{\pi}{3}$. 8. n. 9. $-\sin\theta\mathbf{i} + \cos\theta\mathbf{j}$.

10. $\mathbf{r}\omega^2\operatorname{cosec}^2\alpha$. 11. Always perpendicular.

12. $(ct + e^{-ct} - 1)\mathbf{g}/c^2 - (e^{-ct} - 1)\mathbf{u}/c$.

13. 3π s. Two complete oscillations, amplitude $4\frac{1}{2}$ m. $4\sqrt{5}$ m s^{-2}.

14. $c(\theta - \sin\theta)\mathbf{i} + c(1 - \cos\theta)\mathbf{j}$.

15. $b\hat{\mathbf{u}} - b\theta\hat{\mathbf{n}}; b\theta\dfrac{d\theta}{dt}\hat{\mathbf{u}}; b\left[\left(\dfrac{d\theta}{dt}\right)^2 + \theta\dfrac{d^2\theta}{dt^2}\right]\hat{\mathbf{u}} + b\theta\left(\dfrac{d\theta}{dt}\right)^2\hat{\mathbf{n}}$.

EXERCISE 6(b) (page 158)

1. $4(\mathbf{i} + 2\mathbf{j} + 3\mathbf{k})/\sqrt{14}$. 2. $\sqrt{6}$ rad s^{-1}. 3. $2(\mathbf{i} + 5\mathbf{j} - 3\mathbf{k})/\sqrt{6}$.

4. $\frac{2}{5}\sqrt{(910)}$, parallel to $(1, -3, -9)$. 5. $-4\mathbf{i} + 2\mathbf{j} - 4\mathbf{k}; 6\mathbf{i} - 4\mathbf{j} + 5\mathbf{k}$.

EXERCISE 6(c) (page 166)

1. If $\mathbf{a} = k\hat{\mathbf{n}}$, circle $ks = \psi$; if $\mathbf{a} = k\hat{\mathbf{t}}$, straight line. 2. 5.

5. $\dfrac{1}{v}\sec\psi + \dfrac{k}{g}\tan\psi = C$. 8. $mg(3 + \sqrt{2})$.

EXERCISE 7(a) (page 179)

1. $\tan^{-1}(\frac{4}{3})$. 2. $15°, 75°; 1 : 2 + \sqrt{3}$. 3. $1 : 7 + 4\sqrt{3}$.

4. 3 : 4; 9 : 16. 5. 190 m, 205 m. 8. $\tan^{-1}(\frac{2}{5})$ or $\tan^{-1}(\frac{38}{5})$.

9. $\tan^{-1}(\frac{4}{15}); \frac{2}{3}$ m. 10. $\frac{1}{7}(\sqrt{65} - \sqrt{5})$ s. 11. 1, 19; 0.8, −17.2.

12. 21.8°, 31°. 13. $\sqrt{[g(a^2 + 4h^2)/2h]}; \tan^{-1}(2h/a)$.

14. $\tan^{-1}(4)$; 13 : 40. 15. $\cos(2\beta - \alpha) = 3\cos\alpha$. 18. $(v^2\sqrt{3})/9g; (4v^2\sqrt{3})/9g$

19. $\dfrac{2\lambda u^2\sin\theta}{g}(1 + \lambda\cos\theta)$. 20. $\cos^{-1}\{[V + \sqrt{(V^2 + 8v^2)}]/4v\}$.

21. 3040 m, $\cos^{-1}(\frac{5}{8})$. 22. $\frac{1}{12}\sqrt{3}$.

EXERCISE 7(b) (page 187)

1. 21.56 N, 9.8 N; 18.62 N, 12.74 N; 15.68 N. 3. $1\frac{2}{3}$ cm below top of sphere

4. 7 m s^{-1}. 5. $5mg$. 6. $mg; \frac{4}{3}a$. 10. $\dfrac{\pi}{3}$.

12. $\sqrt{140}$ m s^{-1}; (a), (c).

EXERCISE 7(c) (page 200)

1. 37.5 m. 2. Not quite. 3. $\sqrt{(8ga)}$. 8. $m\sqrt{[2gh(1+f^2)]}$; $2f\sqrt{[h(H-h)]}$

11. $\dfrac{g}{2\omega^2}\left(1+\dfrac{a^2\omega^4}{g^2}\right)$. 12. $\dfrac{u}{g}\sqrt{(u^2+2gh)}$; $u/\sqrt{(u^2+2gh)}$.

13. $\dfrac{V}{g}\sqrt{(V^2-2gb)}$. 14. 60°. 15. $\dfrac{2V\sin\theta}{g(1-e)\cos\alpha}$.

EXERCISE 7(d) (page 210)

1. $\dfrac{dr}{dt}=\pm\Omega r$. 2. $\dfrac{1}{2\lambda r^2}=\dfrac{1}{\mu\theta}+C$. 4. $2\pi k$. 5. $k(e^{\omega t}-1)/\omega$; $2mk\omega\, e^{\omega t}$.

8. $r=a\,e^{\theta}$. 9. $\dfrac{1}{\lambda}\log_e\left(1+\dfrac{\lambda u\sin\alpha}{g}\right)$; $U^2\sin\alpha\cos\alpha(g+\lambda U\sin\alpha)^{-1}$.

10. $A=-B=mE/eH^2$.

EXERCISE 8(a) (page 221)

1. $32m$; $\sqrt{(32/5)}$. 2. $12m$. 3. $39m$. 4. $8m$. 5. $11m$; $11m$.

6. $M(\frac{1}{3}a^2+d^2)$. 7. $M(\frac{4}{3}a^2-2ad+d^2)$. 8. $\frac{2}{3}Ma^2$. 9. $\dfrac{a}{3}\sqrt{14}$; $\dfrac{a}{3}\sqrt{10}$.

10. $\frac{5}{3}Ma^2$; $\frac{2}{3}Ma^2$; $\frac{2}{3}Ma^2$. 11. Ma^2. 12. $\frac{1}{2}Ma^2$. 13. $M(a^2+c^2)$.
14. $\frac{1}{2}M(a^2-b^2)$. 15. $\frac{1}{6}Mb^2$. 16. $\frac{1}{3}Ma^2$. 17. Mb^2. 18. $\frac{2}{3}Ma^2$.

EXERCISE 8(b) (page 232)

1. $\frac{8}{3}Ma^2$. 2. $\frac{2}{3}Ma^2$; $Ma^2(\frac{8}{3}+2\cos\alpha)$ or $Ma^2(\frac{8}{3}-2\cos\alpha)$. 3. $\frac{4}{3}Ma^2$
4. $M\left(\dfrac{a^2}{4}+\dfrac{l^2}{3}\right)$. 5. $M\left(\dfrac{a^2}{4}+\dfrac{l^2}{12}\right)$. 6. $\frac{1}{2}M(a^2-\frac{1}{6}b^2)$. 7. $\frac{1}{36}M(2a^2+b^2)$
8. $\frac{3}{10}Ma^2$; $\frac{3}{20}M(a^2+4h^2)$; $\frac{3}{80}M(4a^2+h^2)$. 9. $a\sqrt{\frac{7}{5}}$. 10. $a\sqrt{\frac{2}{5}}$; $a\sqrt{\frac{83}{320}}$.

11. $a\sqrt{\frac{2}{3}}$; $a\sqrt{\frac{5}{12}}$. 12. $\dfrac{2a}{3}$. 13. $a\sqrt{\frac{2}{3}}$. 14. $\frac{1}{2}\pi^2a^2$; $\frac{1}{4}a\sqrt{6}$.

15. 1.94 kg m^2.

EXERCISE 8(c) (page 241)

1. $\sqrt{(15g/14a)}$. 2. $\sqrt{(2ga/3)}$. 3. $2\pi\sqrt{(28a\sqrt{2}/15g)}$. 4. $\sqrt{(20g/7a)}$.
5. $2\pi/3$. 6. $2\pi\sqrt{(5a/3g)}$; $2\pi\sqrt{(17a/9g)}$. 8. $2\pi\sqrt{(7l/3g)}$.

9. $a(a^2 + 4b^2) : b(b^2 + 4a^2)$. **11.** 32 : 21. **12.** 40π N m.

13. 100 rad s^{-1}. **14.** $\sqrt{[2Mgh/(M + m)]}; \dfrac{Mgha}{2G - Mga}$. **15.** $\frac{1}{8}gt^2$; $2mga$

16. $\dfrac{4Mk^2g}{n\pi}\left(\dfrac{mr}{Mk^2 + mr^2}\right)$. **17.** $\dfrac{mga^2(1 - \mu)}{I + 2ma^2}$.

18. $\frac{33}{16}Ma^2$; $\sqrt{[64mg/(33M + 16m)a]}$. **21.** 11 300 r.p.m.

23. $\frac{2}{5}l$. **24.** $\sqrt{[2gh(2m - M)/(n + M + 2m)]}$.

EXERCISE 9(a) (page 252)

1. $\frac{1}{3}g$, $\frac{4}{3}mg$. **3.** $\frac{1}{35}g$. **5.** $\sqrt{[(8m - 4M)gx/(4m + M)]}$.

7. $\dfrac{m \cos\alpha \sin\alpha}{M + m\cos^2\alpha}$. **9.** $\dfrac{2m_1m_2g\sin\alpha}{(m_1 + m_2)}$.

EXERCISE 9(b) (page 261)

5. $u \log_e 2 - \dfrac{gM}{2A}$.

EXERCISE 10(a) (page 279)

3. $W\left(\dfrac{a}{2a - x}\right)\cot\alpha$. **4.** 60°; $2W/\sqrt{3}$, $W/\sqrt{3}$.

5. $W\sqrt{3}$, W, W, $W\sqrt{3}$; 30°. **6.** $\frac{1}{2}W\left(1 + \dfrac{a^2}{l^2}\right)$. **7.** 45°; $\frac{4}{15}W$.

10. $\tan^{-1}\left(\dfrac{2 - \mu^2}{4\mu}\right)$. **16.** 15°. **17.** 4400 N, 160 N, 4240 N.

18. The insect can detach a pair of legs at 'opposite' vertices, but no other pairs.

19. $Wab\tan\theta/(c + a\sec\theta)$. **21.** $(a + b)/(h - a\cot\alpha)$.

EXERCISE 10(b) (page 296)

1. $\frac{1}{4}(W_1 + W_2)$, $\frac{1}{4}(W_1 - W_2)$. **2.** $\frac{1}{2}W\cot\alpha$, 0.

3. $\frac{9}{8}W\tan\theta$, $\frac{43}{8}W$, $\frac{13}{8}W$, $\tan^{-1}(\frac{13}{9})$.

5. In AB, thrust $\dfrac{1}{2\sqrt{2}}(3U + V)$; in AE, tension $\frac{1}{4}(3U + V)$; in DE, tension

$\frac{1}{4}(U+3V)$; in DC, thrust $\frac{1}{2\sqrt{2}}(U+3V)$; in BC, tension $\frac{1}{2}(U+V)$; if $U > V$, in BE, tension $\frac{1}{2\sqrt{2}}(U-V)$ in EC, thrust $\frac{1}{2\sqrt{2}}(U-V)$.

6. $\frac{6}{5}W$, $\frac{4}{5}W$; in tension, AB, $0.41W$, BC, $1.1W$, BE, $0.90W$, in compression, AE, $1.27W$, ED, $1.02W$, DC, $1.36W$, BD, $0.85W$.

7. $100\sqrt{(91/3)}$ N at $\tan^{-1}(\frac{3}{8}\sqrt{3})$ above horiz; $\frac{1}{3}(800\sqrt{3})$ N; in compression, AC, $200\sqrt{3}$ N; AF, $500/\sqrt{3}$ N; FE, $100/\sqrt{3}$ N; FD, $200/\sqrt{3}$ N in tension, DE, $200/\sqrt{3}$ N, CD, $200/\sqrt{3}$ N, BC, $800/\sqrt{3}$ N, CF, $200\sqrt{3}$ N.

8. $W/\sqrt{3}$; $2W/\sqrt{3}$, along AB; $W/\sqrt{3}$ in each rod; AB, AC in compression.

9. $\frac{3}{2}W$, $\frac{5}{2}W$. Thrusts: $\sqrt{3}W$ in AD, W in DE and EF, $2W/\sqrt{3}$ in BF, $5W/\sqrt{3}$ in CF. Tensions: $\frac{1}{2}W\sqrt{3}$ in AB, $5W/2\sqrt{3}$ in BC, W in BE.

10. $2W$, $2W$, W. Thrusts, BD, CE, $W\sqrt{2}$, CD, W. Tensions AB, $2W$; BC, AD, BE, W.

EXERCISE 10(c) (page 307)

1. $0 < x < a$, $S = wx - \frac{7}{2}wa$, $M = \frac{1}{2}wx^2 - \frac{7}{2}wax$, $a < x < 4a$, $s = wx - \frac{3}{2}wa$, $M = \frac{1}{2}wx^2 - \frac{3}{2}wax - 2wa^2$.

2. $S = \dfrac{Wx^2}{l^2} - \dfrac{W}{3}$; $M = \dfrac{Wx^3}{3l^2} - \dfrac{Wx}{3}$.

3. $3aw$; $2a^2w + axw$; $0 \leqslant y \leqslant x$, $M = \frac{1}{2}w(4a^2 + 2ax - 6ay + y^2)$, $x \leqslant y \leqslant 2a$, $M = \frac{1}{2}w(2a-y)^2$.

4. If $x < l$, $S = \dfrac{Wx}{3l} + w$, $M = \dfrac{Wx^2}{6l} + w(x-y)$.

If $l < x < 3l$, $S = \dfrac{Wx}{3l} - W$, $M = \dfrac{Wx^2}{6l} - (W+w)(x-l) + w(x-y)$.

5. $2Wl$ at C; $6W$.

6. $0 < x < 2$, $S = -500$, $M = -500x$;
$2 < x < 4$, $S = 500$, $M = 500x - 2000$;
$4 < x < 6$, $S = 2500$, $M = 2500x - 10\,000$;
$6 \leqslant x \leqslant 8$, $S = -3750$, $M = -3750x + 27\,500$;
$8 \leqslant x < 10$, $S = -43\,750 + 5000x$, $M = -43\,750x + 2500x^2 + 187\,500$.

EXERCISE 11(a) (page 312)

3. $\frac{11}{3}mg$; $\frac{1}{3}mg\sqrt{(\frac{2}{3})}$. 7. $\tan^{-1}(\mu/10)$. 8. $\dfrac{mgk^2}{k^2+b^2}$.

EXERCISE 11(b) (page 317)

3. $\sqrt{[2Fs/(M+2m)]}$. 5. $\sqrt{[2gx/(1+2k)]}$. 6. $\frac{1}{26}mg^2t^2$; $2gt/(13a)$.
8. $\frac{135}{256}mg$, $\frac{301}{256}mg$; 0, $\frac{109}{64}mg$. 10. $\pi\sqrt{[3(D-d)/g]}$.

EXERCISE 11(c) (page 329)

1. $\dfrac{2}{7\sqrt{3}}$. 3. $\frac{3}{4}g\sin\alpha$, $\frac{1}{4}\dfrac{g}{a}\sin\alpha$; $\frac{5}{6}mgk\sin\alpha$, $\frac{1}{6}mgk\sin\alpha$. 5. $\frac{1}{2}\tan\alpha$.
9. $\frac{2}{3}g\sin\alpha$; $\frac{1}{3}mg\sqrt{(1+8\cos^2\alpha)}$.

EXERCISE 11(d) (page 337)

1. J/m. 2. J/m, J/ma. 3. $J/2m$, $3J/5ma$. 4. $2J/ma$.
7. $2m\sqrt{(\frac{1}{3}ga)}$; $\frac{1}{4}mg\sqrt{37}$. 8. $\dfrac{52J}{15m}, \dfrac{-2J}{15m}$. 10. $\dfrac{a\omega(4a-3x)}{4a^2-6ax+3x^2}$; $x=\frac{2}{3}a$.
11. $\dfrac{4M(1+e)\Omega l}{4M+3m}, \dfrac{(4M-3em)\Omega}{4M+3m}$. 12. $\frac{1}{2}mv^2(1-e^2)+\frac{7}{4}mu^2$
13. $e(M+m)=3M$. 14. $\frac{1}{2}l$. 16. $\frac{2}{3}a\sqrt{3}$, $2\sqrt{[ga(1+2/\sqrt{3})]}$.
20. $\frac{32}{9}\left(1-\dfrac{\sqrt{3}}{2}\right)a$. 22. $\dfrac{I\omega_1+mau}{I+ma^2}$. 25. $\mu>\frac{1}{2}$, $\sqrt{\dfrac{5d}{g}}$.

EXERCISE 12(a) (page 354)

2. $\tan^{-1}(\frac{1}{2})$. 5. $\sin\frac{1}{2}\theta=\frac{3}{5}$, stable; $\theta=\pi$, unstable.
8. $\tan^{-1}(\frac{1}{2})$, unstable; $\pi+\tan^{-1}(\frac{1}{2})$, stable.

EXERCISE 12(b) (page 361)

1. Two vertical positions; $4\pi\sqrt{(a/3g)}$. 2. $\pi\sqrt{(5a/g)}$. 3. $2\pi\sqrt{(3a/2g)}$.
4. $2\pi\sqrt{(107a/20g)}$. 9. $\frac{16}{3}\pi\sqrt{(a/3g\sqrt{7})}$.

Index